A Scholar Collects

This project is supported by a grant from the National Endowment for the Arts in Washington, D.C., a Federal agency.

A SCHOLAR COLLECTS

Selections from the Anthony Morris Clark Bequest

Edited by Ulrich W. Hiesinger and Ann Percy

Philadelphia Museum of Art

The material in this catalogue was exhibited at the Philadelphia Museum of Art from October 2, 1980 to January 4, 1981.

Cover: *Allegory of Painting,* c. 1750, by Stefano Pozzi (no. 45)

Library of Congress catalogue card number: 80–82234
Printed in the United States of America

Library of Congress Cataloging in Publication Data
Philadelphia Museum of Art.
A scholar collects.

Catalogue of an exhibit held Oct. 1980 to Jan. 1981.
Bibliography: p.
Includes index.
1. Art, Italian—Italy—Rome (City)—Exhibitions. 2. Art, Modern—17th-18th centuries—Italy—Rome (City)—Exhibitions. 3. Clark, Anthony M.—Art collections—Exhibitions. 4. Art—Private collections—Exhibitions. 5. Medals—Private collections—Exhibitions. I. Hiesinger, Ulrich W. II. Percy, Ann. III. Title.
N6916.P45 1980 709'.45'632074014811 80–82234
ISBN 0–87633–036–7

CONTENTS

DIRECTOR'S PREFACE

THE STAFFS of many museums throughout the world were saddened by the news of the death of Anthony M. Clark in Rome in 1976. He had been an amusing and informative colleague when he was Secretary of the Museum at the Rhode Island School of Design, Curator of Paintings and Sculpture and then Director of the Minneapolis Institute of Arts, and finally Chairman of the Department of European Paintings at the Metropolitan Museum of Art. And he was even more affable and expansive if he were met in Rome during those summers he wisely claimed for his research.

At the Philadelphia Museum of Art that sense of loss at his death was great. It was not because he was a Philadelphian that he was mourned. In fact, before he went to Harvard, he probably spent more time in the Morris Arboretum than in the museum. It was simply that he inspired that sense of colleagueship among museum curators and administrators that Sir Ellis Waterhouse describes elsewhere in this publication. This museum's director at that time, Evan Turner, had long been his colleague in the Association of Art Museum Directors. Arnold Jolles, the Assistant Director for Art, had been his assistant director in Minneapolis and a close friend. Joseph Rishel, Curator of European Art, when he had worked at the Art Institute of Chicago from 1967 to 1972, had helped Clark with the organization of the 1970-71 exhibition, *Painting in Italy in the Eighteenth Century,* which Chicago, Minneapolis, and Toledo shared. Ann Percy, Associate Curator for Drawings, had spent long hours with him in this museum, poring over the Italian drawings they both loved. And there were others who knew and would miss him.

When the residue of his estate had to be settled, it was its executor, John Walsh, now Curator of Paintings at the Museum of Fine Arts, Boston, who decided that Clark's distinguished collection of drawings, prints, coins, medals, sculpture, and other objects, primarily from eighteenth- and early-nineteenth-century Rome, should come to the Philadelphia Museum of Art. Mr. Walsh, who was a close friend of Clark's and had been his colleague at the Metropolitan Museum of Art, selected Philadelphia because he knew that the collection would be understood and appreciated here. Not only was there at the museum Ann Percy, who had demonstrated in her catalogue of an exhibition of Castiglione drawings in 1971 her affection for, and knowledge of, Italian drawings, but there was also in the city Ulrich Hiesinger, who had met Clark in Rome and was devoting himself to late Roman studies. Miss Percy initiated plans for an exhibition drawn from the collection and was joined by Mr. Hiesinger in selecting works for the exhibition and soliciting entries on the individual pieces from Clark's friends throughout the world. Together Miss Percy and Mr. Hiesinger have worked toward this exhibition and this catalogue as a tribute of their respect and affection for Clark. We hope that the exhibition and this scholarly publication are a sufficient expression of our gratitude for the confidence placed by Mr. Walsh in the Philadelphia Museum of Art.

The catalogue is a record of Clark as a private collector of works of art devoted to his very private enthusiasm, Roman life in the eighteenth and early nineteenth centuries. As a curator and director of museums, he formed public collections with an equal passion. He did not forget eighteenth-century Rome in buying for Minneapolis the handsome portrait by Pompeo Batoni of the cheerful and witty pope, Benedict XIV. He went further back into Italian art in buying Castiglione's great *Immaculate Conception* in 1966 or the little panel of *Saint Benedict* by Fra Angelico in that same year. But his interests were broader: he was particularly proud of his purchases of Prud'hon's *Union of Love and Friendship* in 1964 and Girodet's *Portrait of Mlle Lange as Danaë* in 1969. And he did buy a rare nude by Caillebotte in 1967 and a fine painting by Balthus in 1966. His period in New York was shorter but he added among other works to the Metropolitan's collections Sébastien Bourdon's *Baptism of Christ* and Corot's *Honfleur: Calvary*. Certainly these museums, along with that of the Rhode Island School of Design, have very concrete evidence of Tony Clark's brilliance as a collector for public institutions. Now, through this gift from his estate, the Philadelphia Museum of Art has evidence of the more intimate side of his collecting for himself as a scholar and a lover of both art and Rome.

Jean Sutherland Boggs
Director

CURATOR'S PREFACE

The Philadelphia Museum of Art was fortunate to have received in 1978 378 old master drawings, 204 prints, 114 coins, medals, and plaquettes, 24 sculptures, and 13 miscellaneous *objets d'art* from the estate of the late Anthony M. Clark. As the leading connoisseur of and specialist in eighteenth-century Roman painting, Anthony Clark assembled the finest collection of the art of that city and period in private hands in America. For almost twenty years, working from his close and extensive knowledge of many, often lesser-known artists of the period and combing the resources of dealers throughout America and Europe, he sought to acquire examples of the work of as many artists active in his area of interest as possible. After his death, his paintings were sold to benefit the posthumous publication of his books-in-progress and to help establish a fellowship in his field; the rest of his collection was, according to the terms of his will, donated to a public institution. As a result, the Philadelphia Museum of Art has the most complete representation of eighteenth-century Roman draughtsmanship in America, as well as a holding of prints that demonstrates the high interest in reproductive printmaking during that period and a collection of medals that documents various artistic, historical, political, and cultural events of the times.

When the collection was received, an exhibition selected from the more important works from this bequest, accompanied by a scholarly catalogue, was planned for presentation at the Philadelphia Museum of Art and at other institutions in the United States, and possibly Europe. Almost from the beginning, it was determined that the authorship of the catalogue should draw upon the talents of Tony Clark's numerous colleagues and should reflect the spirit of international cooperation that marked his approach to scholarship. That the list of acknowledgments below seems remarkably long is merely an indication of the strong feeling with which so many of his associates remember Tony's contributions as a scholar and a museum professional, as well as his presence as an unforgettable friend.

Fortunately for all involved in preparing this catalogue, Tony Clark kept careful, up-to-date records on the provenance, attribution, exhibition, and publication of his objects. Contributors have thus been able to use his notes for this information, and whereas in a few cases it has been necessary to change his attributions or datings in the light of new research, for the most part his identifications stand. The checklist of drawings, recording the old master drawings in the collection not catalogued here, follows his attributions entirely.

The pleasurable task of selecting the material for the show was shared by Ulrich Hiesinger and myself with two of the major contributors to the catalogue, Mary L. Myers and Edgar Peters Bowron, who subsequently aided our editorial work in endless ways and with great good will and effectiveness. Several specialists in the field of eighteenth-century Italian art, some contributors to the catalogue and some not, have been warmly generous with advice, opinions, and information drawn from their own researches: a particular debt is owed to Tony's good friend and colleague Jacob Bean, as well as to Erich Schleier, Pierre Rosenberg, Andrew Ciechanowiecki, Frederick den Broeder, Italo Faldi, Giancarlo Sestieri, and the late Milton Lewine. The editors are, in addition, most grateful to the following colleagues for their particular contributions: Franco Battistelli, Enrichetta Beltrame-Quattrocchi, Janet S. Byrne, John Daley, Elaine Evans Dee, Cara D. Denison, James D. Draper, Jack Freiberg, Alvar González-Palacios, Michael Hall, Kathryn Hiesinger, Rupert Hodge, Colta F. Ives, David W. Kiehl, Elisabeth Kieven, Lesley Lewis, Manuela B. Mena Marquès, Phyllis Dearborn Massar, Thomas McCormick, Suzanne McCullagh, Herbert Mitchell, Lucia Monaci Moran, Jennifer Montagu, Kerry A. O'Brien, Adolf Placzek, Nancy L. Pressly, Olga Raggio, Joseph Rishel, Herwarth Röttgen, Elizabeth Roth, Ksenija Rozman, Stella Rudolph, Margret Stuffmann, Philip Troutman, and Enrico Valeriani. Ligia Ravé contributed much time to organizing the bibliography and checklist, and Amy Golahny undertook the enormous job of providing lists of the drawings and prints. Deborah Coy, Victor Wiener, Frans Pijnenburg, and Carlo Virgilio provided essential aid in various ways.

John Walsh, in his profound concern for the care and use of Tony's collections, played a vital role in the realization of this project. The Philadelphia Museum is, in addition, indebted to the National Endowment for the

Arts and the Henfield Foundation for their contributions in support of the catalogue's publication.

As always, in any large undertaking, the registrar's office of the museum has provided essential aid, and special thanks go to Rosalie Reed and Irene Taurins. The conservation department has performed an—inevitably—invisible but essential function: with the support of the museum's conservator, Marigene H. Butler, Stephen D. Bonadies undertook an examination of the various media and the watermarks of the drawings, as well as the treatment of many of them preparatory to exhibition and travel; Andrew Lins refurbished the medals with the aid of Susan Schussler, and colleagues outside the museum, Anne F. Clapp and Marjorie B. Cohn, provided help and advice. Without the seemingly limitless energies of the museum's librarian, Barbara Sevy, and her assistant Carol Homan, research would have proved much more difficult. Barbara Phillips and Virginia Butera aided by resolving numerous administrative details, and Will Brown provided excellent photographs of the sculpture and medals. The catalogue's production owes a great deal to George Marcus, head of publications, and especially to the patience and concern of the editor Beryl L. Rosenstock—not to mention the enormous and cheerful contribution made by Eve Oswald, Martha Small, and Dwight de Keyser, who typed and retyped endless copy. Most helpful throughout has been the interest and concern of the head of the museum's print department, Kneeland McNulty. Last, but by no means least, the project would never have been begun, carried on, or concluded without the support and encouragement of three successive directors of the museum: Evan H. Turner, Arnold Jolles, and Jean Sutherland Boggs.

Ann Percy
Associate Curator for Drawings

REMINISCENCES OF ANTHONY CLARK

Tony Clark was one of the largest and friendliest members of a world that embraced both sides of the Atlantic and was made up of people of good will of many nationalities whose concern was with works of art. Scholars, students, teachers, museum men, art dealers, artists, and collectors—not all of them always happy in one another's company—found in Tony a sympathy with their interests and needs, as well as a stimulating attitude toward works of art that was at once profoundly serious and tinged with beguiling light-heartedness. (In the world of the spirit, Saint Philip Neri must have had something of the same quality.) I think the feeling that most of Tony's friends still feel paramount in their recollection of him is one of affection. For many years I felt a summer had been ill spent if it had not included some days in Rome when Tony was there, when one also renewed, through him, the association with many of his other friends, both old and new. The year he died I had not the heart to go to Rome.

Many of the friends Tony made in the last years of his life had little idea that he had begun with a pencil or brush in his hand rather than Ovid, von Pastor, or Voss, and that he was a serious painter until he took his first museum job at the age of thirty-two. In a generous and funny autobiographical sketch that he sent in 1970 to his Harvard twenty-fifth anniversary report he described his gradual remove from painter to art historian between the years of about 1945 to 1955:[1]

> In New York I tried to be a rather Blakean and highly intolerant and intense artist. . . . In Florence [in the summer of 1949] I painted for the first time as an abstract expressionist . . . ; the following winter in Rome I was affected by Ray Spillenger, to whom de Kooning and Kantian Reason were models, and my manner of painting became neither more knowing nor less messy, but more formal. . . . Greece disciplined and ordered my mind although making me no less of a nut: this was the most intense moment of my life. My painting changed to something between 6th century B.C., the cosmopolitan Byzantine, and a strenuously patterned, pragmatic Cubism. With these arduous affiliations and certain anti-New York biases the talent wilted. . . . On March 9th, 1955, I sailed from Naples, not to be a painter but to become a museum man at the Rhode Island School of Design, an incredibly just improvisation of John Maxon. . . . My Providence job at first was half-time, and my liberation from the Muse of Painting was neither Maxon's fault or desire, but a natural settlement.

There was no such liberation from poetry, which Tony talked about very little but wrote more or less steadily for thirty-five years.

A passion for the city of Rome, considered from the earliest times until the end of the eighteenth century, was latterly at the center of Tony's life. He had tried Greece, but it was ultimately Rome as the radiating center of Western civilization that held his allegiance and, above all, the city in the eighteenth century, when the full consciousness of the great Roman past spilled over again into the hearts of artists and visitors from the rest of the world. The central themes of his researches were in eighteenth-century Rome, and his own collection was very much a reflection of this commitment. Whereas, still assembled during his lifetime, the collection showed considerable breadth—his classical coins and pottery and primitive art objects should not be forgotten—it was hardly encyclopedic: Tony's acquisitions tended instead to express an immediacy and anecdotal quality that were among his special strengths as a scholar and friend. This is particularly true of his drawings, which illuminate the variety and human dimension of daily life in Settecento Rome as much as they illustrate the evolution of style in the same period.

In furtherance of his particular Roman devotion a sort of alter ego of Tony came into being, almost by osmosis, and took shape as "Cardinal Muccavacca." The cardinal's personality owed a good deal both to Alessandro Albani and to Winckelmann: he was very active in Settecento artistic circles and was the author of a certain amount of imaginary correspondence. Drawings of him and his entourage, in the spirit of Pier Leone Ghezzi, often adorned Tony's letters. The concept of the "Muccavacca Prize" for this, that, or the other art-historical idiocy defined itself, as the years passed, with increasing clearness. Cardinal Muccavacca was extremely interested in Tony's collection of drawings, engravings, and medals, which represent very much a special side of Tony's personality: for the private collection of a museum director is, of necessity, something about which he has to make rather complicated rules.

Tony was an extremely good museum director. He took more trouble over his staff and their interests and their prospects than any director I have known. This trouble may not in every case have been rewarding, but in the overwhelming number of instances it certainly was. The first charge on a museum director's covetousness must be his museum's needs: it requires an extremely fine moral sense to ensure that you are not encouraging your museum to buy something just because it happens to fit in with your own special field of interest or that you are not buying for yourself, because you happen to be able to afford it, something that ought to become a part of your museum's collection. In this delicate moral zone I give Tony the highest marks.

Tony was also dedicated to the belief that the director of a museum must not abdicate from the pursuit of scholarship. At a time when there was a dangerous tendency for this to happen, it was he who initiated a session at the annual meetings of the College Art Association that should consist of reports from those working in museums rather than in the sometimes less constricted areas of university departments of art history. As he was himself an extremely gifted supervisor of graduate students he was, more than most of us, aware of the professional responsibilities of the historian of art.

At the meeting of the College Art Association in Baltimore in January, 1975, Tony read a brief paper entitled "State of Studies: Roman Eighteenth-Century Art"[2] that revealed the heart of his aspirations. It was perhaps a little overly pessimistic—and also somewhat overly optimistic about a possible future for such studies—but it showed the direction in which his mind was working. In his last few years in New York, when he had an apartment large enough to deploy his books and his Roman collections, he was developing a workshop from which he hoped to finalize those studies that had taken up his summers and the spare moments of a little more than the past twenty years. His days were carefully planned and future work was beginning to fall into shape. To visit him there was to feel as near to being in Rome as it is possible to feel on Park Avenue, and a conversation there with friends would sometimes take on the air of a *crocchio* in eighteenth-century Rome—except that there was, I fancy, a good deal more matter for laughter.

Tony is sincerely missed by many more people than most of us are likely to be missed by, not only for himself, but because he was often the link through whom we renewed our friendship with others. Few people are natural centers of this sort of radiation. Tony was one of them.

Ellis Waterhouse

The author gratefully acknowledges the helpful comments of John Walsh and John Pinto in preparing this preface.

1. Republished in part in *Antologia di Belle Arti,* vol. 1, no. 1 (March, 1977), pp. 123–25.

2. Published in *Eighteenth Century Studies,* vol. 9, no. 1 (Autumn, 1975), pp. 102–107; republished in *Antologia di Belle Arti,* vol. 1, no. 1 (March, 1977), pp. 121–23.

CONTRIBUTING AUTHORS

E.P.B. *Edgar Peters Bowron*
Curator of Renaissance and Baroque Art
William Rockhill Nelson Gallery of Art–Atkins Museum of Fine Arts
Kansas City, Missouri

A.B.V. *Andrea Busiri Vici*

M.A.C. *Mimi Cazort*
Curator of Drawings
National Gallery of Canada
Ottawa

M.C. *Marco Chiarini*
Direttore, Galleria Palatina
Palazzo Pitti
Florence

M.P.C. *Michael P. Conforti*
Chairman, Curatorial Division, and Bell Memorial Curator of Decorative Arts and Sculpture
The Minneapolis Institute of Arts
Minneapolis

M.T.C. *Maria Teresa Caracciolo Arizzoli*
Service de Documentation
Cabinet des Dessins
Musée du Louvre
Paris

F.R.D. *Frank R. DiFederico*
Associate Professor of Art History
University of Maryland

A.E.G. *Amy E. Golahny*
Ph.D. candidate in art history
Columbia University

U.W.H. *Ulrich W. Hiesinger*

L.W.L. *Louise W. Lippincott*
Assistant Curator, John G. Johnson Collection
Philadelphia

D.M. *Dwight Miller*
Professor of Art History
Stanford University

J-F.M. *Jean-François Méjanès*
Conservateur, Cabinet des Dessins
Musée du Louvre
Paris

M.L.M. *Mary L. Myers*
Curator, Department of Prints
The Metropolitan Museum of Art
New York

A.P. *Ann Percy*
Associate Curator for Drawings
Philadelphia Museum of Art
Philadelphia

J.P. *John Pinto*
Associate Professor, Department of Art
Smith College

P.R. *Pierre Rosenberg*
Conservateur, Département des Peintures
Musée du Louvre
Paris

S.R. *Steffi Röttgen*
Bayerisches Nationalmuseum
Munich

S.S. *Stefano Susinno*
Direttore, Soprintendenza Speciale
Galleria Nazionale d'Arte Moderna
Rome

T.W.S. *Thomas William Sokolowski*
Sessional Lecturer, Fine Arts Department
University of British Columbia

P.W. *Peter Walch*
Associate Professor
Department of Art
University of New Mexico

Drawings

DRAWINGS IN EIGHTEENTH-CENTURY ROME

Ulrich W. Hiesinger

THE BREADTH AND VARIETY of drawing practice in eighteenth-century Rome reflects the artistic life of a city that was at once the capital training ground of European artists, a thriving center for connoisseurs, scholars, collectors, and grand tourists, and the seat of an important and productive local school of art.

As evidence of this variety the works of nearly fifty different artists presented here from the Clark collection include drawings of historical and religious subjects, formal portraits and humorous caricatures, academy nudes, landscapes, fanciful views of ruins, and some typical studies after ancient gems and statues and modern works of art. Nearly every stage in preparatory design is represented, from early trial sketches for planned compositions, to highly detailed studies from the studio model, as well as some drawings finished in their own right.

These works represent many of the principal painters and draughtsmen who spent a significant part of their careers in Rome in the eighteenth century. Most, even among the Italian majority, were born and received their first training outside of Rome. Consequently, in addition to works by native Romans, there are still greater numbers of drawings by artists resettled from Tuscany, Naples, the Veneto, Piedmont, and Lombardy, as well as a significant and characteristic representation of artists from France, Germany, and England. A large proportion were members—by "merit" rather than honor—of Rome's official academic body, the Accademia di San Luca, and among them are eleven artists who served one or more terms as *principe,* or head, of that institution.

In representing a broad range of imagery and individual styles, the drawings in this collection also offer a good deal of practical insight into the working methods of artists throughout the century. Many are preliminary designs for known projects; others, like academy studies, relate to equally specific circumstance and purposes. As private studio creations or as drawings carefully finished for the commercial market, these works nearly always convey something of the strengths and deliberateness of the professional's working concerns.

Drawing was an activity given unprecedented attention in the eighteenth century. The staple of artistic training, it served paradoxically in mature practice as both an inseparable preliminary to painting and a medium increasingly to be practiced in its own right. Indeed, eighteenth-century writers credit a remarkably large number of contemporary Roman artists with distinct and separate reputations as draughtsmen. The systematic emphasis placed on drawing in eighteenth-century Rome is made apparent in painting theory, in methods of training and some aspects of artistic practice, and in the importance that drawings themselves acquired as objects for collection and study. It is this context of activity and concern for drawing that forms the subject of this brief essay.

While one's impression of eighteenth-century design theory may be exaggerated by a preponderance of biographical and critical writing from the later part of the century when neoclassicism brought concern for drawing to its height, it is also true that long, prior tradition had established the rule of *disegno,* or design, as a hallmark of the Roman school. *Disegno* is a theoretical concept with lengthy implications. Referring to the linear definition of form, it was said to embody a general principle that underlay and unified all of the visual arts: "the single parent," to paraphrase Francesco Preziado in 1764,[1] "from which each of the three fine arts originate and proceed." Often used in the eighteenth century as a convenient—and technically mistaken—synonym for drawing, *disegno* also conveyed an idea of correctness, or rather the correcting guidance necessary to elevate mere imitation and avoid willful personal mannerism.

This concept of design, with its encouragement to idealism and clarity of form, was central to the doctrine of classicism revived by Carlo Maratta and his followers at the beginning of the eighteenth century. One permanent effect of their effort was to reestablish a habit of deliberate moderation that survived in every succeeding style. Thus, both the "classical" baroque of Maratta's school and the Roman rococo style, as practiced for example by Sebastiano Conca or Corrado Giaquinto, are notable for a restraint that distinguishes them from their more exuberant counterparts earlier and elsewhere. Neoclassicism, a Roman development, was by definition a movement founded upon principles of formal measure and control.

Classicism, then, remained the stronger of two main interrelated and opposing elements in the Roman makeup. The other, more a disposition to certain values than a coherent doctrine, is an evolving hybrid of Baroque and Romantic sentiment. If the first implied a strong historical consciousness and a belief in permanent ideals accessible through study and deliberate method, the second—no less sensible of the weight of the past, but impelled by it in a different direction—sought to affirm individual genius over repeated rule and to stress a sense of freedom and spontaneity in artistic performance.

In regard to the question of establishment values, it is important to remember that artistic authority continued to reside with the great individual masters and was varied accordingly. As an officially sponsored body, the Accademia di San Luca did play an important symbolic role in maintaining certain traditional principles, but even the elevated status it enjoyed from the beginning of the eighteenth century was greatly owed to the personal prestige of Maratta and to the impetus provided by his choice of the academy as a forum. Otherwise the academy represented a largely ceremonial union, routinely avoided by many of its members, and relinquishing for the most part any serious educational function. The chief exceptions to this rule, which provided the most visible expression of academy standards, came through control of membership, with the express sanction this implied for members' work, and through reward of performance in the academy's public competitions.

Student competitions, which had been a feature of Rome's privately run drawing academies in the seventeenth century, were also held irregularly at the Accademia di San Luca under Pietro da Cortona and apparently with some greater frequency under Maratta's leadership in the 1660s and later.[2] It was not until the eighteenth century, however, that these competitions assumed the grand and regular form that was intended as a hopeful symbol of the academy's, and thus Rome's, supremacy and encouragement in the arts. Established in 1702 through funds provided by Clement XI, the Concorso Clementino was at first an annual competition and later, owing both to lack of funds and a suitable number of new participants, was held at three- or four-year intervals. With its prize ceremonies the occasion for elaborate solemnities, the Concorso Clementino stood throughout the eighteenth century and well into the next as the most famous and visible of the academy's activities.

Entries for painters (and architects) in these competitions were restricted to drawings—a finished historical composition prepared on a theme announced in advance, and an *ex tempore* performance carried out under supervision at a set time. Consequently, successful young artists followed the pattern of meeting their first public test and gaining their earliest local fame entirely on their merits as draughtsmen. As in the case of Giuseppe Cades's prize-winning entry of 1766, which Lanzi cites as still being an object of admiration in his time, these performances could sometimes be remembered long after the event.[3]

It was not unusual, either, for talented young painters to support themselves as draughtsmen early in their careers. Their activities covered a wide field that included portrait drawing for visitors, landscapes, both real and invented, and reproductive drawing after paintings and antiquities. As examples one might cite by artists represented here the portrait drawings supplied by Agostino Masucci for Nicola Pio's *Le vite di pittori* . . . in the late teens and early 1720s; the drawings of ancient statues made for sale by Pompeo Batoni in the late 1720s and early 1730s, which first established his reputation in Rome; the employment by Robert Adam of Laurent Pecheux and Antonio Zucchi as draughtsmen in the 1750s; Giuseppe Cades's early livelihood as draughtsman and copyist in the 1760s; or the drawings of Borghese antiquities commissioned for Visconti's catalogue in the 1790s from Vincenzo Camuccini.

Careful, finished reproductive drawings, especially those after ancient works of art, were a characteristic part of local practice that arose from the enormous growth of interest in antiquity and the leading position occupied by Rome by virtue of her rich collections, excavations, and art commerce. Destined for engraving and publication, or private antiquarian collections, such reproductive drawings offered a natural outlet for skills in precise observation and careful technique that were the result of good Roman training. Though often only the temporary resort of aspiring talents, and though an industry largely anonymous by nature, there were also established and celebrated specialists like Giovanni Domenico Campiglia, who made such work their permanent profession.

The training of artists in Rome centered on the studios of individual masters and, despite an easily gained impression to the contrary, appears to have been almost entirely pragmatic in nature, usually requiring in addition to studio experience a good deal of diligent independent study. Beyond the elementary tasks of drawing after studio casts, engravings, and other drawings, one nearly universal aspect of training, which came to be most symbolic of Roman experience, was the intense pursuit of drawing after antiquities and famous works by old masters—especially Raphael—that abounded in the city's galleries and churches. Often sustained for a period of several years, this habitual program was undertaken both by those who remained under the guidance of a master—as is reported for instance of Marco Benefial and Placido Costanzi—and by others, like Pompeo Batoni or Vincenzo Camuccini, who honored a persistent local tradition in choosing to pursue such studies on their own.[4]

Life drawing was also an indispensable part of training, and if, while drawing in the churches, galleries, or countryside, the student could choose to work alone or in common with others, this activity invariably called for some cooperative arrangement. To meet its few basic requirements—a place of assembly, a hired model with suitable platform and illumination, and usually an instructor to set the poses and offer some form of guidance—a variety of private and public facilities for life drawing were available.

The Accademia di San Luca long relegated this aspect of training to the private sphere, and though some sporadic facilities seem to have been offered by the academy in the early part of the century, it was not until 1754 that a regular program of life classes was established. Until then, the one permanent institutional facility for life drawing was that of the French Academy in Rome, which held evening classes in its seat at the Palazzo Capranica until 1724, and thereafter in the Palazzo Mancini. This was a public class, open to outsiders as well as academy *pensionnaires,* and according to numerous sources maintained its popularity even after the official Roman academy came into being. Pierre Subleyras's superbly drawn male nude (no. 22) is possibly a product of this French Academy class.

Most typically, however, life drawing centered on the private academies operated by several of Rome's leading masters.[5] These academies or drawing schools were customarily held in evening hours apart from normal studio practice and though privately sponsored were considered "public" in that for a usual small fee, they were essentially open to all students and not just those privileged to be studio assistants.

Among the most famous private academies in the city were those of Sebastiano Conca, which, begun in the 1720s, was to acquire almost institutional permanence through continued family operation into the nineteenth century; of Pompeo Batoni, which was unquestionably the most celebrated of mid-century; and of Domenico Corvi, whose teaching was sampled at least for a short time by nearly all the leading young painters of the latter part of the century.

Private academies had been established in Rome in the 1600s, and several are recorded by Missirini at the beginning of the eighteenth century in the palaces of Cardinal Ottoboni, Marcello Sacchetti, and Carlo Falconieri.[6] They are among the subjects addressed in new statutes drawn up by the Accademia di San Luca in 1714, which unsuccessfully attempted to gain a wide range of exclusive privileges for academy members. Among them was the "... authority to create their own works, and to instruct youths, and to conduct public Academies, and to disrobe models ..." Another statute seeking to prevent young artists from holding their own unsupervised groups—"It is forbidden for youths to hold meetings, and Academies of art, without the presidence of an appointed Academician"—provides a reminder of the many spontaneous, short-lived arrangements that served as alternatives throughout the century to both the official and the most famous private schools.[7]

Rome's first publicly sponsored drawing academy, the Accademia del Nudo, was founded in 1754 under Pope Benedict XIV. In serving large numbers of Italian and foreign students, this popular academy was to ease the steady increase in demand for such a facility. It, too, was outgrown in time and seems never, in any case, to have threatened to replace the private academies. In 1779, when Antonio Canova visited the official academy school on first arriving in Rome, he estimated a crowd of over 150 students in attendance at one session, producing such stifling conditions that he was forced to leave.[8] It is not to be wondered, therefore, that in the same year the painter J. H. W. Tischbein, another newcomer to Rome, reported finding as many as ten private academies in operation in the city, a possibly unprecedented number that included, in addition to Batoni's and Corvi's, those run by the sculptor Alexander Trippel and the painters Joseph Bergler and L'Abruzzi.[9]

The Accademia del Nudo[10] occupied a ground-floor hall in a wing of the Capitoline palace and was administered by the Accademia di San Luca. As begun, the school held classes three times each week through a summer and winter term of five months each and was closed during the months of October and February. Eventually this academy held its own competitions with prize medals awarded to the best students in modest imitation of the academy's *concorsi.* The "directors" of the school, who posed the models and supervised the work, served for periods of one month at a time and were chosen from among academy members. Included in the list of directors prior to about 1810 are many artists whose own work is sampled here: Stefano Pozzi, Raphael Mengs, Filippo della Valle, Agostino Masucci, Marco Benefial, Giovanni Domenico Campiglia, Pompeo Batoni, Etienne Parrocel, Ignazio Collino, Domenico Corvi, Giuseppe Bottani, Giuseppe Cades, Domenico de Angelis, Pietro Benvenuti, and Vincenzo Camuccini.

Finished drawings of the academy nude—called academies—were regarded in a sense as the touchstone of professional excellence. Far beyond student years, and unrelated to preparations for specific work, academy drawing remained a common exercise for mature artists, who viewed continued study from life as a necessity in maintaining and perfecting their skills as draughtsmen. Academy drawings by the masters often remained in the studio as guides for students, and just as this seems to have been a regular practice by the later seventeenth century, so in the early 1780s we similarly learn that a young painter freshly introduced to Batoni's studio was given several of his master's academies to copy as a first assignment.[11]

Prized by connoisseurs, academy drawings formed an essential category in any representative collection. Batoni could confidently offer one to a patron as a token of regard, and Lanzi reputed that Domenico Corvi's drawn academies were in even heavier demand than his paintings. For the critic academy drawings offered a crucial standard of judgment as Mariette illustrated around 1770 when, in criticizing Raphael Mengs, he saved for the *coup de grace* a remark on the artist's academies: "I have seen some of his drawn academies: they are of ice."[12]

By classical standards, which held the human figure to be the essence of nature, the academy nude represented an objective, irreducible measure of craft and interpretive skill. The spirit of precise, methodical inquiry that largely guided artistic effort in the eighteenth century is appropriately symbolized by the degree of study concentrated on such finished work.

By the last decades of the century, however, there also appeared—to displace somewhat the traditional priority given to careful analytical drawing—a taste for virtuoso performance that was newly expressed in terms of rapid, improvised composition. Cades, Giani, Sabatelli, and Pinelli, all prolific in their graphic output, are among those whose fame initially derived from their spontaneous facility as draughtsmen. Antonio Zucchi might also be remembered as ending his career producing drawings for a ready market of amateur collectors that were cited for their bold brilliance.

To illustrate, though, how inseparable habits of study and free inspiration had become, one might recall Giuseppe Cades's gift for extemporizing deceptively skilled drawings in the manner of the old masters. Cades produced many such drawings for sale, and in 1788 is described as having in stock drawings rendered "in the manner of" but not specifically copying works by Guercino, Pietro da Cortona, Giulio Romano, and Cavalier d'Arpino, among others, whose effect was enhanced by paper smoked, stained, and torn to simulate age. Neither forgery nor reproductive copies, these drawings were created by Cades as erudite amusement, intended "not . . . to create an exact design from a critical standpoint, but to imitate each author in their actual style of drawing, and to design compositions, studies of various figures, and groups, and in every style . . . in short, as he is able to invent."[13]

No less remarkable was an effort to identify the very act of creative invention as a subject for studied exercise. This was realized through a number of private academies first introduced by the Accademia de' Pensieri established around 1790 by Felice Giani,[14] one of the liveliest draughtsmen at the turn of the century. "Pensieri" refer to the first ideas set out by an artist on paper, and it was the aim of Giani's academy to promote free compositional study through regular informal competitions. Participants created drawings on previously announced themes, which were then exhibited anonymously and criticized and discussed at meetings by fellow academy members. Giani's own drawings created for these sessions were reputedly much in demand by collectors and became within a few decades exceedingly rare.

Among the most significant artists who attended this academy, out of a much larger number of young Italians and foreigners, were Camuccini, Benvenuti, Sabatelli, Bossi and Pinelli. Giani's academy seems to have operated for about six years, and it is uncertain whether as separately recorded, the competitions were afterward continued by most of these artists on their own. That the idea certainly survived in Rome is proved by reports after 1814 that an "Academie de Composition" with identical purposes was held each month among members of the Austrian academy at the Palazzo Venezia.[15]

That fascination with the processes of making art that was such a constant factor in Roman practice and training, was also communicated by the collector and critic, who by century's end voiced full appreciation of the value drawing had in providing a unique view of the artist's private working process.

Prior to this, however, drawings had already assumed new significance as a resource of historical and critical study. The development of drawing collections and their use in the eighteenth century is an important part of the Roman background that characteristically involves once more the joint concerns of scholar, historian, collector, and artist.

Most of the large concentrations of Roman eighteenth-century drawing in existence today derive from collections assembled in Rome during the eighteenth century, and it can be seen that through remarkable precedents the Clark collection is linked to a tradition of purposeful, scholarly collecting that engaged the same group of artists at their source. Interest in eighteenth-century Roman drawings was connected at its earliest stage with the systematic study of Italian art, when works by contemporary masters were viewed as a natural extension of progress and evolution from the past.

Among the first collectors who actively sought to incorporate works by contemporary eighteenth-century Roman artists was Nicola Pio (born c. 1677), a self-described "dilettante romano," who intended his drawings to illustrate a series of 225 artists' biographies that he probably began writing in the mid-teens and had completed by 1724. Pio's *Le vite di pittori* . . .[16] covered the history of Italian art from the time of Mantegna and was brought to date through a large, knowledgeable selection of living Roman artists. From a number of them he commissioned, where necessary, the portrait drawings meant to accompany each biography, and from all he solicited examples of recent work. The collection eventually filled twelve volumes, which Pio described in his preface as containing "drawings, academies and landscapes . . . all being carefully considered, revised, judged, and approved by the living artists." As a result, he added "all the virtuosi and dilettanti were very pleased, and all the foreigners came to see it, not only for the curiosity of its many portraits of the famous . . . but also in order to observe the masters who revived good styles and usages and to see at a glance, how painting was lost, recovered, and advanced, and to otherwise study the excellent merit of the great masters, the most lively and frank manners, and the difference of styles, . . . and [especially to learn from] the subject drawings, and the academies which show the perfection of the nude and the basis of art."[17]

Failing in efforts to publish this work, Pio sold his drawings to the French collector Pierre Crozat, whose collection in turn was largely to illustrate a project not unlike Pio's: the famous *Recueil Crozat* whose first volume appeared in 1729 (*see* the print at no. 103 after a drawing by Pietro de' Pietris once owned by Pio).

The comprehensiveness and scientific purpose of Pio's collection was rivaled at about the same time in Florence by Francesco Gabburri (1675–1742), who was similarly engaged in compiling a history that combined biographical information with examples of the artists' drawn work. Though not Roman, Gabburri's collection deserves mention because his inventory of 1722 listed drawings by a good many artists in Rome,[18] including Carlo Maratta, Benedetto Luti, Pietro de' Pietris, and Padre Pozzo. Of particular interest, however, are the drawings Gabburri specifically commissioned for his collection from van Bloemen, Giovanni Paolo Panini, Sebastiano Conca, Marco Benefial, Andrea Locatelli, Filippo della Valle, Gaspare Vanvitelli, Giovanni Domenico Campiglia, and Francesco Imperiali. The drawing commissioned from this last artist in 1722, representing *Jacob and Rachel,* is now among the Clark drawings (no. 15).

Something quite different from an assembly of individual masterpieces, collections like Pio's and Gabburri's recognized the importance of comprehensive drawing collections as a basic resource for art historical study. In emphasizing the value placed upon originals—rather than reproductive prints—in illustrating the work of artists, a number of successful publications, like the *Recueil Crozat* or the volume on Guercino drawings published by Piranesi in 1763, introduced techniques of printing meant to convey, in addition to the compositional schemes of drawings, some of their qualities of line, texture, and tone.

Although the Pio and Gabburri collections were expressly formed for written historical surveys, historians thereafter were also inclined to view in this light other existing collections whose own purposes, though related to artistic instruction, were somewhat different. In fact, the majority of large Roman drawing collections known in the eighteenth century were formed by artists, and in these one cannot always distinguish didactic purpose from the instincts of the connoisseur. The latter, for instance, seems largely to have motivated Benedetto Luti in assembling a drawing collection—mainly of old masters—that in 1722 was reported to contain around 3,000 drawings.[19] Luti's interest in acquiring and caring for his collection was even said to have interfered with his activity as a painter.

Carlo Maratta, a prodigious collector of drawings, seems on the other hand to have built a collection in direct support of his own work and professional studies, and as a means of studio instruction.[20] Included among Maratta's drawings were the collection of Domenichino and purchases from the studio contents of Andrea Sacchi. It is an interesting reflection on the practical view of earlier studio collections, far exceeded by the historically inclined Maratta, that in making his personal bequest of drawings, Sacchi had excluded Maratta from receiving any, reasoning that as a mature artist he was less in need of them than other students.[21] Though prompted by specific need, Maratta agreed to sell his own collection only when age effectively prevented him from working. In 1703 Pope Clement XI acquired Maratta's drawings for himself to keep them from being sold abroad. As Albani family property, the collection remained the most famous in Rome until its sale by Cardinal Alessandro Albani to George III of England in 1762.

Coincidental with the collecting activity of Maratta, and probably directly influenced by him, was the inauguration of a teaching collection of drawings at the Accademia di San Luca.[22] The earlier part of the academy collection, dating from the last quarter of the seventeenth century and comprised largely of academy nudes and perspective and anatomical studies, was the result of gifts by various artists that apparently included Maratta along with Carlo Cesio, Francesco Cozza, and others. Interest soon faltered, however, and additions to the academy collections during the eighteenth century derive mainly from student activity, including prize drawings from academy competitions and life studies that become especially numerous after the founding of the Accademia del Nudo in 1754. Although the absence of regular academy instruction must have played its part, the neglect of existing academy holdings could have only discouraged further additions. In 1708 the academy resolved "to take more diligent precautions for the safekeeping of the drawings deposited in the Academy,"[23] making clear its reason for doing so by threatening apostolic excommunication for anyone taking works of art belonging to the academy. In 1732, while *principe,* Sebastiano Conca is recorded having the collection inventoried, but as later examples prove, indifference at best seems to have been the more permanent rule.

Teaching value seems also to have been anticipated in the drawing collection formed by the German painter Lambert Krahe during his years in Rome from 1736 to 1756. Foreign artists who visited or spent some time in Rome commonly returned home with a sampling of drawings by contemporary masters, but in Krahe's case, acquisitions were carried out on a vast and systematic scale. Acquired later in the century by the Düsseldorf Academy—where Krahe as first director oversaw its cataloguing and partial publication—the collection remains in that city as one of the largest representations of drawings by late-seventeenth- and eighteenth-century masters.[24]

Probably the last great collection of the century was that of the sculptor Bartolommeo Cavaceppi (1716–1799), which Winckelmann praised for its comprehensiveness and chronological ordering.[25] This collection too, at least by bequest to the Accademia di San Luca, was intended for some teaching purposes. None of the one hundred volumes of drawings Cavaceppi left to the academy remained there, however. They became the property of Vincenzo Pacetti (c. 1746–1820)—who had arbitrated rather dubiously as both *principe* of the academy and an executor of Cavaceppi's estate—were passed to his son, and together with the significant additions made by the elder Pacetti, were eventually purchased for the Berlin Kupferstichkabinett.

From what we know of the original contents and the organization of the Cavaceppi collection, there is little evidence of any special systematization as claimed by Winckelmann. It is true, however, that he spoke of only part of the collection, and our knowledge derives from an inventory of 1800 that listed what remained after the sculptor himself had sold nine or ten volumes of drawings and after the theft of another fourteen volumes which occurred while his estate was being inventoried.

The remaining collection contained volumes representing the various Italian and northern schools, mostly of sixteenth- and seventeenth-century drawings; other volumes were devoted to the work of a single master, such as Baciccio or Maratta and his school; while the most common arrangement was according to categories such as "sketches and drawings of figures," "nudes and anatomy," and "views and animals," etc. Substantial numbers of drawing were by Maratta, Calandrucci, de' Pietris, Benefial, and Masucci, and also present were Sebastiano Conca, Luigi Vanvitelli, Locatelli, Passeri, Trevisani, Imperiali, Chiari, Bianchi, and Pier Leone Ghezzi. One notable volume of "academies of various authors" contained fifty-one academy drawings by Costanzi, de Rossi, Le Gros, Benefial, Scaramuccio, Calandrucci, Pecheux, Parrocel, Corvi, and de' Pietris.

Pacetti's diaries document additions he made to the Cavaceppi collection which include some old master drawings but more often those of eighteenth-century artists. Among Pacetti's early acquisitions (1784) were six volumes of prize drawings in architecture for the Concorso Clementino formerly owned by Filippo della Valle (*principe* 1752), and also owed to him was a large and important group of drawings by Panini.

Purchased on several occasions in the 1790s were groups of academies by Batoni and Mengs and others by Sacchi, Trevisani, Luti, and Subleyras.

As had been true throughout the century, drawings from the studio contents of deceased artists could be had from their heirs, and Pacetti utilized such opportunities for the Batoni and Mengs drawings which he bought from their sons. Similarly, Pacetti also bought a group of twenty-five drawings in 1801 from the widow of Cades; twenty-one academies in 1804 out of the estate of Domenico Corvi, who had died the year before; and in 1803 and 1805 he acquired first a group of eleven drawings, and then an entire portfolio of drawings from Benefial's heirs.

With this complementary emphasis on later Roman artists the combined Cavaceppi–Pacetti collection encompassed a group of eighteenth-century artists that would be largely familiar to anyone who already either knew the Clark collection, or had read through Lanzi's last chapter on the Roman school, written at century's end and revised for the definitive edition of 1809.

Revolution and its calamitous effects on the Papal States seemed almost at once to relegate the world of eighteenth-century Rome to a distant part of history. Yet the artistic achievements of that world were still regarded in the early-nineteenth century as an enlightened basis for progress to come. The very artists who advanced in the new century—from Giani and Canova, who both died in the 1820s, to the still younger generation of Benvenuti, Sabatelli, Camuccini, and Pinelli—had themselves shared their youth in the Rome of Kauffmann, Corvi, Cades, and even of Batoni. Through this final link, interest in eighteenth-century Roman art was kept alive, though failing, through three or four decades of the nineteenth century. The indifference to which it gave way by mid-century is typified in the fate of the Cavaceppi–Pacetti collection itself, for by the time it reached Berlin in 1843 little enthusiasm was stirred by its immense representation of Baroque and later art, only disappointment at its minor showings from the Renaissance.

1. Missirini, 1823, p. 248.

2. More about academy activities in the seventeenth century, including sponsored competitions and teaching programs generally in disuse by the eighteenth century, awaits promised publication by Ann Sutherland Harris of a minute-book of academy meetings from 1634–74 (*see* Ann Sutherland Harris, *Andrea Sacchi,* Oxford, 1977, pp. 33–37). Some information extracted from this source was cited with exaggerated conclusions by Goldstein, 1978, pp. 2–4. *See also L'Accademia,* 1974, and Missirini, 1823, p. 159, who cites private academy competitions at the beginning of the eighteenth century as the models for those at the Accademia di San Luca.

3. Lanzi, 1968, vol. 1, p. 423.

4. For Benefial, *see* Missirini, 1823, p. 222; for Costanzi, *see* Pio, 1977, p. 194. Mengs and Batoni are cited in Lanzi's first edition of 1795–96 (pp. 376–77) as proving the value of study in Rome "since there they formed themselves worthy artists without resorting to any studio save that which Rome holds open to all: and these are the perfect exemplars of the Greek sculptors and the Italian painters" (*see* Lanzi, 1968, vol. 1, p. 645).

5. For the Roman private academies in general, *see* Nikolaus Pevsner, *Academies of Art Past and Present,* Cambridge, 1940, pp. 67 ff; and for seventeenth-century Rome with relevant citations from Passeri, *see* Ann Sutherland Harris, "Drawings by Andrea Sacchi: Additions and Problems," *Master Drawings,* vol. 9, no. 4 (1971), pp. 384–85, and pp. 386–87, nn. 7, 8, 10, 17. For remarks on the academies of Conca and Batoni, *see* Clark, 1967 ("Conca"), p. 331, and Clark, 1967, p. 109. For Corvi's academy with a contemporary account, *see* Ferrara, 1974–75, p. 211, n. 12.

6. Missirini, 1823, p. 159.

7. Laurent Pecheux's academy in the 1750s, though run with Batoni's help (Bollea, 1942, p. 367), or that of the Nazarene painters in the beginning of the nineteenth century, might serve as two diverse examples. For the academy statutes, *see* Missirini, 1823, p. 195, nos. 12 and 17.

8. Canova, 1959, pp. 30–31.

9. Heinrich Wilhelm Tischbein, *Aus meinem Leben,* Berlin, 1956, ed. Kuno Mittelstädt, pp. 151–52; *see also* Pevsner, *Academies of Art,* p. 79; Noack, 1907, pp. 99–100; and Noack, 1927, vol. 1, p. 369. Tischbein's exemplary program of study (*see* pp. 151–60) included drawing after the antique and old masters in the daytime and life drawing at Trippel's private academy in the evening. There he remarked on the chance to share conversation on art or on the models with others in the small group, unlike the large formal academies which imposed a rule of silence.

Curiously, it was not overcrowding of the Capitoline school, but its remoteness—the same reason cited when the school itself was relocated in 1804—that evidently caused the painter Stefano Tofanelli and a certain Abbate Conti to open life drawing classes in the late 1780s (*see also* Rudolph, 1977, p. 178, n. 8, which is useful in general for late-eighteenth-century academies).

10. For the history of this academy, *see* Pietrangeli, 1959; Pietrangeli, 1962; and Pirotta, 1969.

11. For Gaspare Landi in Batoni's studio in 1781, *see* G. Tononi, "Lettere inedite di Gaspare Landi," *Strenna Piacentina,* vol. 3 (1877), pp. 133–34.

12. *Abecedario,* 1851/53–1859/60, vol. 3, p. 381. For life drawings in France, *see* Princeton, 1977.

13. Letter of Stefano Tofanelli of 1788, quoted in Clark, 1964, pp. 25–26, n. 12; *see also* p. 12; Lanzi, 1968, vol. 1, pp. 422–23.

14. For a complete account based on contemporary memoirs, *see* Rudolph, 1977.

15. *See* Walter Wagner, "Die Rompensionäre der Wiener Akademie der bildenden Künste 1772–1848," *Römische historische Mitteilungen,* vol. 14, 1972, p. 98.

16. For Pio's collection, *see* the introduction by Enggass, pp. iii-viii in Pio, 1977; and Clark, 1967 ("Portraits"), the latter with particular reference to the large group of Pio's portrait drawings in the Nationalmuseum, Stockholm. This museum also contains many subject drawings from the same source, and is, with the Louvre, one of the major known repositories of Pio's drawings.

Padre Sebastiano Resta (1635–1714) continued during the early-eighteenth century to assemble his collections of drawings into annotated historical volumes, but this material effectively ended before 1700. For Resta, *see* Popham, 1936–37. Grassi, 1979, p. 66, n. 7, cites later literature; *see also* Milan, Biblioteca Ambrosiana, *Cento Tavole del Codice Resta,* Milan, 1955, for facsimile plates from Resta's "Galleria portatile."

17. Pio, 1977, p. 3.

18. Giuseppe Campori, *Raccolta di cataloghi ed inventarii inediti di quadri, statue, disegni . . . ,* Modena, 1870, pp. 521–96. Gabburri's manuscript biographies of artists is in the Biblioteca Nazionale, Florence. For the sale of the drawing collection, and literature on Gabburri, *see* John Fleming, "Mr. Kent, Art Dealer, and the Fra Bartolommeo Drawings," *The Connoisseur,* vol. 141, no. 570 (May, 1958), p. 227.

19. Richardson, 1722, p. 288. The number of drawings given around the time of Luti's death was over 14,000 (Bottari and Ticozzi, 1822–25, vol. 6, p. 165). In 1759 Luti's collection, or much of it, was acquired by an Englishman named Kent, who also obtained the Gabburri collection. Sales of Luti's drawings are recorded in London 1760 and 1762 (*see* F. Lugt, *Repertoire des catalogues de ventes publiques,* The Hague, 1938, vol. 1, nos. 1126 and 1255;

and Fleming, "Mr. Kent," p. 227). On August 11, 1791 Vincenzo Pacetti recorded a purchase of drawings from the "vendità del cav. Luti" (Cassirer, 1922, p. 95), suggesting that a few sheets at least may have joined the collection now in Berlin. For Luti as collector, *see also* Pio, 1977, p. 24; *Abecedario,* 1851/53–1859/60, vol. 3, p. 228; Pascoli, 1730–36, vol. 1, p. 230.

20. For Maratta's collection with literature, *see* University Park, 1975; for its later history as Albani property, *see* Fleming, 1958.

21. For Sacchi's last testament and inventory of his estate, *see* Harris, *Andrea Sacchi,* pp. 115–28.

22. *See L'Accademia,* 1974, pp. 325 ff.

23. Missirini, 1823, p. 172.

24. For the collection now in the Kunstmuseum, Düsseldorf, *see* Illa Budde, *Beschreibender Katalog der Handzeichnungen in der staatlichen Kunstakademie Düsseldorf,* Düsseldorf, 1930, pp. vii ff; also Düsseldorf, 1964; Harris and Schaar, 1967; Düsseldorf, 1969–70.

Krahe is said to have acquired the estate of Pier Leone Ghezzi, one of the considerable eighteenth-century collections about which little is known; many Ghezzi items, however, ended up in the Cavaceppi collection noted below. For Carlo Marchionni's collection, which included works by contemporaries, *see* no. 44.

Other still extant collections by foreign artists are those of Allan Ramsay (National Gallery of Scotland, Edinburgh) and Bertel Thorvaldsen (Thorvaldsen Museum, Copenhagen).

25. For the Cavaceppi collection with Pacetti's later additions, *see* Cassirer, 1922. *See also* Missirini, 1823, p. 292. For a representative selection of the drawings, *see* Berlin, 1969.

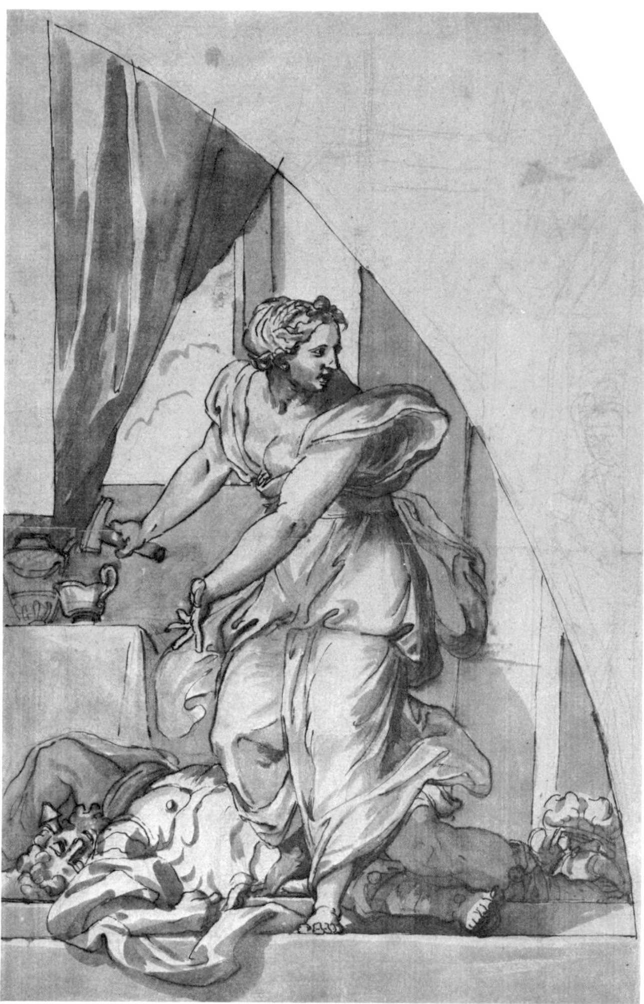

1

Attributed to CARLO MARATTA

Camerano (Marches) 1625—Rome 1713

1. Study for a Lunette: "Jael Slaying Sisera"

c. 1670

Pen and brown ink and brown wash over black chalk on cream laid paper

409 x 268 mm (16 1/8 x 10 9/16")

Watermark: kneeling figure (a knight?) with a cross in a shield

1978-70-329

Provenance: purchased from Adrian Fries, New York, 1958

Exhibition: Minneapolis, 1967, no. 56

Although Carlo Maratta's long and prosperous career was drawing to a close in the early years of the eighteenth century—by 1706 he was barely able to paint[1]—the duration and pervasiveness of his influence on succeeding generations of Roman artists make it appropriate to inaugurate these drawings with a sheet possibly by his hand, and certainly from his studio.[2] Called "art dictator of the age,"[3] Maratta upheld a continuum of Roman tradition that reached back through his teacher Andrea Sacchi to Francesco Albani, Annibale Carraci, and ultimately Raphael and that was to prevail at the close of the Settecento. He produced a vast number of decorations for Roman churches, as did his many pupils, which, along with numerous reproductive engravings after his work (*see* nos. 100, 101), were instrumental in spreading his influence. He was *principe* of the Accademia di San Luca in 1664-65 and *principe perpetuo* from 1701 to 1713, and his reform of its teaching methods from the 1660s onward set the tone for that institution's approach to instruction for at least two hundred years.[4] A prolific and often superb draughtsman—crisp, succinct, vigorous, and full-bodied when he wished to be, especially in his numerous studies of figures, drapery, and parts of the body—he influenced many artists catalogued here, from his direct followers Giuseppe Chiari, Pietro de' Pietris, and Agostino Masucci (nos. 6, 7, 25) to their own subsequent pupils, such as Stefano Pozzi and Giuseppe Bottani (nos. 45-46, 47-50).

The study of *Jael Slaying Sisera* is one of numerous surviving sheets related to Maratta's cartoons for the mosaic decoration of the Cappella della Presentazione in Saint Peter's, a major commission that occupied the artist for years. The subject, Jael killing the Canaanite general Sisera as he flees from the Israelites, is one of a group of Old Testament scenes of Miriam, Joshua, Bileam, Noah, Aaron, Gideon, Isaiah, Elijah, and Moses and occupies a half-lunette over the altar flanking a window; *Judith with the Head of Holofernes* completes the other half of the lunette. The commission was initiated in 1669, and in 1674 canvases were prepared for the cartoons of the *Jael* and *Judith* scenes; however, Maratta's involvement with the project was prolonged into the next decade, possibly even into the 1690s.[5] Work on the cartoons for the chapel dome was incomplete at the time of the artist's death and was carried on by his pupil Giuseppe Chiari.

Many drawn studies for the commission in chalk or ink and wash survive, demonstrating how carefully Maratta worked at adjusting the pose of Jael and the arrangement of Sisera's body before considering his composition resolved; as has often been pointed out, the role of preparatory drawings was of overriding importance in the artist's working method. This sheet can now be added to at least twenty-five known *Jael Slaying Sisera* studies—some possibly executed with studio assistance—scattered in European and American collections.[6]

A.P.

1. *See* Westin and Westin in University Park, 1975, p. 4.

2. Anthony Clark's notebooks show that he considered but later rejected the possibility of the sheet's being a copy or derivation; because it exhibits a certain dryness of execution, Jacob Bean suggests the possibility of a studio hand (in correspondence).

3. Waterhouse, 1976, p. 89.

4. For example, in supervised drawing after the live model and in the institution of competitions for prizes awarded at special ceremonies (*see* especially Ann Sutherland Harris, *Andrea Sacchi*, Oxford, 1977, pp. 34 and 45, n. 58; Goldstein, 1978).

5. Concerning dating and documentation, *see* University Park, 1975, pp. 63–67.

6. The whole group is studied and described by Dowley, 1970. *See also* University Park, 1975, nos. 35–37, figs. 41–44, and pp. 63–67. The collections include the Royal Library at Windsor Castle (*see* Blunt and Cooke, 1960, p. 57, nos. 293–95, fig. 44); the Kunstmuseum in Düsseldorf (*see* Eckhard Schaar, in Harris and Schaar, 1967, pp. 120–21, nos. 311–18, figs. 67–69); and the Real Academia de San Fernando in Madrid (*see* Nieto Alcaide, 1965, pp. 16–18, nos. 35–42, pls. 22–26), each of which has large numbers of Maratta drawings owing largely to the migrations of the artist's own vast collection during the eighteenth century. Other sheets can be found in the Metropolitan Museum in New York (*see* Bean, 1979, pp. 209–10, no. 275, repr.) and in Würzburg, London, Milan, Melbourne, and Providence, Rhode Island. Drawings for others of the mosaic cartoons, including the flanking *Judith with the Head of Holofernes*, are in several of the above-mentioned collections.

PADRE ANDREA POZZO

Trent 1642—Vienna 1709

2. *Study for the Altar of Saint Louis Gonzaga in Sant' Ignazio, Rome*

c. 1697

Red chalk on cream laid paper

273 x 218 mm (10 3/4 x 8 9/16")

1978-70-393

Provenance: gift of Andrew Ciechanowiecki, 1973

Exhibition: New York, 1976–77

Best known for his ceiling fresco in the church of Sant' Ignazio, Rome, the Jesuit father Andrea Pozzo was perhaps the most imaginative Italian painter, architect, and theoretician practicing in the last decade of the seventeenth century. In 1700 he published the second volume of a treatise on perspective with designs for many of his most important executed works, including two altars in the Roman churches of the Gesù and Sant' Ignazio.[1] In these altars Pozzo combined architecture, sculpture, and precious materials to create illusionistic ensembles of unparalleled scale and richness.

This drawing is of special interest because it appears to be a preparatory study for the altar of Saint Louis Gonzaga in Sant' Ignazio (1697–99). While it bears certain similarities to Pozzo's altar of Saint Ignatius in the Gesù (1695–97), the colossal order of Corinthian pilasters framing the aedicula proves that the setting for the design is actually the transept of Sant' Ignazio.

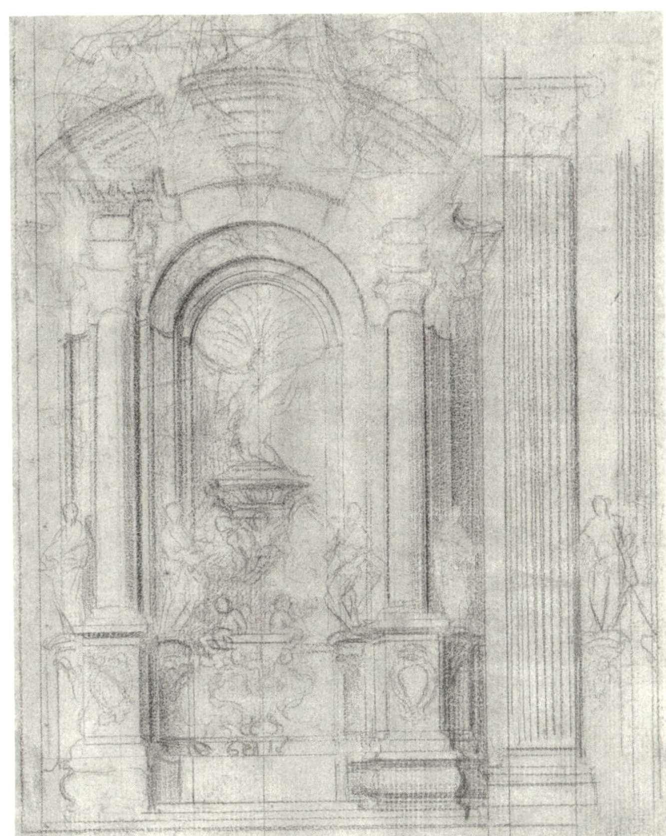

2

In preparing this design for the Gonzaga altar, Pozzo clearly used the earlier Saint Ignatius altar as a point of departure. The sketch repeats the central motif of a free-standing statue of the saint set within a niche flanked by two columns with straight shafts. Pozzo may have borrowed the statues of Virtues flanking the columns from another project for the Saint Ignatius altar, Sebastiano Cipriani's design of 1696.[2] This drawing is also related to the designs for the Gonzaga altar that appear in Pozzo's treatise *Perspectiva pictorum*.... In plate 64, which the artist described as his "prima idea," there are statues of Virtues and spiral columns, but no central niche. Much closer is the design illustrated in plate 65, which contains the Virtues as well as a free-standing statue of Saint Louis Gonzaga kneeling on his reliquary casket, an arrangement that resembles the sculptural group at the center of the drawing. As executed, the design of the altar is further removed from this sketch: the Virtues are eliminated, the number of columns doubled, and the magnificent bas-relief by Pierre Legros the Younger replaces the free-standing sculptural group.

The drawing appears to have been executed in several stages. Using draughtsmen's instruments, Pozzo drew in the outlines of the existing architecture and the dimensions of the niche to serve as a guide. Working freehand, he then rendered the architectural members of the aedicula in perspective, introducing strong passages of shadow to cast the projecting elements of the altar into relief. Finally, he shifted his concern to the design and placement of the sculpture. The study represents an interim stage in the artist's conceptual process, especially striking in its spontaneity and rich in its power of suggestion. Because of its strength and the light it casts on the planning stages of the Gonzaga altar, it constitutes a significant addition to the corpus of drawings by or attributed to Pozzo.

J.P.

1. *Perspectiva Pictorum et Architectorum Andreae Putei e Societate Jesu,* vol. 2, Rome, 1700.
2. Kerber, 1971, fig. 80.

Attributed to CARLO CIGNANI
Bologna 1628—Forlì 1719

3. Diana and Endymion

Verso: *Studies of an Arm, Hand, Head, and Drapery*

c. 1700

Inscribed on recto, apparently by Alessandro Maggiori, in brown ink at bottom center: Il Cignani fece; faint traces below of an old inscription in pencil: C. Cignani; inscribed on verso in brown ink over black chalk at upper left: Carlo Cignani Bolognese / Uno de' primari pittori della sua età discepolo dell' / Albani; and in brown ink in a different hand at center: Io Aless. Maggiori comprai in Bologna il / giorno 4 di Giugno del / 1793.

Recto: brown wash heightened with white gouache over black chalk on faded blue laid paper; verso: red and black chalks

247 x 285 mm (9 3/4 x 11 1/4")

1978-70-235

Provenance: Alessandro Maggiori (Lugt suppl. 3005b), purchased in Bologna, 1793; C. Argentieri (?) (Lugt suppl. 486b: as anonymous mark); P. G. Braschi (?) (Lugt suppl. 2079b: as anonymous mark); gift of John Maxon, 1960

Exhibition: Minneapolis, 1970–71

During the later seventeenth century Carlo Cignani occupied a position in Bologna equivalent to that of Carlo Maratta in Rome. He enjoyed a wide European clientele. Such princely collectors as the Elector of Bavaria and Prince Johann Adam of Liechtenstein especially prized his cultivated, meticulously executed pictures. Cignani was the first president of Bologna's art academy, the Accademia Clementina, and became the only director to be honored with the title of *principe perpetuo*.

The media and manner of drawing employed on the respective sides of this sheet are quite different, and it is by no means certain that both drawings are by the same hand. The chalk details of figures on the verso have a character which is consonant with the relatively little that is known of Cignani's drawing style.[1] The studied contouring of the forms, their careful modeling by a gentle turn of light, and the placidity of the handling indicate an artist of a classical orientation; there is here an unmistakable relationship to the drawing manner

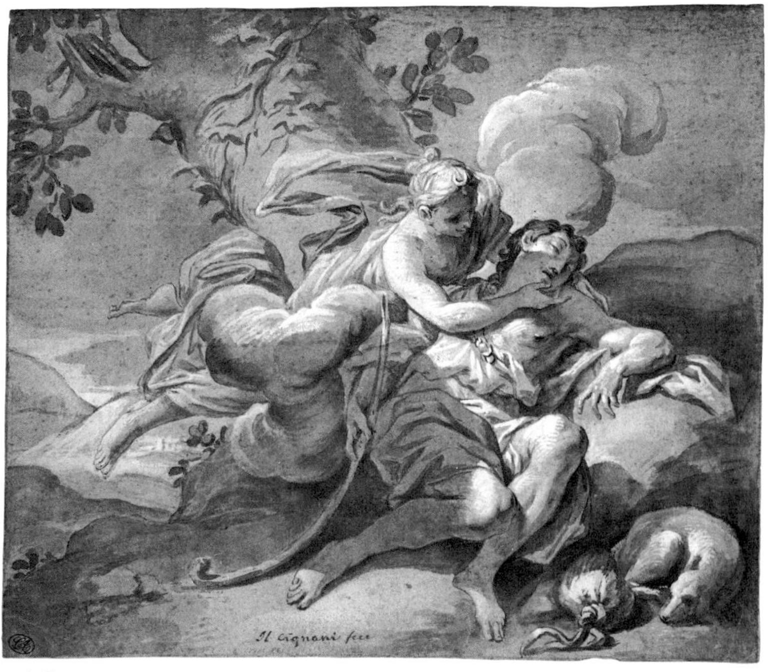

3 Recto

of Domenichino, which suggests a Bolognese lineage. More specifically, the manner of drawing resembles that employed by Cignani in a study of a faun in the Witt Collection, Courtauld Institute Galleries, London,[2] related to a pastoral idyll by the artist recorded in a print by Bartolozzi; however, the detail studies in the Clark drawing cannot be related to any picture by Cignani presently known.

The attribution of the more highly finished *Diana and Endymion* is problematical. Although the suave and rather languorous elegance of the figures relates in a general way to Cignani's work, none of the drawings securely given to him resembles this sheet, either in handling or medium. More significantly, there is a certain coarseness of facial type, especially noticeable in Endymion's broad, flat cheeks and puffy eyes, that is difficult to fit within Cignani's canon. The rendering of the drapery lacks the fine selectivity of pattern and the simple eloquence characteristic of this highly cultivated master, and the contouring of Diana's feet is more superficial than one would expect of him. On the other hand, the drawing is of estimable quality and if not by Cignani must be attributable to a worthy artist of his school.

The inscription on the verso referring to the sheet's purchase in 1793 indicates that it was owned by Alessandro Maggiori, a well-known Emilian collector whose dated notations enable one to trace his collecting activity between 1785 and 1817 in Faenza, Bologna, Rome, and Naples. (For other Maggiori sheets in the Clark collection, *see* nos. 59, 101B.)

D.M.

1. For autograph drawings by Cignani, *see* Kurz, 1955, pl. 23, fig. 23; Renato Roli, *I disegni italiani del Seicento: scuole emiliana, toscana, romana, marchigiana, e umbra*, Treviso, 1969, pls. 55–57; Miller, 1971, pl. 1; and Michael Levey, *The Later Italian Pictures in the Royal Collection*, London, 1974, nos. 449–54, figs. 45–47.
2. Inv. no. 3623.

PIETRO NELLI

Massa di Carrara (Tuscany) 1677—Rome 1740

4. *Portrait of Clement XI Albani*

1701–3

Inscribed on verso in pencil at center: School of Maratta– / Portrait of Pope Clement XI; and at lower left: 2047[?]15R

Red chalk on cream laid paper

427 x 285 mm (16 13/16 x 11 1/4")

1978-70-371

Provenance: purchased from Christopher Powney, London, 1965

Exhibition: Minneapolis, 1967, no. 66

Pietro Nelli was one of the portraitists most in demand in Rome during the first four decades of the eighteenth century. Upon his arrival in the city he became a favorite pupil of Giovanni Maria Morandi (1622–1717), by whom he was treated like a son.[1] He was court portraitist to Pope Clement XI, as is shown by engravings after papal portraits and also by his self-portrait drawing in the series that accompanied Nicola Pio's manuscript bi-

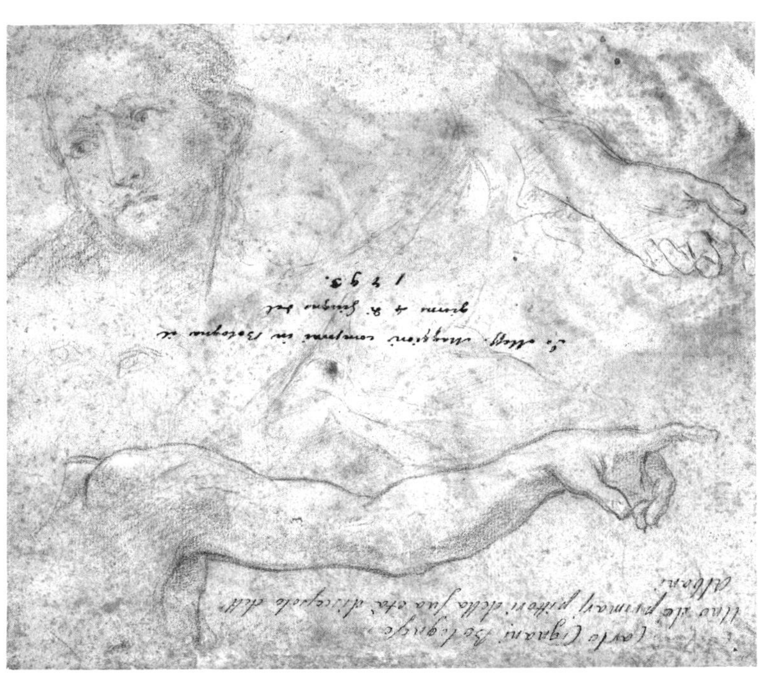

3 Verso

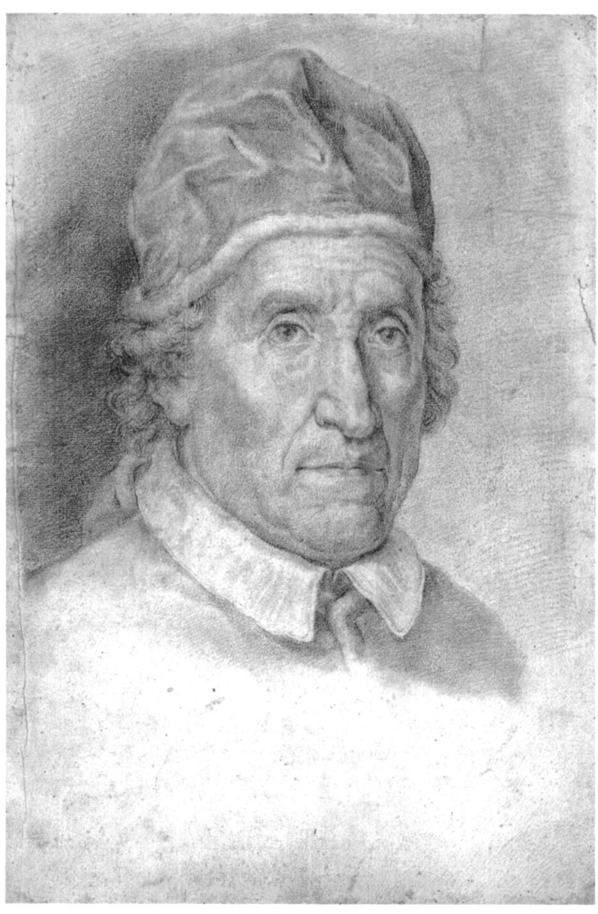

4

ographies (now in the Nationalmuseum, Stockholm[2]) in which the painter holds a sheet almost identical to the Clark drawing with a portrait of the pope wearing the camauro.

One of the earliest portraits of Clement XI painted by Nelli, shortly after the pope was elected in November 1700, is in the Palazzo Albani in Urbino: two others are known through engravings, one by Antonius Birkhard, the other by Gerolamo Rossi. The Clark drawing is almost certainly for a tapestry portrait that is derived in turn from an oil portrait, now lost. The tapestry portrait[3] was one of the first products of the manufactory established by Clement XI, shortly after his election, at the Ospizio (now Istituto Romano) di San Michele in Rome. Clement named as directors of the *arazzeria,* which operated only during the twenty years of his pontificate, the Parisian tapestry maker Jean Simonet and the Roman painter Andrea Procaccini. The first weavings were after Nelli's portraits of Clement, one of which is recorded by the Clark drawing; two others are in the Villa Albani (now Torlonia) in Rome and in the Musée des Arts Décoratifs in Paris, having been dispatched from Rome by Philippe II, duc d'Orléans, regent of France (1715–23).

Nelli also painted portraits of don Orazio Albani, the pope's brother (engraved by Birkhard; presently owned by the contessa Grisi, née Chigi Albani), and of Cardinal Annibale Albani (engraved by Gerolamo Rossi). He portrayed a number of the cardinals created by Clement XI, Innocent XIII, Benedict XIII, and Clement XII, as well as many of the Roman nobility, especially members of the Rospigliosi family. Nelli was elected a member of the Virtuosi del Pantheon in 1712 and of the Accademia di San Luca in 1719.

A.B.V.

1. Information on Nelli's life derives primarily from the recently published manuscript of Nicola Pio (Pio, 1977, pp. 123–24). Concerning Nelli's few drawings known to date, *see* my article in preparation for *L'Urbe.*
2. *See* Clark, 1967 ("Portraits"), p. 13, no. 32.
3. Now in the collection of the Istituto Romano di San Michele, Rome (Gabinetto Fotografico Nazionale, Rome, E43795).

GIUSEPPE GHEZZI

Comunanza (Marches) 1634—Rome 1721

5. A Papal Procession in Piazza San Pietro

1700–10

Inscribed in pencil at lower right: G. Ghezzi

Black and white chalks, squared in black chalk, on grayish beige paper, mounted down

352 x 485 mm (13 7/8 x 19 1/8")

1978-70-286

Provenance: purchased from Carlo and Marcello Sestieri, Rome, 1967

Exhibition: St. Louis, 1972, no. 51, repr.

Giuseppe Ghezzi was one of the major figures of the Roman late Baroque. His first teacher was his father, Sebastiano, a painter and engineer from the Marches who had studied with Guercino. Arriving in Rome in the 1660s, Ghezzi gradually evolved a style appropriate to monumental decoration, one in which narrative essentials are presented economically and in which emphasis lies on expression, gesture, and activity. The naturalism of his art is purposeful; each figure is clearly distinguished and each action precise and measurable. His principal Roman works, combining in equal degree the influences of Guercino, Gaulli, and Maratta, include *The Descent of the Holy Spirit, Saint John Baptizing,* and *The Baptism of Christ* in San Silvestro in Capite (1697); the nave scenes depicting *The Penitent Magdalen, The Resurrection of the Dead, Rebecca and Eliezer at the Well,* and *Adam and Eve Before God* in Santa Maria in Vallicella (1700); and *The Madonna Weeping over the Dead Christ, San Giacomo della Marca,*

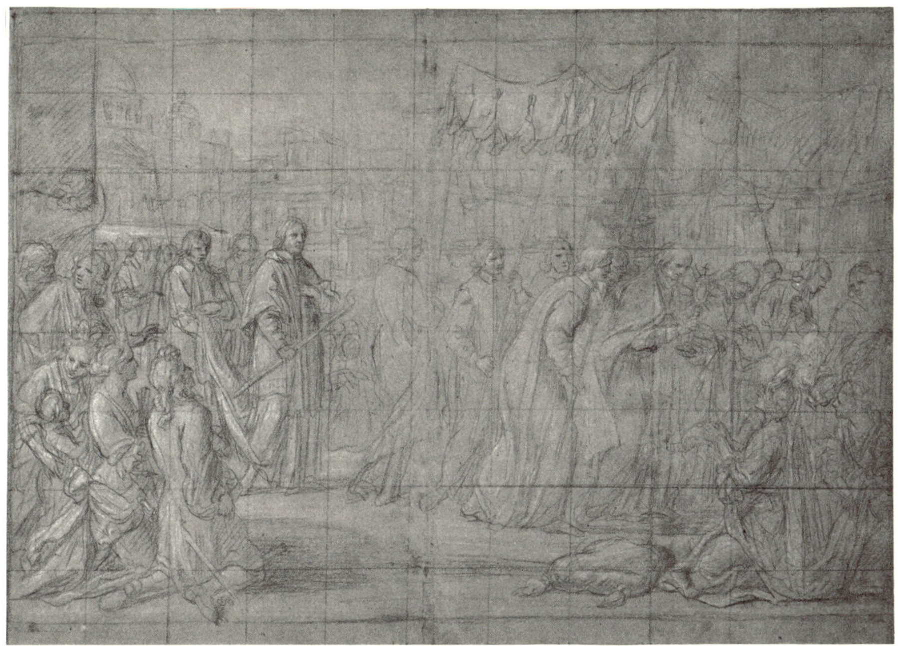

5

and *Saint Nicholas of Tolentino* in San Salvatore in Lauro (c. 1694).[1] Despite the number of altarpieces Ghezzi produced, his contemporary reputation was based largely upon the role he played in the affairs of the Accademia di San Luca and upon his connections with the Roman art market.[2]

Elected to the Accademia di San Luca in 1674, Ghezzi emerged as spokesman for that body with an influence almost equal to that of Maratta in directing the institution. He acted as secretary from 1678 to 1719 and left a valuable record of the academy's activities, especially of its *concorsi* and the award ceremonies held on the Campidoglio.[3] Having been trained in law and philosophy, Ghezzi discovered a natural outlet for his theoretical inclinations through the instruction of young artists. In his writings he frequently emphasized the importance of anatomical studies after the live model, of drapery and perspective studies, of proper modeling and distribution of light and shade, and of "other accessories to perfect theory, the true sustenance of our profession."[4] Thus it was perhaps appropriate that it was Ghezzi who painted for the academy in 1696 the posthumous portraits of two of its founders, Federico Zuccaro and Girolamo Muziano.[5]

Ghezzi and his son, Pier Leone (*see* nos. 12–14), enjoyed the support of Pope Clement XI and of Cardinals Annibale and Alessandro of the Albani family from Urbino. Anthony Clark identified this drawing of a papal procession as a study for a picture in the Galleria Nazionale delle Marche, Urbino, incorrectly attributed there to Pier Leone.[6] The exact subject of the processional scene is not known, but Clark suggested that it might represent a meeting between Clement XI and Queen Maria Casimira of Poland, who resided in Rome during Clement's papacy (1700–1721) from 1699 to 1714. The prominent cardinal to the left appears to be Annibale Albani.

E.P.B.

1. For an introduction to this important, long-neglected painter, *see* the biographies by Pio, 1977, pp. 107–8, and Pascoli, 1730–36, vol. 2, pp. 199–211; also F. Noack in Thieme-Becker, 1907–50, vol. 13, pp. 537–39; Gabrielli, 1934; and Waterhouse, 1976, pp. 81–82.

2. Ghezzi was much in demand as an advisor to collectors. As an appraiser and restorer of old master paintings, his clientele included Queen Christina of Sweden. From 1689 he organized an annual exhibition of paintings from Roman collections to celebrate the feast of Santa Maria di Loreto, held each December 10 in San Salvatore in Lauro, the church of the confraternity of the *marchigiani*. The records of the exhibitions are preserved in a manuscript by Ghezzi in the Museo di Roma ("Notizie dei quadri dei principi in Roma").

3. *See L'Accademia,* 1974, pp. 420–21.

4. G. Ghezzi, *Il centesimo dell'anno MDCXCV celebrato in Roma dall' Accademia del Disegno* . . . , Rome, 1696, p. 10.

5. Stefano Susinno, "I ritratti degli accademici," in *L'Accademia,* 1974, pp. 224, 227, figs. 11, 12.

6. *See* St. Louis, 1972, no. 51; for the painting, *see* Urbino, Palazzo Ducale, *Restauri nelle Marche: testimonianze acquisti e recuperi,* June 28–September 30, 1978, no. 131, repr, p. 508 (inv. no. 955; as by Pier Leone Ghezzi and one of a series of six similar subjects from Palazzo Albani painted c. 1717–20).

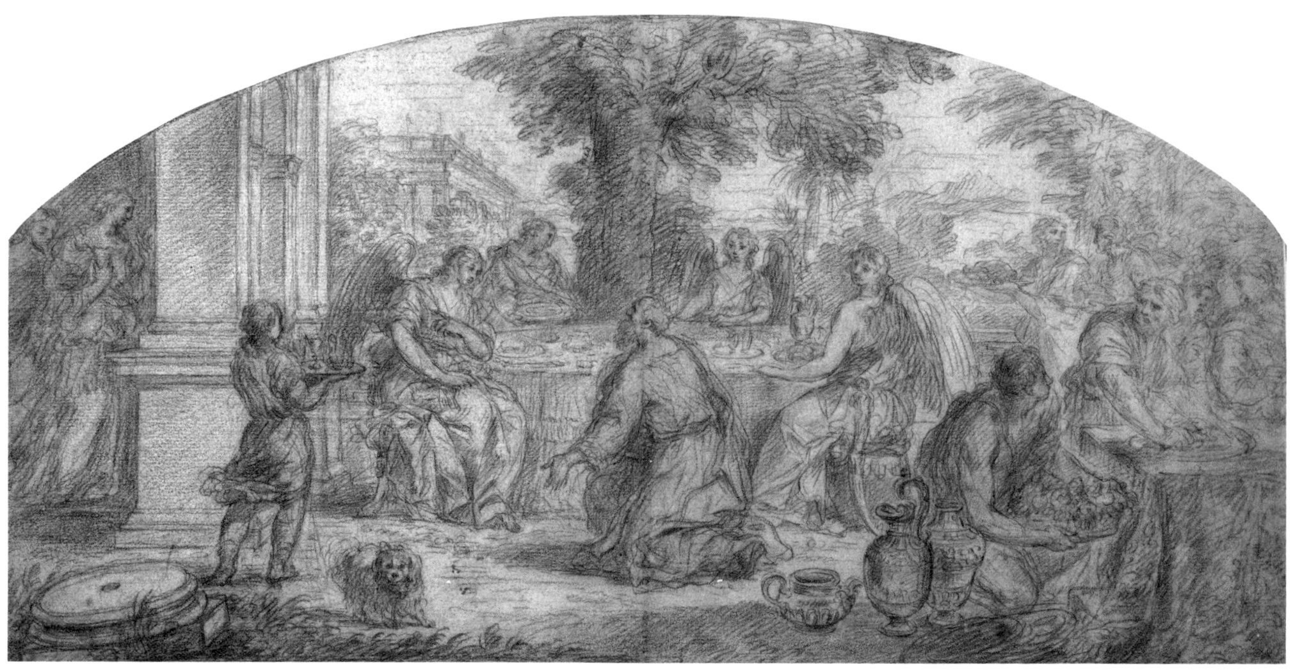

6

GIUSEPPE BARTOLOMEO CHIARI

Rome (or Lucca or Faenza) 1654—Rome 1727

6. *Abraham Entertaining the Three Angels*

c. 1726

Inscribed illegibly on verso, apparently by the artist

Red chalk over black chalk on buff laid paper, mounted down

286 x 570 mm (11 1/4 x 22 7/16")

1978-70-234

Provenance: purchased from Walter Schatzki, New York, 1966

Exhibitions: Minneapolis, 1967, no. 26; Minneapolis 1970–71

Bibliography: Kerber, 1968, p. 85

Among the pupils and successors of Carlo Maratta, the so-called *Maratteschi,* Giuseppe Chiari emerged as his generation's most important and successful continuator of Maratta's late Baroque classicism. The official academic wing of Roman painting during the first quarter of the century was under Chiari's domination, and from 1723 to 1725 he served as *principe* of the Accademia di San Luca. With his masterpiece, the nave ceiling of 1715 for the church of San Clemente, Chiari reestablished in Roman painting the *quadro riportato* tradition—setting an easel painting in a ceiling—for the next fifty years.[1] His oeuvre included many altarpieces in addition to history paintings. Chiari's success as a painter depended largely upon his ability to vary his style according to the demands of patronage: he could be sober, diligent, and noble in grand historical compositions (such as *The Adoration of the Magi,* Gemäldegalerie, Dresden) yet could revert effortlessly to a precious rococo orientation for small-scale cabinet pictures (for example, the four mythologies of 1708 painted for Cardinal Spada, now in the Galleria Spada, Rome). Many of Chiari's paintings have never been properly identified or published, such as the *Sleeping Nymph and Satyr* and *Venus Reclining with Cupid* currently attributed to Luti in the John and Mable Ringling Museum of Art, Sarasota, Florida,[2] or the *Venus, Bacchus, and Ceres* in the Palazzo del Banco di Roma in Rome.

This drawing was first recognized by Anthony Clark as belonging to Chiari, who is not otherwise known to have depicted the theme of Abraham entertaining the angels. Chiari's handling of red chalk derived directly from Maratta's manner, eventually becoming softer and more superficial than that of the older artist. This drawing—the shape of which suggests that it may have been made for an unexecuted or lost chapel lunette—is an excellent example of Chiari's late style. In 1726 the artist worked in the cathedral of Urbino for several months, during which time he also undertook outside commissions;[3] this drawing may be related to one such project. The late date of the composition can be confirmed by comparing its delicate and gently attenuated figures with those in Chiari's altarpiece of 1726 in the church of Santi Apostoli, Rome, depicting *Saint Francis in Ecstasy.*

E.P.B.

1. Waterhouse, 1971, p. 8.
2. Peter Tomory, *Catalogue of the Italian Paintings before 1800, The John and Mable Ringling Museum of Art,* Sarasota, 1976, p. 137, nos. 139–40, repr. p. 136.
3. Kerber, 1968, p. 80.

PIETRO DE' PIETRIS

Premia (Piedmont) 1663 (or 1665)—Rome 1716

7. Flying Angel and Two Putti Holding Drapery

c. 1704

Inscribed on verso in brown ink in an old hand: Originali del sig. Carlo Maratta

Black chalk on blue gray laid paper

265 x 358 mm (10 7/16 x 14 1/16")

Watermark: anchor in a circle

1978-70-385

Provenance: sale, Sotheby's, London, January 28, 1965, in lot 146; purchased from Rockman Prints, New York, 1965

Exhibitions: Minneapolis, 1967, no. 41; Minneapolis, 1970–71

Pascoli and Nicola Pio provide most of the biographical information on Pietro de' Pietris,[1] who came to Rome at an early age from his provincial Piedmontese birthplace, studying under Giuseppe Ghezzi and then briefly with the obscure Cremonese painter Angelo Massarotti (1645–1732) before entering Maratta's studio. De' Pietris was active professionally before the end of the 1680s and, although not remarkably prolific, he produced a respectable number of altarpieces and frescoes for Roman churches, some of which are still *in situ*.[2] He worked for the Ottoboni, Imperiali, and Pallavicini families, as well as for Clement XI, who admired his work and assisted the painter during his final illness. He was also active as a printmaker, etching or engraving his own compositions and providing drawings for reproductive prints by other artists as well (*see also* no. 103).[3] Pascoli describes de' Pietris as a melancholy, solitary, and silent figure who avoided close relationships with his pupils but was a fervent admirer of his master Maratta. He was made a member of the Accademia di San Luca in 1711.

As one might expect of a pupil of Maratta, de' Pietris executed numerous preparatory drawings for his commissions, many of which survive in European and American collections.[4] Predictably, these sheets often bear inscriptions to the older master, as in the case of the *Flying Angel with Drapery,* or are confused with the work of other Maratta pupils, especially that of Agostino Masucci (*see* no. 25). De' Pietris's drawings are often similar in technique and handling to those of Stefano Pozzi as well as Masucci; his style is clearly indebted to Maratta, although his manner, softer and more tentative, lacks Maratta's usual toughness and vigor in the handling of chalk or pen.

Other de' Pietris drawings with which the *Flying Angel with Drapery* can be compared in terms of draughtsmanship and figure types are a double-sided sheet of ink and wash studies of the *Assumption of the Virgin* in the Chrysler Museum in Norfolk[5] and a chalk drawing of the *Virgin and Child with Saints* in Düsseldorf related to an altarpiece in Santa Maria in via Lata, Rome, dating around 1705.[6] The Clark sheet is also similar, especially in the winged figures and putti carrying drapery, to several chalk or ink and wash studies in New York and Berlin for the 1704 title page of a volume on Francesco Albani's frescoes in Palazzo Verospi, Rome;[7] it may be dated tentatively to around the same time.

Two other drawings by de' Pietris are in the Clark collection, both related to known commissions: a study identified by Anthony Clark for the *Assumption* fresco in the dome of Santa Maria alle Fornaci, Rome, of 1712–16 (checklist no. 149) and a rectangular composition of the *Presentation of Christ in the Temple* related to the ovals in Santa Maria in via Lata that Pascoli describes as the artist's last works (checklist no. 148).[8]

A.P.

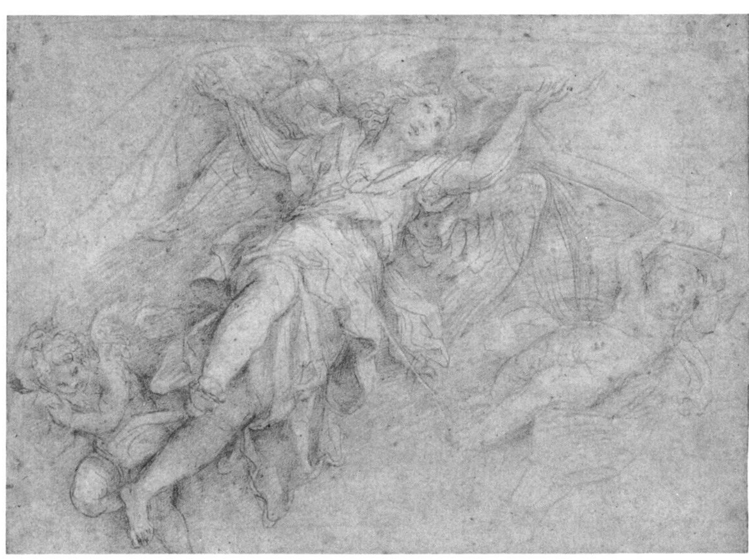

7

1. Pascoli, 1730–36, vol. 1, pp. 223–28; Pio, 1977, pp. 133–34 (varying birth dates of 1663 and 1665, respectively, are given).

2. *See* Pascoli and Pio, *op. cit.*; Gilmartin, 1974; Waterhouse, 1976, p. 104; Enggass, in Pio, 1977, p. 264.

3. Adam Bartsch, *Le peintre graveur,* Vienna, vol. 21, 1821, pp. 289–92; Nagler, 1835–52, vol. 11, pp. 185–86; Le Blanc, 1854–88, vol. 3, p. 182.

4. There are, for example, drawings at Windsor Castle, Oxford, Berlin, Düsseldorf, Stockholm, and Baltimore. *See* Blunt and Cooke, 1960, pp. 85–89, nos. 667–710, figs. 64–68; Anthony Blunt and Edmund Schilling, *The German Drawings in the Collection of her Majesty the Queen at Windsor Castle and Supplements to the Catalogues of Italian and French Drawings,* London, 1971[?], p. 107, no. 362; James Byam Shaw, *Drawings by Old Masters at Christ Church, Oxford,* 1976, vol. 1, p. 177, nos. 656–58, vol. 2, pls. 369–72; K. T. Parker, *Catalogue of the Collection of Drawings in the Ashmolean Museum,* vol. 2, *Italian Schools,* Oxford, 1972, p. 469, nos. 924–25; Dreyer, 1971; Berlin, 1969, nos. 144–49, pls. 77–79; Düsseldorf, 1969–70, nos. 101–3, pl. 86; Clark, 1967 ("Portraits"), p. 13, no. 15, pp. 21–22, no. 218, pls. 4, 15 (another chalk self-portrait, in a decorative surround by another hand, was sold at Christie's, London, July 4, 1972, lot 110, repr.); Clark, 1961, pp. 7–8, fig. 4. A group of ten drawings with old attributions to de' Pietris came to Bowdoin College Museum of Art, Brunswick, Maine, with the collection of James Bowdoin in 1811; probably not all are autograph.

5. Inv. no. 50.49.62; *see* Eric M. Zafran, in Norfolk, Virginia, Chrysler Museum at Norfolk, *One Hundred Drawings in the Chrysler Museum at Norfolk,* March 2–May 6, 1979, no. 26, repr.

6. Düsseldorf, 1964, no. 130, repr. pl. 38; *see* Waterhouse, 1976, p. 104.

7. Bean, 1979, p. 232, no. 304, repr.; Berlin, 1969, nos. 146–49, pls. 77–79; Sabine Jacob, *Italienische Zeichnungen der Kunstbibliothek Berlin,* Berlin, 1975, pp. 110–11, nos. 509–10; repr. pl. 115.

8. Other studies related to the latter commission are at Windsor Castle, Oxford, Berlin, Chicago, and recently on the London market (for these, in addition to the sources cited above, note 4, *see* Joachim and McCullagh, 1979, p. 67, no. 93, repr. pl. 100; sale, Christie's, London, March 28, 1979, lot 207, recto repr., wrongly identified as for de' Pietris's altarpiece in the church). The Metropolitan Museum of Art has recently acquired a handsome ink-and-wash version of the subject (inv. no. 1980.122).

FRANCESCO TREVISANI

Capodistria (Venezia Giulia) 1656—Rome 1746

8. Studies of Three Heads and Drapery

1710–20

Inscribed in brown ink at lower right (in the same manner as no. 25): m 137

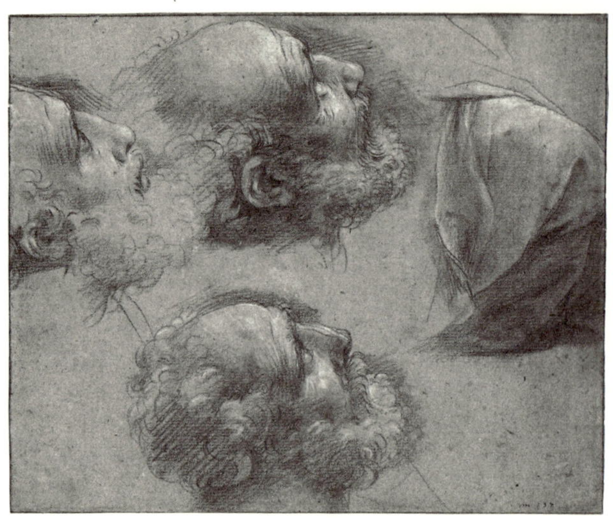

8

Red chalk, some stumping, with touches of white chalk on bluish green laid paper

215 x 253 mm (8 1/2 x 9 15/16")

1978-70-417

Provenance: "Pseudo-Resta" (*see* no. 25, n. 4); purchased from Child's Gallery, Boston, 1958

Exhibitions: Minneapolis, 1967, no. 74; Minneapolis, 1970–71; St. Louis, 1972, no. 55, repr.

Having studied in Venice, Francesco Trevisani settled in Rome in the early 1680s, remaining there the rest of his life and becoming—along with Benedetto Luti, Giuseppe Chiari, and Sebastiano Conca—one of the most prominent artists in the papal city. With the unveiling of his paintings in the Crucifixion Chapel in San Silvestro in Capite in 1696, Trevisani achieved an international reputation that eventually brought him commissions from all over Europe for altarpieces, portraits, and cabinet pictures. He painted the portraits of members of the Jacobite court in Rome and contributed a large number of pictures for the decoration of the new palace being built at Pommersfelden in Germany by the Elector-Bishop of Mainz, Lothar Franz von Schönborn (*see also* no. 9). The high point of Trevisani's career occurred with the completion of his cartoons for the mosaic decorations in the Baptismal Chapel in Saint Peter's.[1]

It was suggested by Anthony Clark that this drawing is related to Trevisani's *Saint Matthew Resuscitating the Son of the King of Ethiopia,* painted about 1730 for the church of San Matteo in Pisa. However, the heads in the drawing are quite different both in physiognomy and pose from those that appear in the painting and in a sketch for it on the London market in 1967;[2] at best, the sheet could only be viewed as a discarded study for the painting. The drawing is, however, associated with a type of figure—a bearded, balding old man posed on one knee and looking up in adoration or supplication—that appears in Trevisani's pictures throughout his career. The type occurs frequently in Trevisani's cartoons for the mosaics in Saint Peter's, which as a group date from 1713 to 1745. One section alone, representing *Baptism by Desire,* contains figures of three old men for which this drawing could have served as an initial study.[3] The drawing can be compared to Trevisani's study for the *Baptism of Constantine* in the Uffizi;[4] both sheets contain three studies of a head seen from somewhat different angles and a piece of drapery, and both can be dated between 1710 and 1720.

F.R.D.

1. For Trevisani, *see* primarily DiFederico, 1977.
2. As *Saint Peter Healing the Sick*; one of a pair of preliminary sketches for the painting. London, Heim Gallery, *Baroque Sketches, Drawings, and Sculptures,* autumn exhibition, 1967, nos. 13 and 14; DiFederico, 1977, pp. 69–70, no. 112, pl. 92.
3. DiFederico, 1977, pp. 66–69, pl. 79.
4. Inv. no. 14151. DiFederico, 1972, p. 10, no. 9, pl. 6.

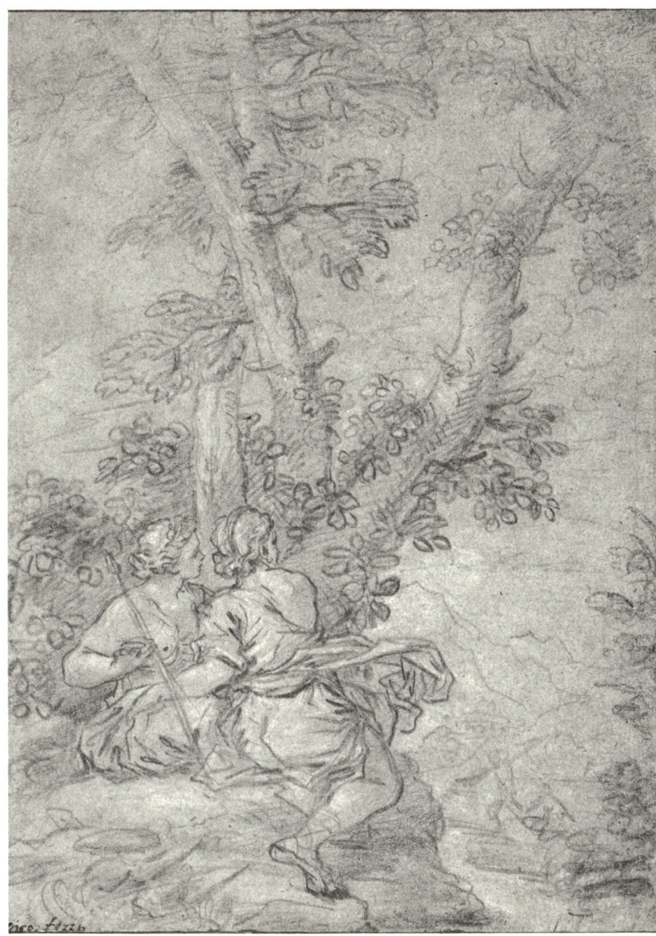

9

BENEDETTO LUTI

Florence 1666—Rome 1724

9. *Jupiter and Callisto* (?)

1710–13

Inscribed in black ink at lower left: Cirro [or Cire] Fezzi [a reworking of the original inscription in brown ink: Cav. Lutti (?)]

Black chalk on blue paper, mounted down

268 x 192 mm (10 9/16 x 7 9/16")

1978-70-323

Provenance: Binney, London, c. 1950; John Maxon, Lawrence, Kansas, 1950; purchased in 1955

Exhibitions: Lawrence, Kansas, University of Kansas Museum of Art, "Old Master Drawings," 1951 (no catalogue; as Ciro Ferri); Minneapolis, 1967, no. 53; Minneapolis, 1970–71

Benedetto Luti enjoyed the protection of the grand duke of Tuscany during his Roman career, being granted the privilege of residing with his family in the Palazzo Firenze and of maintaining a studio in the Villa Medici. Through his connections with the Tuscan court Luti was assured of commissions, and following the death of Carlo Maratta in 1713 his reputation in Rome rivaled that of any other painter. During his career he had serious competition within the city only from Giuseppe Chiari, Sebastiano Conca, and Francesco Trevisani. He worked for the leading Roman families—the Torri, Colonna, Pallavicini, Barberini, and Odescalchi—and received the patronage of such church leaders as Pope Clement XI, Cardinal Ottoboni, Cardinal Augusto Fabbroni, and Padre Cloche, master general of the Dominican order. Although Luti never left Rome after his arrival in 1690, he painted several of his best pictures for foreign nobility, notably Palatine Elector Johann Wilhelm (1658–1716) and Lothar Franz von Schönborn (1655–1729). Delighted with the pair of mythological paintings (*Diana and Endymion* and *Venus and Adonis*) that Luti furnished in 1713 for Schloss Weissenstein at Pommersfelden, Lothar Franz arranged for the painter to be decorated by the emperor Charles VI as a knight of the empire.

Luti was among the painters selected both for the most important papal commission in the first quarter of the century—his is the figure of *Isaiah* in the series of oval prophets in the nave arcade of San Giovanni in Laterano—and for the principal secular commission—the ceilings in the Palazzo de Carolis (now the Palazzo del Banco di Roma, of which Luti's contribution was a

Luna and the Hours). *Principe* of the Accademia di San Luca in 1720, the artist was also prominent as an academician, connoisseur, and collector-dealer.[1]

Anthony Clark owned three drawings by Luti: a preparatory sketch for *The Last Communion of the Magdalen* in Santa Caterina da Siena a Magnanapoli in Rome (checklist no. 101), a black-chalk study of a male nude model (now in a private collection, Kansas City), and the *Jupiter and Callisto*. Clark first identified and connected this quick and spirited sketch with a more advanced version of the composition in the Kunstmuseum, Düsseldorf.[2] No painting of the subject by Luti has been recorded, nor can the design be related to the lost paintings mentioned by Pascoli from the villa of Marchese Torri outside the Porta San Pancrazio in Rome.[3] During his career Luti experimented often with the theme of mythological lovers, and among his paintings and drawings are numerous depictions of Angelica and Medoro, Narcissus and Echo, Venus and Adonis, Diana and Endymion, Bacchus and Ariadne, Atalanta and Hippomenes, and Hercules and Omphale. If the traditional identification of the present scene as the seduction of Callisto by Jupiter (Ovid, *Metamorphoses* 2, 425–45) is correct, the tiny figures engaged in a hunt in the background must be Diana's nymphs.

Luti's treatment of the composition derives equally from Pier Francesco Mola (particularly in the motif of the curving tree trunks), Filippo Lauri, and, as for so many aspects of his art, Pietro da Cortona. The pose of the figure viewed from behind, adapted from Veronese, was a favorite of Luti and was employed by him in several versions of the Supper at Emmaus.[4]

E.P.B.

1. The most recent study of Luti's paintings, with a chapter on the artist as a central figure in the Roman art world, is Bowron, 1979. The best study of the drawings is Dowley, 1962. The artist's pastels have yet to be properly studied.

2. Inv. no. FP 3287. Illa Budde, *Beschreibender Katalog der Handzeichnungen in der Staatlichen Kunstakademie Düsseldorf,* Düsseldorf, 1930, no. 487.

3. Pascoli, 1730–36, vol. 1, p. 231.

4. These include drawings in Düsseldorf and Florence (Dowley, 1962, figs. 7, 8) and in Vaduz (Stiftung Ratjen, *Italienische Zeichnungen des 16.–18. Jahrhunderts,* Munich, 1977, p. 198, no. 92), as well as a painting in the collection of Paul Ganz, New York (A. M. Clark, "Letter to the Editor," *The Art Bulletin,* vol. 45, no. 1 [March, 1963], p. 59 and fig. 2).

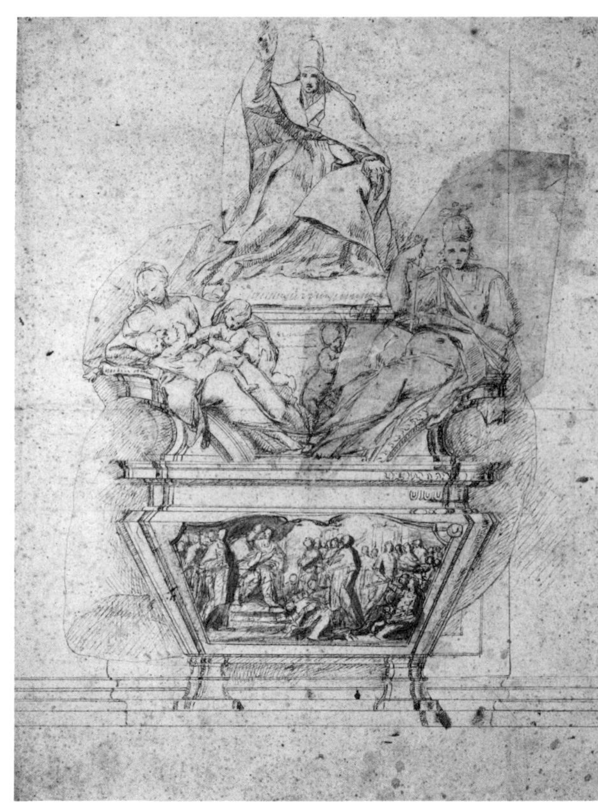

10 Recto

CAMILLO RUSCONI

Milan 1658—Rome 1728

10. Study for the Tomb of Gregory XIII in Saint Peter's

Verso: *Section Drawings of Base of Tomb*

c. 1715

Inscribed on verso in brown ink: 5, and in black chalk: 7

Brown ink over black chalk, brown washes, on cream laid paper, with pasted-on overlay cut from a lighter sheet of cream laid paper

525 x 396 mm (20 5/8 x 15 5/8")

1978-70-400

Provenance: Soutter collection (?); purchased from Swetzoff Gallery, Boston, 1966

Exhibitions: Minneapolis, 1967, no. 2 (as anonymous study for a papal tomb); Regina, Saskatchewan, Norman Mackenzie Art Gallery, and Montreal, Montreal Museum of Fine Arts, *A Selection of Italian Drawings from North American Collections,* January 16–April 3, 1970, no. 76; New York, 1978

Bibliography: Vitzthum, 1970, p. 188, repr. fig. 85; Vitzthum, 1971, p. 91, fig. 31

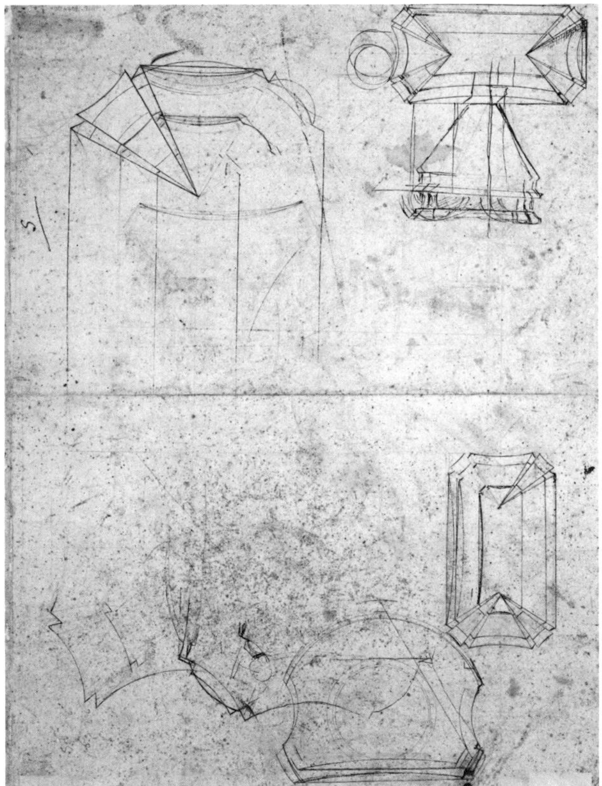

10 Verso

When Camillo Rusconi arrived in Rome around 1686 from Giuseppe Rusnati's workshop in Milan, he was already twenty-eight years old. Though soon accepted by the artistic community and befriended by Rome's foremost painter, Carlo Maratta, he did not begin a monumental work until 1703, when he was asked to execute one of the twelve statues of apostles planned to fill Francesco Borromini's nave niches in San Giovanni in Laterano. Circumstances worked in concert with proof of his abilities, and by 1718 he had finished four of the Lateran statues to universal acclaim. His glorious achievement in translating Maratta's Raphaelesque classicism into the language of monumental sculpture established him as the most sought-after sculptor of his time. His fame brought him students, and their work carried his influence through the third quarter of the eighteenth century.

In the autumn of 1714, after finishing the third of his Lateran figures, Rusconi left Rome for an extended stay in Florence and Milan. In November of that year a papal brief announced that Prospero Antichi's late sixteenth-century tomb of Gregory XIII (pope 1572–85) in Saint Peter's would be replaced by another, under the patronage of Cardinal Boncompagni of Bologna. Rusconi returned to Rome to design this monument. His final *modello* was accepted in July 1715, and the tomb was unveiled in 1723.[1]

This drawing dates from the late spring or early summer of 1715 when the presentation model was being planned. One of four extant designs for the tomb, it depicts the pope seated above figures of Charity and Fortitude, who rest on volutes surmounting the sarcophagus, which bears a relief depicting the institution of the Gregorian calendar.[2] This scheme nearly duplicates that of two early presentation drawings in Düsseldorf, the principal difference occurring in the pose of Fortitude;[3] even within the Clark drawing, the position of this figure has been revised by pasting a separate piece of paper with a new design over the original sheet. Another surviving design, at one time in Malta, is very close to the tomb as finally executed.[4]

Rusconi's early scheme is similar to Antichi's original tomb of Gregory XIII, with its hierarchical placement of sarcophagus surmounted by allegorical figures and the effigy of the pope. In following this late-sixteenth-century arrangement, however, Rusconi at first neglected to take advantage of the seventeenth-century innovation in tomb sculpture of placing the allegorical figures on either side of the sarcophagus, thus lowering the figure of the pope and allowing each element of the tomb to be seen more clearly. He eventually flanked the sarcophagus with volutes carrying the allegorical figures, situating them at raking angles to the wall in a modern, early-eighteenth-century manner. In the final design the figures of Charity and Fortitude, which appear in the Clark drawing, are replaced by Religion and Magnificence; the former supports the tablets of the law in her right hand and holds the book of saints and prophets in her left; the latter rests on a shield and raises a drapery to reveal the sarcophagus relief, in an action that echoes Bernini's tomb of Alexander VII.[5] Despite his other alterations to Antichi's composition, Rusconi's final figure of the seated pope almost duplicates the pose and drapery arrangement of the original sixteenth-century monument.[6]

M.P.C.

1. This chronology is based on Baldinucci, 1950, and on documents in the Archivio Capitolare Lateranense, Rome, "Giustificazione delle statue . . . 1704–14, 1715–29," and Archivio Segreto Vaticano, Rome, Fondo Boncompagni, prot. 568, no. 2. I am indebted to Jennifer Montagu for providing copies of the latter.

2. A drawing for the relief in the Berlin Kupferstichkabinett, is reproduced by Vitzthum, 1970, p. 185, fig. 83.

3. Schlegel, 1969, p. 34. One of the Düsseldorf drawings is reproduced in Düsseldorf, 1969–70, no. 105, pl. 69.

4. Vitzthum, 1970, p. 186, repr. fig. 86 (as in the collection of the late Vincenzo Bonello, La Valletta).

5. The iconography is described in Rusconi's contract drawn up after the completion of his model in July 1715 (Archivio Segreto Vaticano, *see* above, n. 1).

6. The Antichi tomb is reproduced (from an engraving) by Vitzthum, 1970, p. 186, fig. 84.

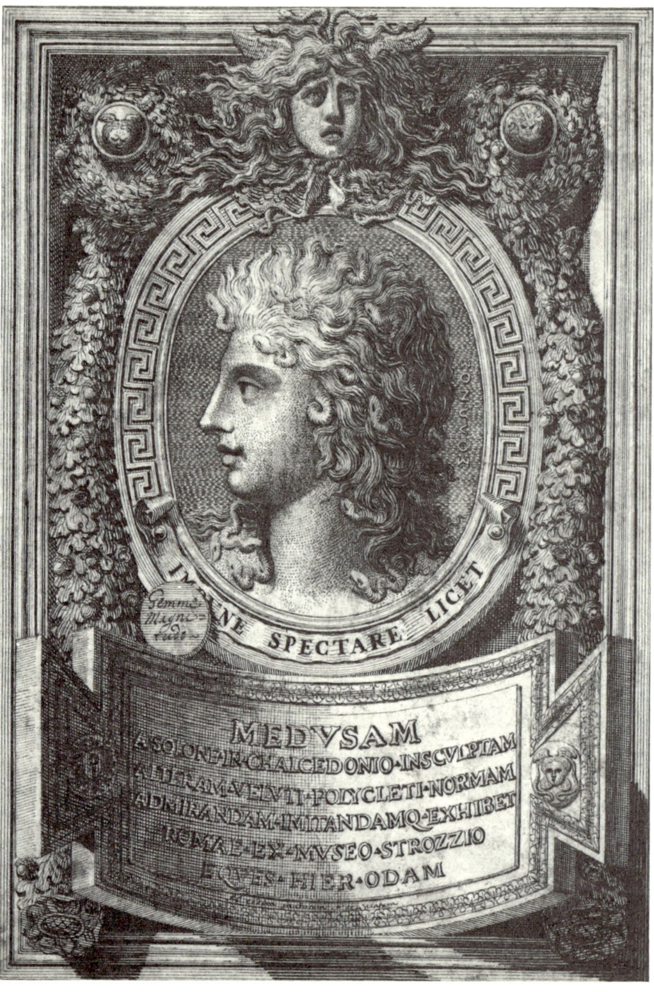

11

GIROLAMO ODAM

Rome 1681 (?)—Rome 1741

11. Design of an Antique Gem ("The Strozzi Medusa")

c. 1715

Signed and inscribed in cartouche: MEDVSAM / A · SOLONE · IN · CHALCEDONIO · INSCVLPTAM / ALTERAM · VELVTI · POLYCLETI · NORMAM / ADMIRANDAM · IMITANDAMQ · EXHIBET / ROMAE · EX · MVSEO · STROZZIO / EQVES · HIER · ODAM; and below: ab eodem inventam et deliniatam

Brown ink on cream paper laid down on a contemporary mount drawn to resemble a frame

409 x 277 mm (16 1/8 x 10 7/8″)

1978-70-373

Provenance: gift of Andrew Ciechanowiecki, 1975

An intellectual as well as an exceptional engraver, Girolamo Odam was educated in ancient and modern literature, philosophy, and mathematics.[1] He studied painting, drawing, and architecture under some of the most esteemed artists of his time, Carlo Maratta, Pier Leone Ghezzi—with whom he later collaborated—and Carlo Fontana. He was an accomplished pastel portraitist and landscape painter although his works are not well known or catalogued today,[2] and he was a renowned antiquary.[3] Odam was beloved by many friends in Rome, among whom were some of the highest nobility. Anthony Clark pointed out that he was patronized by some of the great ecclesiastical families, including the Albani, Corsini, and Ottoboni, and that he was "crucially connected with the careers of a number of important new artists (Imperiali, Masucci, Campiglia, Batoni)."[4] His reputation reached beyond Rome where he was a member of the Accademia degli Arcadii; he was made a member of the Order of Saint George by the duke of Parma.

Unlike most drawings of gems made in preparation for prints, which are often schematic, stiff, and drily executed, this sheet representing an ancient intaglio of the head of Medusa is given a lively and elaborate treatment. The gem, known as the Strozzi Medusa, is a clouded chalcedony that was well known in the eighteenth century. Its discovery in a vineyard on the Caelian hill in Rome was related by Winckelmann in his history of ancient art. Published as early as 1709 in Scipione Maffei's treatise on ancient engraved gems, it was included in most such studies throughout the century, including Stosch's *Pierres antiques gravées* published by Bernard Picart, (*see* no. 19) for which Odam supplied ten drawings, not including the *Medusa*.[5] The inscription on the gem referring to Solon, once believed to be the ancient engraver's signature, is now thought to be a modern addition.

Odam's etching contains some engraving in the hatched background; it exists in two states, the earlier dated 1715, the later 1717.[6] The print follows the style of the drawing closely, as in the use of stipple on the face of Medusa, which gives the profile an unusual, softly modeled appearance. Odam has embellished the gem with a rich mount consisting of a meander design set within an even more elaborate surround of a garland surmounted by a full-face view of Medusa. The inscription on the curved plaque below describes the stone and states that it had been sold from the Strozzi collection. Subsequently it passed through the collections of the antiquary Sabatini (*see* no. 106) and Cardinal Albani (*see* no. 138).

Rich ornamental surrounds were apparently a specialty of Odam. He supplied the drawings (etched by Gaspare Massi) for the surrounds of the illustrated plates in *Carlo Magno: festa teatrale in occasione della nascita del delfino* (Rome, 1729), a volume commemorating the festivities ordered in Rome by Cardinal Ottoboni to honor the birth of the dauphin. The design of these surrounds is an intertwined double meander interrupted at the center of each side by putti supporting an ancient engraved gem, a clever allusion to Cardinal Ottoboni, from whose collection the various gems derived.

M.L.M.

1. On Odam, *see* Orlandi, 1733, p. 261. Clark, 1962, pp. 150–51, establishes his death date and provides further biographical information.

2. Le Blanc, 1854–88, vol. 3, p. 113, lists several prints, including the Medusa and other prints after gems. Although Clark mentioned Odam as a prominent book illustrator, I know only of the *Carlo Magno* described below.

3. He is included in the Vienna version of Pier Leone Ghezzi's *Congress of Antiquaries* (*see* no. 106).

4. Clark, 1962, p. 151.

5. The gem is now in the British Museum; *see* H. B. Walters, *Catalogue of the Engraved Gems and Cameos, Greek, Etruscan, and Roman, in the British Museum*, London, 1926, p. 195, no. 1829, pl. 23, with further bibliography. Odam's drawings for Stosch are quite distinctive from Picart's, as can be seen by comparing this sheet with no. 19; as in the Medusa drawing, he often used stipple to enrich and model the figure, which Picart never did. The gem is dated to the mid-first century A.D. by M.-L. Vollenweider, *Die Steinschneidekunst und ihre Künstler in Spätrepublikanischer und Augusteischer Zeit*, Baden-Baden, 1966, p. 48.

6. Both states are in the Gabinetto Nazionale delle Stampe, Rome, vol. 35-H-13. The state dated 1715 is inv. no. 37319, that dated 1717 is inv. no. 37318. There is an inscription below the plaque in the 1715 state and some of the small medallions differ from those of the 1717 state.

PIER LEONE GHEZZI

Rome 1674—Rome 1755

12. Standing Figure in Clerical Costume

c. 1720

Inscribed on verso in brown ink at upper left: 381

Pen and brown ink on cream laid paper, mounted down

301 x 194 mm (11 13/16 x 7 5/8″)

1978-70-287

Provenance: gift of Fabrizio Apolloni, 1969

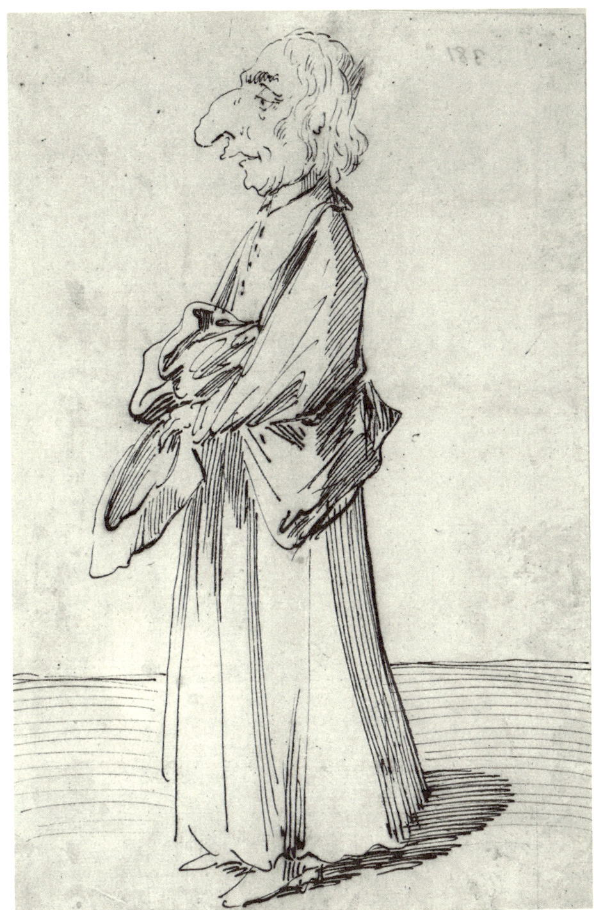

12

During the first half of the eighteenth century there was no more remarkable or engaging artistic personality in Rome than Pier Leone Ghezzi. His accomplishments as a painter and his manifold activities in the artistic society of Rome have today been overshadowed by his fame as the first "professional" caricaturist.[1] Pier Leone was trained by his father Giuseppe (*see* no. 5) and like him became a member of the papal court. Appointed a knight of the Order of Christ by Pope Clement XI, Pier Leone served as a director of Clement's tapestry manufactory at the Ospizio di San Michele (*see also* no. 4), as superintendent of museums, and as painter of the Apostolic Chamber after the death of Giuseppe Passeri in 1714. He was deeply involved in antiquarian matters and was familiar with the leading archaeologists of his day. He studied medicine and anatomy and was active as a picture restorer and dealer-agent in the Roman art market. An accomplished musician, he formed a *società borghese,* or civilians' musical society—as contrasted with aristocratic or clerical groups—that met weekly and included composers, instrumentalists, and singers from various walks of life. Ghezzi's personality and varied activities made him a popular figure in cultivated circles, especially among the foreigners who flocked to Rome.

His primary celebrity, however, derived from his graphic works, of which—not counting archaeological and decorative drawings and book illustrations—about three thousand sheets have survived.[2] The bulk of these drawings are caricatures, preserved in bound volumes belonging to the Vatican Library, the Gabinetto Nazionale delle Stampe in Rome, and the print rooms of the British Museum, Berlin, Dresden, and Leningrad. Two dismembered volumes containing approximately two hundred drawings, once the property of Carlos III, king of Spain, and, until 1971, of the dukes of Wellington, have until recently been the source of most single sheets by the artist to appear on the market.[3]

The greatest single repository of Ghezzi's caricatures is a group of eight folio volumes in the Vatican Library. Ghezzi called this collection "Il mondo nuovo" and divided its satirical repertory into distinct categories: the papal court, families of patrons and friends and their servants, music lovers attending his academy of music, civil servants, members of the clergy, artists, the common people of Rome, and foreigners grouped according to their professions.[4]

The present drawing is traditionally said to represent Francesco de' Ficoroni (1664–1747), a noted collector of antiquities, member of the Roman art world, and author of a variety of books on ancient Rome. The cleric's garb does not preclude this identification, as Ficoroni was apparently an abbot, although nothing is presently known about his clerical career. The sheet is typical of the sketches from life that Ghezzi used to create his famous caricatures. Its format, with the sitter in the foreground against a neutral background, a minimum of attributes indicating his profession, was frequently employed by the artist between 1710 and the early 1720s.[5]

E.P.B.

1. The most important recent studies of Pier Leone Ghezzi as a painter are Clark, 1963; Clark in Chicago, et al., 1970–71, no. 81; and Lo Bianco, 1977. For Ghezzi's drawings, *see* Bodart, 1967, and Bodart, 1976. The archaeological drawings have been studied by Guerrini, 1971.

2. Bodart, 1976, p. 13.

3. Two volumes containing one hundred and fifty-two caricature drawings by Pier Leone Ghezzi, belonging to the Rt. Hon. Lord Braybrooke, were sold at Sotheby's, London, December 10, 1979.

4. Rome, Vatican Library, Cod. Ottob. Lat. 3112–19. On April 24, 1747, Ghezzi sold his collection of architectural drawings and prints and the eight volumes of "Il mondo nuovo" (Bodart, 1976, pp. 22, 24, 26, n. 37).

5. Bodart, 1976, p. 21, figs. 17, 19.

13. *John Martin, Joseph Henry of Straffan, Lord Bruce of Tottenham, and Henry Willoughby, Later Lord Middleton*

c. 1751–53

Inscribed on verso in brown ink at upper left (in a late-eighteenth-century British hand, the same as no. 14); Henry, Martin, Lord Bruce & L[d] Middleton

Pen and brown ink, faint traces of black chalk, touches of color, on light brown laid paper, mounted down on Japanese tissue

322 x 222 mm (12 11/16 x 8 3/4″)

1978-70-289

Provenance: H. D. Molesworth, London; purchased from Hans Calmann, London, 1962

Exhibition: Minneapolis, 1967, no. 43

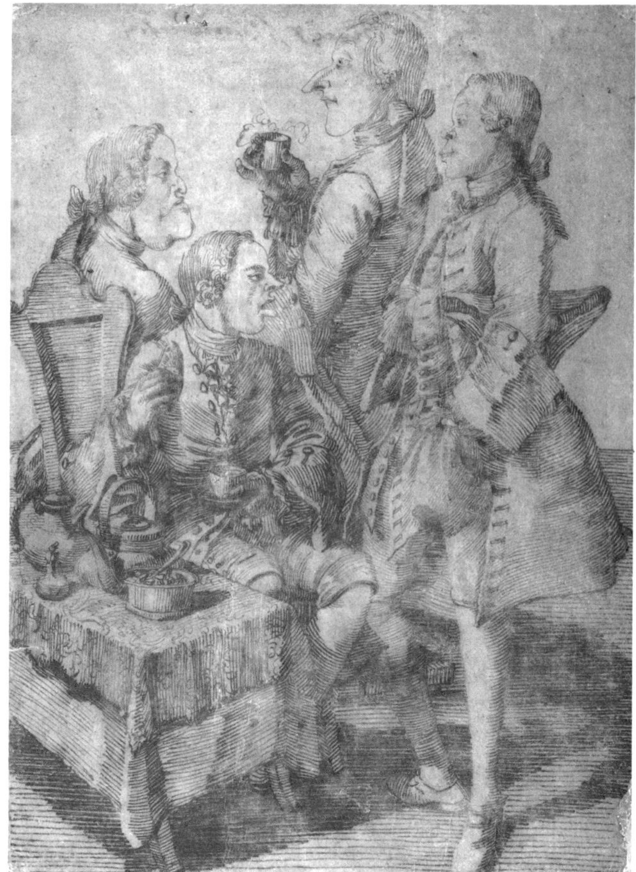

13

Ghezzi's caricatures and gently satirical portraits offer an engaging impression of eighteenth-century Roman life: his work comprises the richest iconographic source of the period. He recorded the activities of the common people as well as of those in the upper strata of society, and had a keen eye for the queer and amusing events of everyday life. His usual procedure was to execute from life one or more quick sketches of his subjects and then to reconstruct the scene in the studio, employing more or less stock poses. One of the volumes of Ghezzi caricatures in the Vatican Library contains numerous notations of this kind made by the artist in the most varied circumstances.[1]

This caricature of four British grand tourists taking tea, drawn toward the end of the artist's life, when his line had grown less crisp and lively, is probably one of those works fashioned from individual sketches of the sitters. John Martin is seated at the left, facing Lord Bruce and Henry Willoughby, later Lord Middleton standing opposite.[2] The fourth member of the party is Joseph Henry of Straffan, County Kildare. Henry was a friend of the Irish statesman, James Caulfield, first earl of Charlemont, to whom he bore a striking resemblance (*see* no. 14). In another caricature Ghezzi drew Joseph Henry standing alone in the middle of Roman ruins, holding a guidebook and identified as a "Cavaliere inglese dilettante delle antichità." This sheet was once bound in a volume of caricatures belonging to the duke of Wellington and is currently in the Metropolitan Museum of Art.[3]

Ghezzi was called "il famoso cavaliere delle caricature," and his caricatures, among the most brilliant examples of a genre that originated in Italy in the art of Annibale Carraci, bore immediate influence upon the English caricature print of the eighteenth century. His designs first appeared in England in a portfolio of Italian caricatures engraved by Arthur Pond and published in London from 1736 to 1747 (*see also* p. 111 and no. 106).[4] Sir Joshua Reynolds, who traveled to Italy in 1750, was inspired to draw and paint a number of caricatures in the Ghezzi manner, as was another Englishman, Thomas Patch. Unlike later caricatures—those of Thomas Rowlandson and James Gillray, for example—Ghezzi's drawings are never marked by savagery, cruelty, or personal animosity. Nor, unlike Goya, was he driven to reveal deformity, weakness, and ugliness as dominant aspects of real life. The large measure of sympathy Ghezzi held for his subjects explains why, in the words of Henry Fuseli, he "could not fail of becoming the favourite of a public whose licentiousness of speech he countenanced by equal licentiousness of brush."[5]

E.P.B.

1. Bodart, 1976, p. 21.
2. Although this figure has been traditionally identified as James Martin, a document dated September 26, 1751, at Lucca mentions a "John Martin jun. Esq. of Overbury in the County of Worcester" making a wager with Lord Bruce (information courtesy of Cynthia O'Connor, communicated by Michael Wynne).
3. Inv. no. 1973.67.
4. New Haven, Connecticut, Yale University, Sterling Memorial Library, *The Age of Horace Walpole in Caricature: an Exhibition of Satirical Prints and Drawings from the Collection of W. S. Lewis,* introduction by D. R. Roylance, catalogue by J. C. Riley, October–December, 1973, n.p.
5. Matthew Pilkington, *A Dictionary of Painters from the Revival of the Art to the Present Period,* ed. by H. Fuseli, London, 1810, p. 210.

14. Joseph Leeson and James Caulfield

c. 1751–53

Inscribed on verso in brown ink at upper left (in late-eighteenth-century British hand, the same as no. 13): Leeson & Ld Charlemount [sic]

Pen and brown ink, faint traces of black chalk, with touches of color, on light brown paper, mounted down on Japanese tissue

322 x 223 mm (12 11/16 x 8 3/4")

1978-70-290

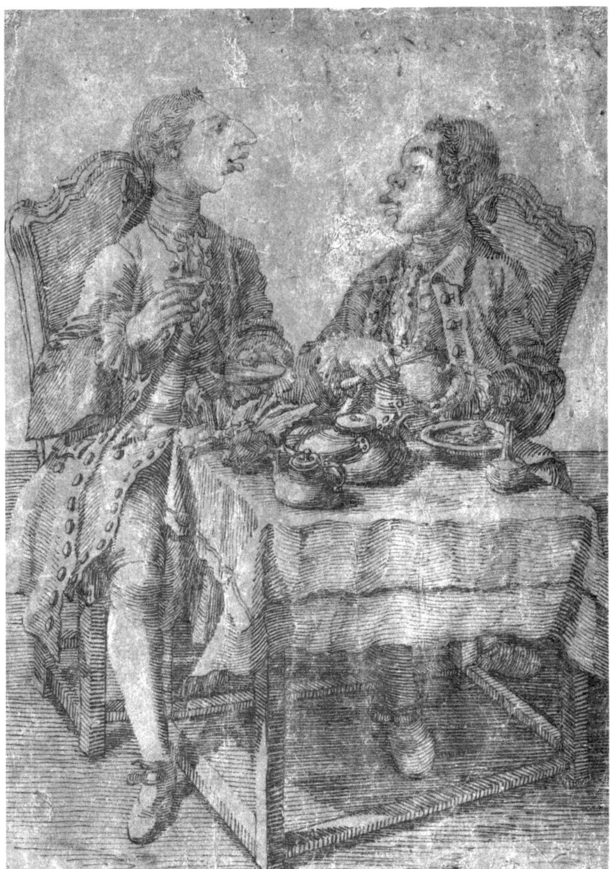

14

Provenance: H. D. Molesworth, London; purchased from Hans Calmann, London, 1962

Exhibition: Minneapolis, 1967, no. 44

This amusing drawing shows Joseph Leeson, Jr. (1730–1801), later second earl of Milltown, taking tea with James Caulfield (1728–99), who was the first earl of Charlemont. Young Leeson was taken to Rome in 1750 by his father, the heir of a prosperous Dublin brewing family and a collector and traveler of note, together with his cousin, Joseph Henry of Straffan, one of the subjects of a companion caricature by Ghezzi (no. 13). During his visit Leeson was painted by Pompeo Batoni in a three-quarter-length portrait that is signed and dated 1751 (National Gallery of Ireland, Dublin). His companion, James Caulfield, who was described by Edmund Burke many years later in 1785 as "the most public-spirited, and at the same time, the best-natured and the best-bred man in Ireland," commissioned two portraits from Batoni between 1751 and 1753. One of these, in the Yale Center for British Art, New Haven, Connecticut, is a splendid example of a portrait format much favored by grand tourists—including a distant view of the Colosseum as a reminder of the sitter's stay in Rome.

A private collection in Ireland contains a replica or copy of the present drawing, in which the sitters have been identified as Joseph Leeson and Joseph Henry of Straffan.[1] The striking similarity of appearance between Henry and James Caulfield is emphasized in the caricatures painted in Rome by Sir Joshua Reynolds in 1751, now in the National Gallery of Ireland, Dublin: these include the famous *Parody on The School of Athens* (which shows the Leesons, Caulfield, Joseph Henry, and other British residents and visitors); *Lord Bruce, Mr. Ward, Joseph Leeson, Jr., and Joseph Henry;* and *Sir Thomas Kennedy, Caulfield, Mr. Ward, and Mr. Phelps*.[2] The features of Caulfield in the present drawing might easily be taken for those of Joseph Henry were it not for the identifying inscription on the verso.

E.P.B.

1. Wynne, 1974, p. 109, fig. 13 (estate of the late Colonel H. T. W. Clements, as attributed to Pier Leone Ghezzi).
2. Sutton, 1956, figs. 1–3.

FRANCESCO FERNANDI, called IMPERIALI

Milan 1679—Rome 1740

15. Jacob and Rachel at the Well

1722

Signed and dated on recto in red chalk at lower right: Fran. D. Imp. F. 1722. Roma; inscribed in pencil at lower right: [illegible word] Day £78; inscribed on verso in brown ink at upper center: No. 443; and in pencil at bottom, presumably in the hand of the collector and biographer Francesco Maria Niccolò Gabburri: Originale di Francisco Imperiali Pittore a Roma. fatto apposta [?] per questa collezione della Citta / [illegible word] e scritta de propria mano [?]

Red chalk over traces of black chalk on beige laid paper

440 x 568 mm (17 5/16 x 22 3/8")

Watermark: deer (?) in a circle

1978-70-307

Provenance: Francesco Maria Niccolò Gabburri, Florence, 1722; Pierre Crozat (?) (Lugt 474); sale, Sotheby's, London, February 22, 1961, lot 14; bought by Carlo Sestieri; gift of Carlo Sestieri, 1963

Exhibitions: Minneapolis, 1967, no. 49; Minneapolis, 1970–71

Bibliography: G. Campori, *Raccolta di cataloghi ed inventarii inediti di quadri, statue, disegni, bronzi, dorerie, smalti, medaglie, avorii, ecc. dal secolo XV al secolo XIX*, Modena, 1870, p. 537 (as made for Gabburri at Rome, 1722, *David al pozzo con Rachele*); F. Noack, in Thieme-Becker, 1907–50, vol. 11, p. 426, as *David and Rachel;* Clark, 1964 ("Imperiali"), p. 229, fig. 49 (as private collection, Rome)

The basic facts of Imperiali's career were set out by Anthony Clark in a fundamental study published nearly two decades ago: "In his mature years Imperiali was known as the author of a modest number of important royal and ecclesiastical commissions, an agent for those seeking drawings of classical antiquities, a knowledge-

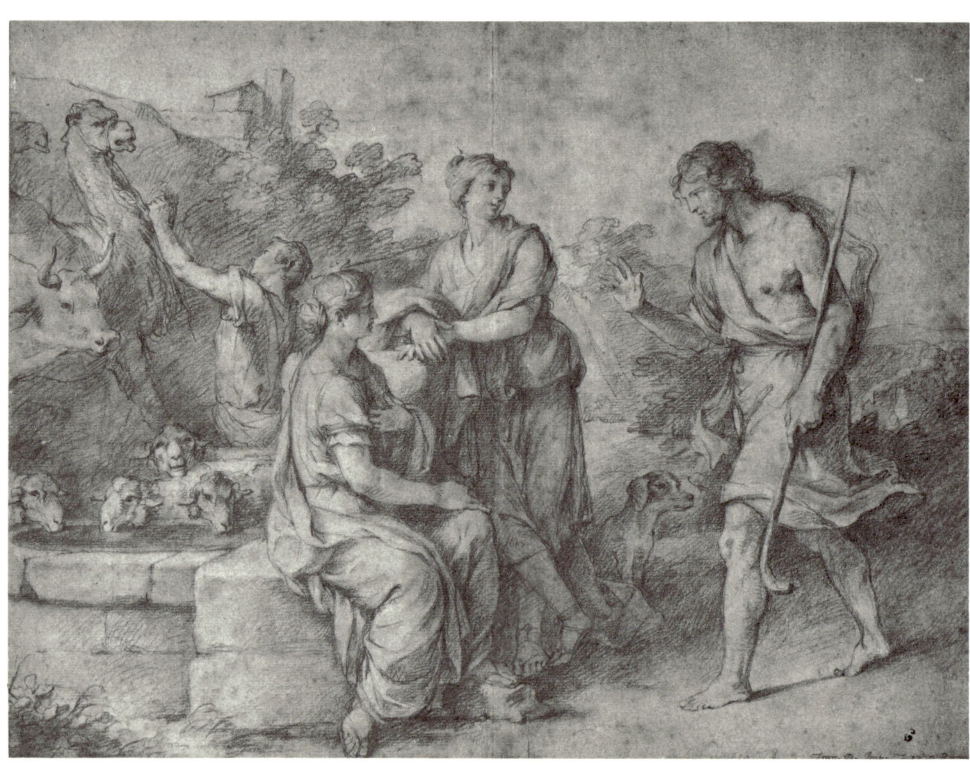

15

able cicerone-teacher of young artists, the protégé of an important cardinal, and the producer of popular works in the minor forms."[1] He was the favorite teacher for foreigners in Rome during the 1730s (including such British artists as Alexander Clerk, William Mossman, William Hoare, Allan Ramsay, and James Russell) and, as Ellis Waterhouse has observed, it is probably significant that his one known Italian pupil was Pompeo Batoni, who subsequently enjoyed considerable British patronage.

According to Nicola Pio,[2] Imperiali arrived in Rome about 1705, following a brief period of training with a minor Milanese painter and a subsequent sojourn in Palermo. In his early Roman years, he produced a number of minor works including studies of animals (examples now at Penicuik, Hopetoun, and Holkham) and in consequence was never admitted to the Accademia di San Luca. In a letter of 1726, however, he is cited as one of the leading history painters in Rome, along with the other "pittori istorici eroici" Giuseppe Chiari, Francesco Trevisani, Sebastiano Conca, and Giovanni Odazzi.[3] Imperiali supplied pictures to Cardinal Ottoboni, to the Elector Clemens August, and to the king of Spain for the decoration of the throne room at La Granja. His ecclesiastical commissions include altars for Sant' Eustachio and San Gregorio al Celio in Rome, and for San Francesco in Gubbio, as well as the two lateral paintings in the chapel of Saints Valentine and Hilary in the cathedral of Viterbo.

Imperiali often depicted Old Testament scenes, particularly those of Rebecca and Eliezer at the well (Palazzo Reale, Turin; Penicuik House, Midlothian, Scotland; Achenbach Foundation for the Graphic Arts, San Francisco) and of Jacob and Rachel. With some variations from the biblical text (Genesis 29:10), the present scene appears to represent Jacob's first sight of Rachel by the well where she had come to water her father's flocks. The sheet contains elements common to both Old Testament subjects mentioned above, however, and has also been related to a *Rebecca and Eliezer at the Well* sold from the collection of Lord Lincoln on March 31, 1939.[4] The drawing corresponds even more closely to an oil *modello* for this painting identified by Anthony Clark on the Roman art market in 1971 and presently in the collection of Fabrizio Lemme, in Rome.

E.P.B.

1. Clark, 1964 ("Imperiali"), p. 229. The first useful study of the painter is Waterhouse, 1958.

2. Pio, 1977, pp. 40–41.

3. Waterhouse, 1958, p. 101 (citing a letter of the abbot Giuseppe Gentile to Lothar Franz von Schönborn, the Elector-Bishop of Mainz, July 20, 1726).

4. Clark, 1964 ("Imperiali"), p. 229. The painting is reproduced in Waterhouse, 1958, fig. 3.

Attributed to ANDREA LOCATELLI

Rome 1695—Rome 1741

16. *A Classical Landscape*

1720–30

Inscribed on verso in pencil: vo / 5 / 14119 / K7951 / 2260 / [rest illegible]

Black chalk, some brownish chalk, on cream laid paper toned gray; edges ruled around in pencil

194 x 312 mm (7 11/16 x 12 1/4")

Watermark: Pro Patria

1978-70-320

Provenance: purchased from Rockman Prints, New York, 1962

Exhibitions: Minneapolis, 1967, no. 52; Minneapolis, 1970–71

The principal source for the life of Andrea Locatelli, the biography by Nicola Pio, informs us that the artist was born in 1695 and not in 1660, as was recently held to be the case.[1] Pio recounts that Locatelli became a pupil of the little-known landscapist "Monsù Alto" at the age of twelve; another contemporary biographer, the collector Francesco Maria Niccolò Gabburri, informs us that at seventeen he began to study with the marine painter Bernardino Fergioni, an equally obscure personality.[2] By the early 1720s Locatelli must have been a full professional; between 1723 and 1725, at the request of the architect Filippo Juvarra, he painted two views of the Castello di Rivoli near Turin that Juvarra had designed for Victor Amadeus II of Savoy,[3] and in 1728 Pier Leone Ghezzi inscribed a caricature of him "A. Lucatelli famoso pittore di paesi."[4] By this time the artist belonged to the circle of "official" patronage in Rome, enjoying the protection of and commissions from Cardinals Albani and Ottoboni and the Colonna and Ruspoli families.[5] Despite this support, he seems to have suffered considerable financial difficulties during his lifetime, perhaps because he worked slowly and was burdened with a large family and poor health.

It is difficult to establish a chronology for Locatelli's oeuvre. He developed a type of idealized Arcadian landscape derived from the Bolognese classical tradition but distinguished by a more decorative and "idyllic" tendency that would eventually culminate in the work of Francesco Zuccarelli. Aside from some specific examples like the Rivoli views and some *bambocciate* and pastorales, he worked in this "idyllic" mode for most of his career. While his paintings at least possess consistent and definable characteristics, his drawings are more difficult to categorize.[6] From the few sheets—no more than ten—that can be attributed to him with some degree of certainty, one gains the impression that for Locatelli drawings were not, as for most artists of the previous century, a method of study and observation leading up to a finished work. Rather, his drawings

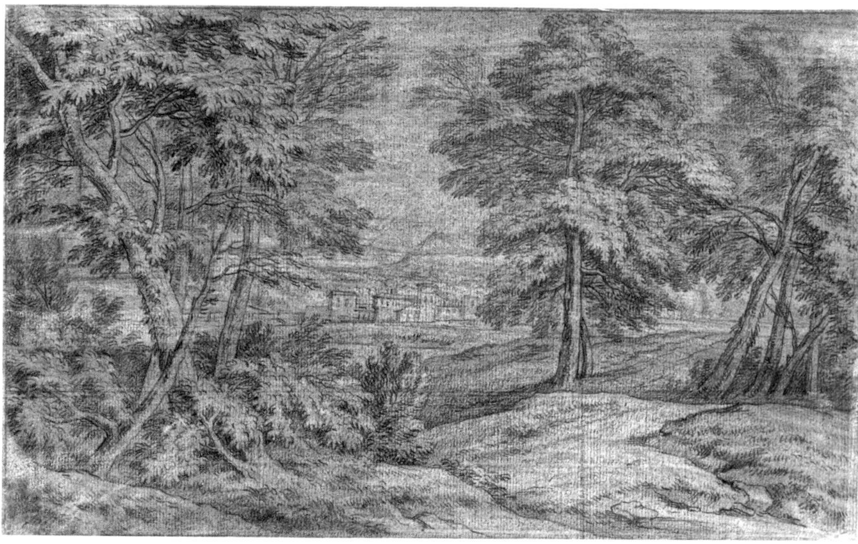

16

were exercises in a different technique related to the same motifs that appear in his paintings. Most of the drawings that can be attributed to him are in wash or pen and ink, and thus the Clark drawing is something of an exception; the strongly classicizing landscape, recalling Domenichino in its balance of the two groups of trees that frame a central opening and reveal a view of buildings and hills in the distance, is also atypical.[7] The use of black chalk recalls the work of Gaspard Dughet, as does the technique of parallel strokes used to define shadows and the nervous rendering of outlines of tree trunks and branches, the latter a mannerism related to the work of many Flemish and Dutch artists active in Rome during the same period.[8] The sheet's departure from most of Locatelli's other known drawings can be attributed to its use of a different technique that lends itself less well to rendering atmosphere and coloristic subtleties. Otherwise, its style and level of quality justify Anthony Clark's attribution to Locatelli, insofar as that artist's drawings are known and understood today.

M.C.

1. Pio, 1977, pp. 185–86. The family name was apparently Lucatelli, although the current spelling as Locatelli is now commonly accepted. In the 1959 *Settecento a Roma* exhibition, Locatelli's birth date was given as either 1660 or 1695 (Rome, 1959, p. 144). This later date is also found on the chalk self-portrait that belongs to the series of portrait drawings intended to illustrate Pio's lives of the artists, today in the Nationalmuseum, Stockholm (on the group, *see* Clark, 1967 ["Portraits"]).

2. Only two paintings and no biographical facts are known for Monsù Alto (*see* Chiarini, 1970). For Gabburri on Locatelli, *see* F. M. N. Gabburri, "Vite di pittori," Florence, Biblioteca Nazionale Centrale, MS Pal. E.B.9.5; *see also* Borroni, 1974.

3. Augusto Telluccini, "Il Castello di Rivoli torinese," *Bollettino d'Arte,* vol. 10, no. 4 (1930), pp. 145–61; vol. 10, no. 5 (1930), pp. 193–216.

4. Rome, Vatican Library, Cod. Ottob. Lat. 3116, fol. 87; published by Busiri Vici, 1967.

5. Pio, 1977, pp. 185–86; on the artist's life and work, *see* Busiri Vici, 1974, and Clark, in Chicago, et al., 1970–71, p. 198.

6. *See* Chiarini, 1972; Busiri Vici, 1974, pp. 188 ff.

7. However, a similar—though not identical—composition is found in a painting reproduced by Busiri Vici, 1974, no. 87.

8. A. Zwollo, *Hollandse en Vlaamse veduteschilders te Rome 1675–1725,* Assen, 1973.

SEBASTIANO CONCA

Gaeta (Latium) 1680—Gaeta 1764

17. Fame and Time

c. 1706

Black chalk with touches of white on green prepared paper, mounted down

375 x 270 mm (14 3/4 x 10 5/8")

1978-70-245

Provenance: purchased from Plinio Nardecchia, Rome, 1961 (as by Pietro Bianchi and supposedly from the Gatty collection)

Exhibitions: Minneapolis, 1967, no. 28; Minneapolis, 1970–71; St. Louis, 1972, no. 56, repr.

Bibliography: Sestieri, 1976, pp. 85, 88–89, repr. p. 88, fig. 13

Trained in the Neapolitan workshop of Francesco Solimena at the close of the Seicento, Sebastiano Conca arrived in Rome in 1706 and was almost immediately drawn into the orbit of Carlo Maratta. In the earliest

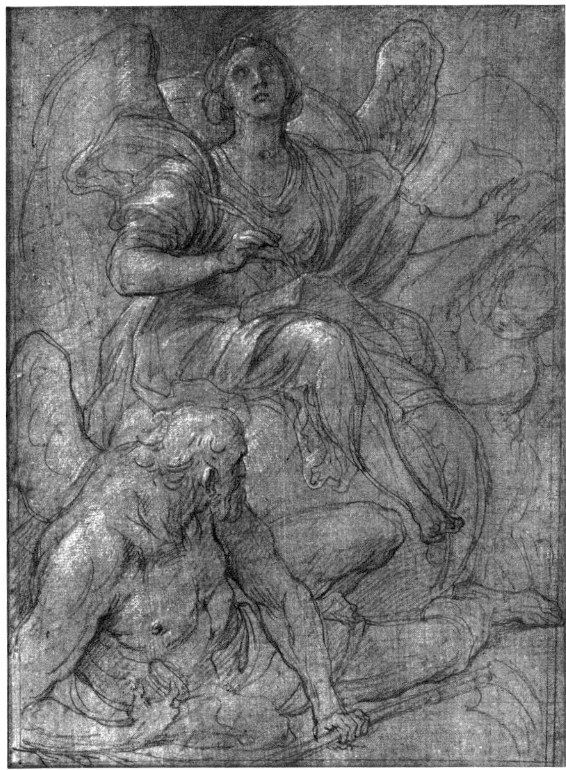

17

works that Conca executed in Rome, the pendant allegories commissioned by Cardinal Fabrizio Spada in 1706, the sumptuous baroque tonality and bravura brushwork of Solimena's mature style have already been tempered and clarified through contact with the academic classicism employed by Maratta and his followers; unfortunately, this admixture was not consistently successful throughout the artist's career.

Conca's most appealing and innovative works are his cabinet pictures, often executed on copper, which mark the earliest appearance in Rome of the French *style fleuri,* or rococo. His large-scale fresco decorations, such as the nave ceiling of the church of Santa Cecilia in Trastevere in Rome (1721–25), though brilliantly effervescent in execution, always fluctuate uncomfortably between the rococo and the late Baroque. A resident of Rome for forty-five years, Conca made only brief trips outside her walls, such as to Turin in the mid twenties to work for the king of Savoy and to Tuscany in 1731–32, where he frescoed the huge *Pool of Bethesda* for the hospital in Siena. Returning to Naples and Gaeta in 1752, Conca painted the ceiling of the church of Santa Chiara in Naples in 1753 (now destroyed). In the works of his final years the artist attempted unsuccessfully to adapt his basically Roman rococo style to the new vogue for neoclassicism.[1]

Conca's 1719 reception piece for the Accademia di San Luca was a painting of a seated figure of Fame, somewhat similar in pose to this drawing.[2] The freer handling of the contours, as well as the more relaxed placement of the figure in the painting, would suggest that the drawing predates it by some years. The conjoined personifications also appear in the multi-figured *Allegory of the Arts* of 1723 in the Schönborn collection at Pommersfelden, and again the looser treatment of these painted allegorical figures does not support a dating contemporary with the Clark drawing.[3] The sheet, which reveals Conca at his most academic, points up an adherence to the canons of late Baroque classicism familiar from the work of the *Maratteschi* in the early decades of the Roman Settecento. Such a close reliance on formulas suggests a very early date. The same mode of composition can be found in the 1706 *Allegory of Music* in the Galleria Spada in Rome; here the poses of the Clark drawing are found repeated in the two central figures, the torso in the figure of Lyric Poetry and Composition and the seated pose in that of Instrumental Music. Although the figures in the Spada allegory are arranged somewhat differently, no other, later work of Conca so clearly approximates the Clark drawing.

The allegories in the Galleria Spada demonstrate by their theme—the road to fame is paved with rules and regulations—the strong theoretical bent that likewise characterized the exercises and lectures presented to students in Conca's own studio in the Palazzo Farnese, as well as the programs initiated by the artist during his tenures as *principe* of the Accademia di San Luca from 1729 to 1731 and 1739 to 1741.

T.W.S.

1. The basic studies on Conca are Clark, 1967 ("Conca"); Sestieri, 1969; Sestieri, 1970 (includes a checklist of works).
2. Repr. Sestieri, 1976, p. 88, fig. 14.
3. Sestieri, 1976, p. 88, dates the Clark drawing around 1719–23, contemporary with the Accademia di San Luca *Fame* and the Pommersfelden *Allegory of the Arts.*

18. Study for a Portrait of Cardinal Antonio Felice Zondadari

c. 1740
Inscribed on verso in pencil at bottom right: 2
Black and white chalks on blue laid paper
427 x 290 mm (16 13/16 x 11 7/16")
1978-70-243
Provenance: purchased from Yvonne ffrench, London, 1967 (as attributed to J. F. de Troy)
Exhibition: Minneapolis, 1970–71

Conca had a wide circle of patrons that included popes, cardinals, and kings. Commissions to decorate the royal residences and chapels of the Elector of Saxony and the kings of Savoy, Poland, Spain, and the Two Sicilies continued throughout his lifetime. His pupils often

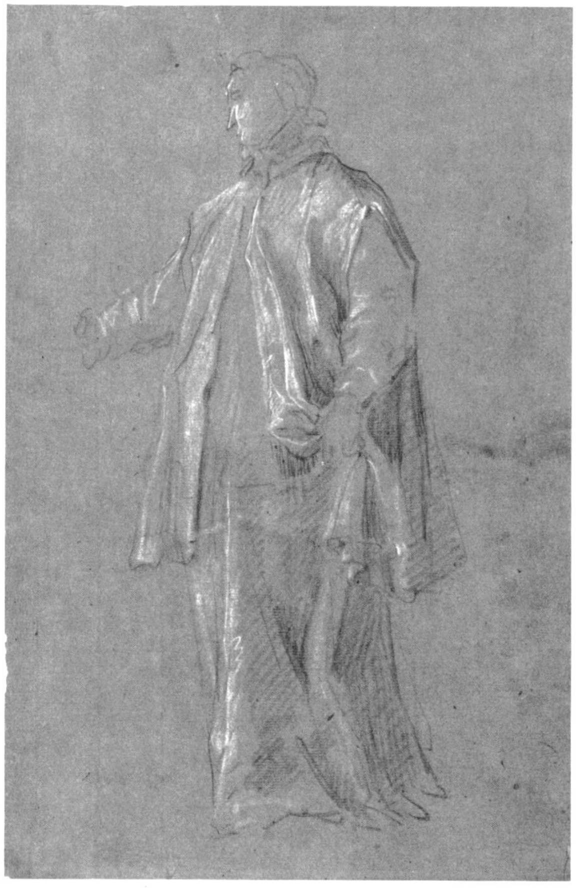

18

profited from these associations, and many became resident court artists, as did Corrado Giaquinto at the court of Spain. Among the artist's cardinalate patrons the most important was Cardinal Pietro Ottoboni; from 1726 until the cardinal's death in 1731 Conca, along with Francesco Trevisani (*see* no. 8), was a member of the Ottoboni household and received a monthly stipend.[1] Cardinal Bentivoglio commissioned Conca to design decorations for the Piazza di Spagna in celebration of the birth of the Infanta, and the artist was especially favored by his fellow Neapolitans Cardinal Tommaso Ruffo and Pope Benedict XIII Orsini.

The drawing of Cardinal Zondadari is a preparatory study for the painting of the *Meeting of Cardinal Zondadari and King Philip V of Spain* in the Bellini collection in Florence.[2] Antonio Felice Zondadari (1665–1737) was the older brother of Alessandro, archbishop of Siena. Having held a diplomatic post during the pontificate of Innocent XII, Antonio was appointed papal nuncio to the court of Philip V by Clement XI. The painting represents the cardinal's presentation to the monarch on May 17, 1706. The drawing can be dated contemporary to the execution of the painting, or around 1740. A flickering use of white heightening enlivens the drawing, which clearly represents a mature artistic statement as compared to the much earlier *Fame and Time* (no. 17). The "three-dimensional" treatment of the figure, which has no parallel among painters of the early eighteenth century, suggests the influence of contemporary sculpture, in particular that of Pierre Legros the Younger. Although the contemporary account is now disproven in which Legros is credited with having induced Conca to "take up the brush" after the latter had abandoned painting in favor of drawing for some four years,[3] Legros's stylistic importance for the young Conca cannot be easily dismissed. The sculptor's use of crisp, linear drapery folds that seem to flap briskly are similar to Conca's treatment of the same forms on a two-dimensional surface. Perhaps suggestive of their association is the fact that Legros had been the previous tenant of the studio in Palazzo Farnese that Conca and his nephews were to occupy for the next one hundred years.

T.W.S.

1. Contrary to the current misconception, Trevisani and Conca received an identical monthly stipend for the years indicated and both appeared under the category of *gentiluomo* in the account books for the Palazzo della Cancelleria during Cardinal Ottoboni's residency (Biblioteca Apostolica Vaticana, "Computisteria Ottoboni").
2. Another version of the painting is in the Galleria d'Arte of the Collegio Alberoni in Piacenza. Clark, 1967 ("Conca"), p. 332, suggested that one of the background figures in *Saint Catherine Imploring Gregory XI to Return from Avignon* in the Nationalmuseum, Stockholm, may also represent Cardinal Zondadari.
3. Bernardo De Dominici, *Vite de' pittori e scultori napoletani,* Naples, 1745, p. 664.

BERNARD PICART

Paris 1673—Amsterdam 1733

19. Designs of Antique Gems

A. *Hercules*

c. 1723

Inscribed on verso in black chalk or pencil at lower right: 2

Red chalk with borders in black chalk or pencil lightly squared in red chalk, on cream laid paper

210 x 149 mm (8 1/4 x 5 7/8") (image only reproduced)

1978-70-383

B. *Aesculapius*

c. 1722

Red chalk with borders in black chalk or pencil on cream laid paper

206 x 149 mm (8 1/8 x 5 7/8") (image only reproduced)

1978-70-382

Provenance: Captain E. G. Spencer-Churchill, Northwick Park; Northwick sales, Christie's,

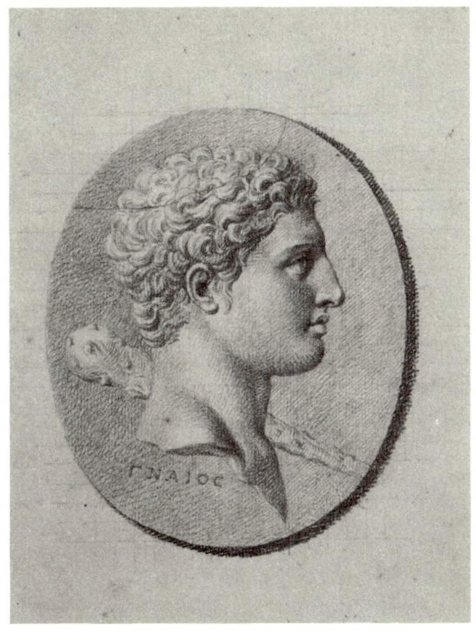

19A

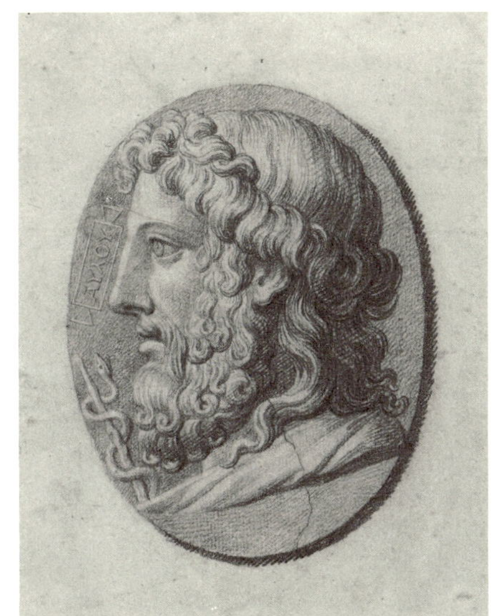

19B

London, May 24, 1965–February 25, 1966, sale and lot number unidentified, from an album with an Italian binding of c. 1810; purchased from Sven Gahlin, London, 1966

Exhibition: Minneapolis, 1970–71

Books of engravings after antiquities of all kinds were an essential part of eighteenth-century classical studies, and the Clark collection contains, in addition to the Odam drawing for the Strozzi Medusa (no. 11), two studies for antique gem engravings by Odam's contemporary and collaborator Bernard Picart. A successful and prolific French Protestant engraver, Picart left his country after the revocation of the Edict of Nantes in 1685 to settle eventually in Amsterdam, where he founded a flourishing publishing house. He is known primarily as a book illustrator and reproductive engraver after both old master and contemporary paintings.[1] These two Picart drawings are preparations in the same direction for his engravings in Baron Philipp von Stosch's *Gemmae Antiquae Caelatae (Pierres antiques gravées),* a sumptuous volume published in 1724 that reproduces seventy ancient gems from European collections.[2]

Baron Stosch (1691–1757), a flamboyant German antiquarian, collector, diplomat, and secret agent for the English, spent most of his adult life in Rome and Florence (*see* no. 106). In 1719, the earliest date that appears on any of the engravings in the publication, he was about twenty-eight years old and in diplomatic service in The Hague. After his return to Rome in 1722, Stosch collaborated with Picart by way of sulphur or paste casts sent to the engraver in Amsterdam.

Although most writers who have discussed the *Pierres antiques gravées* believed that Picart engraved all the plates after drawings supplied by Giralomo Odam and others (*see* no. 11), the catalogue of Picart's work published by his widow specifically states that most of the drawings were executed by Picart himself.[3] The *Hercules* and *Aesculapius* sheets belonged to an album of approximately seventy such studies from which other red-chalk drawings are in the Metropolitan Museum (for plates 7, 45, 55, and 56), the British Museum (for plate 1), and a New York private collection (for plates 25 and 46). An additional sheet representing a chimera, never published, is in a London private collection. The drawings are more simply rendered than the prints, which show the gems framed and well over life-size; the engraved surrounds include titles identifying the subjects, materials, gem engravers, and locations of the gems, as well as small oval configurations reproducing their exact sizes and shapes. Picart signed the *Hercules* and *Aesculapius* engravings at the lower left "B. Picart sculp.," with the dates 1723 and 1722 respectively. A small star at the lower right identifies him as the draughtsman for the design, according to Stosch's preface to the volume.[4]

Although Stosch's scholarship was not without flaws (a small number of the gems he published as antiquities have turned out to be Renaissance or Baroque imitations, and many of the so-called "signatures" engraved on the gems have proven to be post-classical additions), his book became a highly praised model. Its engravings rank among the finest created in a genre of popular and high-quality publications that otherwise included Antonio Francesco Gori's volumes of 1731–32 on the ancient gems in the Medici and other Florentine collections, Pierre-Jean Mariette's 1750 publication of the French royal gem collection, and the catalogue of Marlborough gems of 1780–91, illustrated by Francesco Bartolozzi after the designs of Giovanni Battista Cipriani.

M.L.M.

1. The basic source on Picart's life and work, published by his widow, is *Impostures innocentes ou recueil d'estampes d' après divers peintres illustrés tels que Rafael, le Guide ... et accompagnées d'un discours sur les prejuges de certains curieux touchant la gravure*, Amsterdam, 1734. *See also* A. von Wurzbach, *Neiderländisches Künstler-Lexikon*, Amsterdam, 1963, vol. 2, pp. 326–28, and E. H. Flinn, "The Engravings of Bernard Picart in the Metropolitan Museum of Art," M. A. thesis, New York University, 1971.

2. The book appears in both Latin and French, but is best known by its French title, *Pierres antiques gravées, sur lesquelles les graveurs ont mis leurs noms. Dessinées & gravées en cuivre sur les originaux ou d'après les empreintes, par Bernard Picart. Tirées des principaux cabinets de l'Europe, expliqués par M. Philippe de Stosch*, Amsterdam, 1724. The *Hercules* is plate 23 and the *Aesculapius* is plate 18.

3. *See* n. 1, pp. 4–5.

4. The engraving for *Hercules* and the gem itself are illustrated in Lewis, 1967, p. 323, figs. 5, 6. Both the Hercules and Aesculapius gems are in the British Museum, having passed through the Strozzi and Blacas collections. The Hercules, which is of beryl, is dated to the third decade of the first century B.C. and the Aesculapius, of sard, is considered an antique copy of a fifth-century B.C. original (*see* S. Reinach, *Pierres gravées . . .*, Paris, 1895, pp. 162–63, pl. 133; A. Furtwaengler, *Antiken Gemmen*, Leipzig, 1900, pls. 40, 49, figs. 20, 35; H. B. Walters, *Catalogue of the Engraved Gems and Cameos, Greek, Etruscan, and Roman, in the British Museum*, London, 1926, pp. 182, 200, nos. 1686, 1892, pls. 22, 24. *See also* M. L. Vollenweider, *Die Steinschneidekunst und ihre Künstler in Spätrepublikanischer und Augusteischer Zeit*, Baden-Baden, 1966, p. 45, pl. 42).

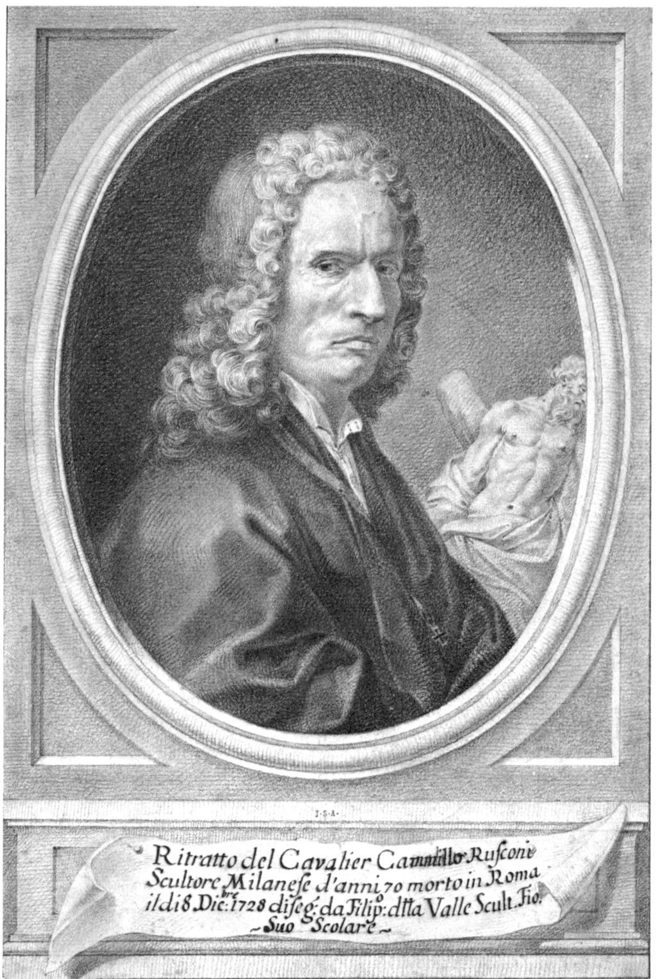

20

FILIPPO DELLA VALLE

Florence 1698—Rome 1768

20. Portrait of Camillo Rusconi

1729

Inscribed on recto in brown ink in cartouche: Ritratto del Cavalier Cammillo Rusconi / Scultore Milanese d'anni 70 morto in Roma / il di 8 Dic: bre 1728 diseg: da Filip:º dtta Valle Scult. Fio. / —Suo Scolare—; Inscribed on verso in brown ink in an old hand: Ritratto del Cav. Cammillo Rusconi Scultore / fatto da Filippo della Valle Scultor Fiorentino / Suo Scolare l'anno 1729 in Roma; and in pencil: 26

Black chalk, some stumping, on cream laid paper

363 x 244 mm (14 1/8 x 9 5/8")

1978-70-423

Provenance: Sir John St. Aubyn (Lugt 1534); sale, Christie's, London, July 4, 1972, lot 111; purchased from David Peel & Co., Ltd., London, 1973

Exhibition: David Peel & Co., Ltd., London, *From Classic to Neo-Classic*, May 9–25, 1973, no. 14, repr.

Rusconi's foremost pupil was Filippo della Valle, who joined him shortly after arriving in Rome in 1725, after the death of his uncle and early teacher G. B. Foggini (*see* no. 21). Della Valle was to develop a subtle sculptural style occasionally influenced by Mannerist works[1] as well as by contemporary French portraiture.[2] His style also embraced an archaeological understanding of ancient sculpture;[3] however, his most enduring debt was to his Roman master, Rusconi. The academic character of his designs, his planar conception of drapery, and his facile manner of carving that often permitted expressive claw-chisel grooves to be left unlustered on the marble surface are all based on Rusconi's example. Della Valle consciously emulated his master, even to the end of his career. For his last commission—the *Saint Theresa* of 1745 in the nave of Saint Peter's[4]—he evoked Rusconi's memory by virtually copying the pose of the older artist's famous statue of *Saint John* in the Lateran. (On Rusconi, *see* no. 10.)

Della Valle wrote a flattering biography of Rusconi in 1732,[5] and he probably executed this portrait, one of the very few finished drawings in his oeuvre, shortly after the older artist's death. Rusconi is depicted in informal studio attire, wearing the cross of a cavalier of the Order of Christ, into which he was admitted in 1718, after completion of his Lateran sculptures. Near him is his statue of *Saint Andrew,* finished in 1709, the first of his four Lateran apostles and the work that established him as the premier sculptor in Rome. The oval composition, set in a rectangular frame, follows the seventeenth-century French tradition of portrait engravings. No engraving from this design is known, however, and della Valle may have executed the drawing simply to pay personal homage to his friend and teacher after his death.

M.P.C.

1. For example, in his *Temperance* in the Corsini Chapel, San Giovanni in Laterano, Rome, of about 1732.
2. *See* his *Clement XII* in San Giovanni dei Fiorentini, Rome, of before 1750.
3. As in his monument to Lady Walpole in Westminster Abbey, London, of about 1740.
4. For a chronology of della Valle's work *see* Honour, 1959.
5. Bottari and Ticozzi, 1822–25, vol. 6, pp. 178–83.

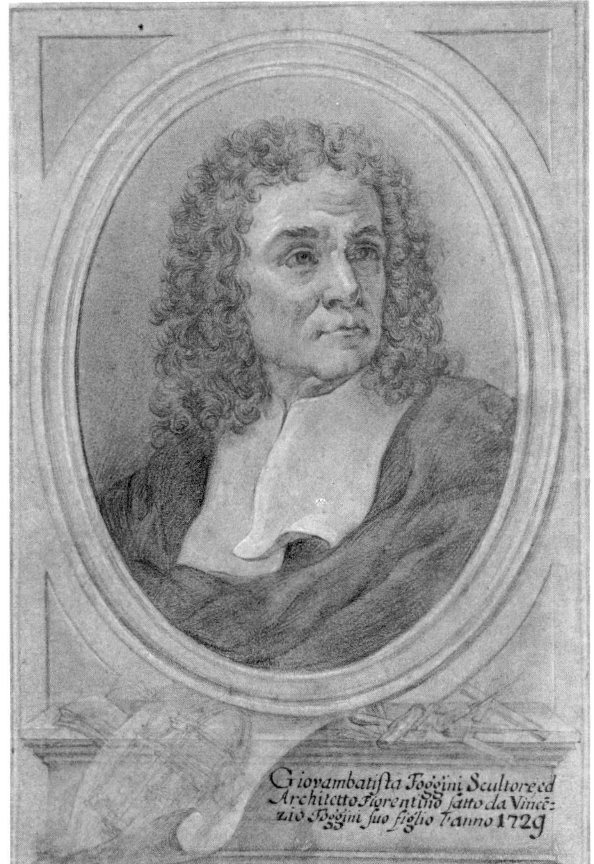

21

VINCENZO FOGGINI

Active Florence, c. 1725–55

21. Portrait of Giovanni Battista Foggini

1729

Signed and dated in brown ink at lower right: Giovambatista Foggini Scultore, ed / Architetto Fiorentino fatto da Vincē= / zio Foggini suo figlio l'anno 1729; inscribed on verso in brown ink at upper center: [illegible] Sig. Gio. Batta Foggini [illegible] scolaro / in Roma di Ercole Ferrata e di Ciro Ferri e morì in Firenze il d. 12 / Aprile 1725. d'anni 73. Disegnai [?] / fino all'ultimo sospiro; and in pencil: 19

Black chalk, some stumping, touches of white chalk, on blue laid paper

364 x 242 mm (14 5/16 x 9 1/2")

1978-70-277

Provenance: gift of Mrs. Charles E. Slatkin, 1965[1]

Bibliography: Florence, 1977, no. 102

In 1673 the sculptor Giovanni Battista Foggini (1652–1725)[2] and the painter Anton Domenico Gabbiani (1652–1726) became the first young Florentine artists to be sent to the recently founded Florentine academy in Rome. This academy had been established by Cosimo III de' Medici on the model of the French Academy in Rome, with a typical program of study emphasizing drawing (taught by the director, Ciro Ferri), classical antiquity, and the great Renaissance and Baroque masters. Foggini also studied in Rome in the studio of Ercole Ferrata, who had worked in Gianlorenzo Bernini's shop and was later strongly influenced by the more classicizing art of Alessandro Algardi.

In 1676 Foggini returned to Florence, quickly making a success of his career. By 1684 he was a professor at the Accademia del Disegno; three years later he was named *primo scultore* of the Casa Serenissima; and in 1694 he was granted the title of *architetto primario* by Cosimo III. The last two positions made Foggini the dominant artistic force in Florence for the remainder of his life. He was personally close to Grand Duke Cosimo and, as *architetto primario,* he directed the grand ducal workshops, an activity that encompassed the designing of all the decorative arts, jewelry, furniture, and other appurtenances for the court.

The most prominent examples of Foggini's work in Florence are the dazzling silver antependium for the high altar of the church of Santissima Annunziata (1680–82), the marble reliefs for the Corsini Chapel in the church of Santa Maria del Carmine (1683–87), and the relief sculpture (finished in 1692) in the Feroni Chapel in Santissima Annunziata. The variety of his production can be studied in the Palazzo Pitti, where many of the smaller objects he designed, such as *prie-dieux,* reliquaries, furniture, and small bronzes, are preserved.

Vincenzo Foggini, Giovanni Battista's eldest son, trained under his father and also went to Rome to study sculpture. Vincenzo's abilities and subsequent career, however, never matched those of his father, and many of his works were based on Giovanni Battista's designs (such as the tomb of Galileo Galilei in Santa Croce, Florence, executed by Vincenzo in collaboration with his brother Giulio).[3]

This posthumous portrait depicts the elder Foggini with the attributes of his dual professions, the sculptor's mallet and the architect's square and calipers. The drawing within the drawing, representing a small building with a centralized plan surmounted by a cupola, is nearly identical to one in Foggini's "Giornale," an album of his drawings in the Gabinetto dei Disegni e delle Stampe degli Uffizi.[4] Foggini never executed such a construction, and it has been suggested that it was a project connected with the grand ducal family.[5]

M.L.M.

1. The Foggini portrait was one of three portraits acquired together from the same source, all laid down in the same manner. The other two are a portrait of Senator Buonarrotti by Tommaso Redi (checklist no. 152) and a self-portrait by Pittoni now in the Minneapolis Institute of Arts.

2. On Giovanni Battista Foggini, *see* Lankheit, 1962, pp. 47–109; Detroit and Florence, 1974, pp. 48–78, 344–63; New York, 1975, pp. 20–23; Florence, 1977.

3. On Vincenzo, *see* Detroit and Florence, 1974, pp. 78–80; Lankheit, 1962, p. 275, docs. 295, 297.

4. Inv. no. 8027A.

5. Florence, 1977, p. 103, no. 102.

PIERRE SUBLEYRAS

Saint-Gilles-du-Gard 1699—Rome 1749

22. *Academic Nude*

c. 1730

Inscribed in brown ink at lower center: Subleras

Black chalk, some stumping, heightened with white chalk on blue gray paper, mounted down

540 x 425 mm (21 1/4 x 16 3/4")

1978-70-408

Provenance: purchased from Mrs. Robert Frank, London, 1960

Exhibitions: Minneapolis, 1967, no. 71; Minneapolis, 1970–71; New York, 1978

It would have been surprising had Anthony Clark, the leading connoisseur and historian of eighteenth-century Roman art, not owned some works by Subleyras, in his century the greatest painter in Rome before Pompeo Batoni. Besides this striking drawing, the collection contained a splendid painting of the *Christ Child in Glory;*[1] in fact, Anthony Clark was first to identify and publish many of Subleyras's paintings.[2] On the other hand, the artist's drawings, the major holdings of which are in the Louvre, the Musée Atger in Montpellier, and the Kunstmuseum in Düsseldorf, are not well known. No general study has yet been made of his graphic style, and such an undertaking would be difficult because of the large number of mistakenly attributed sheets in both public and private collections. Nevertheless, the attribution to Subleyras of this drawing, which bears a later but correct inscription, can easily be confirmed on stylistic grounds. It shares many of the characteristics of the artist's paintings, such as a taste for solid and compact forms, strongly outlined masses, broad illumination, and a kind of modeling that summarizes and simplifies rather than renders details.

Trained in Toulouse, Subleyras received the Grand Prix in painting of the Académie Royale in Paris in 1727 and went to Rome as a French Academy *pensionnaire* at the Palazzo Mancini in 1728. He was never again to leave Rome, achieving a brilliant career there, due in part to the protection of Pope Benedict XIV, whose official portrait he painted. A contemporary of Boucher and Chardin, his style is totally lacking in "baroque" qualities and refers back instead to the severe or classicizing artists of the seventeenth century, such as Eustache Le Sueur. In this way Subleyras seems to anticipate certain neoclassical artists, and it is not a coincidence that at the beginning of the reign of Louis XVI some of his finest paintings, today in the Louvre, were acquired for the royal collections.

This drawing shows as much of Subleyras's rigorous provincial training as it does of the seventeenth-century tradition that the French Academy strove to perpetuate.

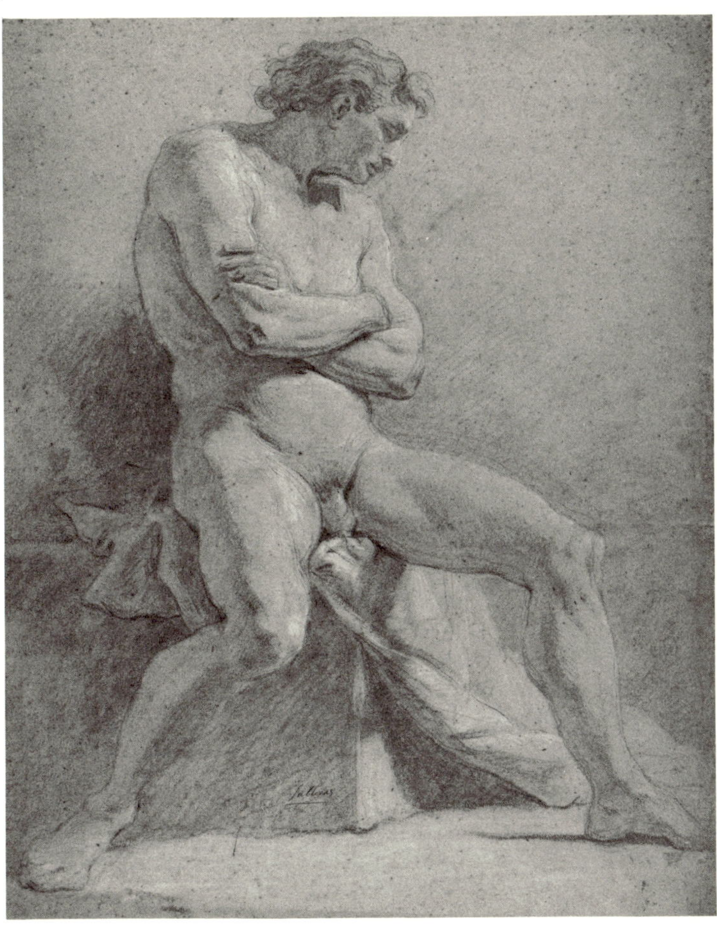

22

Nevertheless, it does not seem to date from the artist's apprenticeship in Toulouse but rather to have been executed during his first years in Rome, around 1730, while he was especially occupied in copying after Raphael and the Carracci.

P.R.

1. Clark sale, Christie's, London, July 6, 1978, lot 58, repr.
2. For example, Clark, 1964–65, where Subleyras's portrait of his wife in the Walters Art Gallery, Baltimore, is correctly attributed.

ETIENNE PARROCEL

Avignon 1696—Rome 1776

23. *Studies for a Portrait of a Cardinal*

c. 1740

Inscribed in pencil at lower right: 1B (probably referring to the price, one baiocco papal currency)

Black and white chalks on grayish beige laid paper

277 x 429 mm (10 7/8 x 16 7/8″)

1978-70-378

Provenance: gift of E. V. A. Everett, Esq., 1966

Exhibitions: Minneapolis, 1967, no. 68; Minneapolis, 1970–71

Despite the writings of Etienne Parrocel's nineteenth-century descendant,[1] and the recent publication of several of Parrocel's religious compositions preserved in Umbria,[2] the work of this artist, known in his time as "le Romain," is still scarcely studied. A member of a brilliant dynasty of artists of which only the founder, Joseph, is somewhat well-known today thanks to the writings of Antoine Schnapper, Etienne Parrocel lived and practiced in Rome from 1717 until his death, although he continued to execute commissions for

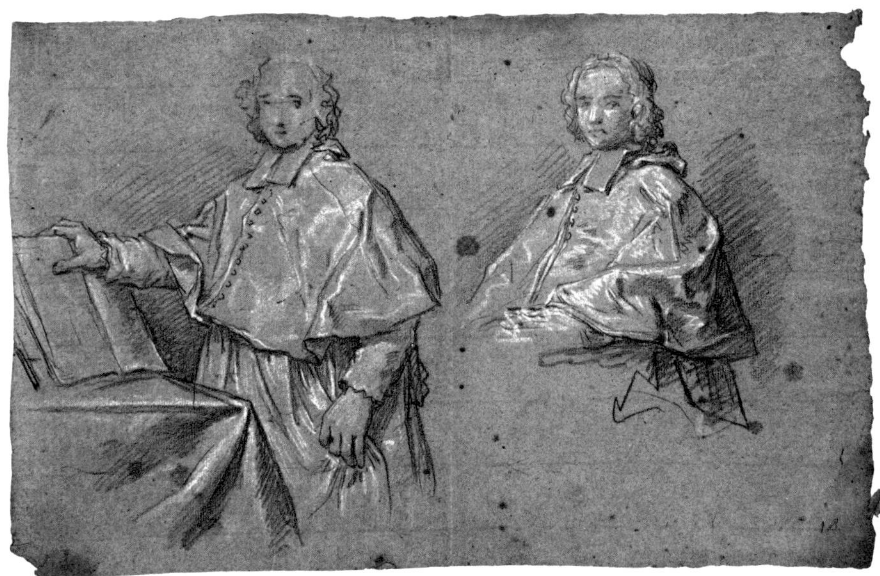

23

churches in the south of France. Considered an Italian by French scholars and a Frenchman by Italians, he has suffered—like the more talented Pierre Subleyras—from a dual nationality that has helped cast his reputation into undeserved oblivion and has left most of his works unrecognized.

The attribution of this drawing, one of the rare sheets by the artist not of a religious subject, is unquestioned, as it belonged to a group of documented sheets in the E. V. A. Everett collection.[3] The subject may represent Cardinal Pierre Guérin de Tencin (1680–1758), as suggested by Anthony Clark. The figure can be compared convincingly with that in an engraving by J. G. Wille after a lost portrait of the cardinal by Parrocel, although the powerful cardinal is seated in the painting but is represented standing in the drawing. Tencin was raised to the purple in 1739 and was in Rome for the second time from 1740—when he played an important role in the election of Pope Benedict XIV—until 1742.

Cardinal de Tencin, a colorful character and an unscrupulous politician—"doux, insinuant, faux comme un jeton, ignorant comme un prédicateur"[4]—was somewhat less notorious than his sister, and probable mistress, Claudine Alexandrine Guérin de Tencin, whose love affairs were scandals but whose salon, the prototype for Mme. Geoffrin's, was frequented by the most enlightened minds of the period. In 1717 she gave birth to an illegitimate child, whom she abandoned, who grew up to become the famed philosopher d'Alembert.

Whoever the subject may be, the Clark drawing—with its zigzagging strokes, the simplicity of its *mise en page,* and the emphasis divided between the face and costume of the sitter in the best Rigaud tradition—adds an element to our understanding of Roman draughtsmanship during the first half of the eighteenth century.

P.R.

1. *See* Etienne Parrocel, *L'Art dans le Midi,* Marseilles, 1884, pp. 322–25; idem, *Monographie des Parrocel: Essai,* Marseilles, 1861, pp. 80–90, especially p. 88.
2. *See* Vittorio Casale, Giorgio Falcidia, et al., *Pittura del '600 e '700, ricerche in Umbria,* vol. 1, Rome, 1976, pp. 44–45.
3. *See* Paris, Galerie Heim, *Cent dessins français du Fitzwilliam Museum, Cambridge,* 1976, no. 76.
4. *Mémoires du Président Hénault, écrits par lui-même, recueillis et mis en ordre par son arrière-neveu M. le Baron de Vigan,* Paris, 1855, p. 395.

LOUIS-GABRIEL BLANCHET

Paris 1705—Rome 1772

24. *View of the Church of San Gregorio al Celio in Rome*

c. 1750

Inscribed on verso in pencil: L. G. Blanchet / A O M / K5227 / 14 / 20 / 51; and in black chalk: L. G. Blanchet

Black and white chalks on gray beige laid paper

226 x 395 mm (8 7/8 x 15 9/16")

Watermark: kneeling knight with a cross in a shield

1978-70-192

Provenance: purchased from Rockman Prints, New York, 1965

Exhibition: Minneapolis, 1967, no. 15

Louis-Gabriel Blanchet, like Pierre Subleyras and Jean Barbault, was one of the few young artists sent to the French Academy in Rome—at the king's expense—who remained in that city for the rest of their lives. Subleyras's rival in the competition for the Grand Prix de Rome in 1727, Blanchet placed second but received his *pensionnaire's* diploma nevertheless. Continually renewing his fellowship, he lodged in the Palazzo Mancini from 1728 to 1752 and thus encountered several successive artistic generations of his compatriots, from Carle Van Loo, François Boucher, and Pierre-Charles Trémolières to the early neoclassical artists.

In addition to the copies normally required of a *pensionnaire,* Blanchet's surviving work consists of palace decorations, portraits, and landscape drawings. In 1732 he painted four overdoors with allegorical subjects for the duc de Saint-Aignan, French ambassador to Rome, of which three can still be traced; to the *Allegory of Painting* exhibited in Rome in 1959 can now be added the allegories of *Architecture* (in the Musée du Berry in Bourges, attributed to Boucher) and *Agriculture* (on the Paris art market), as well as a sketch for the *Allegory of Sculpture* (attributed to Antoine François Callet in the Musée Magnin, Dijon).[1] Of the *Seasons,* each with four putti, once owned by the bailli de Breteuil, ambassador to Rome of the Order of Malta from 1758 to 1777, *Summer* can perhaps be identified with a painting—again attributed to Boucher—in the Muzeum Narodowe in Warsaw. Blanchet is best remembered for his portraits, however, especially those of members of the Stuart dynasty exiled in Rome.[2] Through them he met numerous travelers making the grand tour, as well as artists (he seems to have been one of the contacts between Clérisseau and the Adam brothers), including the architect James Barry, whose portrait by Blanchet is preserved at the Royal Society of Arts in London, and the landscape painter Richard Wilson, in Rome during the 1750s.[3] Anthony Clark correctly reattributed to Blanchet the so-called *Portrait of Mozart* acquired as Batoni by the Christie family in Glyndebourne (Sussex), a portrait that, if the identification of the sitter is correct, would have been painted at the time of the young composer's trip to Italy in 1769–71.[4]

This sheet is completely characteristic of Blanchet's views of Rome and the Roman countryside, distinguished by a common technique (black and white chalks), grayish or brownish paper, and closely similar dimensions. Some are inscribed with numbers, written out in Italian, suggesting that they may have been grouped in albums. It does not seem that they were preparations for engravings, as no examples are known. The attribution of these sheets rests on tradition; as far as we know only one of them is signed,[5] and since none is dated it is difficult to establish a chronology. However, probably on a comparison of these landscapes with those of Richard Wilson, Anthony Clark considered them to date around 1750.

J.-F.M.

1. The paintings are recorded in the Saint-Aignan sale catalogue of 1776; *see* Le Moël and Rosenberg, 1969, especially p. 62. *See also* Rome, 1959, no. 82, pl. 38, and Méjanès, in Cholet, 1973, p. 129, pl. 55.

2. Edinburgh, Scottish National Portrait Gallery, inv. nos. 1836 and 1837; London, Royal Academy of Arts, *France in the Eighteenth Century,* January 6–March 3, 1968, nos. 20 and 21, fig. 251.

3. *See* Brinsley Ford, *The Drawings of Richard Wilson,* London, 1951, pp. 25–26.

4. *See* Edward Speyer, "Mozart at the National Gallery," *The Burlington Magazine,* vol. 28, no. 156 (March, 1916), p. 222, fig. 1b.

5. London, Courtauld Institute Galleries, Witt Collection, inv. no. 3929 (signed: L. G. Blanchet / d'après nature).

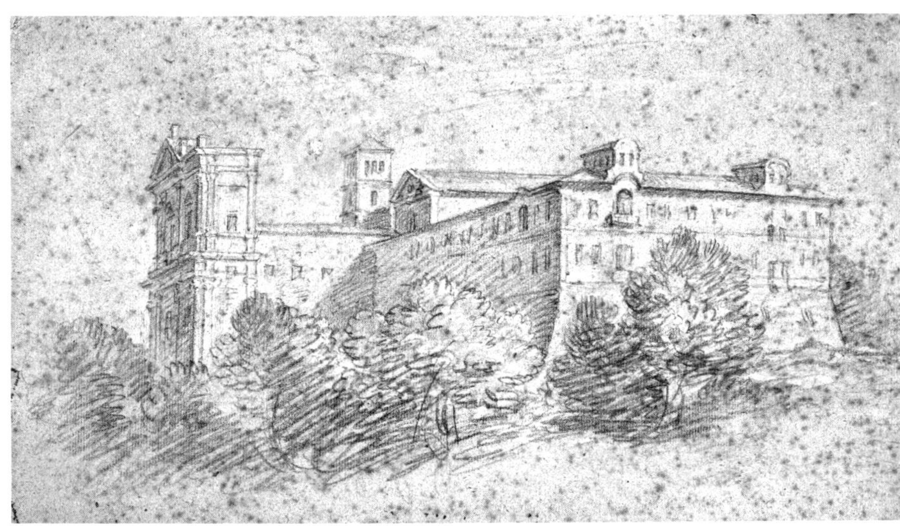

24

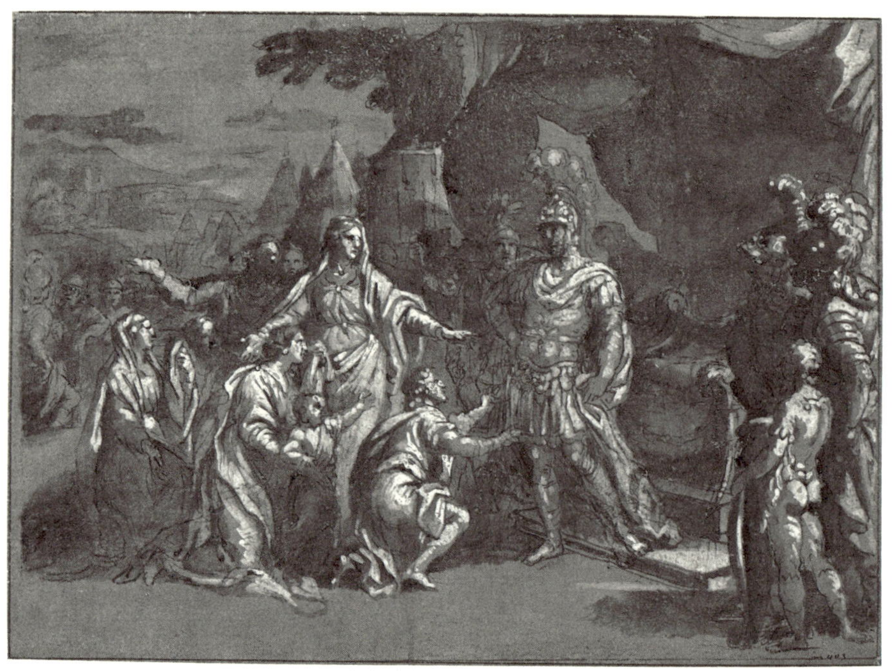

25

AGOSTINO MASUCCI

Rome 1692—Rome 1758

25. *The Family of Darius before Alexander the Great*

c. 1740–45

Inscribed in brown ink at bottom right (in the same manner as no. 8): m 403

Black and red chalk, pen and black and brown ink and brown wash, white gouache heightening on pinkish gray prepared paper, mounted down

229 x 307 mm (9 x 12 1/8″)

1978-70-336

Provenance: "Pseudo-Resta" (*see also* no. 8); Col. Thomas Wildman of Newstead Abbey; William F. Webb; Lady Cheamside; Richard Gatty, Northallerton, Yorkshire; Sotheby's, London, March 18, 1959, lot 66; purchased from W. R. Jeudwine, London, 1960

Bibliography: Clark, 1967 ("Masucci"), p. 262, fig. 9

Agostino Masucci was born in Rome and studied under Andrea Procaccini and Carlo Maratta.[1] By the end of the second decade of the eighteenth century he had begun to execute altarpieces, and by the early 1720s he was well enough established to merit a biography in Nicola Pio's Lives of the Painters. . . .[2] The inscription on Pier Leone Ghezzi's caricature of him of 1722 notes that he will do well "with time."

Proposed for membership in the Accademia di San Luca in 1722 and elected two years later, Masucci eventually emerged in the 1720s and '30s as one of Rome's leading painters of altarpieces and portraits. He was *principe* of the academy between 1736 and 1738, and his pupils included Pompeo Batoni and later Gavin Hamilton.

Masucci was held in great esteem as the principal continuator in his time of the "official" tradition of Maratta, and he transformed the heritage of Baroque classicism into a blunter style usually identified by the unfortunate label of "proto-neoclassicism." This drawing, based on his experience of Renaissance and classical Baroque models, is characteristic of Masucci's mature efforts to rationalize and to distill compositional groupings and space—gains often accompanied, as here, by an air of contrivance and small effect.

The subject of this drawing remains uncertain. A closely related but reversed composition of *Coriolanus and his Family* is in the Mead Art Gallery, Amherst College, Amherst, Massachusetts.[3] Anthony Clark regarded the two drawings as evolving from Masucci's work in completing a painting of Coriolanus left unfinished by Francesco Imperiali upon his death in 1740. Other similar, and for Masucci apparently influential, works by Luigi Garzi have as subjects both Coriolanus and Alexander.[4]

U.W.H.

1. The basic study of Masucci, with literature, is Clark, 1967 ("Masucci"). *See also* the list of works in Waterhouse, 1976, pp. 93–94; and for more recently published drawings, Dreyer, 1971, pp. 202–6, and *L'Accademia,* 1974, p. 350, fig. 25 (prize drawing for the Accademia di San Luca competition of 1707); Williamstown, Mass., The Sterling and Francine Clark Art Institute, *Master Drawings from the Collection of Ingrid and Julius S. Held,* catalogue by L. Giles, E. Millroy, and G. Owens, (traveling exhibition), 1979, no. 25.

2. Pio, 1977, pp. 145–46. Masucci was also a large supplier of portrait drawings for Pio's history; *see* Clark, 1967 ("Portraits"), pp. 10, 12–15.

3. For the most recent comments on the painting of Coriolanus *see A Summary Catalogue of the Collection at the*

Mead Art Gallery, Middletown, Conn., 1978, p. 209 (where its attribution to Benjamin West is still essentially favored).

4. The recto letter-plus-numeral inscription, very like that of no. 8, would appear to relate to the Padre Resta-Lord Somers collection (Lugt 2981; Lugt suppl. 2981) were both drawings—particularly the Masucci—not too late for such a provenance. Such a mark appears on an additional drawing in the Clark collection, by or after Corrado Giaquinto (checklist no. 82), and on another Masucci drawing in the Ashmolean Museum, Oxford (K. T. Parker, *Catalogue of the Collection of Drawings in the Ashmolean Museum,* vol. 2, *Italian Schools,* Oxford, 1972, pp. 515–16, no. 1026).

MARCO BENEFIAL

Rome 1684—Rome 1764

26. Study of a Capuchin Monk

1730–40

Inscribed on recto in black ink at lower right: Del Cav: Benefiale Rom; inscribed on verso in red chalk at lower right: lot [?] 54.

Black chalk with faint touches of white chalk on pinkish prepared paper

278 x 188 mm (10 15/16 x 7 3/8″)

1978-70-184

Provenance: gift of Keith Andrews, 1965

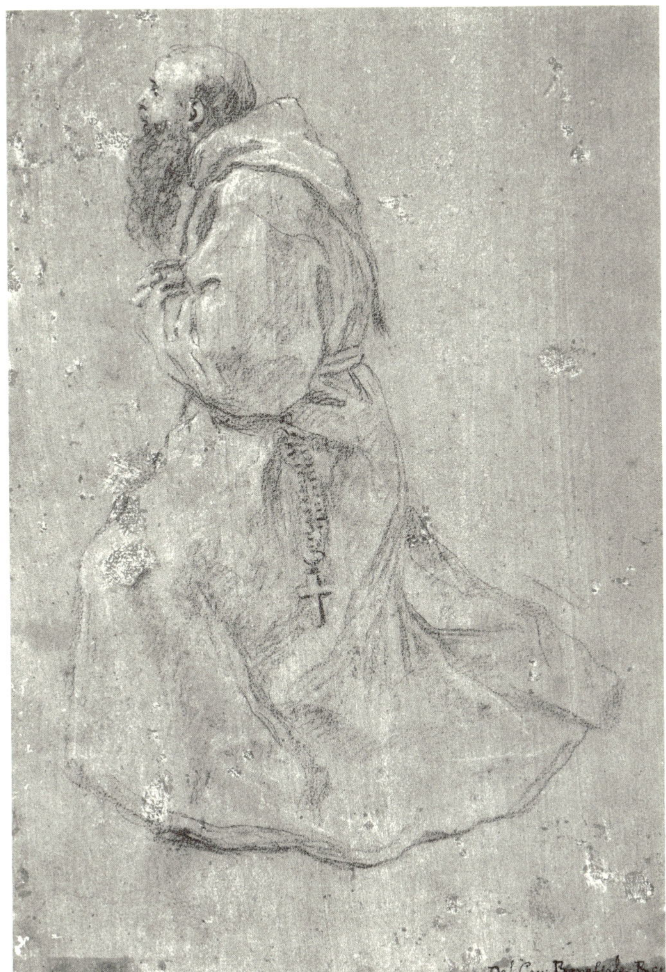

26

The fact that no thorough study of Marco Benefial's life and work yet exists is an accurate measure of the present undeveloped state of research into Roman Settecento painting.[1] Set apart by temperament, intellect, and artistic purpose from most of his Roman contemporaries, Benefial attains in his paintings and drawings a level of distinction that should offer every incentive for the further study of his career. Half a century ago Hermann Voss recognized the significance of the artist's effort to reform Roman painting, and most subsequent writers have noted his intense study of nature and his return to the classical foundations of Raphael and Annibale Carracci. No other Roman painter of Benefial's generation so rigorously interpreted the ideals of the seventeenth-century classical style nor so successfully anticipated the neoclassicism that emerged after 1760 in the work of Mengs, and other artists.

Benefial had a very productive career, a fact frequently obscured by his difficult beginnings and by his activity as a ghost painter for two little-known painters, Filippo Germisoni and Filippo Evangelisti, throughout much of his life. Between 1698 and 1703 he studied with Bonaventura Lamberti, a Bolognese painter who directed his study toward antique sculpture, Raphael, and the Bolognese masters of the early Baroque. Equally important to Benefial's development, however, was the work of Correggio and Lanfranco[2] and, among his contemporaries, of Benedetto Luti and Francesco Trevisani. Despite the steady stream of altarpieces and easel paintings produced in Benefial's studio after about 1718 —the year in which he received the important commission for one of the Lateran prophets—the painter remained an anti-Establishment figure who alienated much of Roman artistic society. He did not become a member of the Accademia di San Luca until 1746 and was expelled from that institution nine years later for his doctrinaire and outspoken criticism of his colleagues.

Benefial's best pictures, as Ellis Waterhouse has observed,[3] show a view of dramatic naturalism that is extraordinarily simple and direct. He invokes a new interpretation of traditional religious imagery, of which the most powerful and arresting examples, all in Rome, are *The Flagellation of Christ* in the church of the Stimmate di San Francesco of 1731, the two *Scenes from the Life of Saint Margaret of Cortona* in the church of Santa Maria d'Aracoeli of 1732, and *The Vision of Saint Catherine of Genoa* in the Galleria Nazionale d'Arte Antica of about 1737.

The beard and pointed cowl, or capuche, worn by the monk, who is perhaps shown as receiving the sacrament, identify him as a member of the Capuchin order.

The figure is reminiscent of that of a kneeling monk by Benefial in a drawing in the Kunstmuseum, Düsseldorf,[4] for one of the ten large canvases the artist painted for the cathedral of Viterbo, destroyed in 1945. The present drawing also appears to be a study for a specific painting, which has yet to be identified.

E.P.B.

1. The most important studies on the artist to date are Noack, 1919; Voss, 1924, pp. 638–42; Paponi, 1958; Falcidia, 1966; Clark, 1966; and Falcidia, 1978. The literature to 1963 has been compiled by E. Borea in *Dizionario biografico,* 1960–, vol. 8, pp. 466–69.

2. Wittkower, 1973, pp. 308, 406, n. 18, pl. 183a, noted the strong Correggio-Lanfranco influence in Benefial's reinterpretation of Raphael's *Transfiguration* in his painting in the church of Sant'Andrea, Vetralla, of about 1730.

3. Waterhouse, 1971, pp. 15–16.

4. Inv. no. FP 13763.

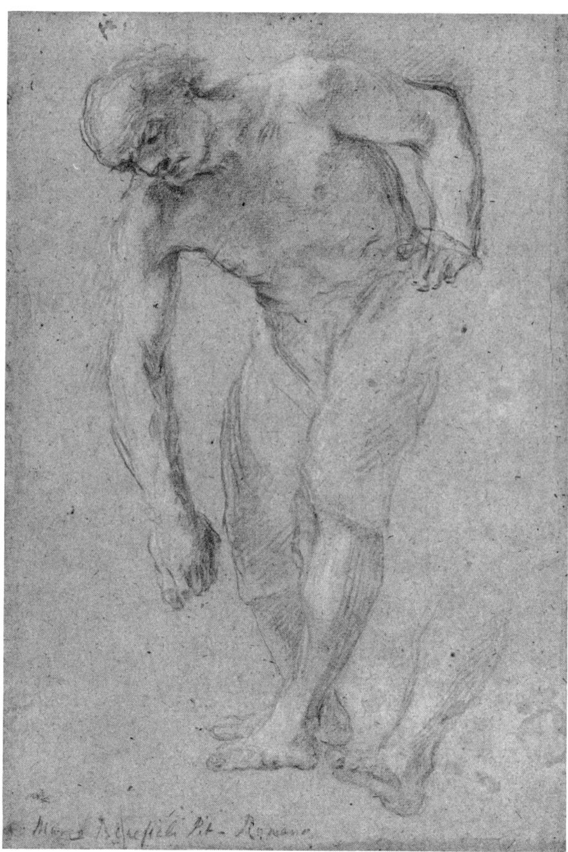

27

27. *Studies of a Soldier for a "Massacre of the Innocents" and a Foot*

1730–40

Signed (or inscribed in a contemporary hand) in black chalk at lower left: Marco Benefiali Pit—Romano

Black chalk, some stumping, with touches of white chalk on gray brown laid paper

414 x 275 mm (16 3/16 x 10 3/4")

1978-70-182

Provenance: John Skippe (1742–1812); James Martin; Edward Holland; Mrs. Rayner-Wood; Edward Holland-Martin; Skippe collection sale, Christie's, London, November 20, 1958, lot 39b; purchased from P & D Colnaghi & Co Ltd, London, 1958

Exhibitions: Minneapolis, 1967, no. 11; Minneapolis, 1970–71

The admirable range of Benefial's talents as a draughtsman will become evident only when the sizeable holdings of his drawings in Düsseldorf, Vienna, and Berlin are properly studied. Executed in a variety of chalks, inks, and washes, these largely unpublished drawings include academic studies of the nude model (the solid basis of his drawing practice), studies after the antique and after other artists, compositional sketches, and studies of individual figures and details. As usual in the Bolognese-Roman tradition, the majority of these drawings are closely related to the artist's work in hand. Anthony Clark distinguished the types and stages of drawings within Benefial's working method as first, minimal compositional sketches in the form of pen, wash, or chalk squibs; second, compositional layout drawings in more developed form; third, figure, drapery, hand, and head studies; and fourth, highly finished *modelli,* often executed in grisaille bodycolor, that immediately preceded oil sketches.[1] Understandably, a greater number of drawings from the more finished third and fourth categories survive than do those from the earlier, more ephemeral stages of work.

Although Popham related this drawing in the catalogue of the Skippe sale to the Santa Maria alle Fornaci *Beheading of Saint John the Baptist* of the 1720s, Clark more plausibly connected the sheet with one of Benefial's several versions of the *Massacre of the Innocents.* This theme probably appealed to Benefial not only for its inherent qualities of movement, drama, and expression but also, as hinted at by his biographers, for its violent nature. He painted the subject a number of times, including a version executed for Cardinal Ferroni in 1730, another currently in the Palazzo Collegio Urbano di Propaganda Fide, and a large, unfinished version in a private collection near Orvieto.[2] Repeated almost schematically throughout the series, the present figure, studied from life, cannot be associated with any particular painting.[3] The same aged model, also naked to the waist though posed in the opposite direction, appears at the extreme right of the *Massacre of the Innocents* in the Galleria Ferroni, Florence.[4] Notable for its powerful use of black chalk and its painterly effect of light and shade, this drawing illuminates Benefial's careful working methods and his intense preparation for every detail of his large-scale compositions. E.P.B.

1. Clark, 1966, pp. 25–26.
2. Voss, 1924, p. 402 (repr.), pp. 640–41; Falcidia, 1978, fig. 49. For a list of Benefial's versions of the theme, *see* Clark, 1966, p. 31, n. 1.
3. John Mortensen, in a letter of July 25, 1975, to Anthony Clark, related the present study to the lost *Massacre of the Shechemites* painted for Benefial's main patron, Count Niccolò Soderini (repr., with a compositional drawing in the Albertina, in Longhi, 1966, pp. 68–70, figs. 62, 63). The attitude of the model in the present drawing is a typical studio pose frequently met in the figures of executioners in Benefial's paintings, but it does not appear to be a specific study for one of Abimelech's soldiers in the canvas painted for Soderini.
4. Repr. Voss, 1924, p. 402.

28. Study for "The Apotheosis of Hercules"
c. 1744
Black chalk and brown wash with white gouache heightening on buff laid paper
405 x 265 mm (15 15/16 x 10 7/16")
1978-70-183
Provenance: purchased from Rockman Prints, New York, 1958
Exhibitions: Minneapolis, 1967, no. 12; Minneapolis, 1970–71

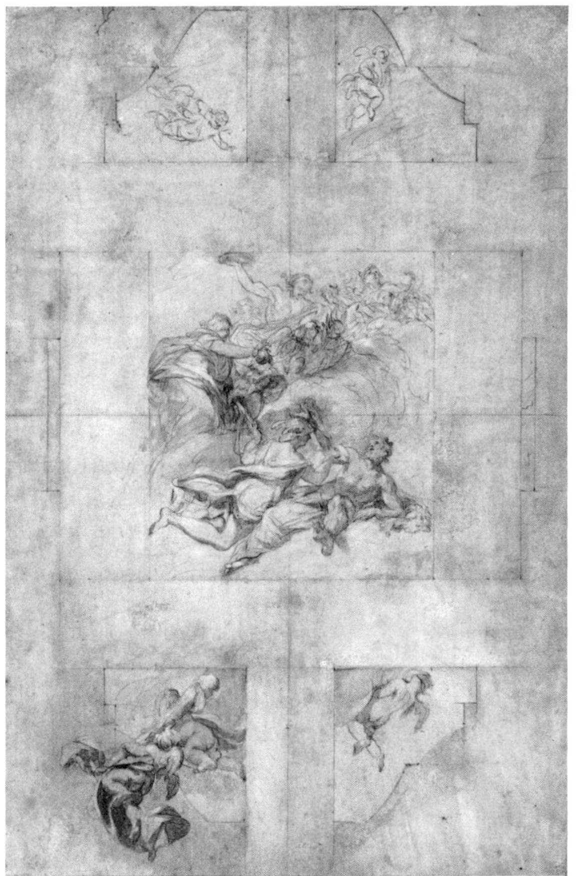

28

Anthony Clark first connected this sketch with Benefial's lost ceiling of 1744 for the Sala Regia in the Palazzo di Spagna, Rome.[1] The *Apotheosis of Hercules* occupies the square central compartment in the drawing, with four smaller sections at the corners containing putti; in one of these sections two putti carry Hercules' club. The subject, known through Ovid's account in the *Metamorphoses,* represents the arrival of Hercules among the assembled gods of Mount Olympus. In the lower half of the principal scene, Mercury introduces the hero, shown reclining on a lion skin in the lower right corner, to the welcoming gods and goddesses on clouds above. Recognizable among them are Hebe at the left, who pours for Hercules the liquid giving immortality and eternal youth; Jupiter, with his eagle, holding aloft a garland; and, at the upper right, Juno beside her peacock. Other deities appear in the background.

Benefial's scheme for the ceiling decoration of the Sala Regia anticipates to a remarkable degree the ceiling design by Cristoforo Unterberger depicting the same subject in the Casino Borghese, Rome.[2]

E.P.B.

1. Notice of the ceiling is given in Noack, 1919, p. 128, who refers to "the ceiling painting *The Reception of Hercules on Olympus* in the large audience hall of the palace of the Spanish Embassy, for which 200 scudi were paid to [Benefial] on November 30, 1744"; *see also* Noack in Thieme-Becker, 1907–50, vol. 3, p. 322.
2. The final, very finished *modello* for Unterberger's central canvas, executed between 1784 and 1786, is in the Walters Art Gallery, Baltimore; Zeri, 1976, vol. 2, p. 538, no. 427.

29. Study for a Group Portrait
Verso: *Head of a King* (not illustrated)
c. 1756
Inscribed on verso in pencil at lower right: 2044 / Lire [?] JR
Recto: brush and gray wash with traces of black chalk on cream laid paper; verso: pencil
232 x 320 mm (9 1/8 x 12 5/8")
Watermark: fleur-de-lis in a double circle
1978-70-185
Provenance: purchased from Leo S. Olschki, Florence, 1965
Bibliography: *One Hundred Items from the Stock of Leo S. Olschki Bookseller,* cat. 142, Florence, 1965, p. 59, no. 80, repr. (as Giuseppe Castiglione, *Saint Francis of Sales Preaching the Gospel to the Chinese*); Clark, 1966, p. 26, pl. 21; Praz, 1971, p. 202, n. 9

This drawing was made as a preparatory study for the group portrait by Benefial in the Galleria Nazionale d'Arte Antica, Rome, that is believed to represent members of the Marefoschi family.[1] The painting, signed and dated 1756, represents a priest preaching to a group of people, two of whom are dressed in oriental costume, set against a conventionally exotic landscape. The frank, realistic depiction of features and poses is typical of the artist, but the portrait's exact identification is puzzling. Mario Praz included the scene among period costume and allegorical portraits in his study of the conversation piece, describing it as "a translation into a domestic masquerade" of the present drawing.[2] Anthony Clark identified the subject as a burlesque of Saint Francis Xavier preaching to the Japanese—"a blasphemous anti-Jesuit painting arranged as a picnic and charade portrait."[3]

Saint Francis Xavier (1506–1552; canonized in 1622) pioneered Christian missionary work in the Far East; he traveled widely through the East Indies, southern India, Ceylon, and Japan but died on an island near the mouth of the Canton river before he could enter China. Despite the stiff gestures of the figure identified as Saint Francis and the wooden countenances of his assembled audience in Benefial's painting, no traces of the comic or burlesque seem evident. Whatever its real subject, the drawing is a tangible reminder of the cult for chinoiserie that reached its height in Rome in the 1750s. The vogue for rich oriental costumes was indulged in plays, operas, ballets, masquerades, and street festivals (*see also* no. 108)—notably at carnival and at the Festa della Chinea, during which the set pieces used for fireworks displays were often in the chinoiserie style.[4]

The drawing implies that originally only the portraits of the preacher, the younger and older seated women, and the standing head of the family at the right were considered. Benefial frequently employed swift, rough sketches of this type in the early stages of developing compositions for both portraits and history paintings. In Clark's judgment it was these brush drawings that especially represented the artist's particular "sureness,... flavor, and . . . fine creative sloppiness."[5]

The *Head of a King* on the verso is possibly the fragment of a cartoon or a copy after an older fresco.

E.P.B.

1. Falcidia, 1964, p. 33, repr. fig. 8. Praz, 1971, p. 202, repr. p. 205, fig. 166; Praz, without citing supporting evidence, identified the sitters as members of the Marefoschi family. *See also* Falcidia, 1978, p. 48, n. 38.

2. Praz, 1971, p. 202, n. 9.

3. Clark, 1966, pp. 26, 32, n. 7, noted the resemblance in the painting of the elderly cleric at the left to Cardinal Passionei.

4. *See* Honour, 1961 (*Chinoiserie*), pp. 118, 261, fig. 75, on Jean Barbault's record of the French Academy's masquerade procession in the 1751 carnival at Rome, in which the *pensionnaires* wore oriental costumes of the type shown by Benefial.

5. Clark, 1966, p. 26.

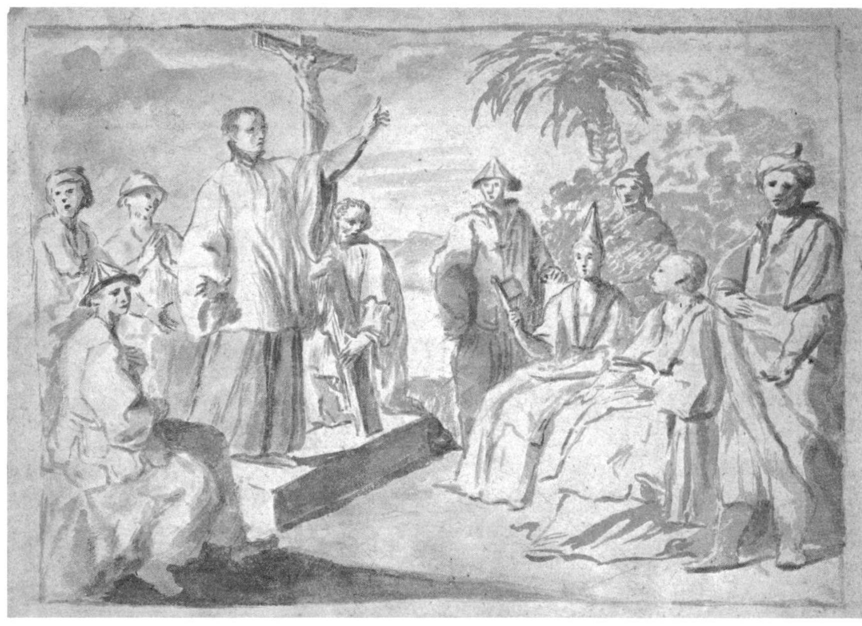

29

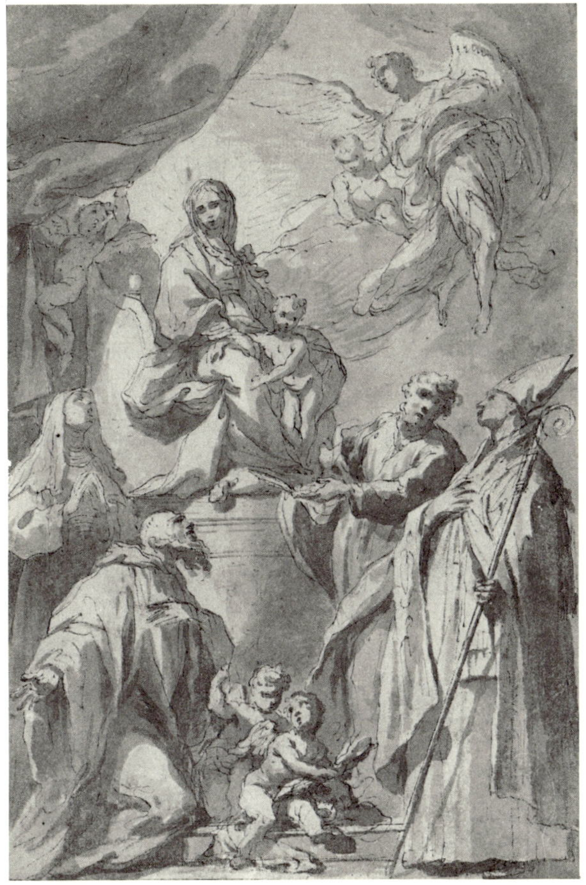

30

POMPEO BATONI

Lucca 1708—Rome 1787

30. Study for "The Virgin and Child Enthroned with Four Beatified Members of the Gabrielli Family"

1732–33

Pen and black ink, gray washes, over faint traces of black chalk on cream laid paper, mounted down

203 x 134 mm (8 x 5 1/4")

1978-70-161

Provenance: purchased from Rockman Prints, New York, 1958

Exhibition: Minneapolis, 1970–71

Bibliography: Faldi, 1971, p. 568

It is not surprising that Anthony Clark's collection of eighteenth-century drawings is richest in the works of his favorite Roman artist, Pompeo Girolamo Batoni. In the same way that he made the entire Roman Settecento almost his own as a field of study, as Ellis Waterhouse has remarked, Clark applied the special talents of his remarkable mind to rediscovering the virtues of this particular Roman painter, whom he studied for over twenty years. Among artists active in Rome in the eighteenth century, Batoni enjoyed the greatest reputation in his own day: by 1740 he was noted; by 1750 he was the most celebrated painter in the city; and by 1760, although Tiepolo was still alive, he was the most famous painter in Italy. Following the deaths of Tiepolo and Mengs, and until his own death in 1787, Batoni was the best-known painter in all of Europe and the last eighteenth-century painter in Italy of really considerable fame.[1] Anthony Clark's introductory essay to the catalogue of the 1967 exhibition in Lucca remains the best available summary of the artist's career.[2]

Batoni had studied briefly in his native Lucca with two minor painters, Giovanni Domenico Lombardi (1682–1752) and Domenico Brugieri (1678–1744), before moving permanently to Rome in 1727, where his contacts with Sebastiano Conca, Agostino Masucci, and Francesco Imperiali, as well as his studies of Raphael's Stanze, the Farnese Gallery, and the city's well-known collections of antiquities, helped form his mature style before the end of the 1730s. Elected to the Accademia di San Luca in 1741, he produced, during the next decades, a variety of imaginative and forceful altarpieces, devotional pictures, and a steady flow of paintings of subjects drawn from classical history and mythology. From the early 1740s he specialized in portraits of foreign visitors to Rome, the category of picture for which he was, and has remained, most famous. For the wealthier British grand tourists Batoni was virtually "the" portrait painter; he also portrayed a variety of other prominent foreign visitors and important local sitters, producing perhaps a dozen portraits a year, of which as many as 250 are still extant.

Partly because so few of the works upon which Batoni's reputation was based have been adequately published, his chronology has never been properly deciphered nor his stylistic position within his century precisely defined. Most writers have noticed that the artist gradually moved toward—and contributed substantially to—a final definition of the neoclassical style that swept Europe in the last quarter of the eighteenth century. Yet his art eludes such definition: Clark himself characterized Batoni simply as "an artist of the grand style of the mid-eighteenth century, that unnamed style between the late Baroque with its brief rococo aftermath and actual neoclassicism."[3] Part of the difficulty lies in Batoni's effortless absorption of the great tradition of Italian art; his work, "full of sonorous echoes of the past"—of Raphael and Poussin, of Guido Reni and Domenichino, of Correggio and Parmigianino, of Annibale Carracci, Bernini, and Pietro da Cortona[4]—is also a fine continuation of the Roman tradition of the first half of his own century, consolidating the accomplishments of artists such as Maratta, Luti, and Trevisani.

The Clark drawings are of particular interest for the light they shed on Batoni's methods as a history painter. He was a superb craftsman, as careful as he was inventive, for whom the drawn study performed a crucial role in the preparation of the final work. The present group of drawings, ranging in date over fifty years from the artist's first public commission to his last, illustrates the full scope of Batoni's draughtsmanship, with the exception of the basis of his earliest fame, his drawings of antiquities made for English travelers.[5] His surviving oeuvre falls within the traditional categories of seventeenth- and eighteenth-century draughtsmanship, including copies of other artists' works, academies (or drawings from the nude), and rough sketches of compositions in the planning stage; there are many studies for individual groups and single figures and rather fewer finished drawings of whole compositions, since Batoni preferred to present oil sketches to patrons commissioning works. Because his drawings exemplify the more academic tendencies of the Roman school in the eighteenth century, it is not surprising that those most frequently encountered are figure and drapery studies in the tradition of Andrea Sacchi and Carlo Maratta.[6]

This drawing of *The Virgin and Child Enthroned,* which is unusual in Batoni's surviving graphic oeuvre because of its technique of pen and wash, is a preliminary design for the artist's first public work in Rome, the altarpiece in San Gregorio al Celio.[7] The canvas, painted for the marchese Forte Gabrielli Valletta of Gubbio, was exhibited publicly in the Palazzo di San Marco, Rome, on August 30, 1733. Gabrielli reportedly had discovered Batoni drawing the ancient bas-reliefs in the Palazzo dei Conservatori and was struck by the beauty of the young painter's copies.[8] He must surely have dictated the subject of the altarpiece for his chapel in San Gregorio, the adoration of the Madonna and Child by four beatified members of his family, the Blessed Pietro and Castora to the left of the throne, and Forte and Lodolfo, bishop of Gubbio, on the right. Contemporary sources mention the studies, models, and cartoon prepared by the industrious Batoni for the painting,[9] and two of these efforts survive, a *bozzetto* in the storerooms of the Gallerie dell' Accademia in Venice and a red-chalk preparatory study for the Camaldolite monk in the foreground in the Museo d'Arte Antica, Castello Sforzesco, Milan.[10] This drawing, one of the earliest by Batoni that has come down to us, should be regarded as one of the key points of reference for the artist's first graphic manner.

E.P.B.

1. For the extraordinary decline of Batoni's reputation in England after his death, however, *see* Francis Haskell, "Pompeo Batoni e gli inglesi," in Lucca, 1967, pp. 70–79.
2. Clark, "La carriera professionale e lo stile del Batoni," in Lucca, 1967, pp. 23–50. For a list of Anthony Clark's writings on Batoni, *see Antologia di Belle Arti,* vol. 1, no. 1 (March, 1977), pp. 125–27.
3. Lucca, 1967, p. 36.
4. Honour, 1967, p. 550.
5. For an excellent résumé of Batoni's early activity as a professional copyist in Rome, *see* Macandrew, 1978.
6. The only general introduction available for Batoni as a draughtsman is Emmerling's brief chapter on the drawings in his volume on the artist (Emmerling, 1932, pp. 74–82).
7. Lucca, 1967, no. 1, repr. pl. 1.
8. Macandrew, 1978, p. 137 (citing Boni, 1787, pp. 33–34).
9. *See* Boni, 1787, p. 34.
10. For the *bozzetto* in Venice, *see* Faldi, 1971, p. 568, repr. fig. 101; for the Milan drawing, first identified by Anthony Clark, *see* Lucca, 1967, no. 77, repr. pl. 77.

31. Studies of Drapery and the Sleeping Christ Child for the Merenda "Holy Family"

c. 1740

Inscribed in pencil at lower right: Studi di Ponpeo [sic] / Batoni valutato / Pauoli [?] 4

Red chalk, a few touches of white chalk, partially squared in red, on yellow prepared paper, mounted down

207 x 305 mm (8 3/16 x 12")

1978-70-165

Provenance: Veuve Galippe; sale, property of Mme. Veuve Galippe, de Vries, Amsterdam, March 27–29, 1923, in lot 515 (as Mengs); Hermann Voss, Berlin, 1932; purchased from Mathias Komor, New York, 1957

Exhibition: Minneapolis, 1967, no. 8

Bibliography: Emmerling, 1932, p. 141, no. Z13, 2 (as for the *Pommersfelden "Holy Family"*)

The source of several Batoni drawings owned by Anthony Clark and exhibited here (nos. 33–40, 43) was an album composed in Rome in the late eighteenth century. It originally contained seventy pages, numbered from 4025 to 4095, each 533 by 380 millimeters (21 by 14 15/16 inches). There is evidence that the album came to England in the nineteenth century, perhaps where it was acquired by Veuve Galippe, the first owner of record. When the volume was sold by Mme. Galippe in Amsterdam in 1923, its 170 drawings were then attributed to Mengs. With 34 drawings removed, the album next surfaced in Berlin in the collection of Fritz Haussmann, where it was studied by Ernst Emmerling. In a manuscript catalogue of the album compiled in 1931 by Emmerling, 107 of the remaining 136 sheets were attributed to Pompeo Batoni. Three additional sheets by Batoni, which seem to have belonged to the album, were in the collection of Hermann Voss in Berlin in 1931 or 1932, and a sketchbook also owned in Berlin during the same years by Hermann Wille may have the same provenance. In the 1950s the album belonged to Countess Finckenstein of Zurich. Several sheets were sold at auction in Zurich in 1958 and in London in November of the same year by Yvonne ffrench (as by Mengs, but subsequently identified as Batoni by Anthony Clark). The remaining contents of

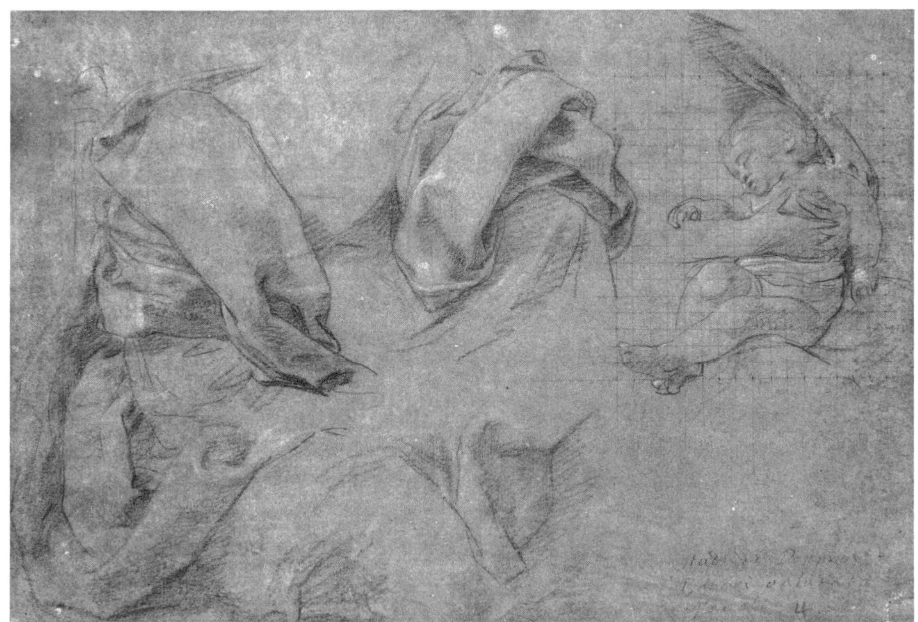

31

the album were acquired by Miss ffrench in 1960 and sold in London in the same year. Several of the Clark Batoni drawings are still on Galippe mounts (nos. 31, 33, 35–40, 43). The four Mengs drawings catalogued here also come from the album (nos. 54–57).

Batoni painted a number of works for the Merenda brothers of Forlì—Giuseppe, an architect, and Count Cesare, auditor to Cardinal Borghese. More than twenty-five canvases by the artist remained in the Merenda collection until the Second World War;[1] several of these paintings have subsequently entered public collections in North America, such as the Art Institute of Chicago, the Bob Jones University Collection of Sacred Art in Greenville, South Carolina, and the Montreal Museum of Fine Arts. This sheet contains studies for the Virgin's drapery and the sleeping Christ Child in Batoni's *Holy Family* painted for the Merenda family around 1740;[2] on the left is a detailed study of the mantle that covers the Virgin's right shoulder and the dress on her right thigh, while the study in the center of the sheet corresponds to the Virgin's mantle at the left knee although Batoni altered the folds slightly in the finished painting.

In 1932 Emmerling connected this drawing with Batoni's *Holy Family* at Pommersfelden (no. 37), where the sleeping Christ Child is seen in a slightly different pose in reverse. Anthony Clark first pointed out the actual purpose of the study and its correspondence to the Merenda painting. An exact and even more painstaking study for the Child, also from the collection of Hermann Voss, is now in the Princeton University Art Museum.[3] For a study of Saint Joseph in the same painting, *see* no. 32.

E.P.B.

1. *See* Marcucci, 1944.
2. Lucca, 1967, no. 3, repr. pl. 3. The painting is in the possession of Count Cesare Farneti Merenda, Forlì.
3. Felton Gibbons, *Catalogue of Italian Drawings in the Art Museum, Princeton University,* Princeton, 1977, vol. 1, p. 16, no. 39; vol. 2, pl. 39.

32. Study of Saint Joseph for the Merenda "Holy Family"

c. 1740

Signed on recto in brown ink at lower right: Pompeo Batoni; inscribed on verso in pencil: Emulo [?] di J. F. Troy; an unidentified collector's mark has been applied in ink by hand

Red chalk, faint touches of white chalk, on yellow prepared paper

204 x 225 mm (8 1/16 x 8 13/16")

1978-70-164

Provenance: purchased from David James, Miami, Florida, 1965

Exhibition: Minneapolis, 1967, no. 9

The attitude of Saint Joseph, gazing thoughtfully upon his wife and the sleeping Child, corresponds nearly exactly with the figure in the *Holy Family* painted by Batoni for the Merenda family about 1740. This study, presumably made from the model, would no doubt have been followed by detailed studies of the head, hands, and drapery. At the extreme left of the sheet appears a rough sketch for a passage of drapery over a sleeve. Batoni's choice of red chalk on warm-toned paper is typical of his individual studies of figures and drapery in the 1740s.

E.P.B.

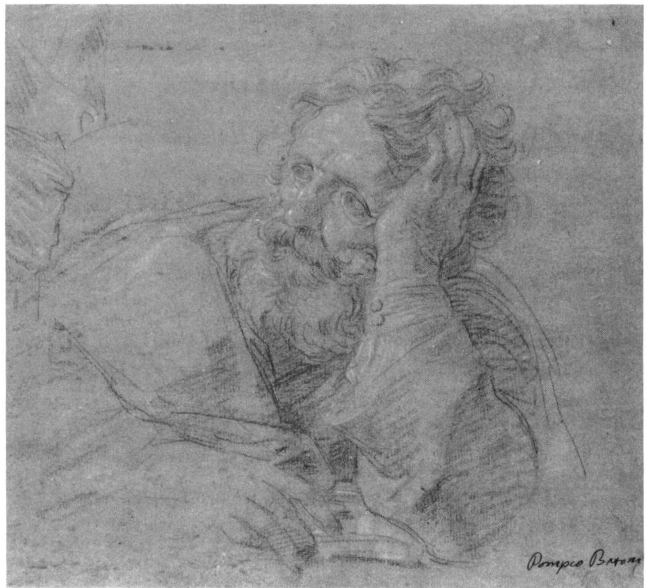

32

33. Study of Hercules for "The Choice of Hercules"

1740–42

Red chalk, squared in red, on beige laid paper, mounted down

284 x 212 mm (11 3/16 x 8 3/8″)

1978-70-159

Provenance: Veuve Galippe; sale, property of Mme. Veuve Galippe, de Vries, Amsterdam, March 27–29, 1923, in lot 515 (as Mengs); Fritz Haussmann, Berlin, 1931; Countess Finckenstein, Zurich, 1950s; purchased from Yvonne ffrench, London, 1960

Exhibitions: London, Alpine Club, *Exhibition of Old Master and Early English Drawings, Presented by Yvonne ffrench at the Alpine Club Gallery,* November 7–19, 1960, no. 24; Cleveland, 1964, no. 8, repr.; Minneapolis, 1967, no. 6; Minneapolis, 1970–71; New York, 1978

Bibliography: Emmerling, 1931, p. 83

A letter of May 27, 1740, from Batoni to Marchese Ludovico Sardini mentions, without describing the exact subject, a picture with three figures ordered by a Marchese Gerini in Florence at a price of 150 scudi. A second letter of December 15, 1742, states that the painting, presumably *The Choice of Hercules* in the Galleria d'Arte Moderna, Palazzo Pitti, Florence,[1] which is signed and dated 1742, had recently been sent to Gerini.[2]

The theme was widely represented in Renaissance and Baroque art. Hercules, usually depicted seated under a tree, is divided in choice between the invitations of two female figures personifying Virtue and Vice. Other versions of this subject by Batoni exist in the Liechtenstein collection in Vaduz, the Galleria Sabauda in Turin, and the Hermitage in Leningrad; a sheet with sketches for the Liechtenstein version, dating about six years after the Florence picture, is in the Yale University Art Gallery, New Haven.[3]

Batoni selected a muscular model, young and beardless, to assume the exact pose of the seated Hercules in the painting. Annibale Carracci had made this pose standard for most representations of the theme more than a century earlier, in a picture that is today in the Galleria Nazionale, Museo di Capodimonte, Naples.[4]

E.P.B.

1. Florence, 1972, p. 34, repr.; repr. Lucca, 1967, pl. 14.
2. Lucca, 1967, no. 14 (citing letters in the Archivio di Stato, Lucca, Archivio Sardini).
3. E. Haverkamp-Begemann and Anne-Marie S. Logan, *European Drawings and Watercolors in the Yale University Art Gallery, 1500–1900,* New Haven and London, 1970, vol. 1, pp. 165–66; vol. 2, pl. 163.
4. Donald Posner, *Annibale Carracci: A Study in the Reform of Italian Painting around 1590,* London, 1971, vol. 2, pp. 40, 41, pl. 93a.

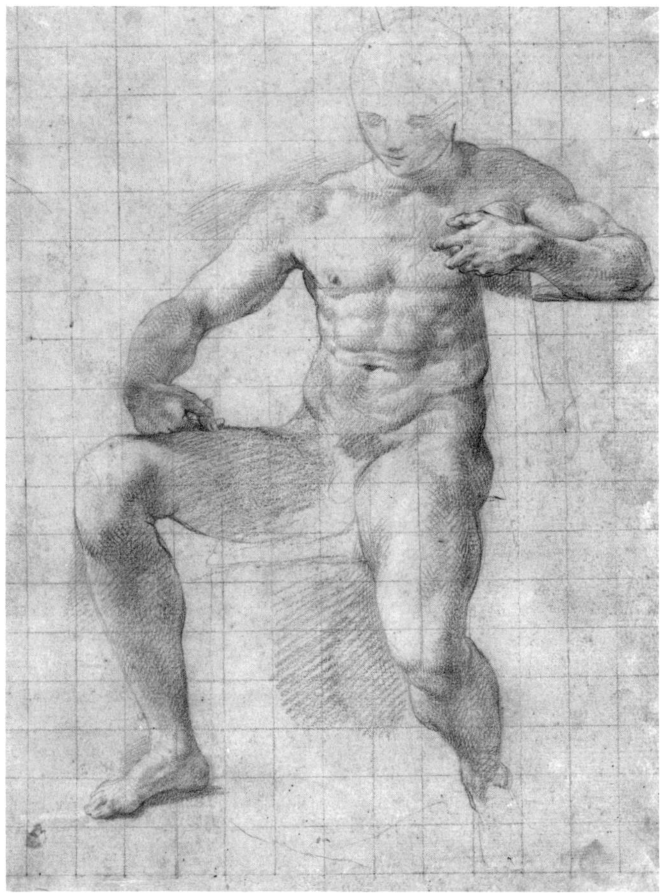

33

34. Studies of an Angel for the "Annunciation" in Santa Maria Maggiore

Verso: *Studies of Drapery, a Female Nude, and a "Rest on the Flight into Egypt"* (not illustrated)

c. 1743

Inscribed on verso in pencil and partially erased: Annunciation / St. Maria Maggiore, and, in another hand: 105

Red chalk, squared in red, on yellow prepared paper

242 x 115 mm (9 1/2 x 4 9/16")

1978-70-160

Provenance: Veuve Galippe; sale, property of Mme. Veuve Galippe, de Vries, Amsterdam, March 27–29, 1923, in lot 515 (as Mengs); Fritz Haussmann, Berlin, 1931; Countess Finckenstein, Zurich, 1950s; purchased from Yvonne ffrench, London, 1960

Bibliography: Emmerling, 1931, p. 13; Emmerling, 1932, pp. 77, 141, cited under no. Z12

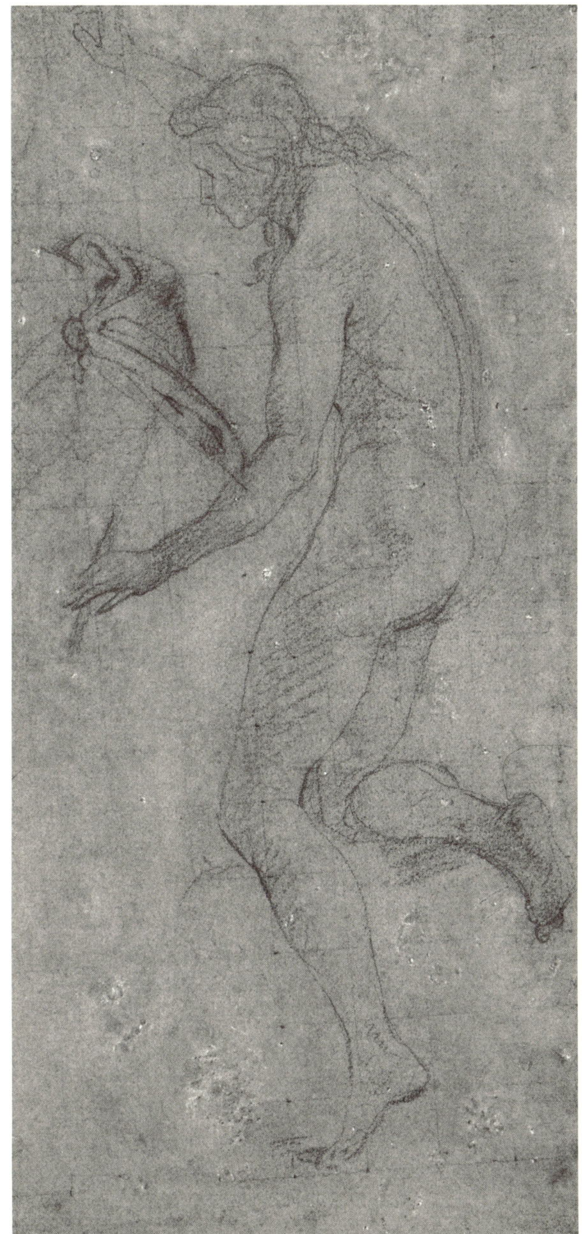

34

The Galippe album contained two preparatory drawings for the altarpiece of the *Annunciation* painted about 1743 for Santa Maria Maggiore, Rome.[1] The first of these sheets, a red-chalk study of the angel set within an oval sketch of the whole composition and squared for transfer, was among those sold in London in 1958 and is currently untraced. Its figure is close to the painting in finish and proportions.

This drawing is a careful study from life showing the pose adopted for the angel in the final painting. Here, however, Batoni has studied different positions for both arms, resulting in a change that enables the angel in the painting to direct the Virgin's as well as the spectator's attention to the presence of the Holy Spirit. This reversal of the attitude of the arms intensifies the internal linear rhythms and emphasizes the swirling movement of the oval composition. Batoni used the upper left portion of the sheet to experiment with the drapery across the angel's left shoulder.

Two further preparatory drawings for the Santa Maria Maggiore *Annunciation* are known, both at the Musée des Beaux-Arts et d'Archéologie, Besançon. One is a study for the Virgin that corresponds almost exactly with the painted version;[2] the other contains several studies of the two putti in the center of the composition.[3]

E.P.B.

1. The date according to Clark in Lucca, 1967, p. 26. Repr. Voss, 1924, p. 410.
2. Inv. no. D. 1014.
3. Inv. no. D. 2290.

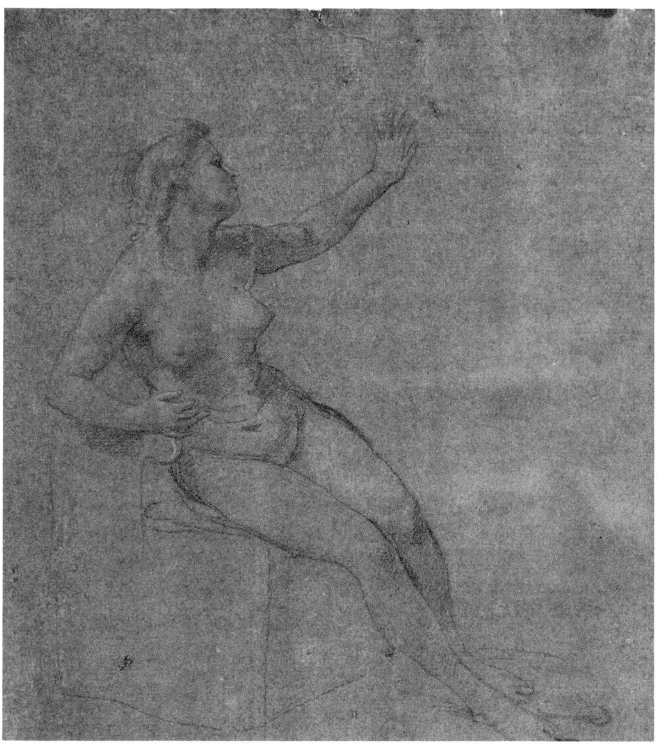

35

35. Study of the Figure of Lasciviousness for "Allegory of Lasciviousness"

1744–46

Red chalk, a few faint touches of white chalk, on yellow prepared paper, mounted down

215 x 197 mm (8 7/16 x 7 3/4")

1978-70-173

Provenance: Veuve Galippe; sale, property of Mme. Veuve Galippe, de Vries, Amsterdam, March 27–29, 1923, in lot 515 (as Mengs); Fritz Haussmann, Berlin, 1931; Countess Finckenstein, Zurich, 1950s; sale, L'Art Ancien, Zurich, 1958, cat. 35, lot 369 (as Mengs); purchased from Yvonne ffrench, London, 1958

Exhibitions: London, Alpine Club, *Old Master Drawings Presented by Yvonne ffrench at the Alpine Club*, 1958–59; Minneapolis, 1967, no. 10

Bibliography: Emmerling, 1931, p. 7; Lucca, 1967, p. 132

By February 1747 Batoni had finished a pair of allegorical canvases for the collector Bartolomeo Talenti of Lucca, *Time Orders Old Age to Destroy Beauty* (National Gallery of Art, London, initialed and dated 1746) and *Allegory of Lasciviousness* (The Hermitage, Leningrad, initialed and dated 1747).[1] The commission was first recorded in Batoni's letter to Talenti of July 4, 1744, promising that the subject would be "della mia fantasia." In a letter several days later the artist described the subjects of the respective pictures as "Il Tempo che distrugge la Bellezza" and "La Lascivia." On July 24, 1745, Batoni wrote that the pictures were partially begun; their completion by early 1747 therefore provides a *terminus ante quem* for the present drawing.[2]

The pose of the model in this study corresponds closely with the figure of Lasciviousness in the Hermitage composition, although for the painting Batoni altered slightly the position of the head and the outstretched arm. The model's feet, summarily indicated in this sheet, were the objects of a more detailed study in a second drawing (no. 36). In the checklist of the 1967 Minneapolis exhibition, Anthony Clark noted the extreme rarity of Roman drawings from the female model.

E.P.B.

1. For the London picture, *see* Michael Levey, *The Seventeenth and Eighteenth Century Italian Schools, National Gallery Catalogues,* London, 1971, p. 10; repr. in Clark, 1959, p. 238, fig. 36 (as on the London art market). The Leningrad picture is reproduced in Lucca, 1967, pl. 28. The paintings were discussed by Clark, 1959, p. 236.

2. Lucca, 1967, pp. 301–8, letter nos. 917–18, 923–24.

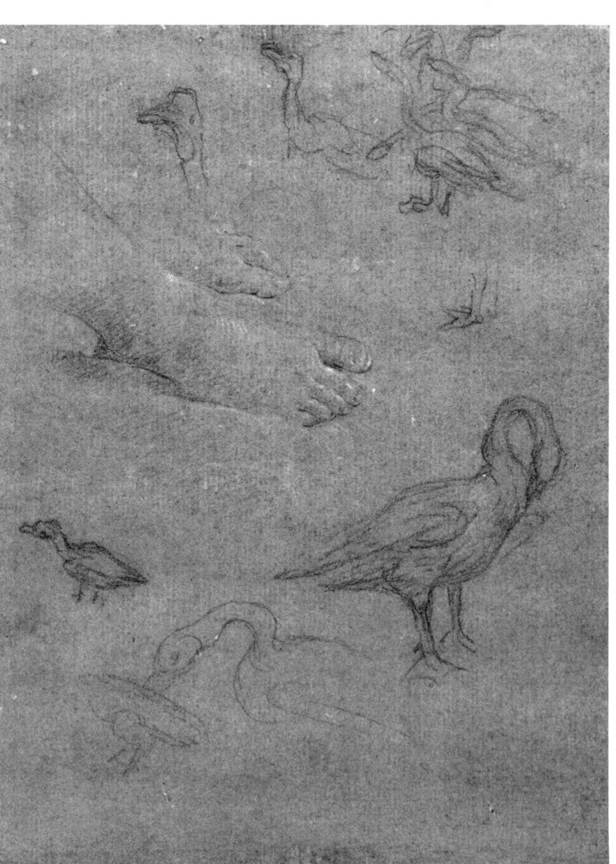

36

36. *Studies of the Feet of Lasciviousness for "Allegory of Lasciviousness" and of the Swans for "Mercy and Truth"*

1744–46

Red and black chalks, touches of white chalk, on yellow prepared paper, mounted down

212 x 154 mm (8 7/16 x 6 1/16")

1978-70-167

Provenance: Veuve Galippe; sale, property of Mme. Veuve Galippe, de Vries, Amsterdam, March 27–29, 1923, in lot 515 (as Mengs); Fritz Haussmann, Berlin, 1931; Countess Finckenstein, Zurich, 1950s; sale, L'Art Ancien, Zurich, 1958, cat. 35, lot 368 (as Mengs); purchased from Yvonne ffrench, London, 1958

Exhibition: London, Alpine Club, *Old Master Drawings Presented by Yvonne ffrench at the Alpine Club,* 1958–59

Bibliography: Emmerling, 1931, p. 71

The allegorical painting *Mercy and Truth*—for which the red-chalk drawings of swans on this sheet are preparatory studies—with its companion painting *Justice and Peace*[1] illustrates Psalm 85:10, "Mercy and truth are met together, righteousness and peace have kissed each other." In the middle distance of the finished work, painted for the Merenda family between about 1745 and 1748, Batoni showed a swan piercing its breast to feed its young with its blood. Intended to amplify the attributes of the allegorical figure of Mercy, the motif may have been adopted from, if not actually confused with, the more traditional image of the pelican and its young, which are both a symbol of the sacrifice of Christ and a common attribute of Charity.

This sheet also includes carefully rendered studies in black chalk of the feet belonging to the figure of Lasciviousness in the Hermitage *Allegory of Lasciviousness* of 1747 (*see also* no. 35).

E.P.B.

1. London, P & D Colnaghi & Co Ltd, *Old Master Paintings and Drawings,* June–August 1979, nos. 20, 21, repr. The paintings are now in the Montreal Museum of Fine Arts.

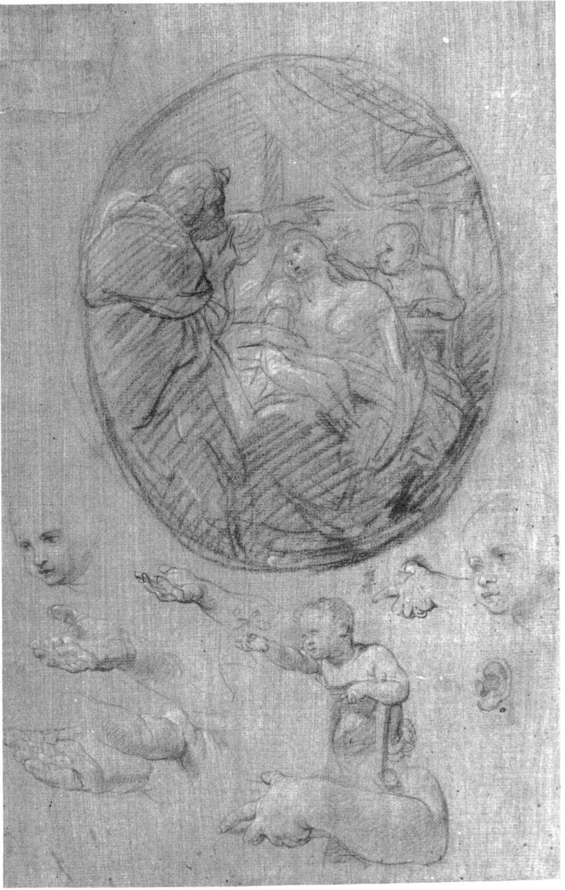

37

37. *Studies for the Pommersfelden "Holy Family"*

c. 1747

Red chalk, touches of white chalk, on grayish green prepared paper (upper left corner replaced), mounted down

388 x 250 mm (15 5/16 x 9 7/8")

1978-70-163

Provenance: Veuve Galippe (Galippe album, no. 4064); sale, property of Mme. Veuve Galippe, de Vries, Amsterdam, March 27–29, 1923, in lot 515 (as Mengs); Fritz Haussmann, Berlin, 1931; Countess Finckenstein, Zurich, 1950s; purchased from Yvonne ffrench, London, 1960

Exhibitions: London, Alpine Club, *Exhibition of Old Master and Early English Drawings, Presented by Yvonne ffrench at the Alpine Club Gallery,* November 7–19, 1960, no. 20; Minneapolis 1967, no. 4; Minneapolis, 1970–71

Bibliography: Emmerling, 1931, p. 79; Emmerling, 1932, p. 141, cited under no. Z12

In Batoni's *Holy Family* of 1747 at Schloss Weissenstein, Pommersfelden,[1] the infant Baptist, who plays with a goldfinch on a string, is shown restrained by Joseph from disturbing the sleeping Virgin and Child.

The main elements of the painting's circular composition are indicated in the upper half of the present sheet, with the notable difference that the Virgin is shown awake.

In the lower half of the drawing, Batoni's chief concern was with the attitude and gesture of the young Saint John. Several studies of his raised right arm and hand are interspersed with those of his left arm and head. The lower half of Saint John's body is obscured in the finished painting and was, therefore, omitted in the sketch at the right of center.

E.P.B.

1. Repr. Emmerling, 1932, no. 90.

38. *Study for the Shield of Aeneas in "Venus Bringing Arms to Aeneas"*
c. 1748
Red chalk on cream laid paper, mounted down
208 x 206 mm (8 3/16 x 8 1/8") (image only reproduced)
1978-70-169
Provenance: Veuve Galippe (Galippe album, no. 4045); sale, property of Mme. Veuve Galippe, de Vries, Amsterdam, March 27–29, 1923, in lot 515 (as Mengs); Fritz Haussmann, Berlin, 1931; Countess Finckenstein, Zurich, 1950s; purchased from Yvonne ffrench, London, 1960
Exhibitions: London, Alpine Club, *Exhibition of Old Master and Early English Drawings, Presented by Yvonne ffrench at the Alpine Club Gallery,* November 7–19, 1960, no. 30; Minneapolis, 1970–71
Bibliography: Emmerling, 1931, p. 43

Presumably on the order of Prince Joseph Wenzel von Liechtenstein (1696–1772), Batoni painted in 1748 the *Venus Bringing Arms to Aeneas* now at Schloss Vaduz, Liechtenstein. Directly inspired by Pietro Testa's etching of the same subject (Bartsch 24)—which contains, however, a shield of entirely different character—the painting was paired with a companion representing the *Choice of Hercules.*[1] Virgil (*Aeneid,* VIII, 608–25) describes in detail the scene in which Venus presents her son with the arms made by Vulcan at her request. The shield, fashioned of iron, gold, silver, and blue enamel, was decorated with a complete pictorial history of Aeneas's descendants through the time of his son Ascanius.

Although in the painting the shield is shown turned slightly, in this drawing Batoni depicts it full face. The artist carefully followed Virgil's description of the shield's decoration, omitting only a few details and occasionally condensing the action of various episodes into a single scene. The following events of Roman history are shown in the compartmentalized scenes around the perimeter of the shield, starting at the base and proceeding counterclockwise: the she-wolf suckling the twins Romulus and Remus in the cave of Mars; the rape of the Sabine women; the punishment of the Sabine Mettius Curtius, whose body was bound between two chariots and torn apart for breaking faith with Rome; the peace ceremony with sacrificial rites; an attempted attack on the capitol; the sacred geese on the Capitoline raising the alarm against the attacking Gauls; Horatius Cocles saving Rome from capture by the Etruscan king Lars Porsenna; and the Roman festival of the Lupercalia. In the upper half of the center compartment, Batoni depicted the battle of Actium (31 B.C.), in which Octavian defeated the forces of Mark Antony and Cleopatra. The lower scene portrays Octavian's triumphal return to Rome from the East two years later.

These figures, on the shield divinely wrought,
By Vulcan labored, and by Venus brought,
With joy and wonder fill the hero's thought.
Unknown the names, he yet admires the grace;
And bears aloft the fame and fortune of his race.[2]

E.P.B.

1. Emmerling, 1932, pp. 124–25, nos. 144, 152; Voss, 1924, pp. 415 (repr.), 648, 649.
2. J. Dryden, trans., *The Aeneid of Virgil,* ed. by R. Fitzgerald, New York, 1964, lines 973–77.

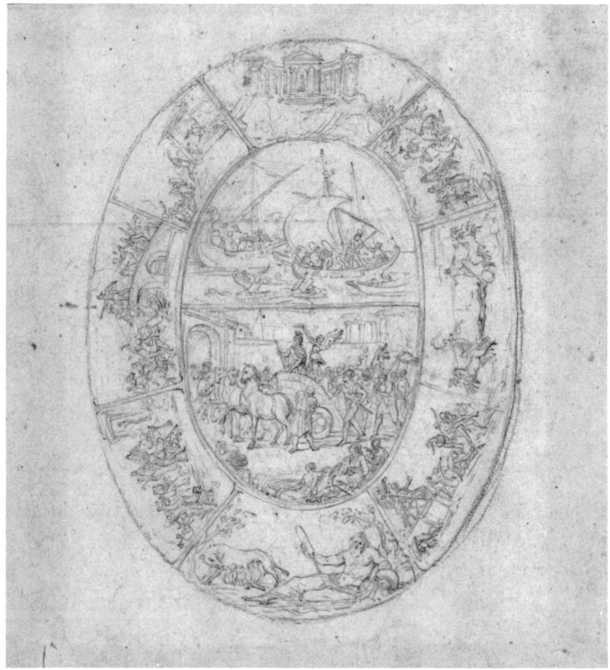

38

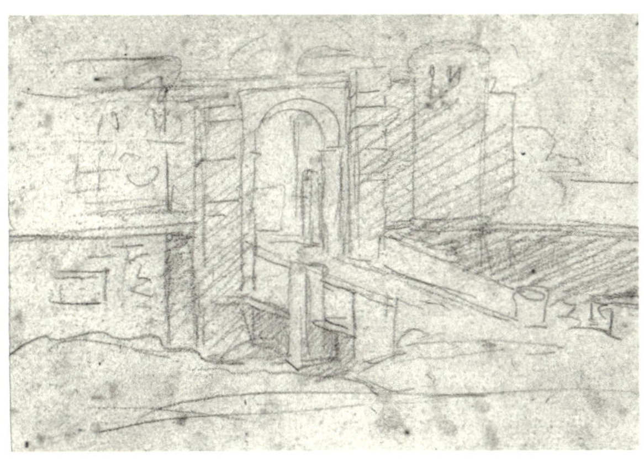

39A

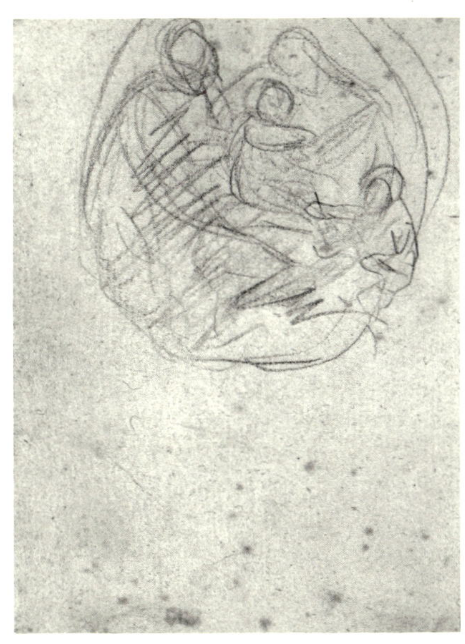

39B

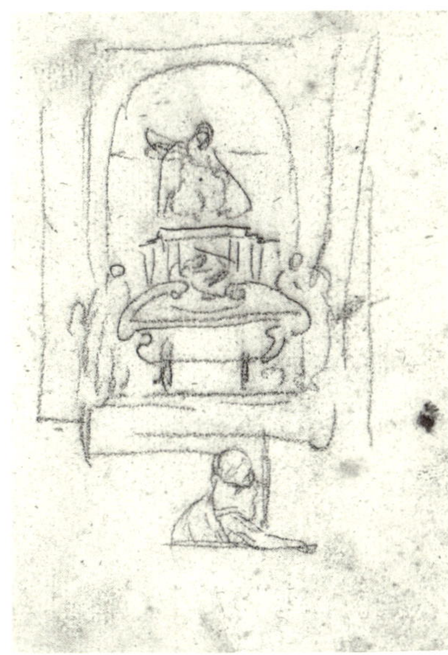

39C

39. *Pages from a Sketchbook*

1740–50

A. *A City Gate*

Verso: *A Bridge; A Woman Leaning on a Pedestal* (not illustrated)

Recto: red chalk on cream laid paper, set into mount; verso: black and red chalks

96 x 136 mm (3 13/16 x 5 3/8")

1978-70-175[s]

B. *Compositional Study for the Pommersfelden "Holy Family"*

Verso: *Draped, Standing Figures* (not illustrated)

Recto: red chalk on cream laid paper, set into mount; verso: black chalk

133 x 96 mm (5 1/4 x 3 13/16")

1978-70-175[o]

C. *Studies of Bernini's Tomb of Urban VIII in Saint Peter's and of a Woman Leaning out of a Window*

Verso: *Studies of Figures* (not illustrated)

Red chalk on cream laid paper, set into mount

136 x 96 mm (5 3/8 x 3 13/16")

1978-70-175[t]

Provenance: Veuve Galippe (Galippe album, nos. 4041[c] [1978-70-175[s]], 4036[c] [1978-70-175[o]], 4041[d] [1978-70-175[t]]); sale, property of Mme. Veuve Galippe, de Vries, Amsterdam, March 27–29, 1923, in lot 515 (as Mengs); Fritz Haussmann, Berlin, 1931; Countess Finckenstein, Zurich, 1950s; Yvonne ffrench, London, 1960; gift of John Maxon, 1960

Exhibition: Minneapolis, 1967, no. 3

Bibliography: Emmerling, 1931, p. 45

These small sketchbook pages were mounted on folio sheets in the Galippe album (*see* no. 31). Most of the twenty-five Batoni drawings (originally numbered 4025[a] to 4044[d]) owned by Anthony Clark from the dismembered sketchbook date from the 1740s; several today retain the old mounts, a few with the original numbering. The drawings consist mainly of quick red- or black-chalk sketches from everyday life, studies from the model, records of the papal tombs in Saint Peter's, Roman monuments, landscape studies, and preliminary ideas for commissions initiated in the early 1740s. In spite of the ephemeral nature of these sketches, Batoni's energetic and economical handling reveals itself capable of producing powerful descriptive effects with a few strokes of the chalk.

E.P.B.

40. *Studies of a Putto for the "Martyrdom of Saint Lucy"*

c. 1759

Black chalk, faint traces of white chalk, on blue prepared paper, mounted down

440 x 300 mm (17 5/16 x 11 13/16")

1978-70-174

Provenance: Veuve Galippe (?);[1] gift of Keith Andrews, 1968

These studies, excellent examples of the swift, bold chalk sketches Batoni used to refine the attitudes and gestures of his figures, are related to one of the flying putti bearing palm branches in the *Martyrdom of Saint Lucy* of 1759, now in the Museo de la Real Academia de San Fernando, Madrid.[2] Although the pose is quite close to the one finally adopted in the finished canvas,

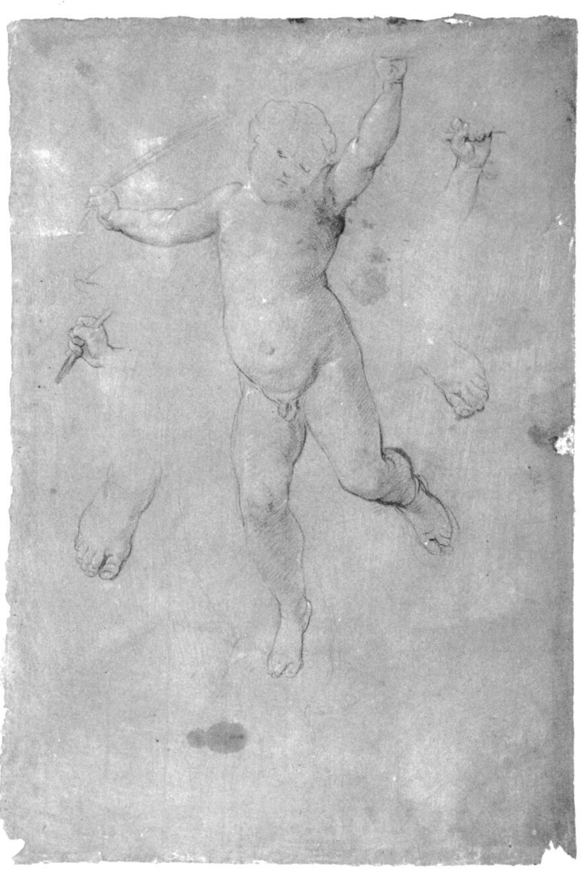

40

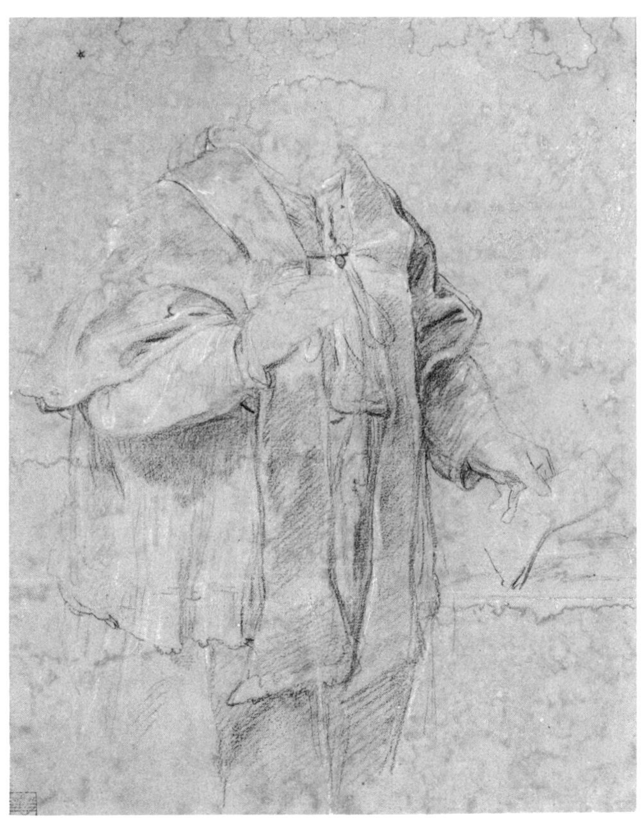

41

the putto is foreshortened slightly. The surrounding studies of his hands and feet reveal Batoni's careful attention to relatively minor details.

Other chalk studies for the painting are in the Musée Wicar, Lille,[3] and the Musée des Beaux-Arts et Archéologie, Besançon.[4]

E.P.B.

1. Although this drawing and cat. no. 43 have not been previously identified as part of the Galippe album, they are both mounted on sheets of the same distinctive paper with which drawings known to have belonged to the album are backed, and it may be assumed that they share the same provenance.
2. F. Labrada, *Catalogo de la Pinturas. El Museo de la Real Academia de Bellas Artes de San Fernando,* Madrid, 1965, p. 14, no. 702.
3. Inv. no. 2324.
4. Inv. no. D. 3065.

41. Study of Drapery for a Portrait of Pope Clement XIII

c. 1760

Inscribed on verso at lower left, erased and almost illegible: P. Davidsohn [?]

Black chalk, with touches of white chalk, on blue prepared paper

255 x 200 mm (10 1/16 x 17 7/8″)

1978-70-168

Provenance: Paul Davidsohn (?), Grunewald-Berlin, before 1920s; Spencer, London; Janos Scholz (Lugt suppl. 2933[b]), 1937–62; purchased from Seiferheld Gallery, New York, 1962

Exhibitions: Minneapolis, 1967, no. 5; Minneapolis, 1970–71

When it was in the collection of Janos Scholz, this forceful study was attributed by Hermann Voss to Bartolomeo Cesi. Its correct identification as a preparatory study for the vestments in Batoni's *Portrait of Pope Clement XIII,* now in the Gallera Nazionale d'Arte Antica, Rome, was made by Anthony Clark at the time he acquired the drawing. In the finished canvas as in the drawn study, the pope is standing before an armchair bearing his coat of arms; his right hand is raised in blessing while in the left is held a letter. Batoni was primarily interested in the arrangement of the pontiff's stole, his mozzetta, or cape, and his rochet (a knee-length, pleated tunic of white linen with tight sleeves). The face, which would have been developed from life studies, has been disregarded, and the hands are only

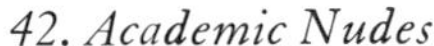

summarily indicated. The contemporary criticism that Batoni's portrait overemphasized the richness of the pope's vestments can be traced to difficulties inherent in the standing pose itself: "It is extremely difficult," Clark once observed, "for a man in the rich vestments of an eighteenth-century pope to look anything but ridiculous unless seated on the throne, and this was how Mengs showed Clement XIII."[1]

Carlo Rezzonico (1693–1769), who ruled as Pope Clement XIII from 1758 to 1769, was engaged throughout his pontificate with formidable problems concerning the distribution of power between the church and state. He refused to yield ground to governments seeking to obscure lines of demarcation, and energetically opposed "enlightened" views on religion and the church. Clement's greatest difficulties arose from the widespread persecution of the Jesuits (*see also* no. 50), a political and ecclesiastical struggle that eventually forced his successor, Pope Clement XIV, to dissolve the the Society of Jesus in 1773 to avert a threat of schism.

E.P.B.

1. Lucca, 1967, p. 45. For Mengs's portraits of Clement XIII, *see* Zeri, 1976, vol. 2, p. 534, pl. 277.

42. Academic Nudes

A. *Male Nude, Leaning on a Pedestal*
1765
Signed in brown ink at lower right: Pompeo Batoni 1765.
Black chalk on blue prepared paper
525 x 387 mm (20 11/16 x 15 1/4″)
1978-70-171

B. *Male Nude, Leaning on a Ladder*
Black chalk on blue prepared paper
538 x 390 mm (21 3/16 x 15 3/8″)
1978-70-170
Provenance: David Allan, Edinburgh (?); sale, property of David Allan, Edinburgh, February 6, 1797, lots 76–77 (?); sale, Sotheby's London, February 22, 1961, lot 10; purchased from Marcello and Carlo Sestieri, Rome, 1961

Although individual studies of heads, limbs, hands, and drapery dominate Batoni's graphic oeuvre, his largely unpublished academy drawings—studies of male nudes drawn from studio models in poses not specifically related to planned compositions—are also important not

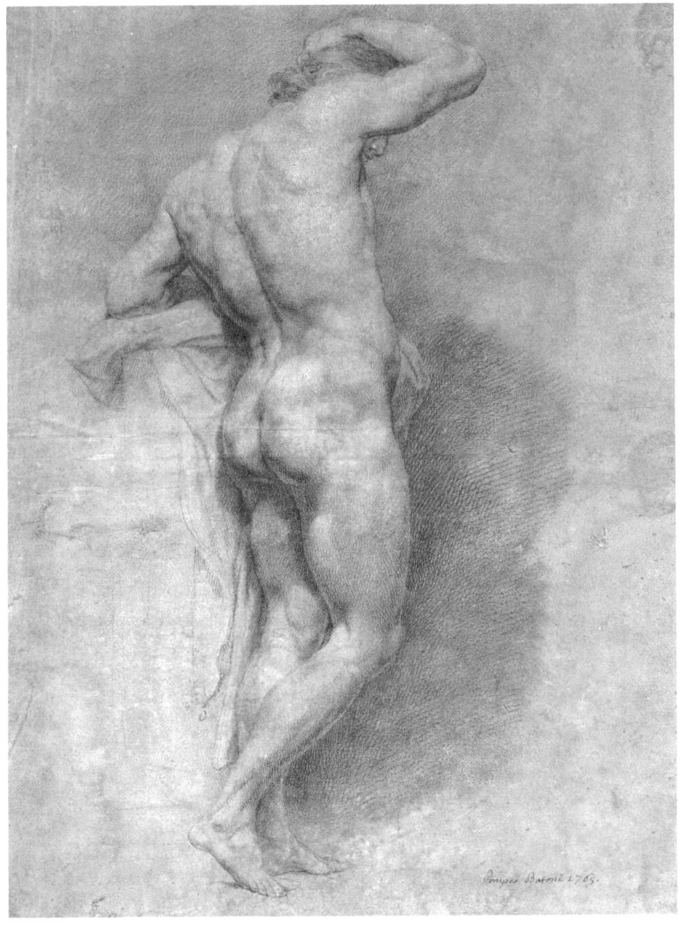

42A

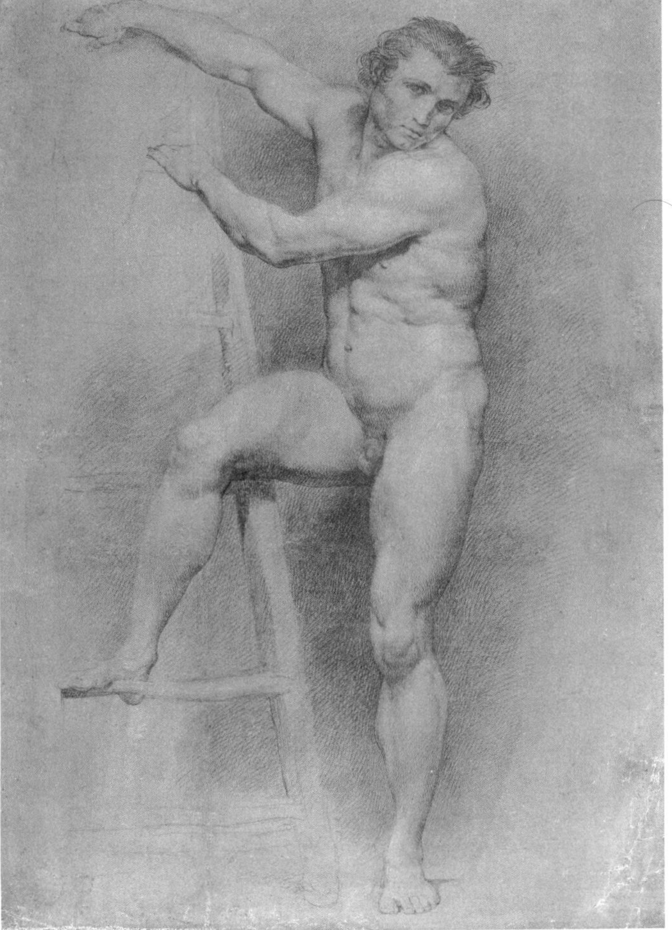

42B

least on account of their technical distinction. He made these accomplished studies all his life: in his earliest years in Lucca at the drawing academies of Giovanni Domenico Lombardi and Domenico Brugieri; in Rome, shortly after his arrival in 1727, at Sebastiano Conca's evening drawing academy; and during his mature years when he held private life-drawing classes in his own studio. He even willingly drew in the life classes of contemporaries in Rome, such as those organized by the French painter Laurent Pecheux (*see* no. 60).[1]

In Rome the practice of making highly finished red-chalk studies of male nudes, established perhaps around 1630,[2] flourished throughout the later seventeenth and eighteenth centuries. In the eighteenth century, drawing classes focusing upon the live model were thought to be the foundation of artistic instruction, and in Paris, for example, the Académie Royale de Peinture et de Sculpture enforced its own monopoly on life-drawing instruction.[3] In Rome, on the other hand, despite the efforts of the Accademia di San Luca to dominate this aspect of artistic education through its Accademia del Nudo, most life-drawing instruction continued to take place in the studios of individual artists, whether academicians or not.[4]

Batoni's surviving academy drawings, for reasons that are not clear, date largely from the 1760s and 1770s.[5] These are evenly divided between drawings in red chalk on white paper and in black chalk on tinted paper, usually with white heightening; each is characterized by consummate technique and faultless anatomical description. The realism of these studies is purposeful; rarely does one encounter the aggressive or exaggerated poses characteristic of Roman academy drawings of the first half of the century.[6] The view of the model from behind, his face almost entirely hidden, is typical of the poses preferred by Batoni in these years. The technical finesse and the mastery of the model's heavily muscled anatomy reflect the artist's thorough knowledge of antique sculpture, acquired in the 1730s when he supported himself in Rome as a professional copyist.[7]

The subtly contoured crosshatching used to model the figure's musculature, as well as to define the backgrounds was probably achieved by reworking, smoothing, and refining rapid, less precise sketches from life. The extrême detailing and polish of these late academy drawings, many of which are signed, suggest that they are not the common product of a day's work in the studio but are instead demonstration pieces, virtuoso examples of the artist's skill as a draughtsman.[8] It is evident that Batoni endeavored to create as brilliant an impression as possible through the cold precision of these drawings, investing them with the monumental and severe qualities that characterize his style of history painting in these years.

E.P.B.

1. Fleming, 1962, pp. 163–64.

2. Ann Sutherland Harris, "Drawings by Andrea Sacchi: Additions and Problems," *Master Drawings,* vol. 9, no. 4 (1971), pp. 384–85, summarizes briefly the origin and development of academy studies in Rome and emphasizes the need for further study of the subject.

3. Princeton, 1977, pp. 18–19. This catalogue's excellent essay by James H. Rubin is the best introduction to eighteenth-century life drawing available.

4. Batoni took his turn in directing the life classes of the Accademia del Nudo in 1756, 1758, and 1759.

5. For the published academies in Berlin and Vienna, *see* Berlin, 1969, pp. 14–15, nos. 14–18, and A. Stix and L. Frölich-Bum, *Beschreibender Katalog der Handzeichnungen in der graphischen Sammlung Albertina,* Vienna, 1932, vol. 3, nos. 950–52.

6. Batoni's later life drawings correspond markedly in style with the French *académies* from the same period (c. 1760–80; *see* Rubin in Princeton, 1977, pp. 31–34), which suggests that certain developments in eighteenth-century artistic education were international in character.

7. For Batoni's activity as a copyist after the antique, *see* Macandrew, 1978.

8. Emmerling, 1932, p. 80.

43. Studies of Christ and Apostles for "The Last Supper"

1782–83

Black and white chalks with traces of brown chalk on blue prepared paper, mounted down

428 x 285 mm (16 7/8 x 11 1/4")

1978-70-172

Provenance: Veuve Galippe (?, *see* no. 40, n. 1); gift of Keith Andrews, 1968

During the years 1780 to 1786 Batoni was engaged in producing seven very large canvases for the Basílica dō Sagrado Coração de Jesus in Lisbon.[1] The altarpieces were commissioned by Maria Francesca di Braganza, queen of Portugal, through the Portuguese ambassador to the Holy See, who closely attended the execution of the work in Rome. The first of these paintings, *The Devotion to the Sacred Heart of Jesus* assigned to the principal altar, was substantially under way on October 20, 1781 (when it was examined in Batoni's studio by Pope Pius VI) and was finished and dispatched to Lisbon the following year. In May 1782, the Portuguese ambassador negotiated the contract for three additional altarpieces depicting *The Last Supper, The Incredulity of Saint Thomas,* and *The Foundation of the Basilica by Queen Maria I in the Presence of Saint Theresa.*

In July 1784, the ambassador contracted for three more altarpieces for the basilica, *Joseph's Dream, The Vision of Saint John the Evangelist,* and *Saint Francis Receiving the Stigmata in the Presence of Saint An-*

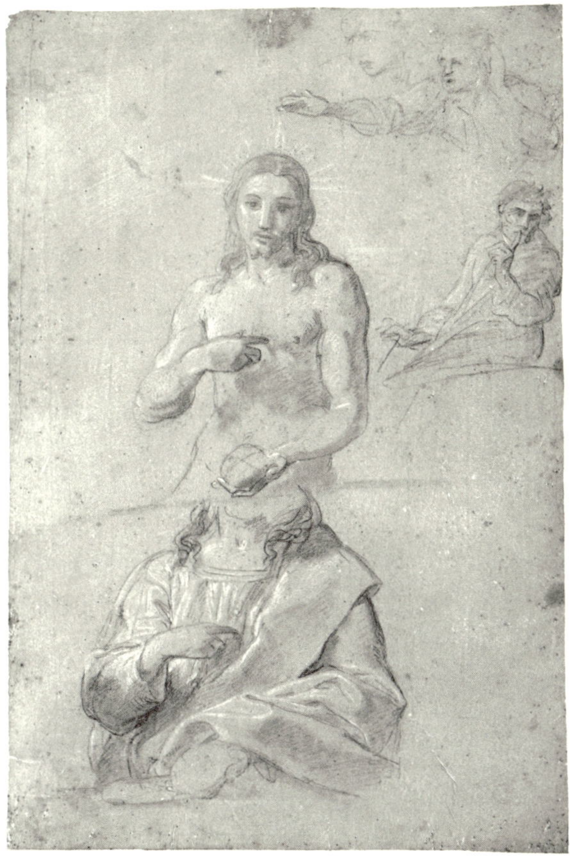

43

thony of Padua, all of which were completed before June 1786. The aged Batoni undoubtedly employed considerable studio assistance for this enormous commission; Anthony Clark suggested the intervention of the painter's son Felice, while Riccardo Averini identified the principal assistant as Felice Giani, who is known to have worked in his studio between 1780 and Batoni's death in 1787 (*see* no. 82).[2]

One of the finest pictures in the series is *The Last Supper,* designated for the altar in the left transept of the basilica, for which Batoni carried out these studies. The artist had begun the painting by August 15, 1782, and had finished it by July 17, 1783, according to reports of the Portuguese ambassador negotiating the arrangements.[3] This sheet reflects a change, typical of Batoni's late work, toward a more "painterly" draughtsmanship. His touch has lightened appreciably, and the soft, delicate hatching used to render the model's body and drapery creates a heightened effect of atmosphere.

E.P.B.

1. The fundamental study, from which this brief account is derived, is Averini, 1973. For the commission, *see also* A. de Lucena, *A arte sacra em Portugal,* Lisbon, 1946, pp. 187–206.
2. Clark, in Lucca, 1967, p. 28; Averini, 1973, p. 83.
3. Averini, 1973, pp. 96–97.

CARLO MARCHIONNI

Rome 1702—Rome 1786

44. Two Sheets of Studies for a Caricature

1750–70

A. *A Fat Man, Seated and Standing, Holding a Portrait of a Donkey*
Inscribed on verso, in pencil: Carlo / Marchionni / Berliner 325 / Same Face
Brown ink over black chalk on cream laid paper
246 x 195 mm (9 11/16 x 7 11/16")
Watermark: GB
1978-70-332

B. *A Fat Man Holding a Portrait of a Donkey; Studies of the Man's Head*
Inscribed in pencil at upper left: Louis Silvestre [?]
Brown ink and wash over black chalk on cream laid paper
280 x 196 mm (11 x 7 3/4")
Watermark: double-headed eagle with a coronet
1978-70-333

Provenance: purchased from Yvonne ffrench, London, 1965 (with checklist no. 108)
Exhibition: Minneapolis, 1967, no. 58, a, b

Carlo Marchionni, along with Ferdinando Fuga (1699–1781), Luigi Vanvitelli (1700–1773), and Tommaso Temanza (1705–1789), ranked as one of the most important architects of his generation. He won first prize in the Concorso Clementino at the Accademia di San Luca in 1728 and was eventually to become the "official" architect to Cardinal Albani, perhaps as early as 1734.[1] A rather traditional and conservative designer, Marchionni's principal commissions were the Villa Albani (1743/46–63, *see* no. 138) and the new sacristy of Saint Peter's (1776–84); he also participated in such sculptural projects as the monument to Benedict XIII in Santa Maria sopra Minerva. An occasional collaborator of Luigi Vanvitelli, he became *architetto soprastante* of the Fabbrica di San Pietro after the latter's death in 1773 and was *principe* of the Accademia di San Luca in 1775–76.

Marchionni collected drawings and paintings—including works by contemporary and older artists such as Pietro and Jan Frans van Bloemen, Giovanni Battista Busiri, Pier Leone Ghezzi, and Pietro Bianchi[2]—and was himself a caricaturist of considerable charm. An inventory of his collection[3] lists five volumes of his own caricatures; three such volumes are today in the Museo di Roma and another in the Vatican Library,[4] comprising in all about four hundred sheets. The Martin-von-Wagner-Museum of the University of Würzburg also owns a number of drawings by the artist[5] that were originally bound. These sheets caricature the many dif-

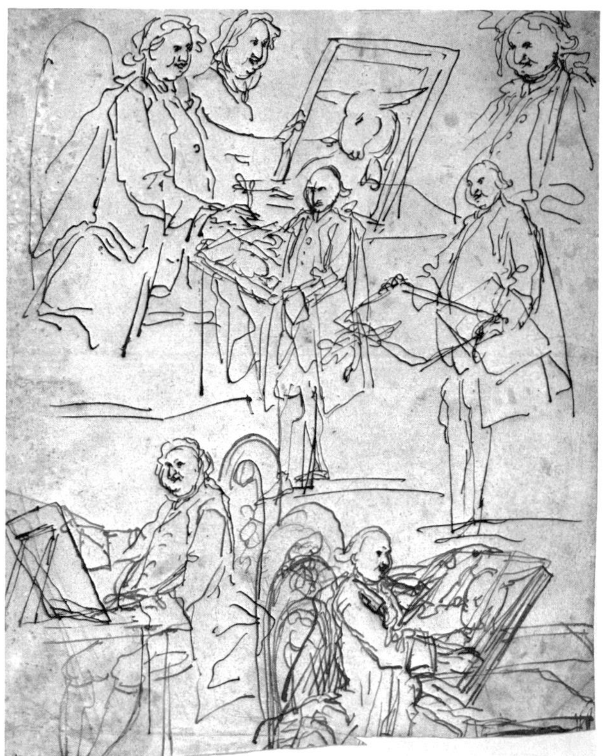

44A

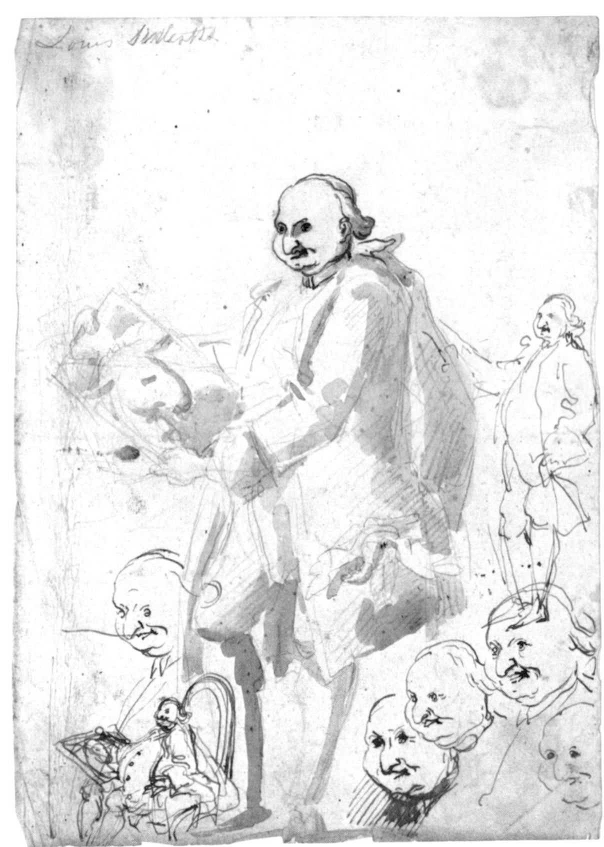

44B

ferent individuals who crossed Marchionni's path—gardeners and tradesmen, hermits, sailors and priests, his fellow artists, friends and family, beggars and dwarfs, nobles and servants—and are often accompanied by careful identifications and descriptions, many humorous or satirical in tone. Nevertheless, Marchionni generally imparts a more genial than satirical quality to the exaggeration of physical peculiarities or defects; rather than attempting to moralize, he appears to have wished only to chronicle in humorous vignettes the figures that attracted or amused him over the years.

These caricatures probably span a long period, as they were drawn in various places—Rome, Civitavecchia, Terni, Ancona—and in more than one style, from a tight pen and ink manner with straight linear hatching, obviously influenced by the caricatures of Pier Leone Ghezzi (two volumes of which Marchionni is known to have owned), to a softer, more atmospheric rendering using gray wash with the pen and ink.[6] These two sheets, therefore, are difficult to date precisely. They are obviously preliminary sketches;[7] Marchionni's typical caricatures are more finished and are often worked up with wash. The identity of the subject is equally elusive: was he a professional artist or an amateur? The same unidentified head appears in two Würzburg sketches.[8] The significance of the chicken protruding in some instances from the fat man's coat pocket is also puzzling.

A.P.

1. Blunt, 1969, pp. 162, 165. On Marchionni, *see* especially Gaus, 1967; Berliner, 1958–59; Storrs, 1973, nos. 65–68; Piccolini, 1942–43; Meeks, 1966, especially pp. 26, 56–57.
2. *See* Clark, 1964 ("Introduction"), p. 47.
3. Referred to by Clark, ibid., p. 47.
4. Vatican Library, Cod. Rossiana 619.
5. Berliner, 1958–59. Other Marchionni drawings, architectural, decorative, and miscellaneous, are in the Cooper-Hewitt Museum, New York, and the Villa Albani at Rome (*see* especially Gaus, 1967, pp. 171–87).
6. Marchionni's production of caricatures must have begun at least in the 1740s as he depicts figures who died in the early 1750s.
7. A third sheet in the Clark collection, similar to the two exhibited here, shows thumbnail sketches of a cupola and a portion of a wall with an arch, as well as a number of heads (checklist no. 108).
8. Berliner, 1958–59, p. 325, figs. 80-81, dated 1745–55. The subject looks a bit like Batoni, except that his face is rounder and his nose more hooked (compare the Batoni self-portraits of the early 1770s reproduced in Lucca, 1967, nos. 48–49).

STEFANO POZZI

Rome 1699—Rome 1768

45. Angel Carrying a Scroll

c. 1746

Inscribed in pencil at lower center: della Sacrestia N° 15 [cancelled] 5

Black and white chalks on blue laid paper

330 x 273 mm (13 x 10 3/4")

1978-70-391

Provenance: gift of di Falco, Naples, 1967 (as Sebastiano Conca)

Exhibition: Minneapolis, 1970–71

Although Stefano Pozzi was one of the most important Roman artists of his generation, he has been almost entirely ignored by modern historians.[1] Born in Rome on November 1, 1699 (not 1707 or 1708, as is generally stated),[2] in 1716 he won first prize for drawing in the Concorso Clementino at the Accademia di San Luca.[3] We have no further information about his career until 1736, when Pascoli mentions him as a pupil of Andrea Procaccini;[4] later he studied with his slightly older contemporary Agostino Masucci. Although Pozzi's art was strictly dependent on the tradition of Maratta, he drew on other sources for certain graceful details, a lively sense of color, and spirited invention. He knew, besides the important examples of Conca and, later, of Batoni, the Roman works of Sebastiano Ricci (represented in his own parish);[5] the early styles of Francesco Trevisani and Michele Rocca; certain more rococo Gaulli followers, such as Giovanni Odazzi and, later, Lodovico Mazzanti; and, as can be seen in his representations of subjects connected with the Olivetan order,[6] the monumental simplicity of Subleyras.

Of Pozzi's important commissions, a number are still *in situ* in Roman churches. These include the ovals between the windows in San Silvestro al Quirinale (before 1736) and works in San Francesco di Paola, Sant' Ignazio (1736 and c. 1765), Santissimo Nome di Maria (c. 1742), and Santa Maria Maggiore (c. 1743), as well as the ceiling of Sant' Appollinare (c. 1748). Pozzi also produced decorative commissions, including a ceiling in Palazzo Altieri (c. 1732),[7] the library designed by Vanvitelli for Cardinal Prospero Colonna in Palazzo Sciarra-Colonna (c. 1743–50), murals in the state apartments of the Palazzo Colonna (1758), and fresco decorations in the Vatican Palace (1757–65) and in the Palazzo Doria Pamphili (1767–68). Among his highest achievements are a number of small paintings on copper, produced for private collectors, with Arcadian or mythological subjects imbued with a veiled eroticism.[8]

In 1732 Pozzi became a member of the Congregazione dei Virtuosi del Pantheon, of which he was made regent in 1739. In 1736 he was admitted to the Accademia di San Luca, where he held various offices, including those of inspector of the paintings exported from the Papal States and *professore* at the Accademia del Nudo on the Campidoglio (he was made the first director of the school in December 1754).[9] In 1758 he became Agostino Masucci's successor as *custode delle pitture,* which placed him in charge of the decoration of the Vatican Palace, of the Scuola del Mosaico attached to Saint Peter's (for which he executed a monumental copy of Raphael's *Transfiguration*), and of the temporary decorations for feast days, canonizations, and the like.

The *Angel Carrying a Scroll* must have its source in the decorations for a canonization. According to Anthony Clark's notebooks, it was one of a group of drawings attributed to Sebastiano Conca—including six other angels with scrolls,[10] two cherubs with palm branches, nine figures of Virtues, and a scene of Saint Camillus de Lellis at the bedside of a sick man—that belonged in 1967 to the Neapolitan dealer di Falco. The last drawing relates to another group of sheets that appeared on the Roman art market in 1974,[11] which included a Saint Catherine, three angels with symbols of martyrdom, and six additional Virtues. Two more compositions in this group, similar in every respect to the di Falco *Saint Camillus,* represent episodes from the lives of Saints Catherine de' Ricci and Fidelis of Sigmaringen. Catherine de' Ricci (1522–1589), Fidelis of Sigmaringen

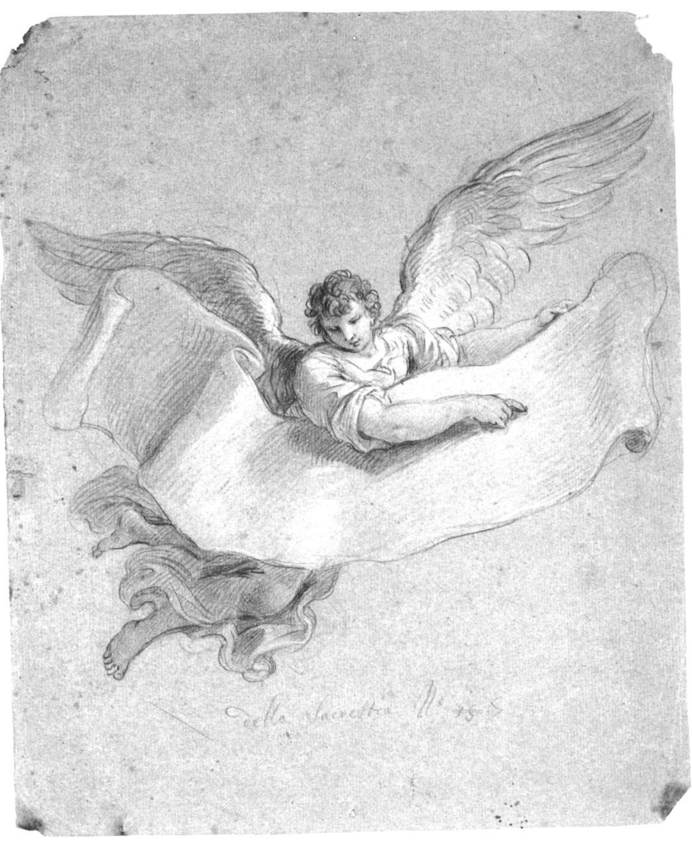

45

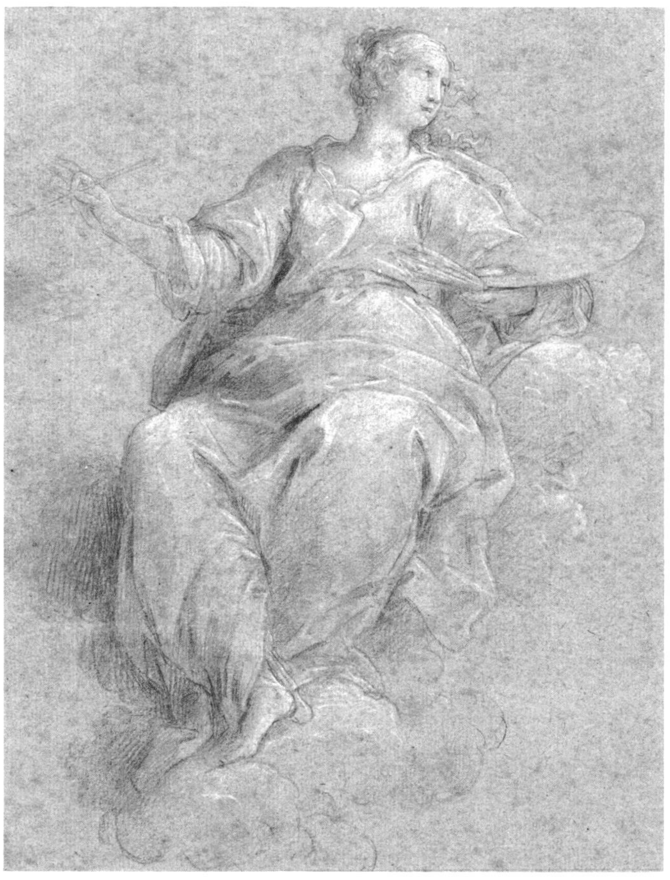

46

(1577–1622), and Camillus de Lellis (1550–1614) were all beatified during the eighteenth century, but at different times (in 1732, 1729, and 1742 respectively); they were, however, canonized by Benedict XIV at a single ceremony held in Saint Peter's on June 29, 1746. It may be suggested, then, that both groups of drawings—including the *Angel* from the Clark collection—refer to a single decorative scheme executed by Pozzi for that solemn occasion and subsequently lost or destroyed.

S.S.

1. His primary biography to date is Thieme-Becker, 1907–50, vol. 27, p. 340. For other works by Pozzi, *see also* Faldi, in Rome, 1959, nos. 528–29; Blunt and Cooke, 1960, p. 90, nos. 712–20; Clark, 1961, pp. 8–10; Salerno, 1965; Bruno Molajoli, *Guida artistica di Fabriano,* Fabriano, 1968, p. 156; Vasco, 1973; Giovanni Carandente, *Il Palazzo Doria Pamphili,* Milan, 1975, p. 276; Giogio Falcidia and Bruno Toscano, in Casale, et al., 1976, pp. 45–46; Röttgen, 1976, pp. 195, 206, n. 10, p. 208, n. 49; Spinosa, 1978, pp. 14–17, p. 23, n. 21 and fig. 17. Articles on Pozzi's drawings and on his late works for the Vatican Palace by, respectively, the present writer and Geneviève and Olivier Michel for *Antologia di Belle Arti* are in press at this writing.

2. Pozzi's correct birthdate was discovered by Geneviève Michel, whose archival researches on the Pozzi family have not yet been published.

3. The drawing, a red-chalk copy of an antique statue is still preserved at the Accademia (inv. no. A288).

4. Pascoli, 1730–36, vol. 2, p. 407.

5. Cf. the *Transfiguration* in the vault of the sacristy of Santi Apostoli.

6. In the church of Santa Caterina at Fabriano, in the chapel of the Blessed Bernard Tolomei at Monte Oliveto Maggiore, and, especially, in a large painting of the Blessed Bernard of about 1744, formerly in the university church at Perugia and now in the left transept of the church of Santa Francesca Romana in the Forum in Rome.

7. The vault of the Gabinetto di Toletta in the *appartamento nobile* on the second floor.

8. *See,* for example, Rome, 1959, nos. 528–29.

9. *See* Pirotta, 1969, p. 328. Pozzi held the same post in November 1759, January 1761, April 1764, and March 1766.

10. One is now in the Fabrizio Lemme collection in Rome. (Giancarlo Sestieri kindly made photographs of the group available to me.)

11. Sale, Christie's, Rome, November 12, 1974, lots 51–55.

46. An Allegory of Painting

c. 1750
Black and white chalks on faded blue laid paper, mounted down
302 x 182 mm (9 1/8 x 7 1/8″)
1978-70-392
Provenance: sale, Sotheby's, London, June 21, 1912; sale, Christie's, London, July 15, 1958, lot 168 (as Batoni); gift of Hans Calmann, 1958
Exhibition: Minneapolis, 1970–71

It is difficult to establish even an approximate chronology for Pozzi's drawings as presently known; many of them must have been produced as works of art in their own right for a public of mostly foreign amateurs and collectors, and only a few can be definitely related to finished paintings.[1]

In his drawings, as in his paintings, Pozzi had a predilection for noble compositions in which seated young women, sumptuously clad or barely veiled, represent allegorical or mythological figures. These subjects and religious themes constitute the two poles of his traditional, classicizing manner. His most mature achievement in the former category is certainly the *Friendship Embracing Peace* of around 1762–66, painted for the royal palace at Caserta, for which there is a finished preparatory drawing in the Baltimore Museum of Art.[2] Pozzi used the same type of composition in a number of works, such as in the personification of Religion represented at the lower left on Nolli's map of Rome of 1748, in the *Three Cardinal Virtues* on the ceiling of Cardinal Prospero Colonna's library in Palazzo Sciarra-Colonna, and in the *Religion* and *Faith* in a vault of the Museo Sacro in the Vatican.

The personification of Painting, a subject dear to academic painters, helped legitimize and strengthen their social prestige by emphasizing the intrinsic nobility of their profession. In the field of Roman drawings, the most illustrious precedent of this self-celebratory theme is no doubt Maratta's *Painting Raised up by Annibale Carracci and Received in the Temple of Glory,* now in the Louvre,[3] which Pozzi could have known through the engraving by Pietro Aquila. In addition to the drawing catalogued here, Pozzi represented the same personification in at least two other allegorical sheets, both belonging to the group of drawings that came to Düsseldorf in 1756 and both with a winged genius representing the genius of Fine Arts (*Genius Bonarum Artium et Amor Virtutis,* as Mengs shows him in a roundel flanking the *Parnassus* in the Villa Albani).[4] Having come to grips in these drawings with a theme that Mengs was later to develop in a more cultivated and doctrinaire manner in the Stanza dei Papiri of the Vatican Library (*see* no. 54), Pozzi went on to expand the motif in his vault fresco in the Museo Profano in the Vatican of 1765, where he replaces Painting with a victorious Minerva who presides as a putto rescues fragments of statuary—standing for the remains of antiquity—from Time, symbol of inexorable destruction.

This sheet is typical of Pozzi's drawing style, characterized by a light, broken line and suggestions of transparencies and pictorial values that are attained by contrasting white heightening against a background of gray blue paper.[5]

S.S.

1. A *Guardian Angel* in the Museu Nacional de Arte Antiga, Lisbon (inv. no. 1069), is connected with one of the ovals in San Silvestro al Quirinale, Rome (before 1736). A sheet sold at auction in Milan (Finarte, Cat. no. 297, December 4, 1978, lot 128) is a study for one of the six paintings commissioned by Cardinal Flavio Chigi about 1761 for the chapel of his family palace. A drawing in the Louvre, Cabinet des Dessins (inv. no. 3788), is for the undated *Madonna del Rosario* in the church of Santa Maria Assunta, Roccantica.
2. Mentioned by Clark, 1961, p. 8, n. 11; inv. no. L381105. Spinosa, 1978, p. 23, fig. 17, reproduces the painting. Pozzi seems also to have supplied *modelli* for the tapestry series with four Virtues donated by Benedict XIV to the church of San Pietro in Bologna and still *in situ,* signed by the tapestry maker Pietro Ferloni (1745–47).
3. Cabinet des Dessins, inv. no. 3371.
4. Inv. nos. FP 3389 and FP 3383; the latter is reproduced in Düsseldorf, 1969–70, no. 112, fig. 87. *See also* Röttgen, 1977.
5. Some of the artist's best sheets can be found today in the Kupferstichkabinett of the Kunstmuseum in Düsseldorf, in the Royal Library at Windsor Castle, and in a few American collections. Pozzi's drawings in America can be found in Baltimore in the Gilmor Collection belonging to the Peabody Institute, where they were studied by Anthony Clark in 1961 at the Baltimore Museum of Art (*see* Clark, 1961, pp. 8–10, figs. 6–7); in New York at the Metropolitan Museum of Art (inv. no. 87.12.131 for a ceiling in the Quirinal Palace recently identified by Geneviève and Olivier Michel), at the Cooper-Hewitt Museum (inv. no. 1938.88.7201), and in the Janos Scholz collection, ultimately to come to the Pierpont Morgan Library; and at the Art Institute of Chicago (inv. nos. 1922.3661 [Joachim and McCullagh, 1979, p. 84, no. 131, repr. fig. 155] and 65.420).

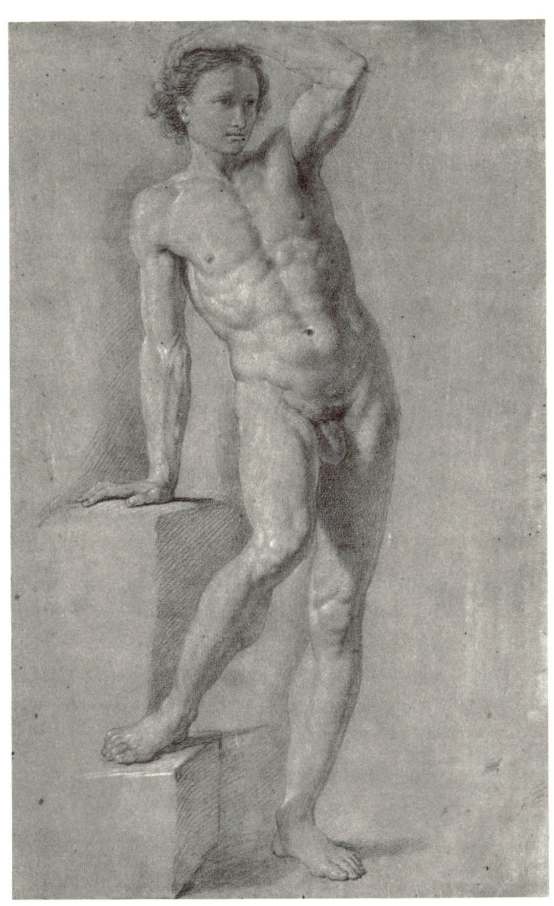

47

GIUSEPPE BOTTANI

Cremona 1717—Mantua 1784

47. Standing Male Nude, Left Hand on Head

c. 1760–70

Inscribed on verso in brown ink: 61

Red and white chalks on red orange prepared paper

432 x 270 mm (17 x 10 5/8″)

Watermark: fleur de lis in a circle with initials G^A^C

1978-70-197

Provenance: collection of the artist's heirs, Rome; Angelo di Castro, Rome, 1969; gift of Erich Schleier, 1969

When the Cremonese painter Giuseppe Bottani arrived in Rome in 1735 at the age of eighteen, he chose to join the school of Agostino Masucci (*see* no. 25), who was the last remaining direct disciple—albeit a late one—of Carlo Maratta. Of the various artistic circles then active in the capital, Masucci's was the most authoritatively traditional, consistent with Bottani's own youthful formation—by way of his first master, the Florentine Vincenzo Meucci, a pupil of the Bolognese Gian Gioseffo dal Sole—within the tradition of Guido Reni and late Bolognese academicism.[1]

Bottani's pursuit of traditional studies after Raphael's Stanze, the Farnese Gallery, antique sculpture, and the live model coincided with the anti-Baroque reaction of Batoni, Mengs, and Gavin Hamilton. He consequently enjoyed a prosperous career that culminated in his election to the Accademia di San Luca in 1758. During more than thirty years spent in Rome, Bottani executed a number of important commissions for the city and for the papacy, including altarpieces for the church of Santa Trinità dei Missionari in Rome (1743) and for the cathedral of Orte (c. 1752). He sent works to various cities in Tuscany, including Pontremoli, the cathedral (1745) and the Armenian church (1757) in Livorno, and the cathedral (1769) in Pescia. He also received major commissions from two princely families in Rome, the Rospigliosi and the Doria Pamphili; for the latter, he executed a monumental *Hercules at the Crossroads* as part of a new decorative program for their palace near the Collegio Romano (c. 1767–68).[2]

In 1769 Bottani was named director of the academy in Mantua and moved there with his brother Giovanni, also a painter. He was influential in the diffusion of the Roman grand manner throughout the Po valley, which, applied in particular to religious subjects, intermingled there with the more traditionalist currents of a growing neoclassical taste.

Bottani's activity as a draughtsman constitutes one of the most evident formal links between the doctrinaire and programmatic classicism of the late eighteenth century and the previous century.[3] The more than three hundred surviving sheets that date throughout his long career[4] provide an excellent example of the conscientious working methods of an academic artist in Rome at mid century. These sheets—often prepared in tempera with delicate tones ranging from rose to gray—illuminate the entire process of pictorial invention from the hastily sketched original idea to carefully finished figure studies and details of hands, heads, or drapery. Their refined, deliberately purified style derives from Maratta and his direct followers but has correspondences with the drawings of Sassoferrato and such Emilian artists as Carlo Cignani and Marcantonio Franceschini.

In Rome Bottani had also served as professor at the Accademia del Nudo on the Campidoglio. The many male[5] academic nudes to be found among his drawings must be connected with this activity.[6] From their high quality—they bear no resemblance to the uncertain efforts of the pupils—we may infer that Bottani went on drawing from the nude well into his maturity, quite possibly as a guide and model for the students in his charge.

In this drawing the model strikes the attitude of a Praxitelean Apollo Lykeios, with a hand on his head (arranged to allow study of the muscle tension in the upraised arm and torso), a pose that occurs frequently in one of the fundamental sources for painters of the period, the Farnese Gallery. Bottani's treatment of the motif reflects not only attention to an earlier tradition[7] but also to Winckelmann's latest dicta on calm and noble simplicity. An academic nude similar to the one exhibited here, from the same source, is in the collection of Erich and Mary Schleier, Berlin.

S.S.

1. On Bottani, *see* Chiara Perina [Tellini], in *Dizionario biografico,* 1960–, vol. 13, pp. 405–6, with bibliography; *see also* Marrini, 1766, vol. 2, pt. 2, pp. xxxi–ii; Perina [Tellini], 1961; Susinno, 1970; Susinno, 1971; Perina Tellini, 1973; Susinno, 1976; Borea, 1977; Susinno, 1978.

2. Repr. Susinno, 1978, p. 311, fig. 6.

3. *See* Faldi, 1977, p. 507.

4. The large group of drawings in Rome that passed to Giuseppe Bottani's descendants through the female line and were only dispersed on the market in 1969 does not seem to be identifiable with the collection in Milan mentioned by Perina as belonging to descendants of Giovanni Bottani through the female line (Perina [Tellini], 1961, p. 59, n. 43). The 130 or so sheets now in the Gabinetto Nazionale delle Stampe in Rome are from the former collection (*see* Susinno, 1976, p. 34, n. 6).

5. Female models were forbidden, and the students had to make do with men who, with the necessary adjustments, could serve as models for heroines or female saints (*see* Susinno, 1978, p. 309).

6. Bottani is mentioned as directing the life classes of the Accademia del Nudo in April 1764 (Pirotta, 1969, p. 330) and is called "professore primario" of the school in the decree appointing him director of the Mantuan academy (Perina [Tellini], 1961, p. 58, n. 13). A sketchbook in the Istituto Nazionale di Archeologia e Storia dell'Arte in Rome (MS 4), consisting of about thirty pages of academies and anatomical details and inscribed with Bottani's name in Greek letters, seems to belong to the period of his early training instead of to this late activity (*see* Perina [Tellini], in *Dizionario biografico,* 1960–, vol. 13, p. 406).

7. Compare a similarly posed male nude by the seventeenth-century painter Andrea Sacchi (repr. Blunt and Cooke, 1960, pl. 26).

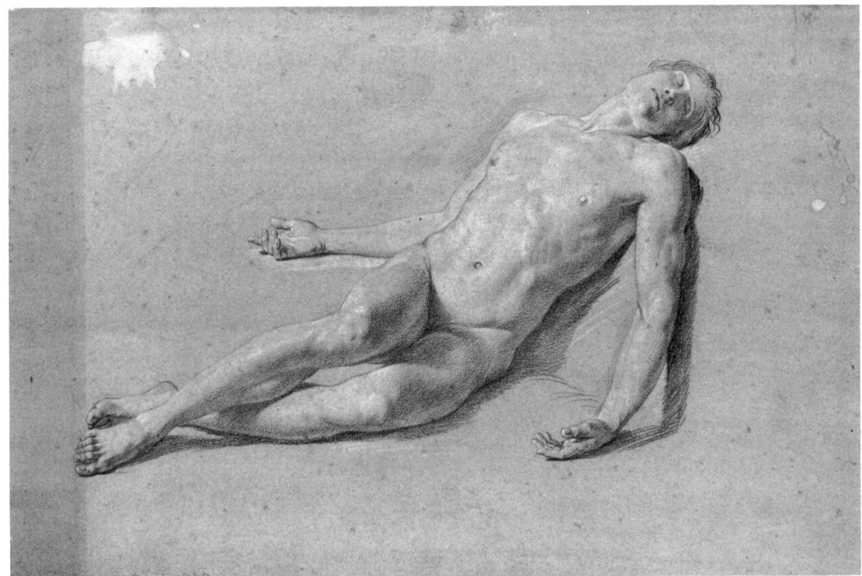

48

48. Reclining Male Nude Posed as a Dead Christ
c. 1757
Red and white chalks on yellowish prepared paper
269 x 397 mm (10 5/8 x 15 5/8")
1978-70-196
Provenance: collection of the artist's heirs, Rome; purchased from Angelo di Castro, Rome, 1969

The model in this academy has assumed the classic pose of Christ supported by Mary at the foot of the Cross, a motif that was virtually codified by the Carracci. Bottani may well have known the *Pietà* that Annibale executed in 1599–1600 for Cardinal Odoardo Farnese,[1] now in the Museo di Capodimonte in Naples, with an excellent copy in the chapel of the Palazzo Doria Pamphili in Rome. This famous work had already served as a model for Giovanni Battista Gaulli in a *Pietà* painted for Cardinal Chigi in 1667, which since 1967 has belonged to the Galleria Nazionale d'Arte Antica in Rome.[2]

The figure can be compared with two preparatory studies for a dead Christ in the Gabinetto dei Disegni e delle Stampe degli Uffizi, traditionally attributed to Pompeo Batoni and included in the Batoni exhibition in Lucca with the observation that they share stylistic features in common with Bottani's drawings.[3] However, the treatment of the nude figure in the Bottani drawing is much less dramatic: in his attitude of peaceful abandon, the dead Christ might almost be a sleeping Endymion. This impression is confirmed by the style of the drawing which, like much of Bottani's work, is characterized by a light, sure line that concentrates on essentials and defines forms with extreme purity. The sense of redundancy in the Uffizi drawings, which should probably be ascribed to the circle of the Florentine painter Giovanni Domenico Ferretti, is entirely lacking.

Bottani depicted a Pietà in a painting of 1757, which was sold as Batoni in the principe di Fondi sale in Naples in 1895;[4] however, its attribution to Bottani is confirmed by an old signature or inscription on the back of the canvas, as well as by a preparatory drawing of the Madonna's hand holding a cloth in the Fabrizio Lemme collection in Rome.[5] In the same year the artist sent a *Death of Saint Francis Xavier* to the church of San Nicolò at Pontremoli,[6] which demonstrates a passing interest on his part in Marco Benefial's mode of realism; the figure of the dying saint, reclining upon a straw pallet, must have originated in an academic study similar to this drawing.

S.S.

1. *See* Donald Posner, *Annibale Carracci: A Study in the Reform of Italian Painting around 1590,* London, 1971, vol. 2, p. 52, no. 119, repr. pl. 119a.

2. *See* Robert Enggass, *The Painting of Baciccio: Giovanni Battista Gaulli (1639–1709),* University Park, Pennsylvania, 1964, pp. 5–6, 155, repr. fig. 3.

3. Lucca, 1967, nos. 64–65; inv. nos. 5793S and 5794S.

4. *See* Susinno, 1978, p. 312, n. 13. The painting was formerly in the Meldolesi collection, Rome; a photograph exists in the photo archives of the Bibliotheca Hertziana, Rome.

5. Gabinetto Fotografico Nazionale, Rome, F 23887; this detail is quoted almost literally from Gaulli's Chigi *Pietà.*

6. *See* Perina [Tellini], 1961, p. 54. An autograph copy in the Parasacchi collection at Pontremoli is reproduced by Perina Tellini, 1973, p. 14, fig. 3.

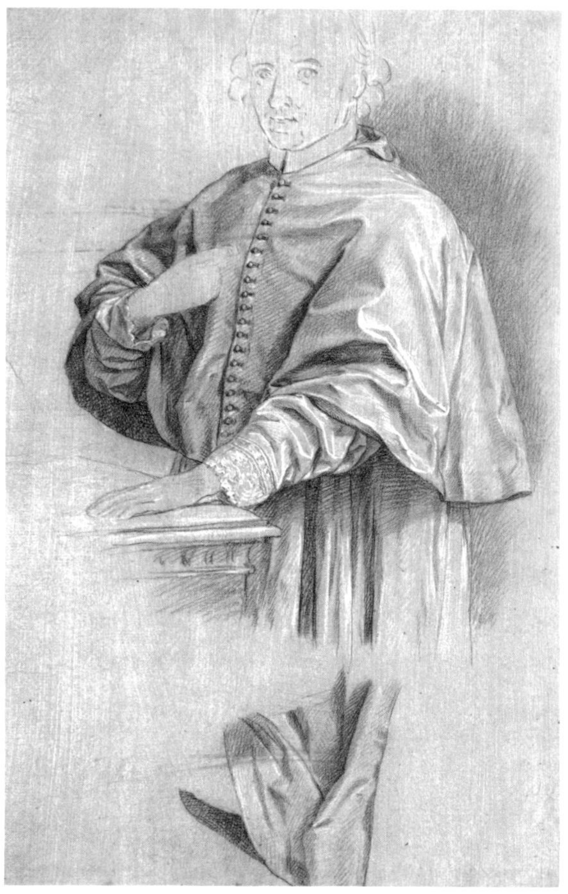

49

49. Studies for a Portrait of a Cleric

c. 1753–63
Red and white chalks on grayish prepared paper
406 x 260 mm (16 x 10 1/4")
1978-70-201
Provenance: collection of the artist's heirs, Rome; gift of Angelo di Castro, 1969
Bibliography: Susinno, 1978, p. 312, n. 13

In the earliest biography of Bottani, the abbot Marrini mentions his work as a portraitist, from which a small but significant group of paintings survives.[1] Though certainly inferior both in quality and success, Bottani's activity must have been comparable in some ways to Batoni's portrait work. Among Bottani's clients, like those of Batoni, were numerous foreigners on the grand tour and, on a more modest level, provincial nobles from Pontremoli or Livorno anxious to acquire in Rome a distinguished portrait as a sign of social prestige.

Marrini mentions in particular the portrait of the Neapolitan cardinal Giuseppe Spinelli (1697–1763),[2] who received the red hat from Clement XII in 1735. Until 1753 Spinelli was archbishop of Naples where he had the apse of the cathedral rebuilt, employing artists who had worked in Rome such as Paolo Posi, Stefano Pozzi, and Corrado Giaquinto. If, as seems possible, this drawing is an advanced preparatory study for Spinelli's portrait, it can be dated between 1753, the year Cardinal Spinelli arrived in Rome as the newly appointed bishop of Palestrina, and 1763, the year of his death in that city. The prelate's rank is indicated by the mozzetta, or elbow-length hooded cape worn by cardinals and by bishops in their dioceses. (The square biretta, which should be clasped against the chest in the right hand in the drawing, is actually represented in a separate study of the hands only, formerly in the di Castro collection in Rome.[3]) The smaller study on this sheet shows an alternate position for the left arm, raised perhaps instead of the right arm to hold the biretta. The head must also have been the subject of a separate study. Here the features are barely indicated; they are not, however, incompatible with Cardinal Spinelli's physiognomy as we know it from an engraving by Nicola Billy, derived from the first official portrait of the new cardinal, painted by Domenico Duprà in 1735.[4]

The composition—simple and severe, with no background and with a single distinctive feature serving to point up the exalted rank of the sitter—follows a formula reserved for the highest members of the ecclesiastical hierarchy. It belongs to a typically Roman tradition of portraiture that had continued more or less unchanged from Raphael to Maratta and that was taken up in the eighteenth century by such gifted artists as Antonio David in the 1730s[5] and Batoni in his vigorous portrait of Cardinal Colonna di Sciarra of about 1750.[6] Similarly, at the end of the century Antonio Cavallucci's portrait of Cardinal Pignatelli (after 1794)[7] fits comfortably within the context of contemporary international portraiture practiced by Angelica Kauffmann and Anton von Maron, without altering, however, the structure of an official genre that left little room for compositional invention.

S.S.

1. *See* Susinno, 1976, pp. 40–44; Susinno, 1978, pp. 310, 312. Marrini's biography was published in 1766.

2. "Many portraits from the hand of this fine painter are to be found in Poland, Denmark, England, and a number of Italian cities, especially Livorno; and one must not fail to mention the portrait of Cardinal Spinelli, which may be admired in Rome in the possession of the relatives of that prelate" (Marrini, 1766, vol. 2, pt. 2, p. xxxii, n. 7). For Cardinal Spinelli, *see* Moroni, 1840–61, vol. 68, pp. 290–92.

3. Gabinetto Fotografico Nazionale, Rome, F 24037; black and white chalks on red prepared paper, 262 x 375 mm.

4. Repr. in Busiri Vici, 1977, p. 6 (for the original painting by Duprà, *see* pp. 4–5).

5. For David and for enlightening general considerations on the portraiture, official and otherwise, of the Roman Settecento, *see* Clark, 1963 ("Neo-classicism").

6. Exhibited Chicago, et al., 1970–71, no. 68.

7. *See* Röttgen, 1976, p. 204 and fig. 44.

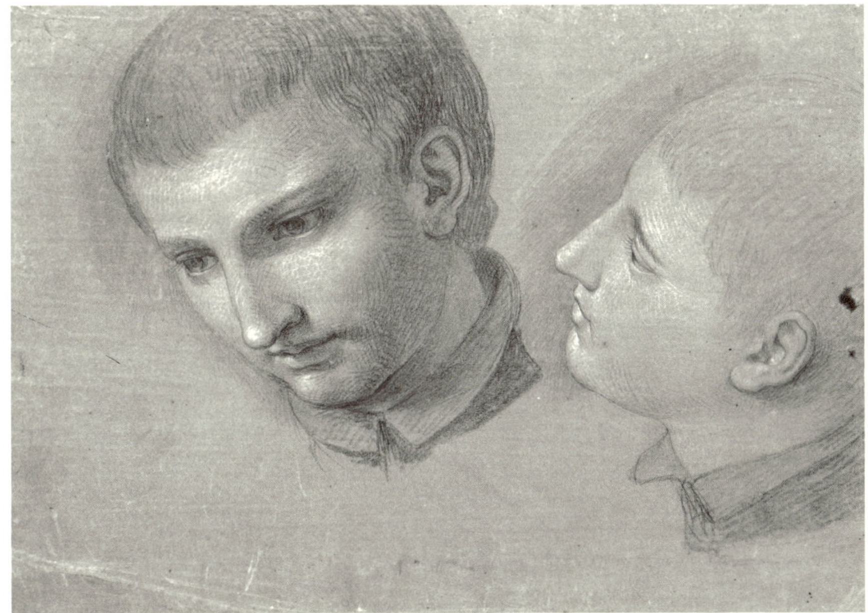

50

50. Studies of Heads for "Saint Louis Gonzaga and Saint Stanislas Kostka Adoring the Madonna and Child"
c. 1750–65
Inscribed on verso in pencil: di Giuseppe Bottani; numbered on verso in brown ink: 181
Black and white chalks on gray prepared paper
281 x 397 mm (11 1/16 x 15 9/16")
1978-70-200
Provenance: collection of the artist's heirs, Rome; purchased from Angelo di Castro, Rome, 1969
Exhibition: Minneapolis, 1970–71

This drawing poses the problem of the relationship between Giuseppe Bottani and his younger brother Giovanni (Cremona 1725—Mantua 1803), his pupil and assistant who succeeded him in 1784 as director of the academy in Mantua.[1] Giovanni lacked an individual artistic identity; his entire activity took place within his brother's workshop except during the last and least important years of his career. The sheet is a preparatory study of the two heads of Saint Louis Gonzaga and Saint Stanislas Kostka for a painting now in the chapel of the diocesan seminary in Pontremoli that shows the two Jesuit saints adoring the Madonna and Child. Although the painting, which sources ascribe to Giovanni,[2] is conventional in execution it contains parts, such as the head of the child Jesus, that are of considerable quality. This preparatory drawing, however, which is the only known sheet that can be connected with the painting, has all the refinement of Giuseppe's drawing style, recognizable in the sure line of the contours, the closely crosshatched shading, and the precise definition of detail. The painting was most likely a mutual effort based on Giuseppe's drawing; other works that the less-gifted Giovanni had the honor of signing must have been similar collaborations.

Bottani must have been inspired for the subject by the exquisite painting of about 1765 in the first chapel on the right in the church of Sant' Ignazio in Rome, which can be attributed to Stefano Pozzi.[3] The rather rare theme bears witness to a renewed interest in the Society of Jesus, especially in connection with youth and with educational institutions, just at the time in which anti-Jesuit polemics, which were to result in the suppression of the society in 1773 (*see also* no. 41), were at their height.

S.S.

1. For biographical information on Giovanni Bottani, *see* Perina [Tellini], 1961, p. 58, n. 16, and Chiara Perina [Tellini], in *Dizionario biografico*, 1960–, vol. 13, pp. 405–6; and, especially, Chiara Perina [Tellini], in E. Marani and Chiara Perina [Tellini], *Mantova, le arti*, vol. 3: *Dalla metà del secolo XVI ai nostri giorni*, Mantua, 1965, pp. 604–6.

2. *See* Pietro Bologna, *Artisti e cose d'arte e di storia pontremolesi*, Florence, 1898, p. 93; Susinno, 1970, pp. 81–86. The picture was painted for the church of San Colombano (now called San Francesco and attached to the seminary at Pontremoli); it should be dated, like most of Bottani's work in Pontremoli, to the 1750s or early 1760s.

3. *See* Giovanni Martinetti, *S. Ignazio*, Rome, 1967, p. 61. The painting is also reproduced as the work of an anonymous eighteenth-century artist in Francesco Calvo, *Roma: S. Ignazio (Tesori d'arte cristiana*, Bologna, vol. 5, fasc. 89, December 23, 1967), p. 252, fig. 1. *See also* Minor, 1980, p. 61, n. 2, who discusses the various attributions of the painting without specifically identifying it as the work of Pozzi.

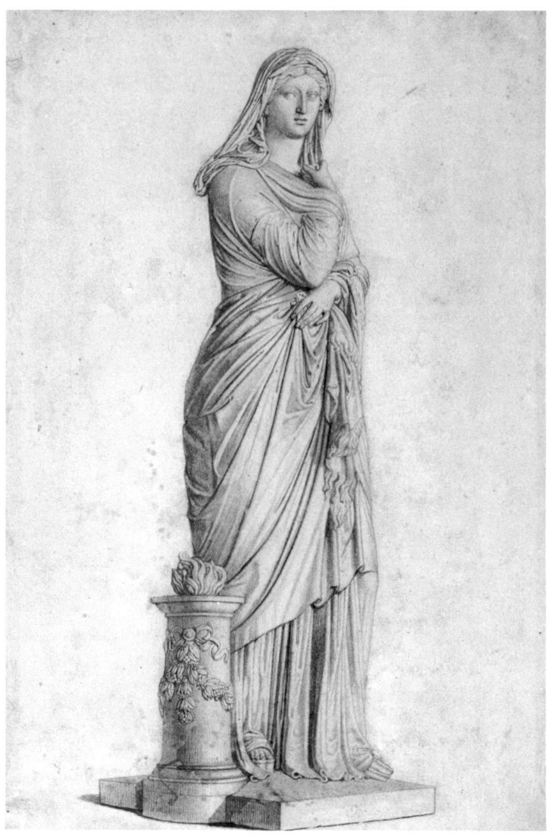

51

GIOVANNI DOMENICO CAMPIGLIA

Lucca 1692—Rome 1772 (?)

51. Statue of a Roman Woman, So-called "Vestal Virgin"

c. 1760

Inscribed indistinctly on the statue base: 97; inscribed on verso in black chalk at lower left: K 5061 and in pencil at lower right: SES

Black chalk on buff wove paper

329 x 217 mm (12 15/16 x 8 9/16")

1978-70-223

Provenance: purchased from Rockman Prints, New York, 1961

Exhibition: Minneapolis, 1967, no. 23

Trained as a painter in Florence where he practiced portraiture, Giovanni Domenico Campiglia was principally known as a draughtsman and engraver whose work over a long career centered on the illustration of antiquities both on private commission and for officially sponsored publications.[1]

Campiglia is first documented in Rome when he took first prize in the competition of the Accademia di San Luca in 1716. Subsequently employed by the academy making designs for engravings, he also began to make drawn copies of antique sculptures and gems in Roman collections. In the 1720s he produced drawings, in company with the young Pompeo Batoni, for the graphic collections assembled by Richard Topham (1671–1730) which offer a characteristic measure of the patronage Campiglia was to enjoy from private, often English, sources. In addition to projects of this kind, he also seems to have developed a specialty in drawing group portraits of visitors to Rome.

Campiglia's fame was established with the commission from the grand duke of Tuscany for drawings of antiquities to illustrate the six volumes of Anton Francesco Gori's *Museum Florentinum,* which appeared between 1731 and 1742. Campiglia was also engaged from 1734 onward in providing the drawings and some of the engraved plates for Giovanni Bottari's celebrated *Musei Capitolini,* published between 1741 and 1755.

In 1739 Campiglia was named superintendent of the Calcografia Camerale, the papal printing office, where he remained employed until pensioned in 1772. Thereafter the record of his activity ceases.[2]

This drawing reproduces a statue of a woman (*Pudicitia*) now in the Louvre,[3] the location of which at the time Campiglia knew it—probably in a Roman collection—is unknown. As an accurate if discreetly flattering portrayal of its subject, it is typical of the very precise, highly finished drawings that earned Campiglia a reputation among the best professional copyists.

The use of wove paper indicates a relatively late date for this drawing. Probably once part of a series, it may have been among the substantial numbers of Campiglia drawings owned by William Lock (1732–1810) which, as Macandrew noted,[4] were sold at Sotheby's on May 3, 1821 ("the works of . . . Campiglia, consisting of Antique Statues, Busts and Bas-reliefs very highly finished in black chalk").

Many of Campiglia's drawings survive in the Gabinetto dei Disegni e delle Stampe degli Uffizi; in the Gabinetto Nazionale delle Stampe, Rome; in the library of Eton College (Topham Collection); and in the Walker Art Gallery, Liverpool.

U.W.H.

1. For Campiglia, *see* S. Prosperi Valenti in *Dizionario biografico,* 1960–, vol. 17, pp. 541–43; Macandrew, 1978.

2. Campiglia became a member of the Accademia di San Luca in 1740 and directed life classes at the Accademia del Nudo in April 1757 and November 1760 (Pirotta, 1969, p. 329). For his self-portrait at the academy, *see L'Accademia,* 1974, p. 248, figs. 27 and 28; and for his reception piece, *Genius of Painting, see* Faldi, 1977, pp. 504–8, fig. 8.

3. *See* Charles Clarac, *Musée de sculpture antique et moderne,* vol. 4, Paris, 1850, p. 344, no. 1885; Salomon Reinach, *Répertoire de la statuaire grecque et romaine,* vol. 1, Paris, 1930, p. 168, no. 3 (repr.). According to Clarac the earlier designation of this statue as a Vestal was based upon the altar, since removed, which was part of a restoration by Girardon. The left hand and leg were also restorations.

4. Macandrew, 1978, pp. 138–39, p. 143, n. 24.

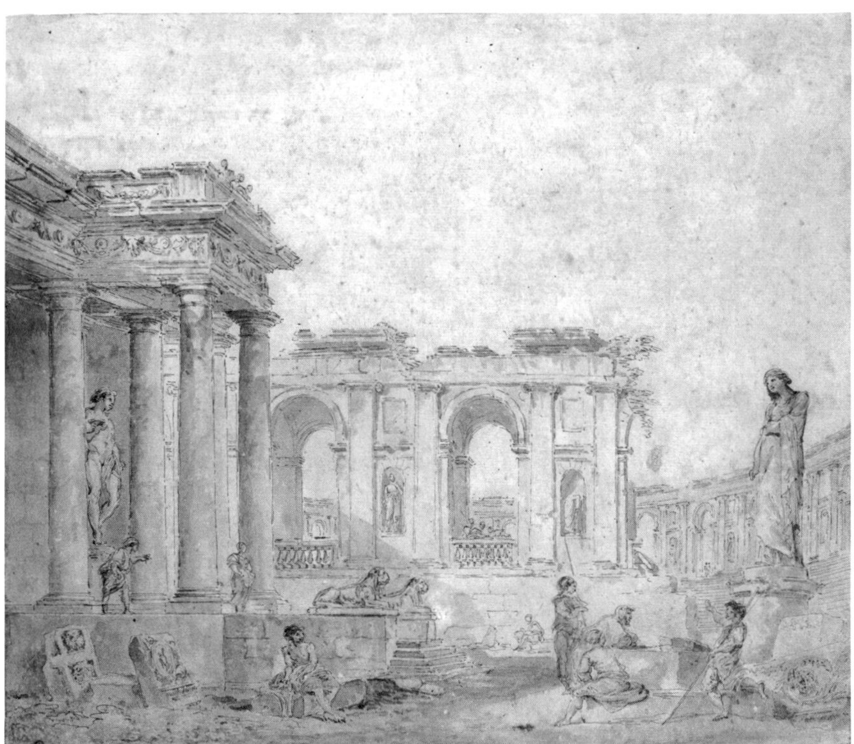

52

HUBERT ROBERT

Paris 1733—Paris 1808

52. *Architectural Fantasy*

c. 1755–60

Black ink, gray wash, blue and green watercolor on buff laid paper

280 x 320 mm (11 1/16 x 12 5/8")

Watermark: powder horn in a scrolled shield

1978-70-376

Provenance: Marcia, Baroness Fauconberg and Conyers and Countess of Yarborough; Earl of Yarborough; purchased from P & D Colnaghi & Co Ltd, London, 1964 (as G. P. Panini)

Exhibition: Minneapolis, 1967, no. 6 (as G. P. Panini)

Imaginary views that combine classical ruins, statuary, and casually disposed figure groups ranked among the most typical products of Roman art in the eighteenth century and remain today one of its few universally recognized achievements. This drawing has been hitherto attributed to Giovanni Paolo Panini (1691–1765; active in Rome from 1711), the painter most responsible for the development of this genre in Italy. Though very close to Panini's manner, the drawing seems actually to belong among the early works of the French painter Hubert Robert, the most important figure to emerge from the host of native and foreign artists who succeeded to and practiced Panini's style of view painting both during and after his lifetime.[1]

A number of Robert's idiosyncracies in figural drawing are especially evident, as well as an ease and fluidity of draughtsmanship that seem typical of Robert, and in contrast to the more staccato methods of Panini.

Robert spent eleven years in Italy, mainly in Rome, and experience gained there of the works of Panini and Giambattista Piranesi (1720–78) was to be of lasting importance for his subsequent career in France.[2] Robert first came to Rome in 1754 as a student at the French Academy, where Panini taught as professor of perspective. Panini's influence on the young painter seems to have been immediate and profound, as the academy director Charles Natoire carefully noted in a letter of 1759.[3] At least one dated drawing from that year[4] attests to Robert's known activity in drawing directly after Panini's work.

This composition corresponds specifically to no known painting by Panini but is related to a long series of ruin landscapes with preaching apostles or sibyls that appear in his oeuvre in the late 1720s and, with a broadened format, become increasingly numerous in the late 1740s and early 1750s.[5] Though an absence of dated drawings from Robert's very first Roman years makes the dating of this sheet uncertain, it may perhaps represent one of his earliest links to Panini. Robert's drawing seems to be a free composition inspired by and close to the manner of his master.

By the same hand is a nearly identical sheet in the National Gallery of Scotland, Edinburgh.[6] More confined spatially, the latter drawing contains some minor differences in its perspective and in the arrangement of figures, possibly reflecting a slightly later stage in the evolution of the same composition.

U.W.H.

1. The drawing was exhibited as by Panini in 1967. Anthony Clark in manuscript notes compared this sheet to the Edinburg drawing cited below (catalogued as Panini) and quoted a letter of Richard P. Wunder of January 22, 1965, in which the drawing is ascribed to Panini. Victor Carlson in verbal communication was the first to point out its similarities to Hubert Robert and suggested a possible date in the early 1750s. Independent communication from Marianne Roland-Michel also raised the possibility of Robert's authorship. For a recent study of Robert's drawings, with literature, *see* Washington, 1978–79, with introductory remarks by Carlson on pp. 18–26. For Panini's drawings, *see* Arisi, 1961, figs. 345–87. For Panini drawings reattributed to Robert, *see* Middlebury, Vermont, Middlebury College, *Architectural Ornament, Landscape and Figure Drawings collected by Richard P. Wunder,* 1975, nos. 32 and 33; Christie's, sale catalogue of the Richard Wunder collection, London, July 7, 1976, lots 148 and 149.

2. At the time of his death Robert owned twenty-five paintings by Panini, a collection reportedly ". . . considered by Hubert Robert as the treasure of his studies; repeating daily that he owed to them, after Nature, the greatest part of his success." (Alexandre Paillet, in the 1809 sale catalogue of Robert's estate, cited by Jean Cailleux, "Hubert Robert, dessinateur de la Rome vivante. 1757–1765," *Actes du XXIIe Congrès International d'Histoire de l'Art,* Budapest 1969 [published 1972], vol. 2, p. 59). For Piranesi and Robert, *see* Rome, 1976, no. 171–84.

3. *Correspondance,* 1887–1912, vol. 11, p. 262; also p. 388 for a further letter of July 8, 1761.

4. *See* Washington, 1978–79, p. 19; *Old Master Drawings Presented by Adolphe Stein and Lorna Lowe* (sale catalogue, H. Terry-Engell Gallery), London, July 3–15, 1972, no. 140, pl. 82. This work offers strong support for the attribution to Robert of the Clark drawing.

5. Arisi, 1961.

6. Keith Andrews, *National Gallery of Scotland, Catalogue of Italian Drawings,* Cambridge, 1968, p. 86, no. D963, fig. 608.

DOMENICO CUNEGO

Verona 1726—Rome 1803

53. Preparatory Study for an Engraving of "Hebe" after Gavin Hamilton

c. 1767

Red chalk, some stumping, on cream paper, mounted down

349 x 277 mm (13 3/4 x 10 7/8")

1978-70-433

Provenance: purchased from Rockman Prints, New York, 1959

Exhibition: Minneapolis, 1967, no. 78 (as Giovanni Volpato)

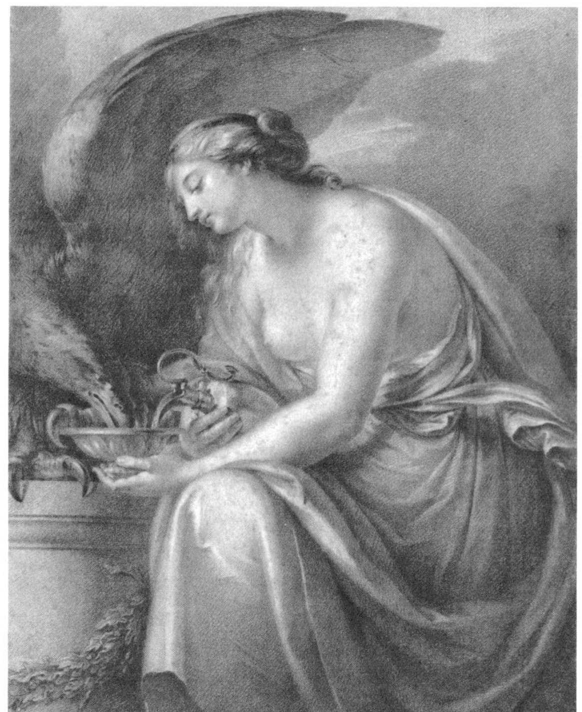

53

Domenico Cunego came to Rome in 1761 as part of the retinue of James Adam and Charles-Louis Clérisseau; he was engaged to engrave for Adam Clérisseau's drawings of the ancient ruins at Spalato, and within several years he also became active as the principal engraver of Gavin Hamilton's paintings. Hamilton (1723–1798), a Scot educated at the University of Glasgow, had been in Rome since the 1740s when he had studied as a painter with Agostino Masucci. In 1748 he had accompanied James Stuart and Nicholas Revett to Naples in order to study the antiquities, most particularly the paintings at Herculaneum. Hamilton supported himself primarily as an art dealer and archaeologist, and many of the important art works that came to British collections in the eighteenth century passed through his hands—examples are the collection of antiquities formerly at Lansdowne House and such Renaissance paintings as Raphael's *Ansidei Madonna* and Leonardo's *Virgin of the Rocks,* both now in the National Gallery, London. He also sold to Pius VI many works of ancient sculpture that the pope contributed to the formation of the Museo Pio-Clementino (*see* no. 110).[1]

Hamilton's grave, intellectual paintings were crucial to the development of the neoclassical style in Rome; as Waterhouse pointed out, his classical historical picture *Andromache Weeping over the Body of Hector* was planned before Mengs's *Parnassus* ceiling for the Villa Albani and therefore "has a claim to be the earliest important composition which can genuinely be called neo-classical."[2] *Andromache Weeping,* exhibited in 1762, became in 1764 the first composition engraved by Cunego, who thereafter continued to engrave Hamilton's paintings before they were sent off to their purchasers, thus ensuring a wide circulation of the painter's major historical compositions. Cunego and Giovanni Volpato (1733–1803), to whom this drawing was formerly attributed, also engraved for Hamilton the *Schola Italica Picturae* of 1773, a series of forty engravings after paintings of sixteenth- and seventeenth-century artists that included Michelangelo, Raphael, Andrea del Sarto, Parmigianino, Correggio, Titian, Veronese, the Carracci, Domenichino, Guercino, Caravaggio, and Guido Reni. The eclecticism of this choice reflected Hamilton's own taste in painting and in his art dealings.

This drawing is a preparatory study for Cunego's engraving after Hamilton's painting of *Hebe* in the collection of the marquess of Exeter at Burghley House (with an old but incorrect attribution there to Angelica Kauffmann).[3] Hebe, daughter of Jupiter and Juno, goddess of eternal youth and beauty, and cupbearer to the gods, is seen "giving drink to the eagle of Jupiter." The painting, along with another version now at the Stanford University Museum of Art,[4] has been dated by Françoise Forster-Hahn to the later 1760s.[5] An engraving by Cunego dated 1767 of *Juno* forms a natural pendant to the engraving of *Hebe,* and both were probably created at the same time.[6]

M.L.M.

1. On Hamilton, *see* Waterhouse, 1954. On his activity as an archaeologist and art dealer, *see* Irwin, 1962.

2. Waterhouse, 1954, p. 69.

3. Giovanni Volpato, to whom this drawing was attributed by Anthony Clark, engraved only six works by Hamilton, five of which were single allegorical figures, while Cunego engraved eleven, most of which were after Hamilton's major historical subjects. The dimensions of Cunego's engraving are virtually the same as this drawing, and the engraving follows the drawing exactly. The Cunego engraving exists in many collections (in the Metropolitan Museum of Art, the British Museum, and the Gabinetto Nazionale delle Stampe, Rome) but it has been impossible to trace the Volpato version. The latter is listed by Le Blanc, 1854–88, vol. 4, p. 152, no. 65; Anthony Clark must have seen an impression of it but stated that he had never seen the Cunego print. The copper plate for Cunego's engraving (Le Blanc, 1854–88, vol. 2, p. 75, no. 27) is in the Calcografia Nazionale, Rome.

4. Formerly identified incorrectly as Lady Emma Hamilton as Hebe and therefore misdated to 1786, when Gavin Hamilton accompanied Lady Hamilton to Naples and painted her several times. *See also* London, 1972 (*Lady Hamilton*), no. 35, pl. 3.

5. Forster-Hahn, 1975, pp. 369–70.

6. The engravings are of the same size and format; the inscriptions at the bottom of both prints that give Latin and English titles and the painter's and engraver's names are executed in exactly the same way (the *Juno* is reproduced by Forster-Hahn, 1975, p. 366, fig. 48).

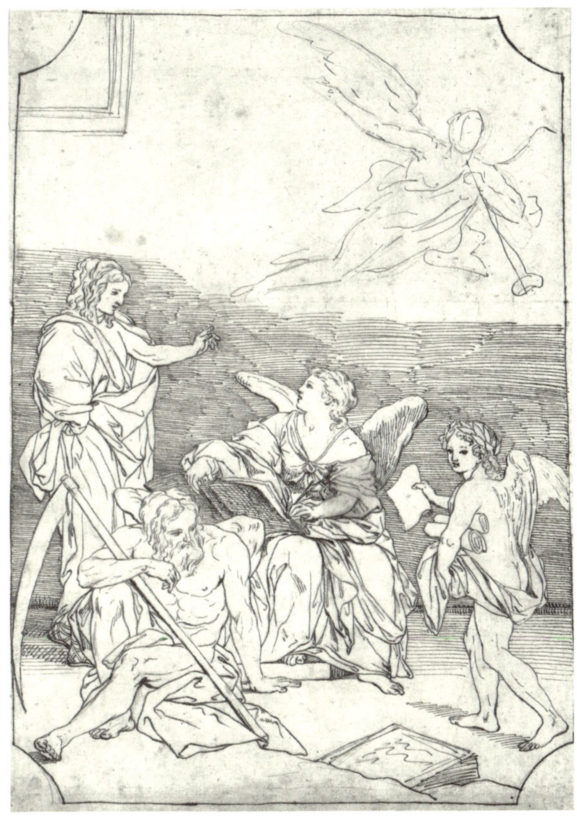

54 Recto

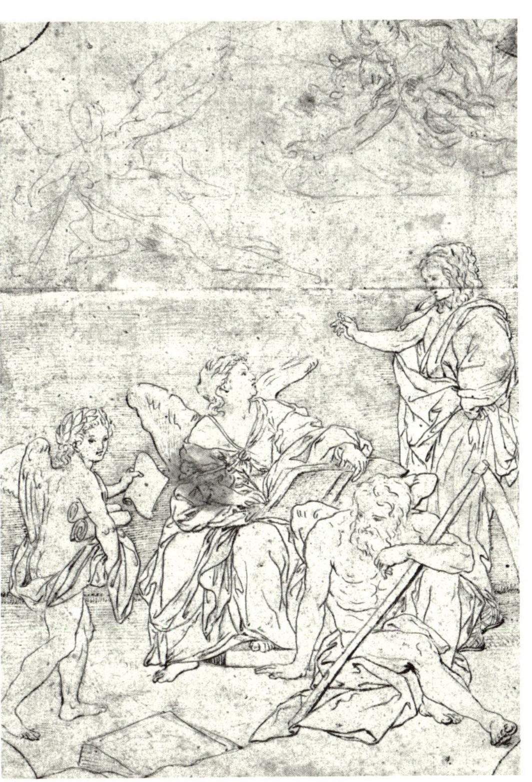

54 Verso

ANTON RAPHAEL MENGS

Aussig (Czechoslovakia) 1728—Rome 1779

54. *Study for the Central Part of the Ceiling in the Stanza dei Papiri, Vatican Library*

Verso: *Tracing of Recto Composition with a Study of a Mythological Scene (Pan, Venus, and Cupid)*

1771–72

Recto: pen and brown ink over traces of red chalk on cream laid paper, set into mount; verso: black chalk

332 x 239 mm (13 1/16 x 9 7/16")

1978-70-339

Provenance: Veuve Galippe;[1] sale, property of Mme. Veuve Galippe, de Vries, Amsterdam, March 27–29, 1923, in lot 515; Fritz Haussmann, Berlin, 1931; Countess Finckenstein, Zurich, 1950s; purchased from Yvonne ffrench, London, 1960

Exhibition: Minneapolis, 1967, no. 62

Bibliography: Röttgen, 1980 (in press)

A writer of fundamental importance in the fields of art history and theory, Anton Raphael Mengs was one of the major exponents of academic neoclassicism as well as a highly influential model for the succeeding generation of European painters. Mengs, son of the Dresden court painter Ismael Mengs, studied first with his father, who took him to Rome in 1740; after three years of studying and copying the frescoes of Raphael and Michelangelo, he returned to Dresden and in 1744 was named court painter to Augustus III. Between 1746 and 1749 he was again in Rome, where he converted to Catholicism; in Dresden from 1749 until 1752, he was made first painter to the court of Saxony before leaving a third time for Rome, there to become the good friend of Winckelmann upon the latter's arrival in 1755. During the Seven Years War, Mengs lost his state pension and was forced to work on private commissions in Rome, including portraits of British travelers. In 1757–58 he painted, with Anton von Maron's help, the nave ceiling fresco of Sant' Eusebio in Rome, and he completed his best-known work, the *Parnassus* ceiling in the Villa Albani, in 1761, the same year he was called to Spain as court painter. Mengs returned to Italy by 1770 and was elected *principe* of the Accademia di San Luca in 1771. During the next year he decorated the Stanza dei Papiri in the Vatican Library and returned to Madrid in 1774 after spending several months in Naples and Florence. In 1776, because of his poor health, he received the king's permission to settle permanently in Rome, where he died in 1779.

This sheet is the only known study for the main group of figures in the central ceiling fresco that Mengs executed on the commission of Pope Clement XIV in 1772 for the Stanza dei Papiri of the Vatican Library. The artist's preparatory studies for the fresco are documented to 1771. The study differs from the finished work not only in formal elements but also in ways indicating that the subject, not yet fully developed, was altered in the course of execution. His most significant change in the fresco was the transfer of the drawing's figural group—winged History, shown writing in a book, together with Time, Janus, a genius, and a fame —to a setting in the Belvedere courtyard. This is made clear by the view of the Museo Clementino, only founded in 1771, which one entered from the courtyard at this stage of construction.[2] The widening of the composition to accommodate the view also led Mengs to reverse the group of figures.[3]

The distant source for the figure of History, considerably altered by Mengs, was a painting by Solimena alluding to Louis XIV. The more immediate model employed by the artist, however, was an offshoot of this composition referring to Charles III of Spain, and ultimately the figure was based on Cesare Ripa's History, similarly depicted with wings.[4] The drawing is not technically uniform: whereas the main group is rendered in the stiff pen technique typical of Mengs's compositional sketches—and was perhaps done with studio assistance—the more freely drawn figure of the hovering Fame exhibits all the characteristics of a preliminary sketch, probably added in connection with the changes in the background.

S.R.

1. On the Galippe album, which contained a number of drawings by Batoni and Mengs and to which this sheet (as well as nos. 55–57) belonged, *see* no. 31. All the Mengs drawings catalogued here are on Galippe mounts, trimmed so that the Galippe numbering unfortunately has been lost. It is difficult to guess how many drawings by Mengs were originally in the album. Of twenty-one sheets attributable to the artist and acquired from the album by Anthony Clark, sixteen are counterproofs, and of these at least five seem to have been copied after Mengs.

2. A drawn plan for this view is in the Biblioteca Comunale in Fermo (repr. in Luigi Dania, *La pittura a Fermo e nel suo circondario,* Fermo, 1967, fig. 58).

3. A copy of the composition is reproduced in London, 1972, no. 195, pl. 25.

4. Cf. von Kutschera-Woborsky, 1917, pp. 44–46; Lazareff, 1925; von Einem, 1973, p. 32, n. 134.

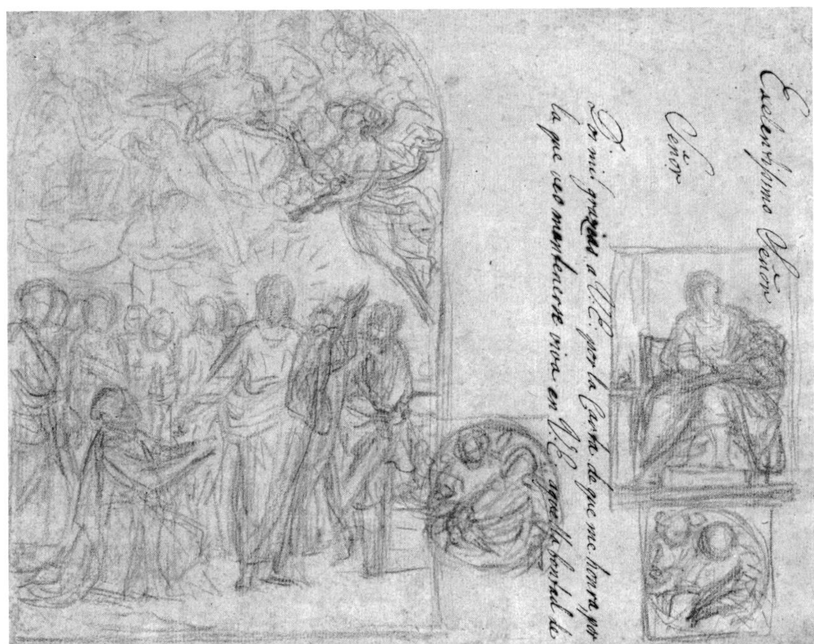

55

55. Studies for "Christ Presenting the Keys to Saint Peter" and Other Compositions

1772

Inscribed in brown ink with the beginning of a letter written in Spanish by Mengs: Exelentissimo Señor / Señor / Doi mil grazias a V: E: por la Carta de que me honra, por / la que veo mantenerse viva en V: E: quella bontad de

Black chalk on cream laid paper, mounted down

192 x 243 mm (7 5/8 x 9 9/16")

1978-70-340

Provenance: Veuve Galippe; sale, property of Mme. Veuve Galippe, de Vries, Amsterdam, March 27–29, 1923, in lot 515; Fritz Haussmann, Berlin, 1931; Countess Finckenstein, Zurich, 1950s; purchased from Yvonne ffrench, London, 1960

Exhibition: Minneapolis, The Minneapolis Institute of Arts, "Contemporary and Ancient Art," April 7–21, 1963, no. 25

Bibliography: Incisa della Rocchetta, 1932, p. 270, repr.

The commission for Mengs's altarpiece of *Christ Presenting the Keys to Saint Peter* was received by the artist in September 1772 from the Reverenda Fabbrica di San Pietro; apparently it was sought as a replacement for Francesco Vanni's 1603 painting of *The Fall of Simon Magus* after a version of the same theme by Batoni had been rejected by the Fabbrica.[1] Two other drawings, quite different from this example, can be connected with the commission for the Saint Peter's altarpiece: an early sheet of ink sketches related to the composition is in the British Museum, and a chalk drawing, which shows only the lower portion of the composition, is in the Albertina, Vienna.[2] A grisaille *bozzetto* for the painting belongs to the descendants of Sigismondo Chigi.[3]

Although this drawing generally agrees more closely with the *bozzetto* than with the sheet in Vienna, which presents a markedly different group with some figures kneeling or bending, the differences between the drawings and painted *bozzetto* suggest that they were not separated by a great period of time. It can be assumed that all of the surviving preliminary studies are datable shortly before or after the commission was granted. The sketch on this sheet for an enthroned figure writing in a book is closely connected to the painting in the Stanza dei Papiri in the Vatican Library (*see* no. 54), which was completed in November 1772. Thus the entire page of sketches can be dated to the second half of that year. No painting related to the two circular compositions with half-length figures—perhaps showing Christ being comforted by an angel—has yet been identified in Mengs's oeuvre, but related designs are found on other sheets of studies datable to the same period (*see* no. 56).

S.R.

1. For the documentation of the commission, *see* Hautecoeur, 1910, p. 452; Incisa della Rocchetta, 1932; Belli Barsali, 1973. *See also* von Einem, 1973, pp. 33–36, 39.

2. London, The British Museum, Print Room, inv. no. 1960-7-16-27/28. Vienna, Graphische Sammlung Albertina, inv. no. 4625 (*See* Alfred Stix, *Beschreibender Katalog der Handzeichnungen, Graphische Sammlung Albertina*, vol. 4, *Die Zeichnungen der deutschen Schulen*, edited by H. Tietze, et al., Vienna, 1933, no. 1920).

3. Repr. by von Einem, 1973, opp. p. 36.

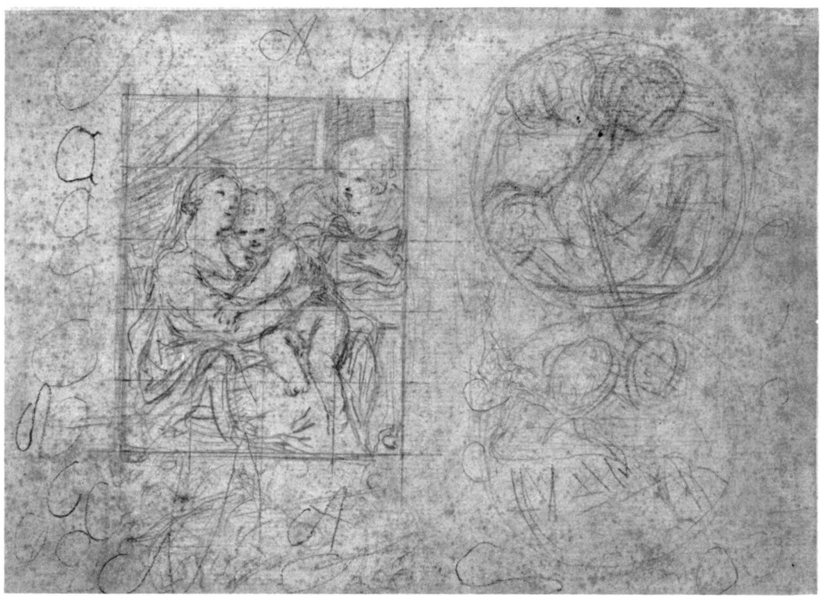

56

56. *Studies for a Holy Family and Other Compositions*
Verso: *Studies for a Holy Family with Saint Elizabeth and Other Figures* (not illustrated)
c. 1772
Recto: black chalk, partially squared, on cream laid paper, set into mount; writing exercises, probably by a child, in black chalk throughout; verso: black chalk
162 x 224 mm (6 3/8 x 8 13/16")
1978-70-342
Provenance: Veuve Galippe; sale, property of Mme. Veuve Galippe, de Vries, Amsterdam, March 27–29, 1923, in lot 515; Fritz Haussmann, Berlin, 1931; Countess Finckenstein, Zurich, 1950s; purchased from Yvonne ffrench, London, 1960

The squared composition of the Holy Family at the left of this sheet appears in another drawing in the Albertina,[1] but no painting by Mengs related to these studies can be identified. We know that the artist was occupied with the theme of a half-figure Madonna and Child during this period, as is demonstrated by engravings after one such composition.[2] A related work is the contemporary tondo composition now in the National Gallery in London.[3] Mengs's increased attention to these Raphaelesque images can be traced to his copying, in a work now lost, of Raphael's *Madonna della Sedia* in the Palazzo Pitti during his stay in Florence in 1770.

The sketches on the recto of this sheet may be dated to around 1772, as the upper tondo composition, which Clark tentatively identified as *Christ Comforted by an Angel (or Angels)*, relates to number 57, which can be securely dated in that year. This subject, with various alterations, appears five times on three different sheets in the Clark collection (nos. 55–57) and cannot be identified exactly. S.R.

1. Vienna, Graphische Sammlung Albertina, inv. no. 4622. *See* Alfred Stix, *Beschreibender Katalog der Handzeichnungen, Graphische Sammlung Albertina,* vol. 4, *Die Zeichnungen der deutschen Schulen,* edited by H. Tietze, et al., Vienna, 1933, no. 1896.
2. By Domenico Cunego, dated 1773, and Manuel Esquivel Sotomayer, dated 1802. *See also* Nagler, 1835–52, vol. 9, p. 121, and vol. 17, p. 87.
3. Inv. no. 1099 (chalk on paper mounted on canvas); *see* Honisch, 1965, p. 136, no. 350.

57. *Studies for "Christ Comforted by an Angel," "The Dream of Saint Joseph," "The Madonna and Child Enthroned with Saints," and "Saint John the Baptist in the Wilderness"*
c. 1772
Black chalk and brown ink on cream laid paper, mounted down
228 x 191 mm (8 15/16 x 7 1/2")
1978-70-341
Provenance: Veuve Galippe; sale, property of Mme. Veuve Galippe, de Vries, Amsterdam, March 27–29, 1923, in lot 515; German art market, 1926; gift of Yvonne ffrench, 1960

This sheet can be dated from the connection of its two tondo compositions with other drawings by Mengs. The circular composition of *Christ Comforted by an Angel,* which may be related to the theme of Christ on the Mount of Olives, appears in two other sheets of the Galippe album (nos. 55 and 56); dating of number 55 to

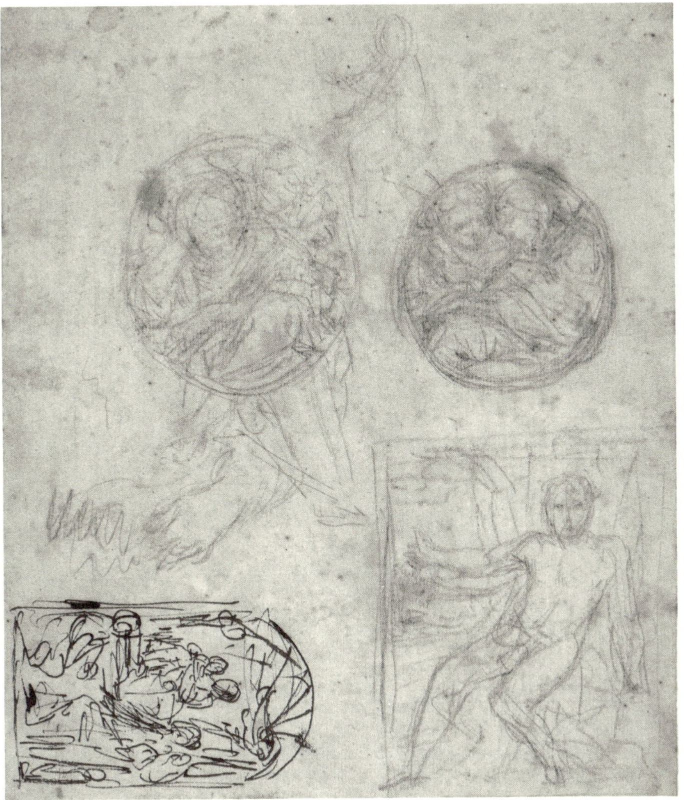

57

1772 is established by its study for *Christ Presenting the Keys to Saint Peter*. Another sheet with ink and black-chalk studies in Philadelphia shows a circular composition for Christ comforted by an angel.[1] No painting of this theme by Mengs is known, but there can be no doubt that the two tondo compositions in this sheet were conceived as pendants. Although a *Dream of Saint Joseph* by Mengs in tondo form has not survived, one is listed in the inventory of the artist's estate.[2] Two autograph versions of the theme are closely related in composition to the drawing; both can be dated to the years 1773–74.[3]

The hasty compositional sketch of a *sacra conversazione* with an angel playing a musical instrument, obviously influenced by Raphael and Andrea del Sarto, cannot be related to other known drawings or paintings. The other quick compositional sketches on the sheet can be related to the painting of *Saint John the Baptist* that appeared on the New York market in 1974 (whereabouts unknown). Mengs's brother-in-law, Anton von Maron, seems to have been involved in the execution of this painting, which can thus be dated to 1772–73, or during the period of Mengs's sojourn in Rome of 1771 to 1773. The inspiration of the composition was Raphael's painting of the subject, located in the eighteenth century in the Tribuna of the Uffizi, which Mengs could have known during his stay in Florence in 1770. S.R.

1. Pennsylvania Academy of the Fine Arts, inv. no. 289 (formerly on deposit at the Philadelphia Museum of Art). The sheet is related to an unfinished painting in the collection of Pius VI, now lost.

2. Rome, Archivio di Stato (to be published in the present writer's forthcoming monograph on Mengs).

3. Sarasota, Florida, John and Mable Ringling Museum of Art; repr. in William E. Suida, *A Catalogue of Paintings in the John and Mable Ringling Museum of Art*, Sarasota, 1949, p. 266, no. 328. Vienna, Kunsthistorisches Museum (inv. no. 124); repr. in *Kunsthistorisches Museum Wien*, Vienna, 1973, pl. 136.

DOMENICO CORVI

Viterbo 1721—Rome 1803

58. Academic Nude, Seated

1760–70

Inscribed on verso in brown ink: n. 18—

Black chalk, some stumping, and faint traces of white chalk on tan laid paper

555 x 425 (21 7/8 x 16 3/4")

Watermark: C F in a circle topped by a fleur-de-lis

1978-70-263

Provenance: purchased from Libreria Querzola, Rome, 1962

Exhibition: Minneapolis, 1967, no. 36

One of the chief exponents of the Roman classical tradition in the second half of the eighteenth century, Domenico Corvi was especially admired for his graceful handling of color and light and for the strength of his draughtsmanship. Lanzi noted Corvi's incomparable command of anatomy, perspective, and design—strengths that, in his 1785 *Self-portrait* in the Galleria degli Uffizi, the painter himself wished to underscore by portraying himself painting an academy of Hercules in the presence of a cast of the Medici Venus, theoretical treatises, and schematic figure drawings. Corvi's academy drawings were avidly sought by his contemporaries and, if Lanzi is to be believed, were valued even more highly than his paintings.[1]

In addition to offering private drawing instruction in his own studio, Corvi played an active role in the Accademia del Nudo of the Accademia di San Luca. He frequently supervised the students in attendance there, setting the poses of the models, arranging the drapery and props as required, and correcting the students' work. He directed the life-model classes in 1757, 1760, 1775, 1777, 1778, 1792, 1801, and 1802.[2]

This drawing exemplifies the high quality of Corvi's academy drawings, which occupy a prominent place within his largely unstudied graphic oeuvre. Although similar poses, lighting, background, and devices for the model's support are found in his other life drawings,

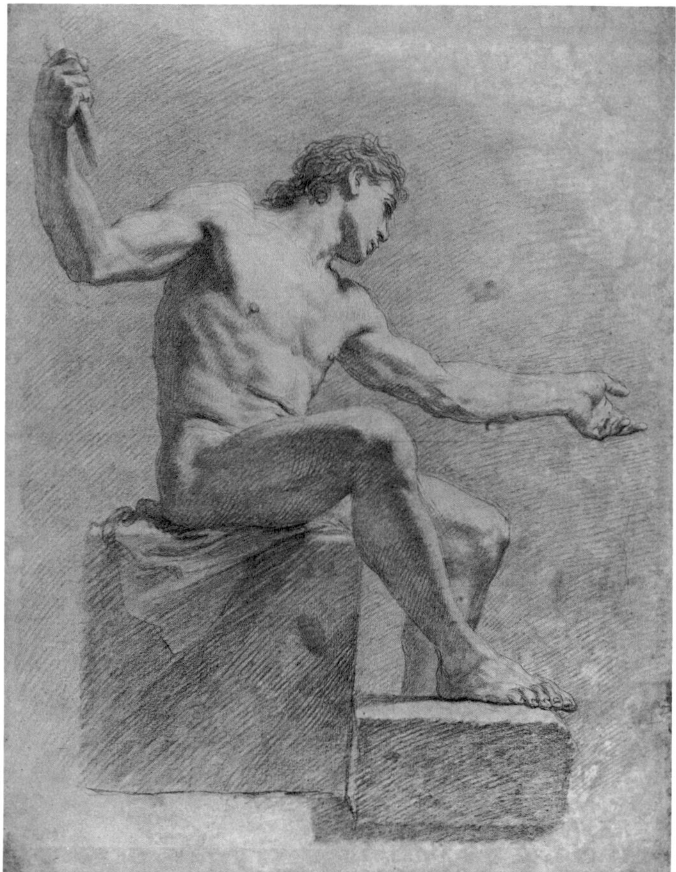

58

this sheet is a particularly fine example of his masterful understanding of anatomy. A deftness of shading and precision of contour are combined with stumping to create an image of sophisticated and refined strength.

Corvi's academies cannot be dated precisely according to stylistic criteria, since evidence of his evolution as a draughtsman is limited. One is tempted, nonetheless, to place this sheet at the time of his early maturity in the 1760s. The youthful model and his energetic pose may be compared, for example, to the figure types and poses in the four canvases now in Vedana—especially the *Gideon and the Fleece*—executed around 1758, probably for the now-destroyed Roman church and convent of Santa Chiara al Quirinale.[3] The problem of dating is complicated, however, by the existence of two less precise and articulated red-chalk academy drawings in the Cooper-Hewitt Museum, New York, one of which is inscribed by its former owner, Alessandro Maggiori, "il Corvi da giovane."[4]

E.P.B.

1. Lanzi, 1968, vol. 1, p. 422. For the Uffizi *Self-portrait, see* Clark, 1963 ("Neo-classicism"), p. 358, fig. 7. In an earlier *Self-portrait* painted for the Accademia di San Luca, Corvi also portrayed himself in the act of painting a male nude model (Stefano Susinno, "I ritratti degli accademici," in *L'Accademia,* 1974, p. 260, pl. 8).

2. Pirotta, 1969.

3. Faldi, 1970, p. 80, figs. 306–9. The paintings are today in the Certosa of Vedana (Belluno).

4. Inv. no. 1896-16-7. For other Maggiori drawings in the Clark collection, *see* nos. 3, 59. Maggiori's inscription notwithstanding, Anthony Clark did not accept an early date for the Cooper-Hewitt academy drawings.

59. *Study of a Boy's Head*

1770–90

Inscribed on recto by Alessandro Maggiori in dark brown ink at lower right: Il Corvi fece; inscribed on verso in brown ink: Io A. Maggiori acquissai [?] in Roma / nel 1817.

Black chalks with some stumping, faint traces of white chalk on blue laid paper

197 x 170 mm (7 3/4 x 6 11/16")

1978-70-262

Provenance: Alessandro Maggiori (Lugt suppl. 3005^{b}), purchased in Rome, 1817; C. Argentieri (?) (Lugt suppl. 486^{b}: as anonymous mark); P. G. Braschi (?) (Lugt suppl. 2079^{b}: as anonymous mark); gift of Hans Calmann, 1960

Exhibitions: Cleveland, 1964, no. 10 (repr.); Minneapolis, 1967, no. 35; Minneapolis, 1970–71

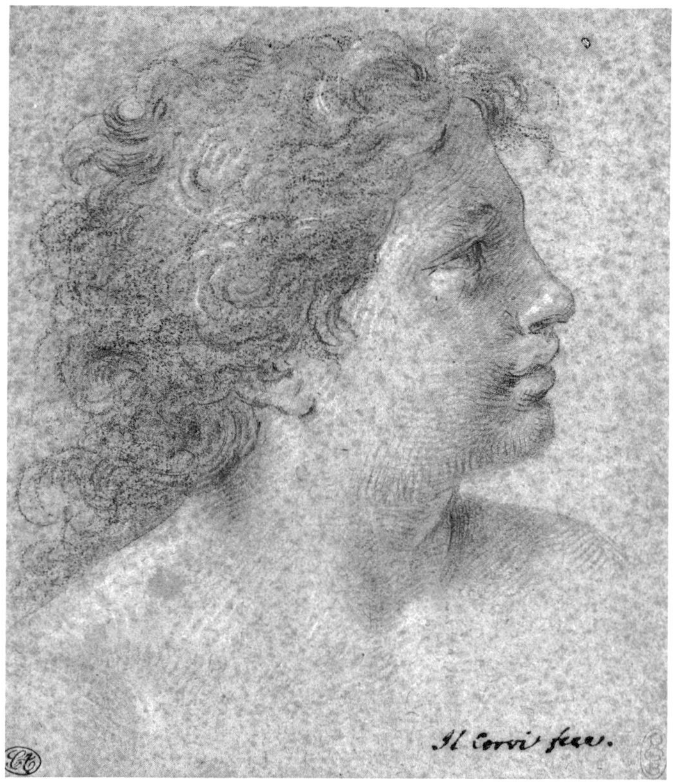

59

Corvi's early Roman activity remains obscure. In 1750 he won a first prize in painting in the competition held at the Accademia di San Luca, and his rise to prominence began shortly afterward. He was elected *accademico di San Luca* in 1756,[1] the same year that he received his first major commission, which was for the decorations in the church of the Gonfalone in Viterbo. In addition to works presumably executed for Santa Chiara al Quirinale, Rome, Corvi painted for the Roman churches of San Marcello, Santa Caterina da Siena in via Giulia, San Marco, Santa Maria Maggiore, and San Salvatore in Lauro. He also worked for a number of important Roman families including the Doria, Altieri, Barberini, and Borghese, and for many other clients in the Papal States, Piedmont, Tuscany, and Lombardy.[2]

Corvi's style combined influences from Seicento Bolognese painting (promoted by his master, Francesco Mancini) and from the mainstream of contemporary Roman painting represented by Mengs and Batoni. In the 1760s and 1770s he developed a theatrical manner joining an exhilarating illusionism with energetic poses, soft harmonies of light and color, and a compositional richness that might be termed a neoclassical "return" to the baroque. Corvi was sympathetic to the evolving taste of his century, however. A comparison of his *Sacrifice of Iphigenia* (Palazzo Borghese, Rome) of 1771–72 with the *Sacrifice of Polyxena* (Palazzo Comunale, Viterbo)[3] of approximately two decades later demonstrates his intensified pursuit of a more decidedly classical style and his movement toward a sober, meditated form of art that parallels the extreme phases of European neoclassicism. Corvi's reputation was secure in his own lifetime—on a visit to Rome in 1765, the Frenchman Joseph Lalande praised him as one of the best painters in the city after Batoni and Mengs[4]—and he was an effective and influential model for his pupils and other younger artists.

The subject of this charming study, obviously drawn from life, cannot be related to any specific painting by Corvi. The model's features resemble those of a number of adolescent boys found in the artist's works throughout his career.[5]

E.P.B.

1. *L'Accademia,* 1974, p. 140.
2. The most useful study of the artist is Faldi, 1970, pp. 78–84, 351–75; but *see also* Clark, in Chicago, et al., 1970–71, no. 80.
3. Faldi, 1970, figs. 311, 325.
4. Lalande, 1769, vol. 5, p. 263.
5. Faldi, 1970, figs. 305, 308, 309, 322, 325.

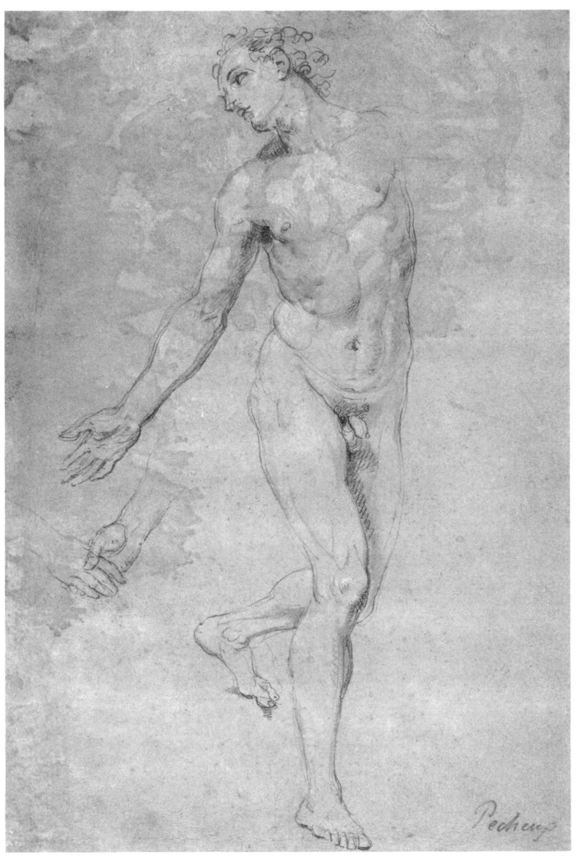

60

LAURENT PECHEUX

Lyons 1729—Turin 1821

60. *Studies for "Venus and Adonis"*

1766

Signed at lower right in black chalk: Pecheux; inscribed on verso at top in blue chalk: 518

Black chalk, some stumping, on bluish gray prepared paper

282 x 191 mm (11 1/8 x 7 1/2")

1978-70-379

Provenance: purchased in Milan, 1960

Exhibitions: Minneapolis, 1967, no. 69; Minneapolis, 1970–71

Unlike many of his compatriots, who came to Rome as *pensionnaires* of the French Academy, Laurent Pecheux arrived in 1753 unaided except by letters of introduction to Natoire, the director of the academy, to Bartolomeo Guibal, then in Mengs's studio, and to Charles-Louis Clérisseau. He became a friend of Clérisseau and through him was hired as Robert Adam's teacher for figure drawing. Through Guibal he met Mengs and was able to draw in the master's studio, although not to study with him formally; Batoni became a close friend and was invited to help lead a life class Pecheux had organized. Official recognition of his talents came with election to the Accademia di San Luca and the Accademia di Belle Arti in Parma in 1762 and to the Accademia Clementina in Bologna two years later. That year Pecheux began a trip to Venice and the principal Venetian, Emilian, and Tuscan cities. He was called to Parma as court portraitist in 1765 but returned to Rome the following year.

Pecheux remained in Rome for eleven more years, working in the Palazzo and Casino Borghese and in the Palazzo Barberini, making occasional journeys to execute portraits for the Neapolitan court and to study the excavations at Herculaneum and Pompeii. In 1777 he accepted the posts of court painter and director of the academy at Turin. In so doing he ignored the advice of friends like Batoni and Mengs who pointed out that with Batoni an old man and with Mengs in ever poorer health, Pecheux could play an important role in Roman painting.[1] In Piedmont, Pecheux established a solid academic practice and left his influence on an entire generation of Piedmontese artists.

After Pecheux's return to Rome from Parma in 1766, one of the first efforts recorded in his manuscript list of works was a painting of *Venus and Adonis,* now in Lyon,[2] for which this drawing shows a study of Adonis. Although it was painted after thirteen years' experience in Rome, and although it reveals the artist's admiration for the neoclassical principles of Batoni and Mengs, Pecheux's *Venus and Adonis* exhibits only in small degree the cool, exaggerated classicism of his later work. Instead the painting combines the lessons of his journey through Emilia—where he studied artists such as Correggio and Francesco Albani—with echoes of the rococo scale and prettiness that he knew from his youth in France.

This study differs slightly from the figure in the finished painting, which shows Adonis's shoulders set at a greater angle and his torso more emphatically twisted. The study of two hands at the left of the sheet was not used in the painting, as Cupid's outstretched arm eventually obscured Adonis's right hand. It is probable that this drawing, in which most contours are restudied, was taken from life.

M.L.M.

1. Bollea, 1942, p. 380 (information from Pecheux's autobiography).

2. Pecheux wrote an autobiography and a list of his paintings, published in the standard monograph on the artist, Bollea, 1942. For the *Venus and Adonis, see* Bollea, 1942, p. 75, fig. 16, p. 395, no. 36, p. 403, no. 6; *see also* Rome, 1959, no. 437. The painting is signed and dated Laur. Pecheux de Lyon faisoit 1766. It was acquired by the Musée des Beaux-Arts of Lyons from the artist's heirs in Turin. The signature on the drawing appears to be the same as that on the painting and is therefore acceptable as genuine.

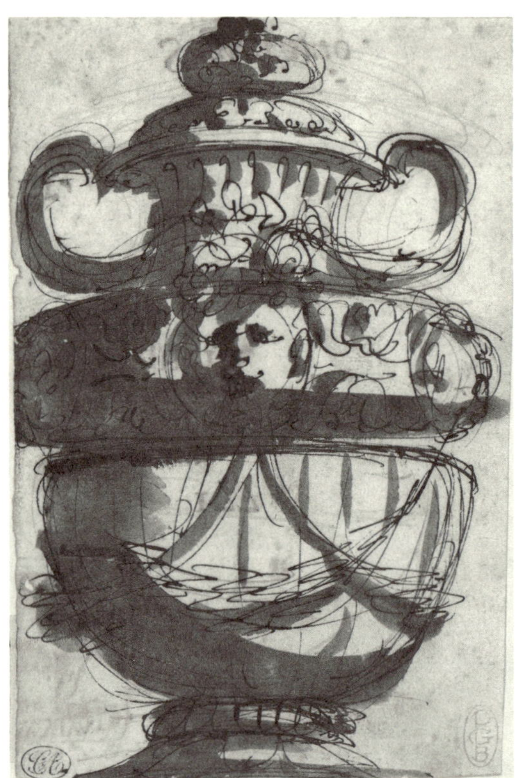

61

Attributed to IGNAZIO COLLINO

Turin 1724—Turin 1793

61. Study of a Vase

1770–80

Inscribed on verso in pencil, erased: Bozzetti di Collini

Pen and brown ink with brown wash over traces of black chalk on cream wove paper that is a printed form of the Piedmontese Royal Secretariat, bearing the open date 177–

156 x 99 mm (6 3/16 x 3 15/16″)

1978-70-242

Provenance: C. Argentieri (?) (Lugt suppl. 486^b: as anonymous mark); P. G. Braschi (?) (Lugt suppl. 2079^b: as anonymous mark); P & D Colnaghi & Co Ltd, c. 1950, as G. B. Piranesi; gift of John Maxon, c. 1955

Exhibition: Providence, 1957, no. 118 (as G. B. Piranesi)

In 1744 Ignazio Collino is documented as studying drawing in the studio of the Savoyard court painter Claudio Beaumont, and soon afterward he entered the studio of Francesco Ladatte, the French-trained, rococo-mannered sculptor to King Charles Emmanuel III. Collino was given a royal pension and was sent to Rome in late 1748 to study the ancient monuments. Pleased with his work there, Charles Emmanuel also sent the artist's younger brother Filippo (1737–1801) to Rome for instruction and to serve as Ignazio's assistant.

Two marbles commissioned by the king from Ignazio were exhibited in Rome in 1759 and were widely praised, most significantly by Cardinal Alessandro Albani and Placido Costanzi, then *principe* of the Accademia di San Luca. The next year Ignazio was elected *accademico di merito* of the Accademia di San Luca, as was Filippo three years later. When the brothers returned to Turin in 1767 they introduced into its rather provincial court the then avant-garde style of neoclassicism and proceeded to furnish the royal palaces and churches with examples of their work. The two brothers afterwards collaborated throughout their careers, and as they often co-signed their works it is nearly impossible to distinguish their separate hands. It was always Ignazio, however, who retained the greater position and renown. In 1783 he was appointed first sculptor to King Victor Amadeus III of Savoy, a position he held for the last decade of his life.[1]

This drawing was attributed to Piranesi until 1961, when Hylton Thomas suggested that the attribution was incorrect. The following year the sheet was removed from its mount, revealing on the verso the stamp of the Piedmontese Royal Secretariat with the date 177– and an erased inscription including Collino's name. The current attribution thus depends on the inscription and not on a comparison with Collino's drawings, which are virtually unknown. The style of this vase, however, is compatible with what is known of Collino's work. He is documented as having provided not only figural sculpture and reliefs for royal palaces and churches, but ornamental sculpture as well. Examples are the tomb sculptures executed by the Collino brothers for Kings Charles Emmanuel (reigned 1730–73) and Victor Amadeus (reigned 1773–96), both of which projects incorporated decorative elements. Although such neoclassical elements as fluting, masks, and garlands are employed, the vase in the Clark drawing remains rather baroque in the complexity of its basic form and outline and in the combination of its many decorative elements. It is quite unlike the severely restrained classicism of vases designed by French artists (some in Rome) as early as the 1750s, such as those by Louis-Joseph Le Lorrain around 1752, J. F. de Neufforge of 1755–56, and Joseph-Marie Vien around 1760,[2] all of which it postdates by some twenty to thirty years. The Collinos' sculpture, although quite advanced for Turin during the period and certainly much more neoclassical in style than the work of Ladatte, still retained baroque and rococo elements throughout the 1770s and beyond. As John Fleming pointed out, it was only with the example of Canova's work toward the end of Filippo Collino's life in the 1790s that the Collino brothers' sculpture moved toward a truly neoclassical mode.[3]

M.L.M.

1. On the Collino brothers, *see* Fleming, 1963; Baudi di Vesme, 1963–68, vol. 1, pp. 332–45; and Strambi, 1964, with previous bibliography.
2. *See* Eriksen, 1974, pls. 310–18, 297, 298, 323 respectively.
3. Fleming, 1963, p. 193.

ANTONIO ZUCCHI

Venice 1726—Rome 1795

62. Arcadian Scene

c. 1775

Inscribed on recto, illegibly, in black chalk; inscribed on verso in pencil: 15/2, and 156

Pen and black ink, red washes, over traces of black chalk on heavy cream laid paper

214 x 210 mm (8 3/8 x 8 1/4")

1978-70-438

Provenance: gift of John Maxon, 1963

Antonio Zucchi trained as a painter in Venice under Francesco Fontebasso and Jacopo Amigoni. After 1757 he was apparently employed to engrave plates for Robert Adam's *Ruins . . . at Spalatro* and in 1760 left Venice on a tour of Italy with James Adam and Charles-Louis Clérisseau. Zucchi worked for Adam in Italy, making drawings of antiquities and advising on the purchase of art works, an activity that included his survey, with Clérisseau and Adam, of the drawing collection of Cardinal Albani prior to its sale to George III.[1]

Established in Rome after 1761, Zucchi went to England in 1766 at Adam's invitation and there enjoyed a busy career specializing in painted interior decorations.

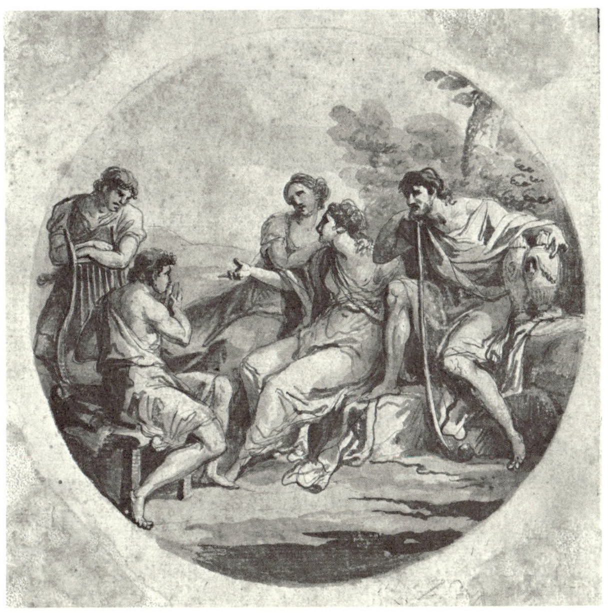

62

The wealth of classical scenes, pastoral landscapes, and architectural fantasies that the artist produced for the gallery of the duke of Northumberland at Alnwick and for Osterley Park, Kedleston Hall, Kenwood, and Syon House—to name only a few of many such projects—was described by Giovanni Gherardo de Rossi as typical of his varied and imaginative output: "Every kind of painting was commendably treated by Zucchi. Besides histories, he painted landscapes, views, ruins; he provided inventions of groups, bas-reliefs, and decorations to sculptors and to modelers in clay, and in the evening hours he created watercolor drawings, so touched with the brilliance of bold skill that they were snatched up by admirers of the fine arts."[2]

Zucchi was a frequent collaborator on decorative projects with Angelica Kauffmann and under her influence seems to have moved from a style of view painting reminiscent of Panini and Clérisseau toward neoclassical groupings of a more intimate and poetic character. Zucchi married Angelica Kauffmann in 1781, and in the following year they resettled permanently in Rome. Described by Kauffmann as her "worthy husband, friend, and best companion," Zucchi lived his remaining years overshadowed by his much younger and more illustrious wife. Ill health caused him to curtail his activity, which centered mainly on the creation of drawings.

This sheet depicts a musical contest carried out between two figures at the left, one of whom rests upon a lyre and listens while the other plays the pipes.[3] In the center a woman gestures as if to express admiration, while beside her a bearded shepherd sits, leaning upon a crook and resting his arm upon a pair of sculpted urns.

Although Zucchi's career in Venice, Rome, and England is well enough known in outline, his large output of paintings and drawings has never been systematically studied. Consequently there is little on which to base a date for this drawing, and equally uncertain is the specific project, if any, for which it was created. Typical in format of the interior panels produced in great numbers during Zucchi's peak years in England, may probably be assigned to the latter part of this period.

U.W.H.

1. For Zucchi with Adam in Italy, *see* Fleming, 1962. For Zucchi's works, with literature, *see* H. Vollmer in Thieme-Becker, 1907–50, vol. 36, pp. 576–77; Delogu, 1930, pp. 166–70; Moschini, 1957; Mayer, 1972, pp. 90 ff. For a signed landscape by Zucchi, *see* Arisi, 1961, p. 296, fig. 416; the two landscapes in the Fitzwilliam Museum, Cambridge, attributed to Zucchi by Delogu are given by Arisi (nos. 37–38) to Giovanni Paolo Panini around 1720. *See* Bregenz and Vienna, 1968–69, nos. 498–502.

2. De Rossi, 1811, p. 84.

3. An old inscription on an earlier mat, according to Clark's notes, contained the words "La disputa dell. . . ."

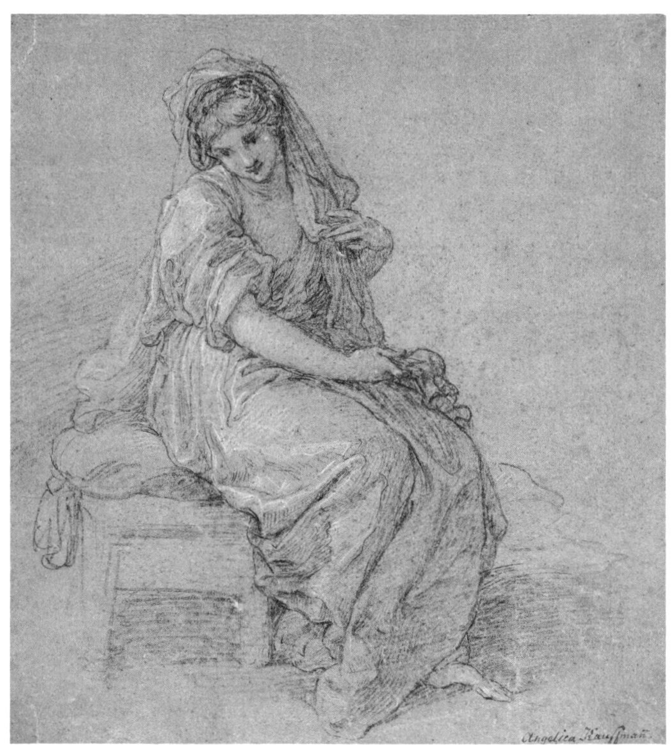

63

MARIA ANNE ANGELICA
CATHERINE KAUFFMANN

Coire (Switzerland) 1741—Rome 1807

63. Study of a Seated Woman Wearing a Veil

c. 1770

Signed in brown ink at lower right: Angelica Kauffmañ.

Black and white chalks on blue gray prepared paper

275 x 253 mm (10 13/16 x 9 15/16")

1978-70-311

Provenance: purchased from Mathias Komor, New York, 1964

Exhibition: Minneapolis, 1967, no. 50

Despite Angelica Kauffmann's wide renown as a portraitist and painter of historical and mythological subjects—the international character of her patrons is comparable to that of Batoni, Canova, and Élizabeth Vigée-Lebrun—her oeuvre remains undefined; as a consequence her name can be misassigned to a bewildering variety of late-eighteenth-century drawings and paintings. A precocious artistic and musical talent, she trained early with her father, a minor ecclesiastical muralist active in Switzerland, Austria, and northern Italy; they journeyed together to Rome in 1763. In Italy she met and exchanged portrait drawings with the young Benjamin West,[1] painted Winckelmann's portrait, and made the acquaintance of Cardinal Albani; she also met and nearly became engaged to the painter Nathaniel Dance. This first stay in Rome and Naples was short (1763–65) but crucial to her development as one of the leading practitioners of the neoclassical style.

Kauffmann and her father left for England via Venice and Paris, arriving in London in 1766. Two years later she became one of the two female founding members of the Royal Academy there (the other was Mary Moser, a flower painter). She was a friend of Joshua Reynolds and quickly picked up important portrait commissions, becoming quite the rage in London art circles.[2] After a brief and disastrous first marriage she wed the painter Antonio Zucchi (*see* no. 62) in 1781 and returned to Rome with him in 1782, settling near the Trinità dei Monti. Her elegant neoclassical style was much in demand and, except for extended visits to Naples in the early 1780s, she remained in Rome most of the rest of her life. Of her former circle. Winckelmann had died in 1768 and Batoni was quite old; Cardinal Albani had died in 1779, but that year also marked the arrival of the young Canova in Rome, and he and Kauffmann became close friends. She was also acquainted with Goethe during the latter's sojourn in Rome from 1786 to 1788 and designed illustrations in 1787 for the poet's *Iphigenie auf Tauris* in its second, verse version and for his historical drama *Egmont.* As a token of his regard for the artist, Goethe planted a pine tree in her garden on the occasion of his departure from Rome.[3]

This study of a seated woman, unlike many drawings, may be confidently given to Angelica, as it is close in style to several securely attributed works.[4] The signature, though perhaps added later, is unquestionably genuine. The drawing appears to date to her stay in London, as it is looser than her earlier Italian studies and possesses a markedly French flavor—both in the treatment of drapery and the coquettishness of pose—that is likely to have only fully emerged in her drawing style after she passed through Paris on her way to London in 1766. The sheet is related to two portrait studies in the Witt Collection, Courtauld Institute Galleries, London, of Anne Seymour Damer (1766) and the marchioness Townshend and her son (c. 1780), thus suggesting a date of about 1770.[5]

P.W./A.P.

1. Robert C. Alberts, *Benjamin West: A Biography,* Boston, 1978, pp. 47–48, 426, 478.
2. Ibid., p. 100.
3. On Kauffmann, *see* Clark in Bregenz and Vienna, 1968, pp. 5–17; Brigante Colonna, 1932, especially pp. 99 ff.; Waterhouse, 1962, p. 185; Storrs, 1973, pp. 120–21, and nos. 114–15.
4. Comparable in type are several drawings of seated female figures in the so-called Vallardi album—a group of 137 drawings from Angelica's first Roman period given or sold by her to the Milanese dealer Giuseppe Vallardi (*see* Lugt 1223) in 1800 and now in the Victoria and Albert Museum (*see* Walch, 1977).
5. Inv. nos. 4351, 3553; repr. Bregenz and Vienna, 1968–69, figs. 226, 227.

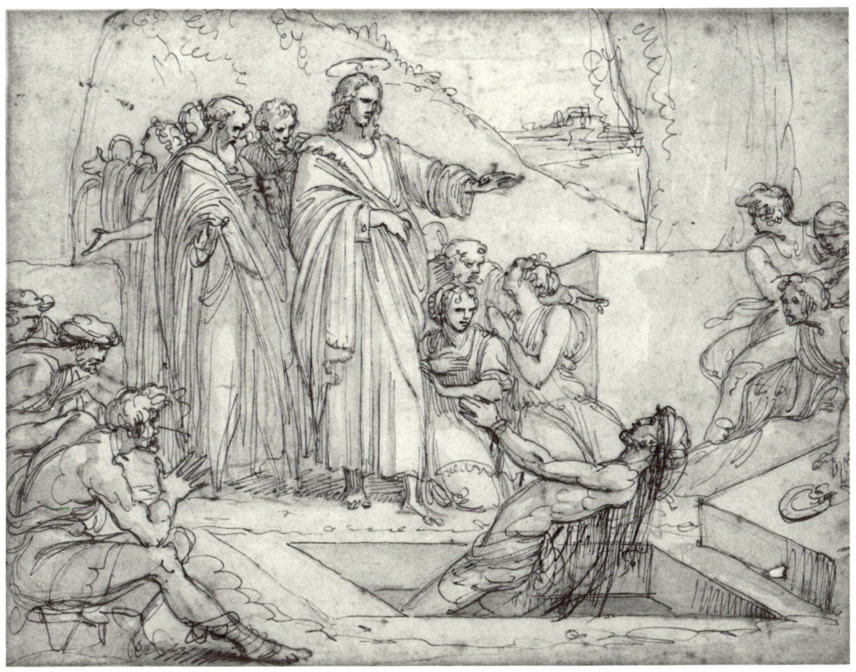

64

GIUSEPPE CADES

Rome 1750 (?)—Rome 1799

64. The Resurrection of Lazarus

c. 1770

Pen and brown ink, brown wash, over black chalk on cream paper, mounted down

185 x 236 mm (7 5/16 x 9 5/16")

1978-70-212

Provenance: Gatty collection; sale, Christie's, London, March 18, 1959, lot 43; purchased from R. E. Lewis, San Francisco, 1959

After the Batoni drawings, the most sizable and distinguished holdings by any one artist in the Clark collection are the drawings of Giuseppe Cades, an artist whom Anthony Clark virtually discovered as a draughtsman.[1] Despite his relatively short career, Cades was an important history painter and decorator in Rome. His paintings and drawings, which could vary in style from the baroque to the neoclassical, often appear to be fifty years ahead of their time in their quality of historical revivalism. His role as a draughtsman in Rome during the last quarter of the eighteenth century, his relation to the Fuseli circle there, and his influence on later draughtsmen-decorators such as Felice Giani are all subjects still to be explored.

This sheet appears to be the only known version of the resurrection of Lazarus produced by the artist. The broad, balanced composition, as well as the freedom in pose and arrangement of the figures, reveals a confident draughtsman who had already absorbed the lessons of the great Renaissance masters. Nonetheless, the drawing's somewhat dry technique and the use of rather uniform parallel hatchings to render such parts as faces and draperies suggest a relatively early date, around the late 1760s or early 1770s; the sheet is closely related, in fact, to a signed, dated drawing of *Hercules* of 1768 in the Nationalmuseum, Stockholm.[2] At that time, hardly past adolescence, Cades—who according to tradition was at one time a pupil of Domenico Corvi—was training himself by drawing after earlier masters and was simultaneously influenced by German, Scandinavian, and French artists who were then flocking to Rome.[3] He was establishing a reputation both in Rome and in southern France and was beginning to receive important commissions. In 1766 he won first prize in the second-class painting competition at the Accademia di San Luca. His painting of the *Virgin* was exhibited in the Hôtel de Ville, Toulouse, in 1775, an event that was followed by many other exhibitions in the region of the French Pyrenees.[4] His commissions of the 1770s included paintings for the church of Santi Apostoli in Rome (c. 1770); for the convent of San Benigno di Fruttuaria, church of Santa Maria Assunta, San Benigno Canavese, Turin (1774); and for decorations, for the Sala di Musica in the Palazzo Senatorio in Rome (1779).

From the 1780s until his death at the age of about forty-nine, Cades enjoyed growing success among his contemporaries. A member of the Accademia di San Luca from 1786, he worked chiefly in Rome and its environs, numbering among his patrons Empress Catherine II of Russia, Lord Arundel, and many religious orders, churches, and convents in various regions of Italy. His most important commissions around Rome included the decorations for two rooms in the Palazzo Chigi in Ariccia with subjects from Ariosto, the ceiling of a second-floor *camerino* of the Casino Borghese depicting a scene from Boccaccio, and decorations in the *appartamento neoclassico* in the Palazzo Altieri. The dispersal of Cades's paintings and drawings after his death, as well as the tendency of nineteenth-century writers to dismiss his work as that of a mere follower of the school of Maratta, resulted in the near-obliteration of his reputation. The 1959 exhibition *Il Settecento a Roma,* followed by the numerous discoveries of Anthony Clark, restored Cades to his deserved position in the history of Roman eighteenth-century painting and draughtsmanship, revealing him as an independent master who, far from concluding an era, appears in retrospect to have anticipated the succeeding one.[5]

M.T.C.

1. Clark, 1964, summarizes the artist's career.

2. Inv. no. NMH 1940/1875. Cades's very early period is documented by a group of signed drawings bearing dates of 1762 and 1763: Paris, Louvre, Cabinet des Dessins, *Rest on the Flight into Egypt,* 1762 (inv. no. 36019); Rouen, Musée des Beaux-Arts, *Angels Playing Trumpets,* 1762 (Fonds Baderou; inv. no. 975-4-1836); Paris, private collection, *Study of a Woman,* 1762; Paris, private collection, *Adam and Eve,* 1762; Rome, private collection, *Christ and the Apostles,* 1763.

3. *See* Clark, 1964, p. 19. Pierre Rosenberg pointed out the relationship between the Clark *Resurrection of Lazarus* and two paintings by Jean Jouvenet: the first, of the same subject (Louvre, inv. no. 5489), was engraved by Jean Audran; the other, a *Christ Healing the Paralytic,* was engraved by Nicolas Henry Tardieu, Cornelius Vermeulen, and Etienne Picart. Through the circulation of engravings, which had considerable importance at the end of the eighteenth century, Roman painters were becoming familiar with French history painting of the seventeenth century (*see also* Caracciolo, 1978 ["Storia"], p. 73).

4. The prize drawing, once thought to be lost, has been found at the Accademia di San Luca; it represents *Tobias Restoring His Father's Sight,* and two preparatory versions are in the Nationalmuseum in Stockholm. For Cades's *Virgin, see Les Expositions de l'Academie Royale de Toulouse de 1751 à 1791,* ed. R. Mesuret, Toulouse, 1972, p. 275; *see also* Caracciolo, 1978 ("Storia"), pp. 74–95.

5. An encapsulation of the components influencing Cades's style is found in Clark, in Chicago, et al., 1970–71, pp. 184, 186.

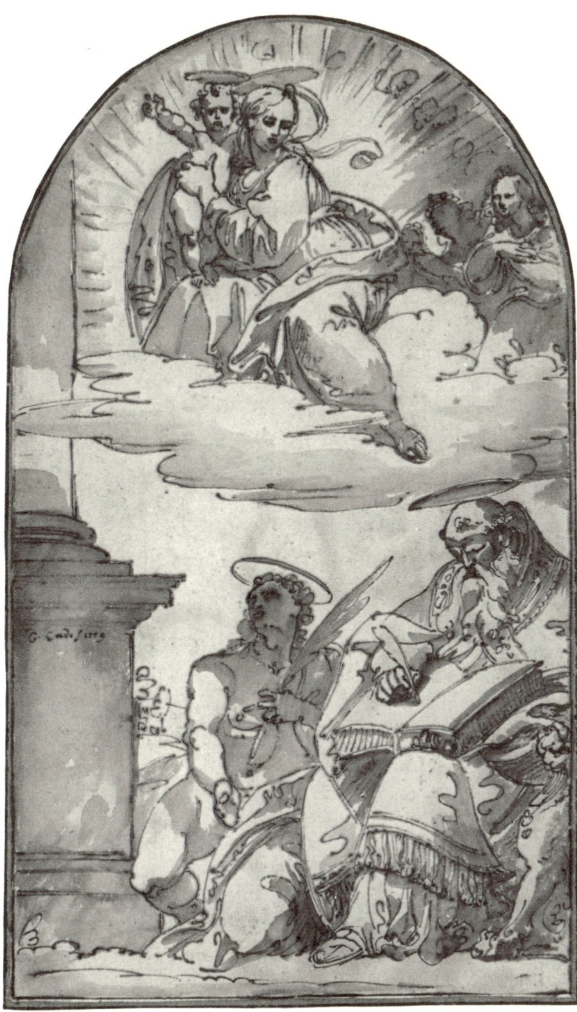

65

65. *The Virgin and Child with Two Saints*

1779

Signed and dated in brown ink at left: G. Cades 1779

Pen and brown ink, brown washes, on cream paper, mounted down

242 x 140 mm (9 1/2 x 5 1/2")

1978-70-210

Provenance: H. S. Reitlinger (Lugt suppl. 2274[a], on mount); sale, Christie's, London, June 22, 1956, lot 15; purchased from Swetzoff Gallery, Boston, 1956

Exhibition: Providence, 1957, no. 45

No painting related to this signed and dated sheet, which documents Cades's manner at the end of the 1770s, is known. The identification of the two saints is likewise problematical.[1] The drawing antedates by two years a painting completed in 1781 for the cathedral of Ascoli Piceno that represents *Saint Peter Appearing to Saints Lucy and Agatha.*[2] In the painting, as in many of Cades's later religious pictures, the foreground figures and the column defining the space to one side recall certain classicizing Bolognese paintings of the seventeenth century, especially those of Guercino, whom Cades particularly admired.[3] This drawing confirms that Cades's interest in Guercino predated his trip to northern Italy and his stay in Cento around 1785–86.

In this mature work the somewhat dry and stiff manner of the early period has disappeared; wash highlights —which in other drawings are often heightened by touches of watercolor or gouache—mold the volumes, while meticulous contours sharply define each shape. Whereas for composition and subject matter Cades most often refers back to the Carracci, Guido Reni, and Guercino, his handling of outline and somewhat récherché figure style demonstrates his continuous, strong ties to the traditions of Roman and Bolognese Mannerism.[4]

M.T.C.

1. Anthony Clark identified the saint seated and writing as Saint Augustine and the martyred saint as Saint Sebastian. The latter bears a marked resemblance to a sheet in the Cades album in Lisbon showing Saint Sebastian bound to a tree (Museu Nacional de Arte Antiga; inv. no. 2142) and to a sketch in the Porto museum for a painting of *The Holy Monstrance Appearing to Saints Sebastian and Nicholas of Bari* (inv. no. 427). On the other hand, the so-called Saint Augustine may actually be Saint Bonaventure of Bagnorea (Bagnoregio), who often appears in Cades's work (*Saint Bonaventure Writing*, formerly in the church of Santa Maria la Nova in Montecelio, now in the Palazzo Venezia, Rome, 1790; a lost *Saints Bonaventure and Francis* related to sheets 2163 and 2192 in the Lisbon album, formerly in Santa Maria la Nova in Montecelio; and a *Saint Francis Praying to the Virgin for Saint Bonaventure* in the church of San Francesco in Bagnoregio, 1796).

2. Now on deposit in the Pinacoteca, Ascoli Piceno.

3. For Guercino's influence on Cades, *see* Caracciolo, 1978.

4. Other drawings related in style, subject matter, or date are in the Art Gallery of Ontario, Toronto (*Virgin and Child with Three Saints;* Purchase 1970), The Hermitage, Leningrad (*Studies for the Costumes of the "Seven Planets,"* 1780; inv. no. 43421; Caracciolo, 1978 ["Storia"], pp. 78–95, fig. 22), and a private collection (two studies for the *Annunciation*; Caracciolo, 1973, pp. 4–5, figs. 8, 9).

66. *Caricature of Pompeo Batoni*

c. 1780

Pen and brown ink on cream laid paper

113 x 83 mm (4 7/16 x 3 1/4")

1978-70-204

Provenance: gift of Giuliano Briganti, 1970

This drawing, which was first attributed to the artist by Anthony Clark and identified by him as a caricature of Pompeo Batoni, is one of a small number of caricatures by Cades known today.[1] The subject does indeed re-

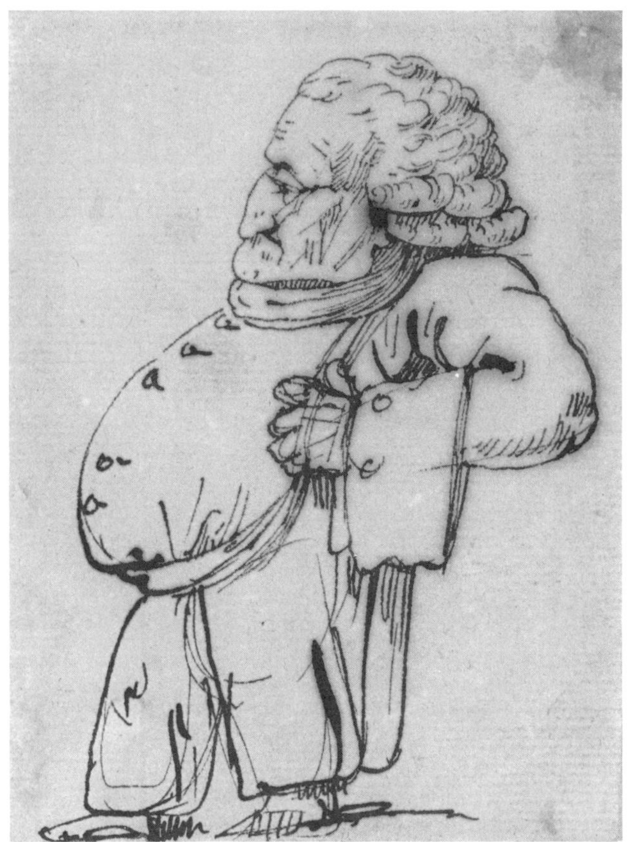

66

semble the self-portraits of the middle-aged Batoni in the Galleria degli Uffizi, Florence, and the Amedeo Cenami collection, Lucca.[2] In Cades's caricature, Batoni seems older, which confirms the dating proposed by Clark of around 1780. The draughtsmanship has more in common with the styles of certain foreign artists who had worked in Rome, such as the French painter François-Andre Vincent or the Swedish sculptor Johan Tobias Sergel, than it does with that of the most famous Roman master of caricature prior to Cades, Pier Leone Ghezzi (*see* nos. 12–14).

M.T.C.

1. A few caricatures by Cades from the Pacetti collection are preserved in the Kupferstichkabinett of the Staatliche Museen, West Berlin. Anthony Clark also owned a self-caricature of the artist with his close colleague, the engraver Tommaso Piroli (c. 1750–1824; *see* checklist no. 28; exh. Minneapolis, 1967, no. 19), which he dated around the same time as the present sheet, as well as the caricature of a Roman scholar or cicerone (checklist no. 27; exh. Minneapolis, 1967, no. 20). A few caricature studies appear at the top of a sheet representing *Saint Anne* on the Roman market in 1967 (Rome, W. Apolloni, *Disegni antichi,* December 5–24, 1967, no. 66).

2. *See* Lucca, 1967, nos. 48, 49, repr.; the former is dated 1772, the latter 1773–74.

67. *Allegory with Minerva Sheltering a Female Figure Holding a Celestial Globe*

1780–90

Inscribed on verso in brown ink in an old hand: Giorgio Vasari 1511–1574; in black chalk: 4010; and in pencil: 7142/4

Pen and brown ink, brown washes, blue and rose watercolor, on heavy gray laid paper; scored at right edge

208 x 267 mm (8 3/16 x 10 1/2")

1978-70-216

Provenance: sale, Sotheby's, London, March 27, 1969, lot 69 (as Bellona and another female allegory); Folio Fine Art Ltd., London, May 1969; sale, Christie's, London, June 29, 1971, lot 190 (as female allegories of Geography and War); gift of Fabrizio Apolloni, 1971

Of all the works by Giuseppe Cades, the mythological subjects remain the least known and most poorly documented. His interpretations of such themes are often complex and difficult to understand, which may be due in many cases to the patrons' intervention. Nevertheless, the artist's special interest in mythology indicates a certain independence of Davidian neoclassicism and an affirmation of his ties with Roman tradition renewed in his own personal terms. Cades's mythological subjects also suggest his rapport with northern artists active in Rome around the 1780s and especially with Angelica Kauffmann and her followers.

Cades's earliest mythologies may have been influenced by Johan Tobias Sergel's Roman works, as well as by those of Fuseli. His drawing of Mars and Venus in the Museo Horne in Florence,[1] for example, may well have been inspired by Sergel's highly acclaimed Mars and Venus of 1774.[2] During the 1780s mythology and ancient history blend in Cades's work like threads in a single discourse. In 1779, in collaboration with Giacomo Quarenghi, he completed the new music room that Don Abbondio Rezzonico, senator of Rome, had commissioned for his palace on the Capitoline.[3] The following year he decorated a ceiling in the Palazzo Ruspoli on the via del Corso with a scene of Venus weeping over the body of Adonis.[4] During the summer months of 1784 he produced some easel paintings with scenes of Ceres for Catherine II of Russia[5] and began to decorate a room with Apollo and the Muses (now destroyed) in the Palazzo Chigi in Piazza Colonna, on the commission of Prince Sigismondo Chigi.[6]

A group of highly finished allegorical or mythological drawings in ink, wash, and watercolor now in the Hermitage may relate, along with this drawing, to the Rezzonico or Chigi commissions, both of which have themes related to music.[7] When it was sold at auction in 1969 the Clark *Minerva* was accompanied by a pen-

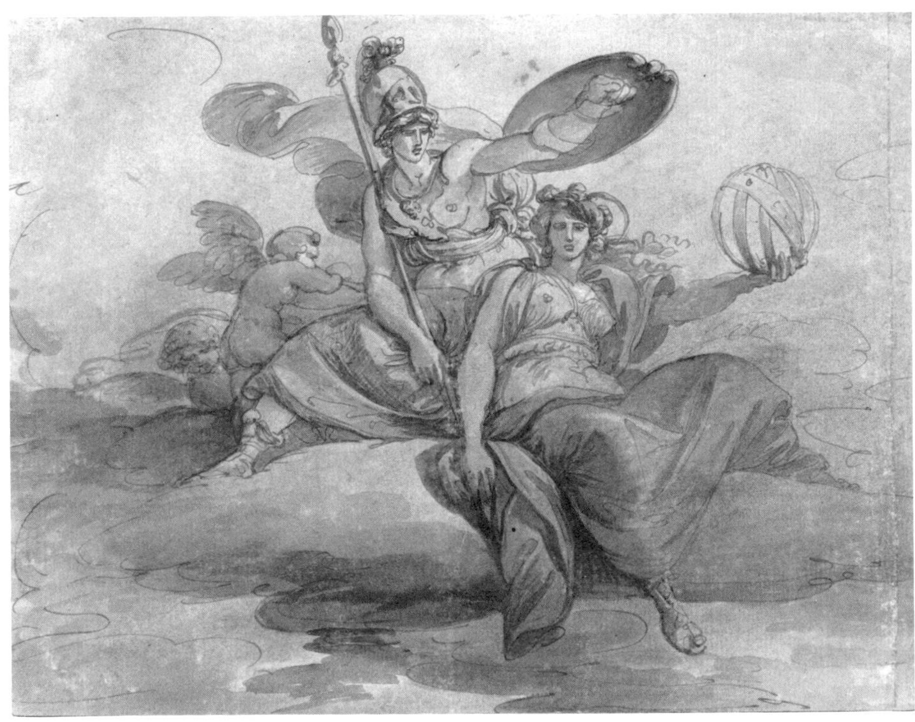

67

dant of about the same size and executed in the same technique, showing *Mercury Crowning a Winged Female Figure.*[8] Unfortunately it is impossible to tell whether the *Minerva* and *Mercury* were originally conceived for either of these commissions and were later changed or rejected; however, they can safely be placed among the mythological and allegorical subjects produced by Cades during the 1780s.

M.T.C.

1. Inv. no. 5589; Clark, 1964, p. 20, repr. pl. 7.
2. The sculpture is now in the Nationalmuseum, Stockholm; for its influence on Roman artists, *see* Hartmann, 1957, pp. 147–48.
3. Pietrangeli, 1963, pp. 244–47; Caracciolo, 1973, pp. 2, 4–5.
4. The attribution of this unpublished ceiling, based on documents, is due to Olivier Michel (who kindly brought it to my attention). Lanzi, 1968, vol. 1, p. 424, notes that Cades had worked for Prince Ruspoli, without, however, specifying the nature of the works executed.
5. *Giornale*, 1784–87, vol. 1, pp. 266–84, 285, 293, 296.
6. Di Macco, 1973–74.
7. Formerly in the Yussupov collection. The subjects include *Two Winged Female Figures* (inv. no. 20560), *Glory and Love* (?) (inv. no. 20561), *Two Muses* (inv. no. 20562), *Apollo and Minerva* (inv. no. 43412), *A Winged Genius* (inv. no. 20559), and *Two Allegorical Female Figures* (inv. no. 20558); *see* M. V. Dobroklonski, *Italian Drawings in The Hermitage,* Leningrad, 1961, nos. 848–51, 853–54.
8. Drawing auctioned at Sotheby's, London, March 27, 1969, lot 70, repr.

68. *Two Studies for Candelabra*

1780–90

Inscribed on verso in black chalk: per [pour?] biscuit Volpato

Pen and brown ink, brown and pink washes, over traces of black chalk on cream laid paper

208 x 233 mm (8 3/16 x 9 1/8″)

Watermark: Pietro M [cut off]

1978-70-218

Provenance: purchased from Plinio Nardecchia, Rome, 1963

Anthony Clark tentatively suggested in his manuscript notes that these two studies of figures supporting candelabra may be preparatory drawings for decorative objects executed either in silver or porcelain. Though there is evidence that Cades did produce designs for sculptures—a red-chalk drawing in the Biblioteca Nacional in Madrid can be identified as a preliminary design for a sarcophagus-shaped fountain celebrating the heroes who died for the Roman Republic of 1798–99—his possible activity as a designer of decorative objects is not documented either through surviving works or records of commissions.[1] The sheet exhibited here thus remains relatively isolated in Cades's oeuvre, although two very close ink-and-wash replicas of the individual figures—slightly more developed in the details of the young man's face and in the drapery of the seated woman—are preserved on two separate sheets in an album of assorted drawings in the Museu Nacional de Arte Antiga in Lisbon.[2] The meticulous detail and clear, precise outlines of the Lisbon drawings confirm beyond doubt the

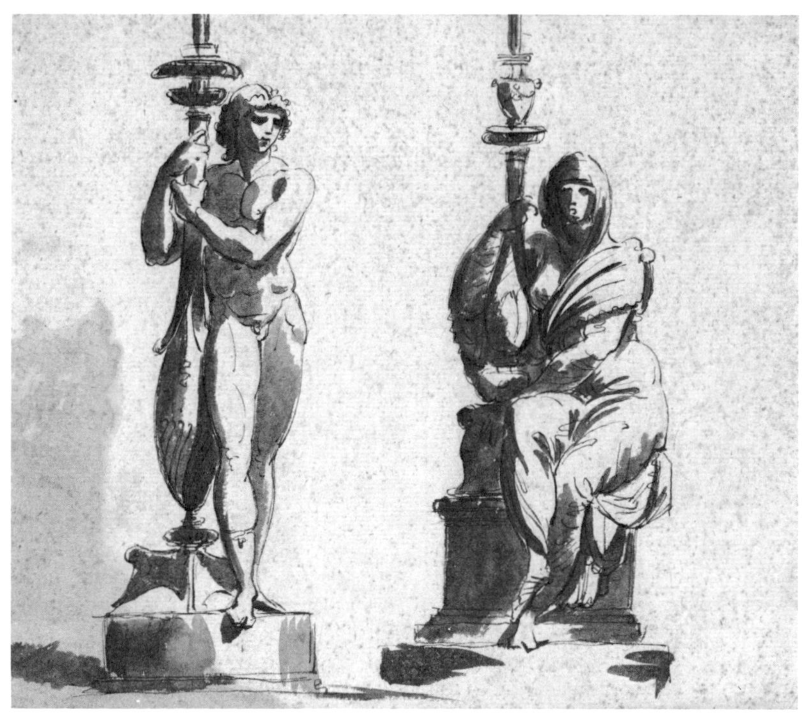

68

attribution of the present sheet to Cades. The experienced handling of the wash used to render the play of light and shadow suggests a dating in the 1780s.

An inscription on the verso suggests that these figures may have been used in preparation for works in biscuit produced at the porcelain manufactory of Giovanni Volpato (1733–1803).[3] Volpato, a native of the Veneto, had been active in Rome since 1771, frequenting, with Cades, the circle of Venetians at Palazzo Venezia and the palace of Don Abbondio Rezzonico. Antonio Canova described in his diary an evening spent in the company of the two artists,[4] and there is otherwise much evidence concerning Cades's involvement with this Venetian milieu;[5] thus, it is a possibility, at present unsubstantiated, that Cades did indeed contribute designs for Volpato's manufactory.

M.T.C.

1. Clark, 1964, p. 24, pl. 15.
2. Inv. no. 2128 (*Nude Youth*, 235 x 110 mm); inv. no. 2129 (*Draped and Seated Woman*, 235 x 110 mm).
3. For Giovanni Volpato's manufactory, located in the via di Santa Pudenziana, Rome, *see* Morazzone, 1935, p. 94; Honour ("Statuettes"), 1967; Biavati, 1977; Canova, 1959, pp. 47–48.
4. Canova, 1959, pp. 56, 137.
5. For example, the decoration of the new music room in the Palazzo Senatorio (*see* no. 67). In 1780, Cades designed the costumes of the *Seven Planets* for a masquerade staged at a ball given by Ambassador Girolamo Zulian on April 17 in Palazzo Venezia to honor the Hapsburg archduke Ferdinand and his wife, Maria Beatrice d'Este-Cybo (*see* Caracciolo, 1978 ["Storia"], pp. 78–95, fig. 22).

69. *Bacchus and Ariadne*

c. 1785–90

Inscribed in pencil at upper right, very faintly: 89

Pen and black ink, with brown washes, over traces of black chalk, on cream laid paper, mounted down

345 x 440 mm (13 5/8 x 17 5/16")

1978-70-213

Provenance: Walker's Gallery, London, 1962; gift of Keith Andrews, 1962

Exhibitions: Cleveland, 1964, no. 99, repr.; Minneapolis, 1967, no. 18; Bregenz and Vienna, 1968–69, no. 132, repr.; Minneapolis, Minnesota, The Minneapolis Institute of Arts, *A Loan Exhibition of Drawings and Watercolors from Minnesota Private Collections,* May 13–June 13, 1971, no. 13, repr.

This drawing is a fine example of Cades's mature style at the end of the 1780s. Related to several late drawings depicting Lucretia and Alexander the Great,[1] it demonstrates the essential linearity of the artist's drawing style as well as his taste for full, very finished compositions. In direct contrast to the Batoni holdings in the Clark collection, most of the Cades drawings are not preparatory studies for paintings but seem to have been produced as ends in themselves. One is reminded that throughout his career Cades made drawings for sale in imitation of —or rather, "in the manner of"—old masters.[2]

The subject is taken from Ovid's *Ars amatoria* (I, ll. 527 ff) and represents the encounter between Bacchus and Ariadne after she had been abandoned by Theseus on the island of Naxos. Bacchus's face and torso seem to have been directly inspired by Annibale Carracci's *Bacchus* in the Palazzo Farnese.

M.T.C.

1. *See* Caracciolo, 1978 ("Storia"), pp. 77–78, 82–83, figs. 10–14.
2. *See* especially Clark, 1964, p. 22.

70. Orpheus Charming the Animals (The Invention of Music?)

c. 1790

Inscribed in brown ink at lower right: Cades

Pen and brown ink, with brown washes, over traces of black chalk, on cream laid paper, mounted down

194 x 334 mm (7 5/8 x 13 1/8")

1978-70-215

Provenance: sale, Christie's, London, July 7, 1959, lot 77; purchased from Rockman Prints, New York, 1959

This example of Cades's allegorical and mythological drawings appears to date somewhat later than the *Minerva* allegory (no. 67), perhaps around 1790. The subject is difficult to identify.[1] The figure in the background appears to be Orpheus charming the animals, but the female figure in the foreground and the *amoretti* wielding hammers at an anvil currently defy identification. The artist repeated the Orpheus group in reverse on a separate sheet now in the Louvre.[2] The Louvre drawing, executed with pen and wash in an assured, neo-Mannerist style, demonstrates the brilliance of Cades's best work, a quality that this drawing lacks. A second, almost identical version of the composition, also owned by Anthony Clark, could be an autograph copy of the present sheet but more likely represents a preliminary stage of work;[3] unsigned, this sheet recalls the quick, rough pencil and pen studies for Cades's *Orlando furioso* scenes in the Camera dell' Ariosto in the Palazzo Chigi, Ariccia.[4] Both drawings demonstrate the style of Cades's preliminary processes, in which he sought to lay out compositions rather than observe detail. Such preliminary drawings were usually followed by more finished, pictorial studies, which immediately preceded transfer of the composition to canvas or wall.

M.T.C.

1. Anthony Clark, in his manuscript notes, refers to a version of the allegory (minus Orpheus) by Cavallucci in the Palazzo Caetani, Rome, of about 1786, and to an *Origin of Music* or *Mercury Playing the Lyre* by Cades owned by a James Byres in 1790.
2. Inv. no. RF 34511. *See* Caracciolo, 1978 ("Storia"), pp. 79, 84, repr. fig. 21.
3. Checklist no. 29. This drawing is on exactly the same paper as the sheet exhibited here and the image is the same

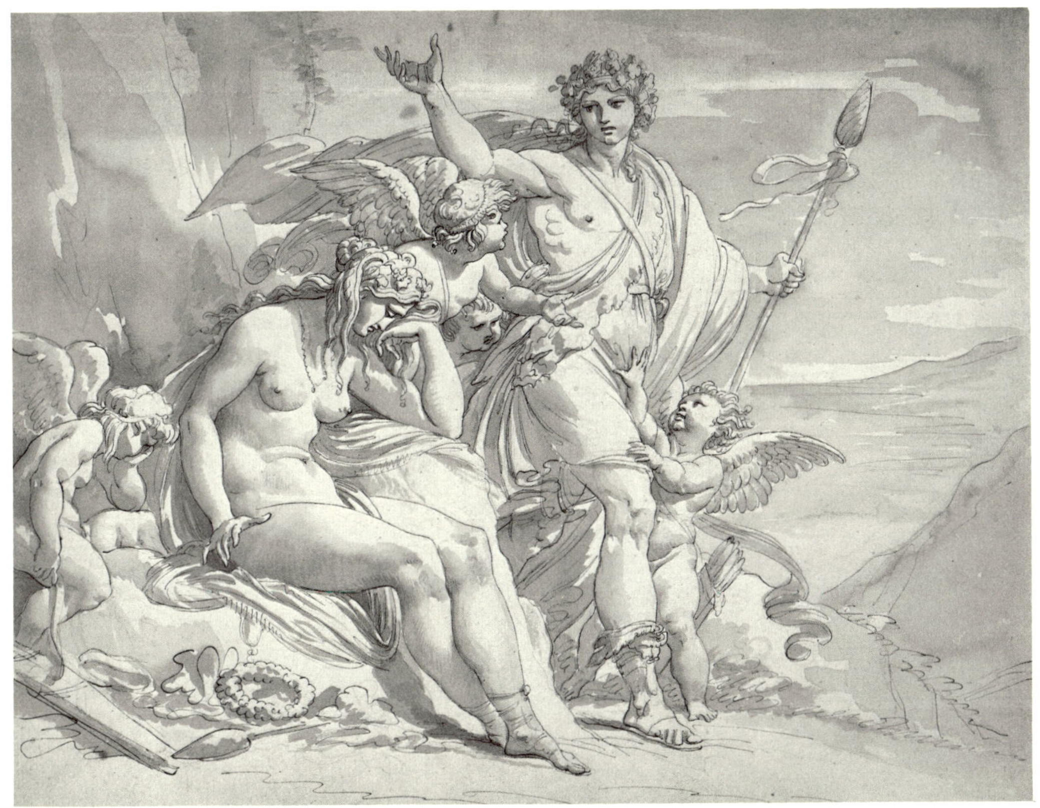

69

size. The sheet bears a watermark, partly cut off, with the initials JH & Z. It was bought from Rockman Prints, New York, in 1958.

4. Di Macco, 1973–74, pp. 355, 363–64, figs. 8, 13–15.

71. Saint Francis Xavier Embarking for India

c. 1790

Signed in brown ink at lower left: Cades. dis.; signed on verso (or inscribed in an old hand) in black chalk: Cades fece

Pen and brown ink and brown washes, over faint traces of black chalk, on cream laid paper

132 x 84 mm (5 3/16 x 3 5/16″)

1978-70-211

Provenance: gift of Helene Seiferheld, 1960

Exhibitions: Minneapolis, 1967, no. 17; Minneapolis, 1970–71

Bibliography: Caracciolo, 1973, p. 9

As Anthony Clark suggests, the central figure of this composition is probably the missionary Saint Francis Xavier, shown embarking from Lisbon in 1541 on a mission to India at the behest of King John III of Portugal and Ignatius of Loyola.[1] The subject is not unusual for Cades, as he often depicted Portuguese and Spanish religious or historical figures, a peculiar propensity for which he, along with Antonio Cavallucci, must have enjoyed some form of official sanction in Roman circles.[2] Public collections in Portugal today contain a number of works by Cades,[3] and the Portuguese church in Rome, San Luigi dei Portoghesi, commissioned from him an altarpiece around the end of the 1790s with a subject from Portuguese history.[4]

From the end of the 1780s to the mid 1790s, with the important commission for five altarpieces for the convent of San Francesco in Fabriano, Cades's output consisted largely of religious subjects. These were drawn especially from sixteenth- and seventeenth-century history, exhibiting something of the "Troubadour Style" that was encouraged officially in French painting at the end of the eighteenth century and was to spread throughout Europe during the course of the next century.[5] This sheet probably dates to the same period, which represents one of the most striking of Cades's official career in Rome; its draughtsmanship reflects the neo-Mannerist interests common to many artists at the time (nos. 83, 96), while the reference to manuscript illumination implied in its small scale places this work within the tradition of medieval or Renaissance "revivalism."

M.T.C.

1. On Francis Xavier, *see* no. 29.

2. *See* Clark, in *Dizionario biografico,* 1960–, vol. 16, pp. 72–78.

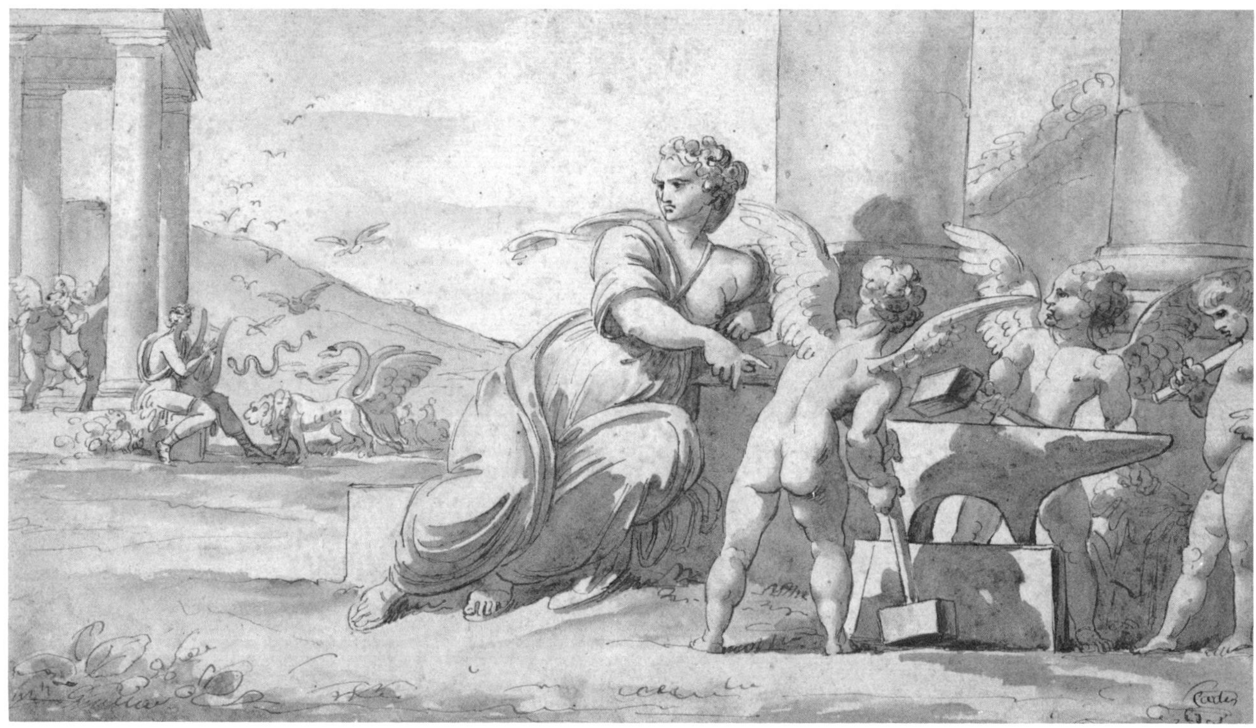

70

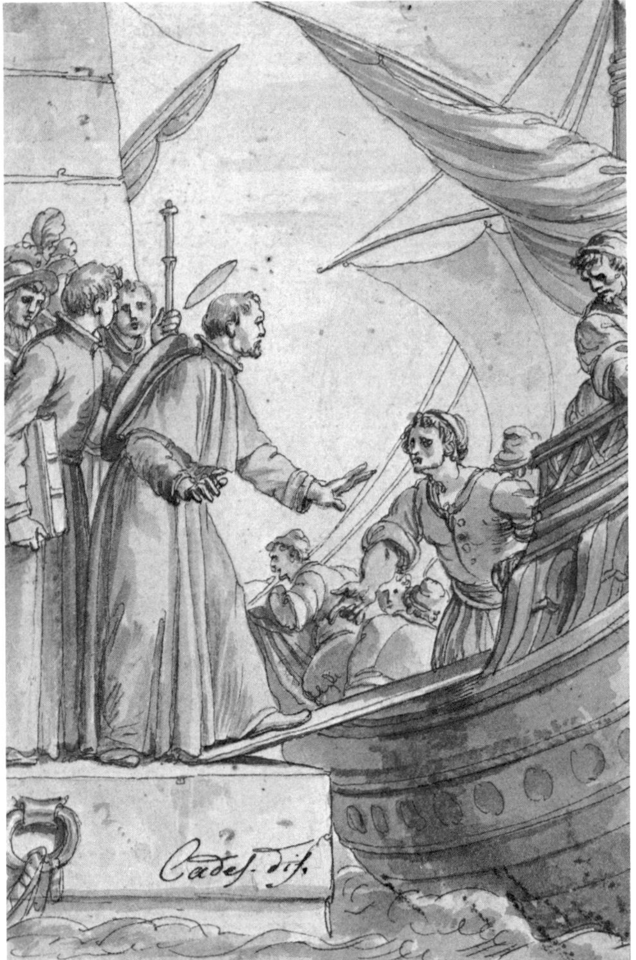

71

72. *Portrait of a Lady*

1788

Signed and dated in black chalk at bottom right: Cades—1788

Black chalk, some stumping, and red wash on cream laid paper

233 x 176 mm (9 1/8 x 6 7/8")

1978-70-207

Provenance: Christopher Powney, London, 1964; purchased from Yvonne ffrench, London, 1965

Exhibitions: London, Alpine Club, *Old Master Drawings Presented by Yvonne ffrench,* May 18–29, 1965, no. 32, repr.; Minneapolis, 1967, no. 22; Minneapolis, 1970–71

Bibliography: Caracciolo, 1973, p. 9

Giuseppe Cades's talent as a portraitist remains little known and poorly documented; in painting we know only the two self-portraits in the Accademia di San Luca in Rome.[1] The three drawn portraits in the Clark collection probably constitute the most important examples of the few that have turned up to date (*see also* nos. 73, 74).[2] Nevertheless, Cades must have been an accomplished portraitist and advanced for his time in avoiding the established Batonian mode, which pre-

3. For example, an oil in Lisbon, Museu Nacional de Arte Antiga (inv. no. 456) and an album containing 126 drawings by Cades from the collection of the Portuguese painter Domingos Antonio de Sequeira (1768–1837). *See also* several canvases in Porto, in the Museu Nacional de Soares dos Reis (inv. nos. 5, 11, 422, 427, 429, 547) and the Museu Romantico (inv. nos. 563, 566).

4. This work, however, never progressed beyond the stage of sketches and drawings; *see* Caracciolo, 1977, pp. 264–65, figs. 17, 20.

5. For example, the drawing dated 1795 of *Christ Appearing to the Blessed Angelina da Marsciano* (Museu Nacional de Arte Antiga, Lisbon) and the painting of *Saint Francis Praying to the Virgin for Saint Bonaventure* of 1796 (Bagnoregio, church of San Francesco; *see also* Caracciolo, 1977, pp. 262–64).

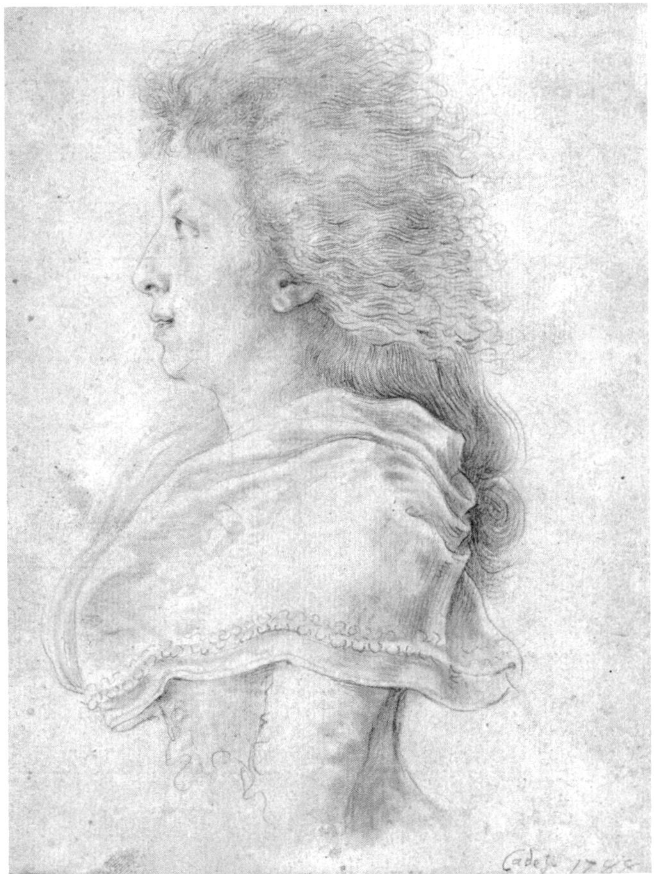

72

sented an idealized likeness of the sitter in a surround of antique paraphernalia.

Although Anthony Clark had suggested that the subject of the portrait might be the countess of Albany, the identification cannot be substantiated. The unusual hairstyle—short, frizzed, and brushed up in front, with long, loose curls in back—was in vogue precisely during the late 1780s and was called "à la hérisson," or "hedgehog" fashion. This is one of Cades's most charming drawings, despite its somewhat rubbed condition.

M.T.C.

1. One dated 1786 (repr. Chicago, et al., 1970–71, no. 76) and the other showing the artist as a youth of about sixteen years.

2. Two portraits of unidentified women are found on folios 16 and 27 of the artist's sketchbook in the Thorvaldsen Museum in Copenhagen; Caracciolo, 1978, pp. 24–47, repr. pp. 32, 34. A portrait of Pope Pius VI and an allegorical portrait of an unidentified king of Spain are preserved in the Cades album in the Museu Nacional de Arte Antiga in Lisbon.

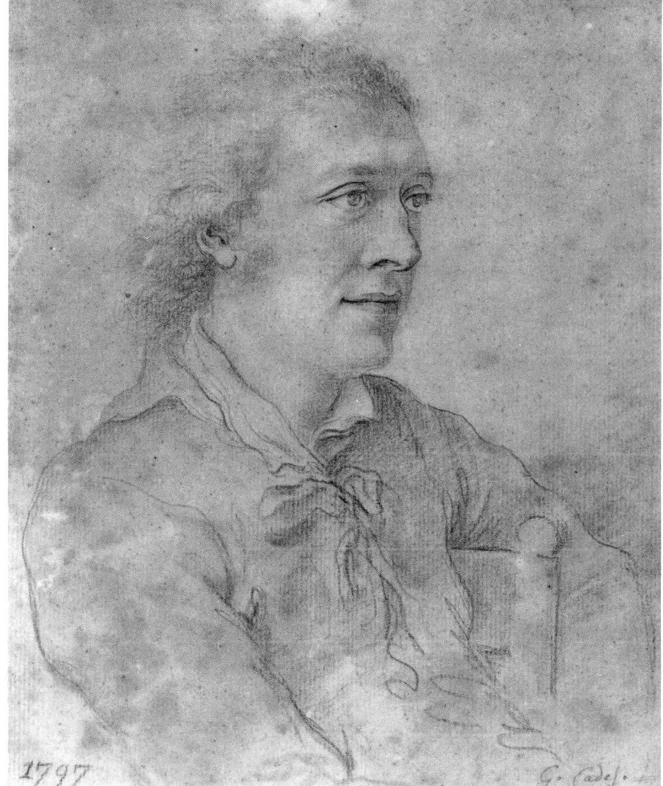

73

73. Portrait of a Man

1797

Signed in black chalk at lower right: G. Cades.; dated in black chalk at lower left: 1797

Black and red chalks on cream laid paper, very discolored

228 x 185 mm (9 x 7 1/4")

1978-70-208

Provenance: gift of Carlo Sestieri, 1964

Exhibition: Minneapolis, 1967, no. 21 (as possibly a late self-portrait)

Despite the very Italian character of its technique and composition, this drawing relates especially to the style of Angelica Kauffmann and her followers and to the work of such French artists as François-André Vincent and Jean-Baptiste Wicar in the last years of the century.

M.T.C.

74. Portrait of a Man, Half-length, Seen from the Front

1790–99

Black chalk on cream laid paper

210 x 175 mm (8 1/4 x 6 7/8")

Watermark: A I
C

1978-70-209

Provenance: purchased from Megna, Rome 1965

Unfortunately, no identification can be suggested for this attractive sheet, nor can it easily be dated.

M.T.C.

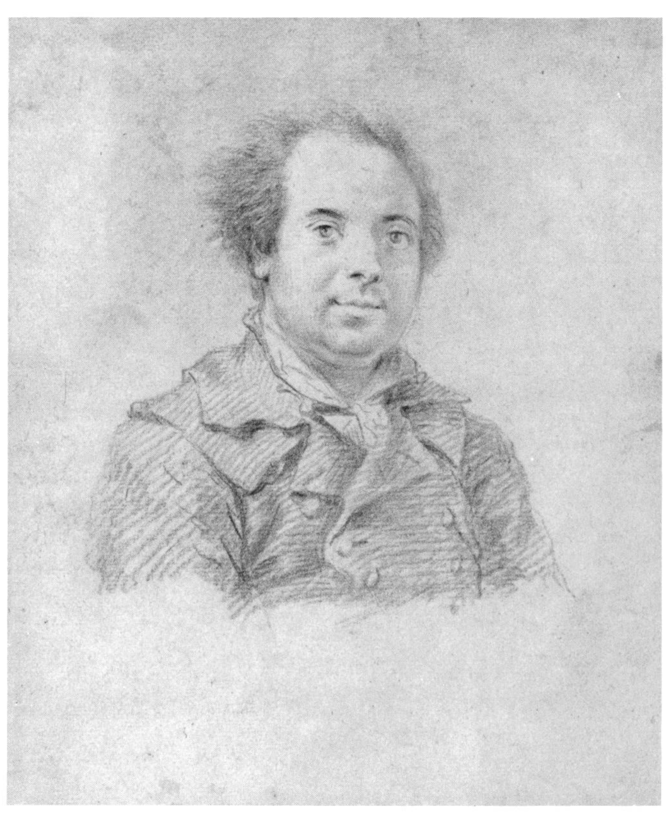

74

TOMMASO MARIA CONCA

Gaeta (Latium) 1735—Rome 1822

75. *Bacchante*

c. 1782–86

Inscribed on verso in pencil in the artist's hand (according to Anthony Clark): No. 64; and, in another hand: French / MVO [?], 29, and #3784

Black and white chalks on light brown laid paper

295 x 197 mm (11 5/8 x 7 1/2")

Watermark: Strasburg Bend

1978-70-256

Provenance: purchased from Rockman Prints, New York, 1964

Exhibition: Minneapolis, 1967, no. 34

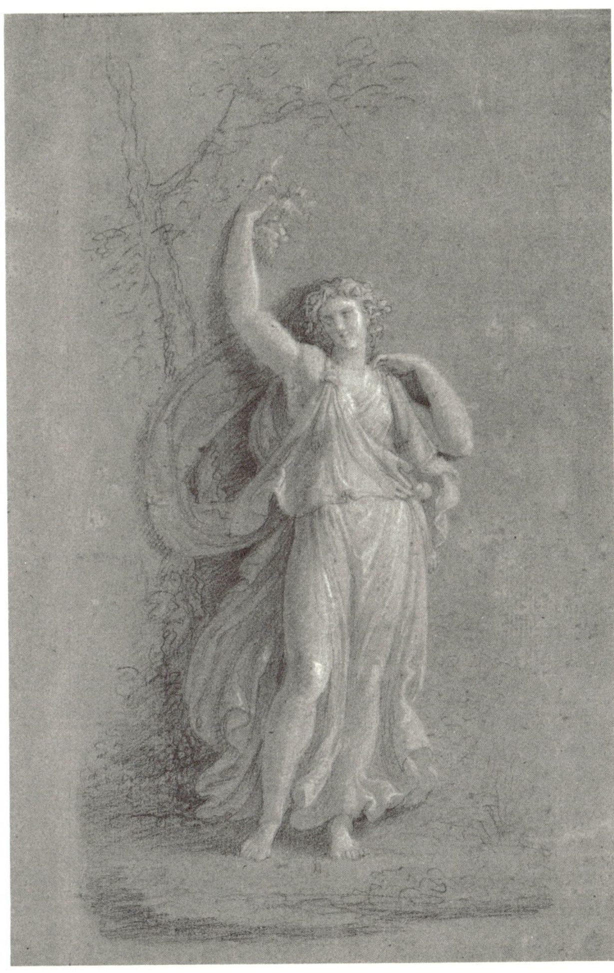

75

Tommaso Maria Conca was the pupil of his uncle, Sebastiano Conca, after the latter's return to Naples in 1752. He went on to become one of the better-known decorators of the late-eighteenth and early-nineteenth centuries.[1] His election to membership in the Accademia di San Luca in 1770 suggests that he had probably arrived in Rome during the previous decade, at a moment when the neoclassical style was in the ascendant. The late rococo manner developed by Sebastiano and passed on to Tommaso was quickly tempered in Rome by the younger artist's infatuation with the Bolognese master Annibale Carracci, and Tommaso's mature work relates to the classicizing styles of the major decorators of the 1780s, such as Cristoforo Unterberger or Domenico de Angelis (*see* no. 80).

From 1782 to 1786 Tommaso worked with the large team of artists decorating the Casino Borghese; he collaborated with Giovanni Battista Marchetti in the Sala Egizia, executing the mythological scenes as well as some of the grisailles. In 1786 he decorated the Sala delle Muse at the Museo Pio-Clementino in the Vatican Palace with scenes of Apollo and the Muses, and in 1789 he painted the dome of the cathedral of Città di Castello (Umbria) with scenes of the city's patron saint acting as intercessor before the Holy Trinity. He also executed for Prospero Antonio Lignani an exact replica of his Egyptian room in the Casino Borghese, a work that was repainted by Giacomo Conca in the nineteenth century. In 1793 he was elected *principe* of the Accademia di San Luca.

Conca designed illustrations for the papal encyclical of Clement XIV *Dominus ac redempter noster,* which dealt with the suppression of the Jesuit order, and he contributed a painting of *Lorenzo de'Medici Giving Aid to Greek Scholars Harassed by Turks* to the Quirinal Palace decorations commissioned to mark the triumphal arrival of Napoleon in Rome in 1813.[2] Although he was an accomplished decorative painter, Conca's altarpieces and cabinet pictures usually appear overworked and congested; his large-scale gestures and stage props, so effective in a high interior frieze or cupola, were poorly adapted to compositions viewed at close range. His most significant legacy is perhaps his work in grisaille, in which he succeeds in adapting a feathery, rococo brushwork to the canon of classical figural types.

Possibly intended for the central panel in the Sala Egizia in the Casino Borghese, this drawing of a bacchante shows Conca in his most evocative and lyrical manner. The figural type reflects an acquaintance with the chorus of accessory figures in ceilings decorated by the Carracci. The inspiration of antique cameos may account for the almost transparent handling that defines the drapery: from it one might guess that Conca knew the works of Josiah Wedgwood. Although Anton Raphael Mengs is often cited as Conca's neoclassical progenitor, the clear, hard forms of the elder painter have little affinity with the ethereal bacchante in this drawing. T.W.S.

1. F. Noack, in Thieme-Becker, 1907–50, vol. 7, pp. 288–89, still provides the most complete information on the artist.

2. *See* Ternois, 1970, pp. 68–69.

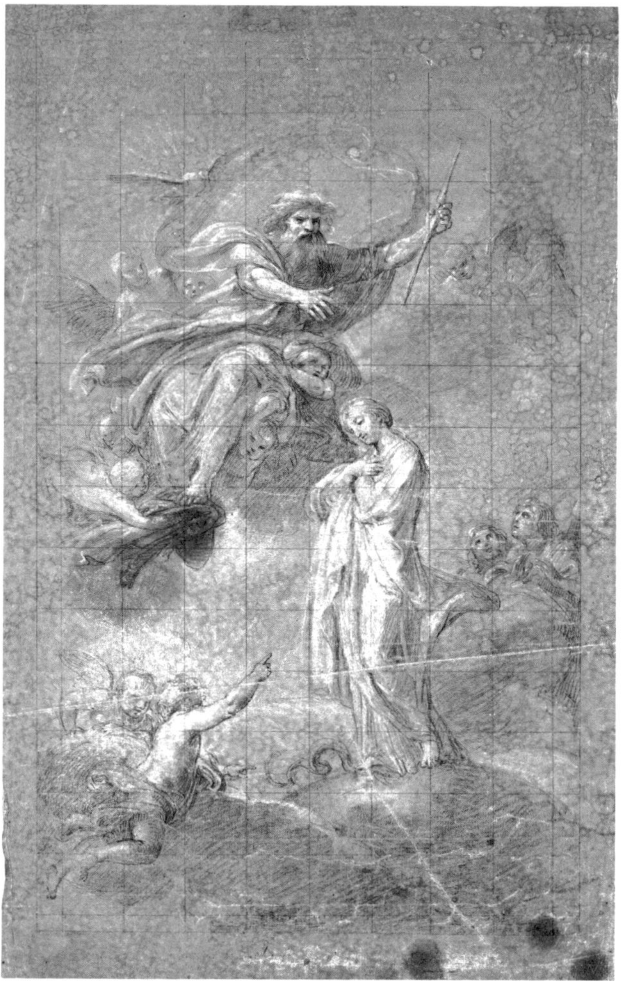

76 Recto

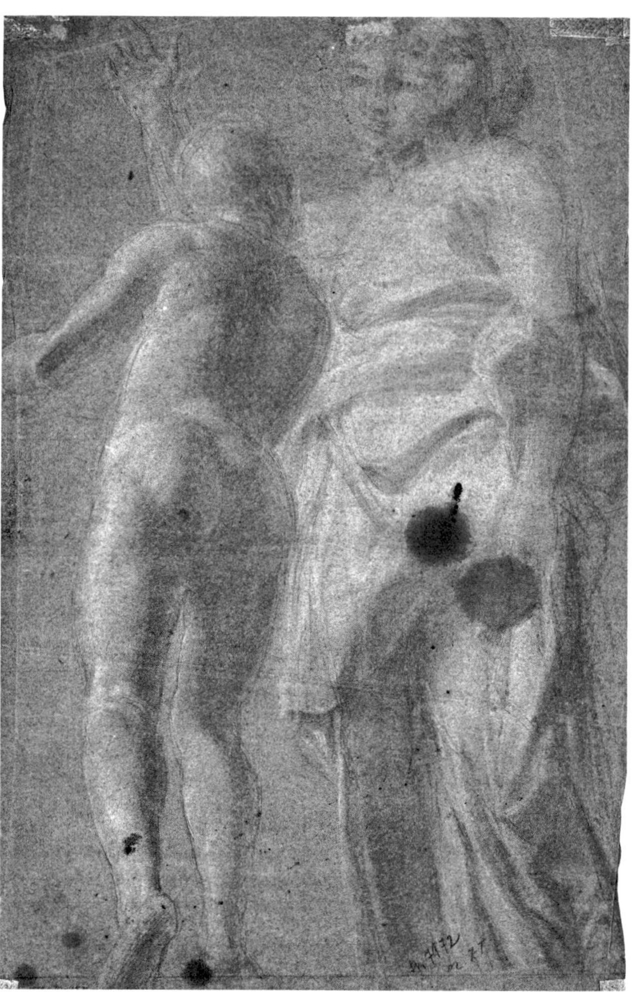

76 Verso

76. *The Virgin with God the Father and Angels*
Verso: *Study of Two Figures in the Sala delle Muse, Vatican Palace*
c. 1786–96
Inscribed illegibly on recto at bottom; inscribed on verso in pencil at bottom: [?] 7972 / n ZT
Recto: black and white chalks, squared in black chalk, on blue laid paper discolored to greenish brown; verso: black and white chalks, rubbed
450 x 287 mm (17 7/16 x 11 5/16″)
1978-70-252
Provenance: purchased from Leo S. Olschki, Florence, 1958

One is tempted to date this sheet to the same period as the decorations of 1786 in the Museo Pio-Clementino, especially in view of the drawing on the verso, which was identified by Anthony Clark as a preparatory study for the Sala delle Muse.[1] However, since no strict chronology has been established for Tommaso Conca's graphic oeuvre, such as guess would be hazardous; moreover, a chalk drawing recently on the Roman market showing an angel and some putti, squared, may possibly be a more developed version of the upper right part of the recto composition and is inscribed "Eques. Thomas Conca inv: et diseg: 1796 . . . Tifern [?]."[2] The most successful part of the Clark drawing's composition, God the Father supported on a cloudbank held aloft by putti, was adapted by Tommaso from a similar grouping in the large fresco of the *Pool of Bethesda* that Sebastiano Conca painted for the chapel of the Ospedale di Santa Maria della Scala Santa in Siena (*see* no. 17).

Another drawing by Tommaso for the Sala delle Muse, of *Homer and Calliope,* is in the collection of Julius Held, Vermont,[3] and a composition study for the ceiling is in the Cooper-Hewitt Museum in New York.[4]

T.W.S./A.P.

1. The figures appear in an engraving by Michelangelo Simonetti and Domenico de Angelis reproduced (as Jack Freiberg kindly informs us) in Paul Letarouilly, *Le Vatican et la Basilique de St.-Pierre de Rome,* London, 1953 (rept. 1963; first published Paris, 1882), pl. 253.

2. Sold Christie's, Rome, November 4, 1978, lot 1178 (information and photograph courtesy of Francis Russell and Speer Ogle). The Clark collection includes an ink com-

position study by Tommaso Conca with a letter draft dated October 1798 on the verso (checklist no. 51); although some similarity exists between the facial types of the ink study and that of the *Virgin with God the Father and Angels,* the different media preclude a firm comparison.

3. Binghamton, State University of New York, University Art Gallery, et al., *Loan Exhibition: Selections from the Drawing Collection of Mr. and Mrs. Julius S. Held,* traveling exhibition, 1970, no. 116, repr.

4. Inv. no. 1938-88-3578; exh. New York, et al., 1978–80, no. 34.

77. The Holy Family Crossing the Nile

after 1816

Inscribed in pencil at lower right: T. Conca / (23)21

Black chalk on beige wove paper

447 x 371 mm (17 5/8 x 14 9/16″)

1978-70-251

Watermark: J. Whatman 1816

Provenance: purchased from Rockman Prints, New York, 1958

Exhibition: Minneapolis, Minnesota, The Minneapolis Institute of Arts, *A Loan Exhibition of Drawings and Watercolors from Minnesota Private Collections,* May 13–June 13, 1971, no. 16, repr.

This sheet represents a preliminary sketch for Conca's work in the Cappella della Madonna in the church of Sant' Eustachio in Rome. Its watermark suggests a dating to the last years of the artist's career, when he was over eighty years old. The boatman, who leans heavily on his oar, recalls a similar figure in Domenichino's *Calling of Saint Andrew* in the church of Sant' Andrea della Valle, Rome, especially in its use of a low viewpoint. Conca's attempt to update his essentially late-rococo figure style with a new sense of solidarity results in some awkwardness: the figures' two-dimensional quality suggests that he was perhaps most flexible and successful when painting in grisaille. A comparison with Sebastiano Conca's drawing of the *Rest on the Flight into Egypt* in the Museo Nazionale di San Martino, Naples, points up the old-fashioned tendencies that Tommaso unsuccessfully tried to submerge. The finished state of this drawing suggests that the artist may have intended it as a presentation *modello* for the patrons of the chapel.

Other black-chalk drawings by Tommaso Conca in this same tight manner largely dependent on careful hatching and cross-hatching are four ceiling designs with putti in the Cooper-Hewitt Museum, New York.[1] They relate to the much earlier commission for the Sala delle Muse of the 1780s, suggesting that the artist's chalk manner remained essentially the same for a number of years.

T.W.S.

1. Two were exhibited in a recent traveling exhibition, New York, et al., 1978–80, nos. 35 and 36, repr.; nos. 1938-88-7187 and -7186; they bear similar inscriptions to the present drawing, to another sheet in the Clark collection (checklist no. 52), and to a number of other Tommaso Conca drawings in the Cooper-Hewitt Museum.

78. The Finding of Moses

1810–20

Inscribed on recto in pencil at bottom left: Raff. Mengs 1728–1779, and at bottom right: E; inscribed on verso in pencil at bottom: 327 (encircled)

Gouache and brown washes on blue wove paper

354 x 497 mm (13 15/16 x 19 9/16″)

1978-70-250

Provenance: Piancastelli (?); Mary Brandegee (Lugt suppl. 1860[c]); purchased from Lucien Goldschmidt, New York, 1959 (as Mengs)

Exhibitions: Minneapolis, 1967, no. 32; Minneapolis, 1970–71

Formerly attributed to Anton Raphael Mengs, this unusually rich and finished drawing presumably dates within the last years of Tommaso Conca's life. Closer in style to the works of artists who make up the later phase of neoclassicism in Italy—such as Felice Giani and Andrea Appiani—than it is to that of Mengs, it retains none of the elements of Tommaso Conca's Neapolitan late-Baroque heritage. The dramatic and colorful effect, as well as the impression of clarity and solidity of form, makes this one of the outstanding sheets attributed to Conca. At present it cannot be related to a particular commission.

T.W.S.

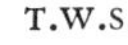

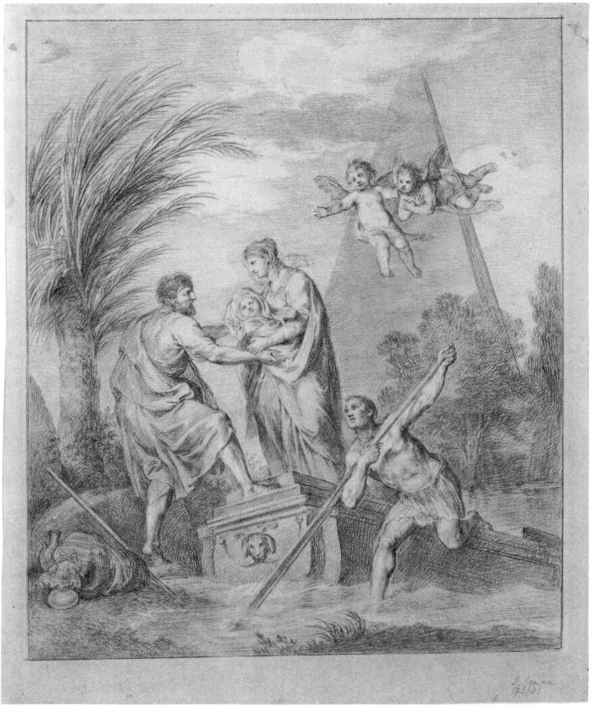

77

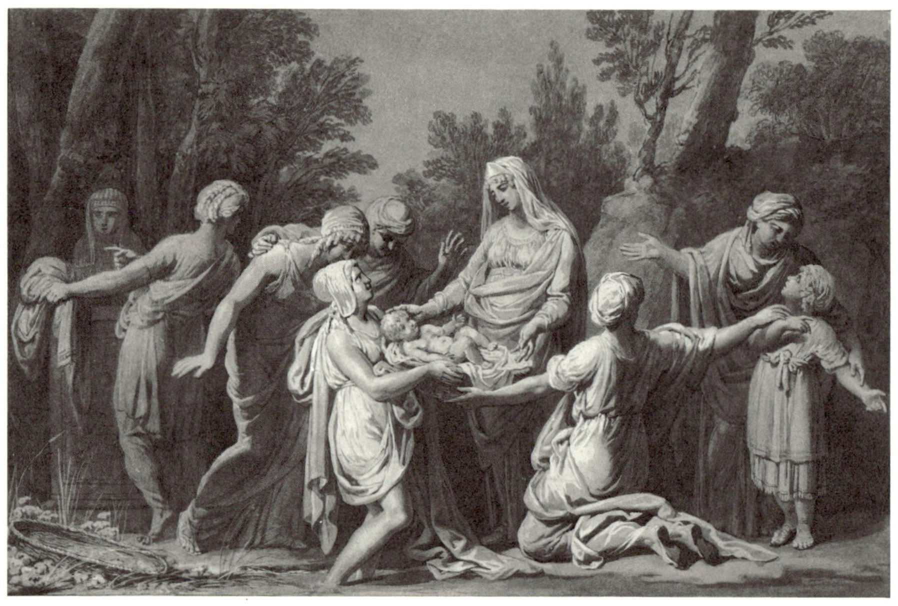

78

ANTONIO CAVALLUCCI

Sermoneta (Latium) 1752—Rome 1795

79. *Study of a Woman's Head*

1770–75

Inscribed on verso in pencil at lower right: I [?] 28800 HL

Red and white chalks on purplish gray prepared paper

210 x 162 mm (8 1/4 x 6 3/8")

1978-70-229

Provenance: purchased from P & D Colnaghi & Co Ltd, London, 1966

Exhibitions: Minneapolis, 1967, no. 25; Minneapolis, 1970–71

Antonio Cavallucci spent most of his short life in Rome, where he was supported by the Caetani family, dukes of Sermoneta. He studied briefly with Stefano Pozzi (*see* nos. 45, 46) and Gaetano Lapis, but among his contemporaries Mengs and Batoni influenced him most. Elected a member of the Accademia di San Luca in 1786, he taught at the Portuguese academy in Rome from 1790. The ceilings and wall decorations for the principal Caetani palaces in Rome and elsewhere are among his best works, but his oeuvre also comprises religious and historical easel paintings, as well as a number of extremely elegant portraits. In Rome Cavallucci produced paintings for the Ospedale Pio (Arciospedale di Santo Spirito in Sassia), for the baptismal chapel in the church of San Martino ai Monti, and for the sacristy of the canons in Saint Peter's. Outside the city he made paintings for Anguillara Sabazia (Latium), Subiaco, Catania (Sicily), Loreto, Borgo San Sepolcro, Rieti, Pisa, and Avignon. The most familiar of these is *The Investiture of Saint Bona* of 1792 in the cathedral of Pisa (a *modello* is at the Museo Nazionale di San Matteo, Pisa). The well-illustrated article recently published by Steffi Röttgen reveals why Cavallucci was thought to be the finest painter in Rome after the death of Batoni.[1]

Cavallucci's paintings show knowledge of old masters and earlier Roman Settecento painters, as well as such Seicento figures as Domenichino. His first works were copies of Guido Reni's *Penitent Magdalen* (Galleria Nazionale d'Arte Antica, Rome) and *Saint Michael Archangel* (church of Santa Maria della Concezione, or the Cappuccini, Rome); in 1787 he traveled to Bologna, Parma, Venice, and Florence, studying among other old masters the Carracci, Correggio, Titian, Fra Bartolomeo, and Andrea del Sarto. Cavallucci responded no less than Mengs and Cades to the Vatican frescoes and to other mature works by Raphael (he, too, made isolated studies from *The School of Athens*[2]). He held a special affinity, however, for the paintings of the young Raphael that were still strongly influenced by Perugino. The postures and physical types of many of his figures appear to derive from such early works as the Mond *Crucifixion* (National Gallery, London), *The Coronation of the Virgin* (Vatican Gallery), and *The Marriage of the Virgin* (Pinacoteca di Brera, Milan). Cavallucci's affinity to the young Raphael is especially pronounced in two of his later works, *The Investiture of Saint Bona* and *The Conversion of the Duke of Brunswick* (Musée du Hiéron, Paray le Monial, Saône-et-Loire).

This delicate and graceful *Study of a Woman's Head,* which confirms the high esteem held by Cavallucci's contemporaries for his drawn heads of women, angels, and the Child Jesus,[3] seems deliberately conceived in the mode of Raphael's Umbrian works. According to Cavallucci's biographers, the two principal sources of inspiration in his life were his religion and his painting, and in this respect he seems to anticipate the Nazarenes who worked in Rome at the beginning of the nineteenth century.[4] Inspired by their religious ideals, members of this brotherhood of German painters embraced with even greater enthusiasm the works of the early Raphael as the best prototype upon which to base their art.

E.P.B.

1. Röttgen, 1976. *See also* the early biographies by Vinci, 1795, and de Rossi, 1796, which must be used with caution; F. Noack, in Thieme-Becker, 1907–50, vol. 6, pp. 225–26; Golzio, 1945; Anthony Clark, in Chicago, et al., 1970–71, p. 188, no. 78.

2. A large (68 x 97″) copy of the center of the composition with Plato and Aristotle and their respective supporters was attributed by Anthony Clark to Cavallucci several years ago (Carew sale, Christie's, London, May 27, 1966, lot 89).

3. De Rossi, 1796, pp. 62–63.

4. Voss, 1924, p. 664: "Cavallucci's art is interesting as an example of the influence of Northern *Empfindsamkeit* and sentimentality upon Roman art of the eighteenth century."

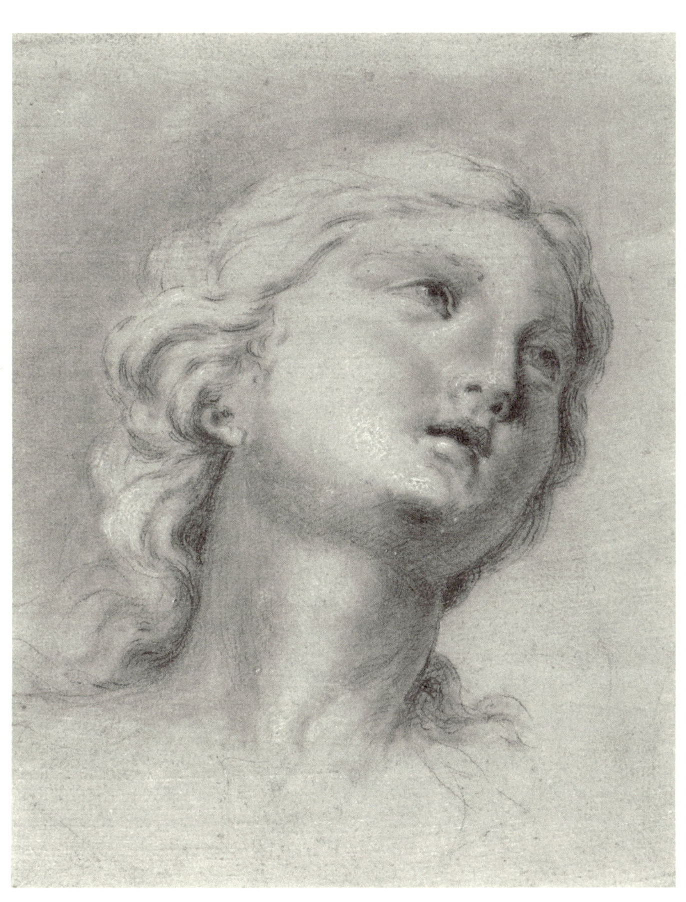

79

DOMENICO DE ANGELIS

Ponzano—Rome [?] after 1803

80. Studies for "The Triumph of Galatea"

c. 1785–90

Black and white chalks on gray blue laid paper

400 x 510 mm (15 3/4 x 20 1/8″)

1978-70-154

Provenance: William F. Webb; Lady Cheamside; Richard Gatty, Northallerton, Yorkshire; sale, Sotheby's, London, March 18, 1959, lot 61 (as Gavin Hamilton); purchased from Alister Mathews, Bournemouth, Hampshire, 1959

Exhibition: Minneapolis, 1967, no. 38

Domenico de Angelis, who remains virtually unstudied as a painter, was active in the second half of the eighteenth century in Rome, where he participated in many of the city's most important decorative commissions, including those for the Palazzo Borghese, the Casino Borghese, and the Gabinetto delle Maschere in the Vatican Palace.[1] A pupil of Benefial (*see* nos. 26–29) and member of the Accademia di San Luca from 1774, de Angelis specialized in subjects from classical mythology and was also engaged in the excavation of antiquities; as a part-time antiquarian he contributed significantly to the growth of the Museo Pio-Clementino's collections under Clement XIII and Pius VI.[2]

This sheet contains studies of the putti for de Angelis's composition of *The Triumph of Galatea*[3] painted for the central vault of the Salone degli Imperatori in the Casino Borghese. The *Galatea,* with its flanking tondi, comprises one of two mythological cycles—the other, in the Sala della Paolina, depicts *The History of Aeneas*—that were executed by de Angelis as part of the casino's comprehensive remodeling, ordered after 1782 by Marcantonio Borghese and carried out by a select group of Rome's leading artists.

Notwithstanding several individual, minor adjustments, these figures represent carefully finished, near-final studies for five of the six putti accompanying Galatea's entourage. Placed symmetrically in the drawing, the figures are given a different arrangement in the painted version, but with one exception their postures remain the same. By exchanging the position of the upper two putti, de Angelis was led to reverse the middle figure completely; placed in the upper right of the fresco, this figure is seen from behind, holding a torch instead of an arrow and moving in the opposite direction.

U.W.H.

1. The brief notices on de Angelis include Rome, 1959, no. 187; Nagler, 1835–52, vol. 1, p. 127; Meyer, 1870–85, vol. 2, p. 48; de Rinaldis, 1948, p. 229; Thieme-Becker, 1907–50, vol. 2, p. 507; *see also Memorie per le belle arti*, 1785–88, vol. 3, p. 29. For the artist's self-portrait in the Accademia

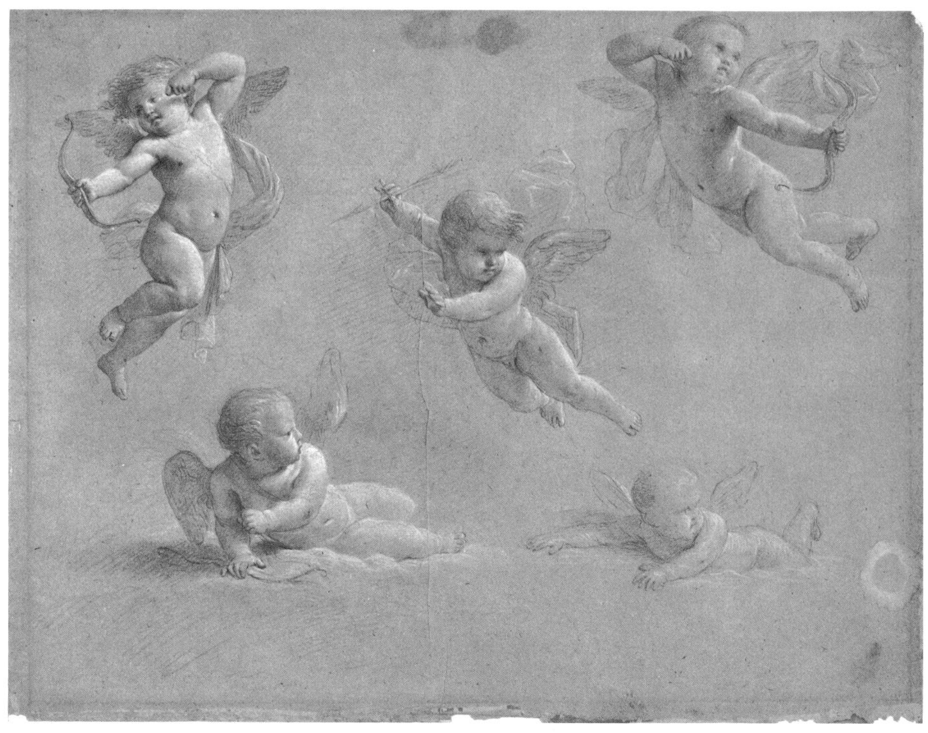

80

di San Luca, *see L'Accademia,* 1974, pp. 241, 258, fig. 36. A recently attributed painting of *Venus Chastising Cupid* appeared at a Sotheby-Parke Bernet sale in New York (June 7, 1978, lot 17, repr.). Entirely different in style is the work of another artist named de Angelis, who in the early nineteenth century (1818) painted in the Vatican Library's Galleria Clementina and Sala Alessandrina. This artist, possibly related, is perhaps the same "de Angelis romano" listed in 1830 among the "pittori di paese" and residing "all'Arco di Pantano n. 7" (de Keller, 1830, p. 97).

2. For de Angelis's role as excavator and antiquarian, *see* Howard, 1973, pp. 54 ff.

3. *See* della Pergola, 1962, pl. 67.

FELICE GIANI

San Sebastiano Curone (Piedmont) 1758—Rome 1823

81. An Angel or Genius

1780–85

Black chalk on cream laid paper

410 x 273 mm (16 1/8 x 10 3/4")

Watermark: fleur-de-lis in a double circle

1978-70-295

Provenance: gift of Andrew Ciechanowiecki, 1973

Felice Giani was an artist for whom drawing served numerous purposes, and his output in that medium was prodigious; over one thousand drawings belong to the Cooper-Hewitt Museum in New York, and there are large holdings in several Italian collections as well.[1] Although the group of Giani drawings in the Clark collection by no means demonstrates the full range of his draughtsmanship, the sheets are especially interesting in that they all seem to date to his less-well-known early period in Rome.

As one of the major house and palace decorators in Italy—his activity lasted from 1786 until just before his death—Giani was employed in numerous cities in central Italy, as well as for a brief time in France. He journeyed constantly; we know from letters and his account book that during the latter part of his career he moved between Bologna, Faenza, Forlì, and Rome, the cities where his lively decorations are found most abundantly in houses, palaces, villas, and theaters. He also worked in Ferrara, Modena, Cesena, Imola, Pesaro, Ravenna, Venice, and Rimini. Occasionally neo-Pompeian in mode, linear rather than painterly in conception, and rapid and superficial in execution, his colorful grotesques or friezes and panels depicting triumphs and allegories of the gods and heroes of antiquity are usually surrounded by monochromatic painted or stucco decorations. These ensembles were executed in collaboration with members of the workshop that either accompanied the artist or traveled in his wake. He seems rarely to have done church decorations or easel paintings.

Much has been written about Giani during the past thirty years, partly because he was one of the most prolific late-neoclassical painters in Italy, and partly because the extravagance and individuality of his style have led art historians to interpret him—loosely—as one of the precursors of romantic painting, particularly as it was practiced in France.[2]

The winged male figure in this drawing, having no attributes, probably represents an old-fashioned angel rather than one of Giani's ubiquitous, later, and more modern "republican" or "imperial" winged geniuses.[3] The sheet must date relatively early in the artist's career, probably near the beginning of his first stay in Rome (1780–98).[4] The handling of the chalk is controlled yet soft, being close to his early Gandolfian manner; the *Two Geniuses with Wreaths* (no. 82) is close in subject and style and is executed on similar paper bearing the same watermark. The present drawing may be copied or derived from a work by an Italian master of around 1600. Such an approach would not be unusual for Giani, who drew copiously but loosely after masters from earlier periods—usually in pen and ink and wash—creating such works as a mode of self-training not only during his early career but throughout his life.

A.P.

1. Massar, 1976, is the primary study of Giani as a draughtsman. (Phyllis Massar has generously shared with me her copious Giani files.) The most detailed accounts of Giani's career and chronology are to be found in Servolini, 1952–53; Faenza, 1979 (with bibliography); and, especially, Acquaviva and Vitali, 1979, who recapitulate much of the documentary information and provide a clear, detailed chronology, as well as extensive bibliography. *See also* Faldi, 1952, on Giani's Roman works.

2. Longhi made this intuitive suggestion (in a note to Corbara, 1950, p. 46). It is difficult to deal precisely with the question of Giani and France, as it is doubtful that his reported works at Malmaison and the Tuileries ever existed; the Villa Aldini at Montmorency, which he decorated in 1812–13, has been destroyed.

3. For works by Giani related specifically to the Roman Republic, *see* Rome, 1973–74, pp. 87–88, nos. 21–25, pl. 20.

4. Ksenija Rozman's researches in the *Stati d'anime,* or Easter parish censuses in Rome (which she kindly shared with me), show Giani listed as residing in vicolo Sant' Isidoro from 1785 through 1798, although he was absent for short periods in 1786–87, 1794–95, 1796, and 1797 (*see* especially Acquaviva and Vitali, 1979, pp. 199–204). Subsequently he lived for the most part elsewhere, primarily in Bologna and Faenza, although he executed important commissions in Rome in 1806, 1811–12 (*see* Ternois, 1970), 1818, and 1821. Near the end of his life—in 1820—he bought an apartment in via Gregoriana.

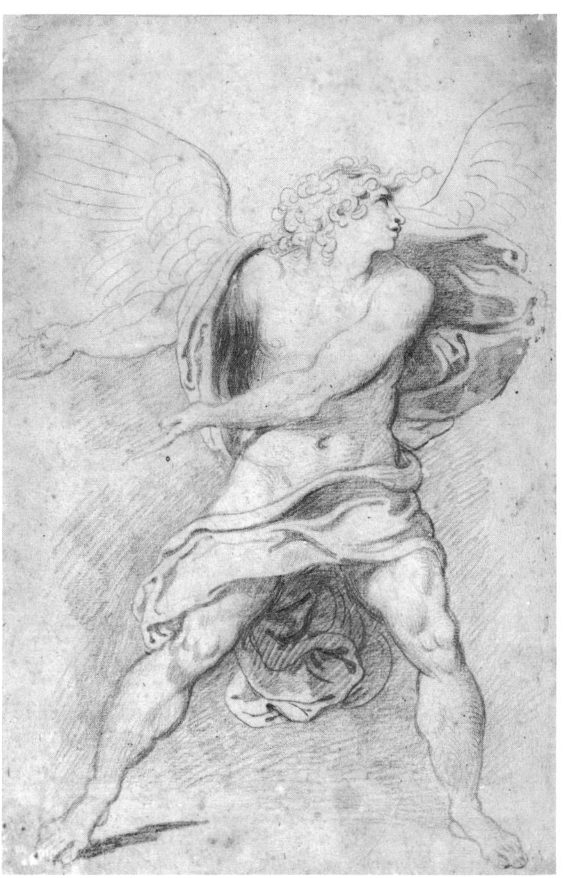

81

82. Two Geniuses with Wreaths

1780–85
Black chalk on cream laid paper
406 x 267 mm (16 x 10 1/2")
Watermark: Fleur-de-lis in a double circle
1978-70-296
Provenance: gift of Andrew Ciechanowiecki, 1974

Giani, in a brief autograph account written in 1820, chronicled his training after he left his provincial Piedmontese birthplace, studies that took place in Pavia between 1775 and 1778, in Bologna in 1778–79, and in Rome in the 1780s. His experience in Bologna seems to have had the earliest real impact, and the tradition of architectural decoration and scenography in that city left a lasting impression on his style. Among his masters in Bologna he lists Ubaldo Gandolfi (1728–1781) and Ubaldo's contemporary and follower Domenico Pedrini (1728–1800; *see* no. 97). The influence of Ubaldo's younger brother Gaetano (1734–1802) is also clearly evident in Giani's early chalk drawings, and Guercino's chiaroscuro and handling of wash seem to have affected his ink drawings.[1] Giani moved from a baroque, soft, and illusionistic manner to a linear, neoclassical style emphasizing frieze-like compositions during the first half of the 1780s.[2] The *Two Geniuses with Wreaths,* as well as the similar *Angel* or *Genius* (no. 81), probably dates to this transitional period.

Giani names his masters in Rome as Batoni, the decorator Cristoforo Unterberger (1732–1798), and the architect Giovanni Antolini (1756–1841)—an early source adds that he drew the nude in the studio of Domenico Corvi[3]—but other influences appear more evident during this period. He must have known, for example, the

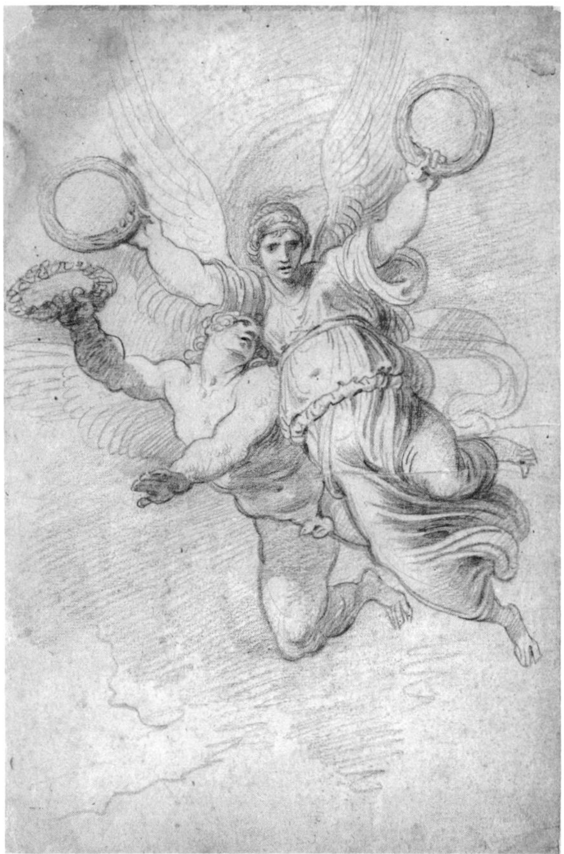

82

drawings of his older contemporary Giuseppe Cades, who worked contemporaneously with him between 1789 and 1793 in Palazzo Altieri. In addition, a strong northern influence seems to affect Giani's developing neoclassicism during the 1780s,[4] probably derived from the major neoclassical figures whose work he could have known in Rome, such as Gavin Hamilton, Jacques-Louis David, Angelica Kauffmann, and John Flaxman (by 1787), as well as from French visitors, winners of the Prix de Rome, such as Jean-Germain Drouais (1763–1788) or Jean-François-Pierre Peyron (1744–1814). An interesting, though as yet unexplored connection exists with works by members of the Fuseli circle in Rome—although most of these artists had left Rome before Giani arrived—especially in terms of a dramatic intensity of approach and a penchant for visionary themes.[5]

The motif of winged geniuses as victories or fames with palms, wreaths, or trumpets appears continually throughout Giani's drawn oeuvre as part of the standard Napoleonic decorative repertory—arms and trophies, standards, fasces, quadrigae, liberty trees and Phrygian caps, altars, etc.—employed by the artist with rare exuberance. Francophile commissions were of considerable importance to Giani's career during and following the period of Napoleon's ascendancy, and it has been suggested that the artist was of Jacobin persuasion.[6]

A.P.

1. *See* Faenza, 1979, nos. 2 and 5, pls. 1, 3, 6.
2. This development is seen in dated works of 1779, 1783, and 1784 exhibited at the recent shows in Bologna and Faenza (Faenza, 1979, nos. 6–8, pls. 1, 7–9).
3. Gasparoni, 1863, p. 10.
4. It has also been pointed out that many of his close friends were northerners (Ottani Cavina, in Faenza, 1979, p. lx).
5. *See* New Haven, 1979.
6. Faldi, 1955, pp. 15–16; *see also* Rudolph, 1977, p. 179 and n. 13.

83. Allegory of Love Triumphant

1785–90

Inscribed on recto, in pencil, at lower left: 6; on verso, in pencil: 291, 83, and p6E [?]

Brown ink and washes over traces of pencil, white gouache heightening, and traces of red brown paint on brown paper, mounted down

385 x 300 mm (15 3/16 x 11 13/16″)

1978-70-298

Provenance: purchased from Swetzoff Gallery, Boston, 1956

Exhibition: Providence, 1957, no. 73

Countless small allegorical scenes like this *Allegory of Love Triumphant* appear in Giani's decorative cycles, making it impossible to date this example on the basis of subject matter. Nonetheless, its crisp, wiry penmanship and the use of two shades of wash of differing densities, as well as the distinctively profiled facial types and curving contours of the figures, connect the sheet closely to the artist's ink drawing of *The Multiplication of the Loaves and Fishes,* dispatched to Bologna in 1789 in acknowledgment of his election two years earlier as *accademico d'onore* of the Accademia Clementina.[1] In the use of white heightening the sheet can be related to a group of large, finished, multi-figure ink drawings dating around the mid-1780s;[2] later in his career Giani relied on the sparkling contrast of rich, dark inks with light papers rather than gouache heightening for such effects.

The *Allegory of Love Triumphant,* in which the omnipotence of Cupid is conveyed by his trampling of literary, scientific, and artistic attributes, is an unusually finished drawing to have served as a preparatory study for a wall or ceiling decoration. In this it resembles the so-called "academy pieces" that figure importantly in Giani's oeuvre, as designs on set themes produced by himself and his friends and critiqued by them as a method of training. A manuscript *memoria* by a much younger colleague of the artist records that Giani founded such an academy in his house in Rome, presumably around 1790, called the Accademia de' Pensieri, which was attended by Camuccini, Benvenuti, Sabatelli,

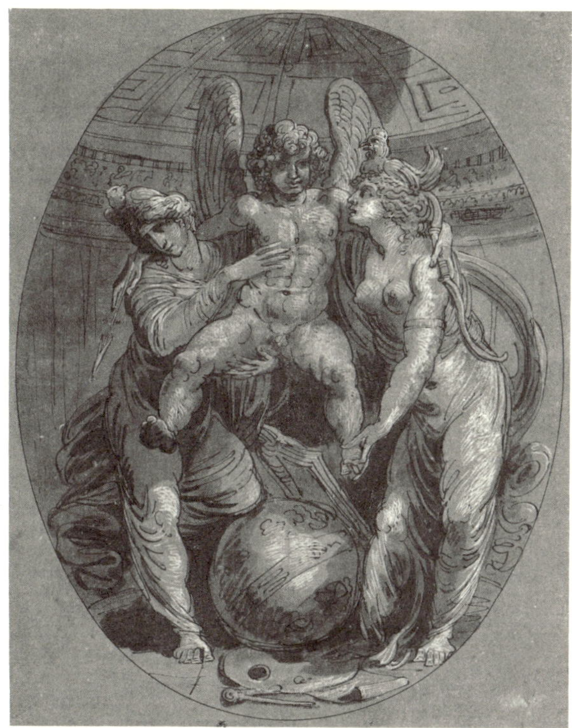

83

and Giovanni Battista dell'Era (1765–1798), among others.[3] The Bolognese Francesco Rosaspina mentions in a letter of 1801 an *accademia pittorica* held in the evening at his own house with Giani, which seems to have endured for at least ten years;[4] in 1803 Antonio Basoli records Giani's participation in the Accademia della Pace in Bologna,[5] and as late as 1822 a letter to Giani from his long-time friend Michele Kock refers to an Accademia della Pace as still meeting in Rome, the evening's subject being a typical one, the death of Count Ugolino.[6] Apparently Giani's special fame was partly founded on his ability to extemporize whole compositions from his imagination, from his familiarity with history and mythology, and from his close acquaintance with the "beautiful style of the ancients." The informal academic exercises would have been one method of keeping his "hand in," and Giani seems to have utilized the practice for some thirty years.

Such drawings by Giani, while adopting the usual forms and compositional devices of neoclassical art, are so exaggerated in expression and gesture and so energetic—not to say eccentric—in draughtsmanship that they deserve to be considered part of the "extravagant" tradition at the turn of the century that encompasses such figures as Fortunato Duranti, Luigi Sabatelli, Antonio Basoli (1774–1848), and Pelagio Palagi (1775–1860). Here the strict antiquarianism and standard of calm, selectively idealized beauty associated with David or Winckelmann gives way to an element of fantasy, a visionary quality, and a neo-Mannerist tendency reminiscent of Fuseli's Michelangelesque *terribilità*[7] or the imaginative and evocative renderings of Roman monuments that make the works of Jean Laurent Le Geay and Piranesi so irresistible.

A.P.

1. Bologna, 1979, no. 543, repr. pl. 346.
2. Faenza, 1979, nos. 6, 8–11 (repr. pls. 7, 9–12).
3. Rudolph, 1977. Drawings of this type by Giani are reproduced by Massar, 1976, pl. 40, and Rudolph, 1977, pls. 2, 3.
4. Acquaviva and Vitali, 1979, pp. 42–43, letter no. 20; the academy at Rosaspina's house is recorded in an etching by Giulio Tomba after a drawing by Giani dated 1811 (Faenza, 1979, no. 139, repr. pl. 115). Giani seems also to have held an academy, called de' Pensieri, in his own studio in Bologna at this time (Acquaviva and Vitali, 1979, pp. 63–64, letter no. 47).
5. Matteucci, 1974, p. 468.
6. Acquaviva and Vitali, 1979, pp. 105–6, letter no. 98.
7. Giani was criticized by an early-nineteenth-century contemporary for this mannered approach to classical antiquity (Ovidi, 1902, p. 6). Longhi isolated the "mannerist" element in Giani's work and related it to a larger European movement involving Reynolds, Blake, Fuseli, and Duranti (note to Golfieri, 1950, p. 28).

84. Figures Performing a Rite before the Arch of Constantine and the Meta Sudans

c. 1798
Ink and watercolor on cream wove paper
300 x 262 mm (11 13/16 x 10 5/16")
1978-70-299
Provenance: gift of Norman Leitman, 1967

This scene depicts an assembly of figures dressed in a loosely classical manner, performing some sort of rite or ceremony before the Arch of Constantine and the Meta Sudans, an antique cone-shaped fountain that once stood in front of the arch.[1] The draughtsmanship is drier and more restrained than is usual for Giani, and this has occasioned some doubts as to the attribution of the sheet. The arch and the tiny figures, however, are rendered very like those in Giani's small painting of the Festa della Federazione (or ceremony to celebrate the new French-instituted Roman Republic) at the Ponte Sant'Angelo in 1798—one of a pair now in the Museo di Roma—and on the basis of this comparison it seems that the present drawing can be given to Giani and dated to about the same time.[2]

The attribution touches upon a thorny question: of the vast numbers of landscape and *veduta* drawings ascribed to Giani it is by no means certain that all can be safely accepted as his work.[3] As was common practice during the period, Giani most probably went with

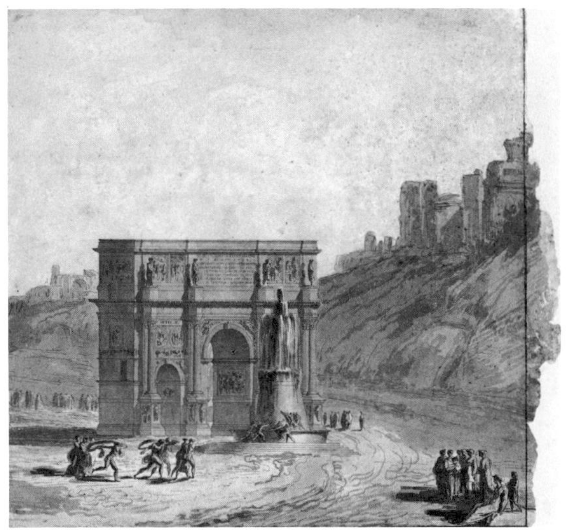

84

a group of companions to draw views through Rome and the Italian countryside. It is reasonable to suppose that the hands of individuals in such a group could be difficult to differentiate, as in the well-known case of Fragonard and Hubert Robert, who drew together as students in the Roman Campagna. The only one of Giani's group who has been identified by name is the Austro-Slovenian painter Francesco Caucig of Gorizia (1755–1828), who lived in Rome from 1781 through 1787 and who shared Giani's apartment in vicolo Sant' Isidoro between 1785 and 1787.[4]

A.P.

1. Erected by the emperor Titus and renovated by Constantine, the last of its remains were not demolished until 1936.
2. The paintings were published by Faldi, 1955. The Clark sheet was once designated as an anonymous eighteenth-century French work.
3. A number of views, especially of Rome and Tivoli, are in the Gabinetto Nazionale delle Stampe, Palazzo della Farnesina, Rome. Others are in the Istituto Nazionale di Archeologia e Storia dell'Arte, Palazzo Venezia, Rome, where, for example, in two albums with views (MS Lanciani 82/1 and 95) some appear to be by Giani, others not (MS Lanciani 96, views of Tivoli ascribed to Giani, appears to be another hand). Frequently the sites are identified by the artists, and those inscribed in Giani's distinctive handwriting seem to be sure attributions. Three albums of views at the Bibliotheca Hertziana, Rome, are putative attributions to Giani, and may be by him or a close follower. Autograph views include an album at the Biblioteca Comunale, Forlì, of charming black-chalk scenes documenting a trip made by Giani and his workshop from Faenza to Marradi in 1794 (some are reproduced in Faenza, 1979, pls. 32–39), as well as several strong ink drawings made in 1813 at Montmorency and now at the Museo Napoleonico, Rome, and the Pinacoteca Nazionale, Bologna (*see* Pericoli Ridolfini, 1964; Faenza, 1979, nos. 140–43, repr. pls. 117–20).
4. *See* Ljubljana, 1978, especially pp. 261–62, 267.

85. *Caricature of a Man Reading the Inscription on a Tombstone*
1790–1800
Inscribed on recto, in Giani's hand, in brown ink: Auridi [?], Carissima Sorella, Romer [Roman?], and, on the tombstone: qui ciace un / uom della / NATURA / AMANTE / Maresciallo / poltroneria; in a different hand, in light red ink: N° 624-2'-30; on verso, in pencil: 20892
Brown ink on buff laid paper
270 x 195 mm (10 5/8 x 7 11/16")
1978-70-294
Provenance: purchased from Christopher Powney, London, 1970

Caricatures rarely appear in Giani's enormous, varied output of drawings, although he occasionally drew genre figures in the manner of his younger contemporary Bartolomeo Pinelli (*see* no. 98). Six character or costume studies in the Museo Civico d'Arte Antica, Turin, share the quick, blunt strokes of this drawing; they can be dated around 1789 because of their close connection to a dated *Self-portrait,* also in Turin.[1] Two drawings in the Uffizi are also related in handling to this group and to the Clark caricature.[2] Both are on the

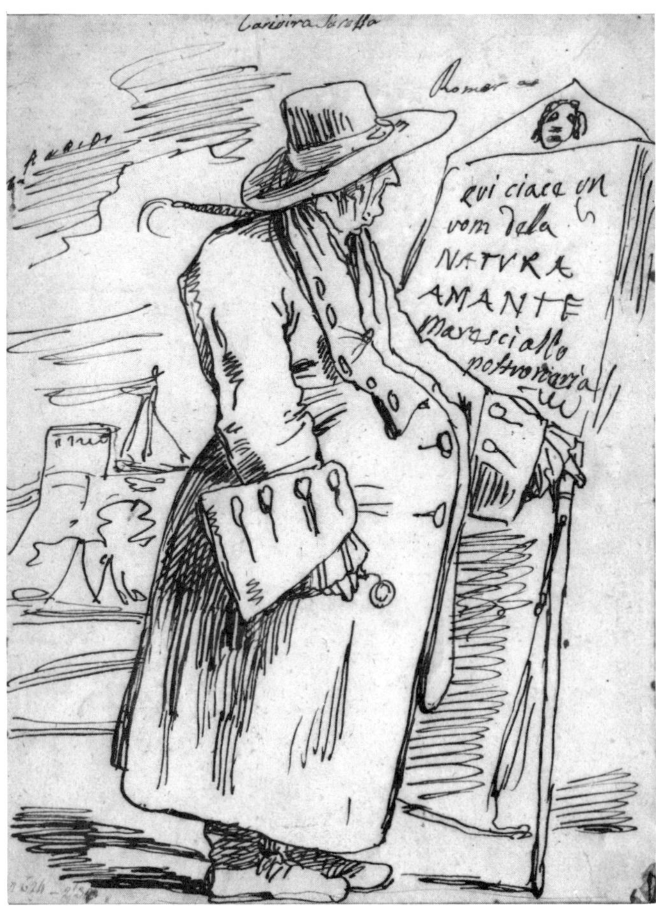

85

same kind of paper; the former shows a seated countrywoman, the latter—which is nearer the Clark caricature in its intensely personal and strange quality as well as its scribbly draughtsmanship—a necromancer at his black art.

The sheet depicts a pot-bellied, pigtailed old man with a walking stick and a pair of spectacles, dressed in a big hat and a very old-fashioned greatcoat, dating probably from around the mid-eighteenth century. He is shown near a harbor gazing at the inscription on a tomb (actually a roughly defined Canoverian stele) upon which is written in Giani's distinctive hand an inscription that translates, "Here lies a man who loved nature, Marshal Lazybones." On the one hand, the drawing's reference to Poussin's *Arcadian Shepherds,* perhaps by way of Castiglione and Tiepolo, is obvious; on the other, the contemporary theoretical dispute over the relationship of art and nature that may have prompted the satire remains tantalizingly obscure.

A.P.

1. Faenza, 1979, nos. 17–23, repr. pls. 18–24.
2. Gabinetto dei Disegni e delle Stampe, inv. no. 9895S, and 9896S. The latter is reproduced in Faenza, 1979, no. 27, pl. 28 (there dated c. 1790–1800).

ANONYMOUS ITALIAN

86. Studies of Two Male Figures in Midair and Two Female Heads

c. 1780
Inscribed on verso, in pencil: DN.–
Brown ink on cream laid paper
263 x 190 mm (10 5/16 x 7 1/2")
1978-70-478
Provenance: purchased from Rappaport, Rome, 1955 (?)
Exhibitions: Providence, 1957, no. 87 (as Angelica Kauffmann); Minneapolis, 1970–71 (as anonymous Roman, c. 1780)

This sheet, considered by Anthony Clark the work of an anonymous late-eighteenth-century artist, was related to early Giani by Enrichetta Beltrame-Quattrocchi and Mary Myers.[1] Indeed the figures, especially their profiles, resemble those in at least two drawings attributed to Giani.[2] On the other hand, the handling of the pen is lighter and less robust than is usual in Giani's work, and it is difficult to relate this sheet precisely to his manner at any period. Various other attributions have been made over the years—to Angelica Kauffmann, Fortunato Duranti, Anton von Maron, and Giuseppe Bernardino Bison—none of which, however, can be accepted with any degree of certainty.

A.P.

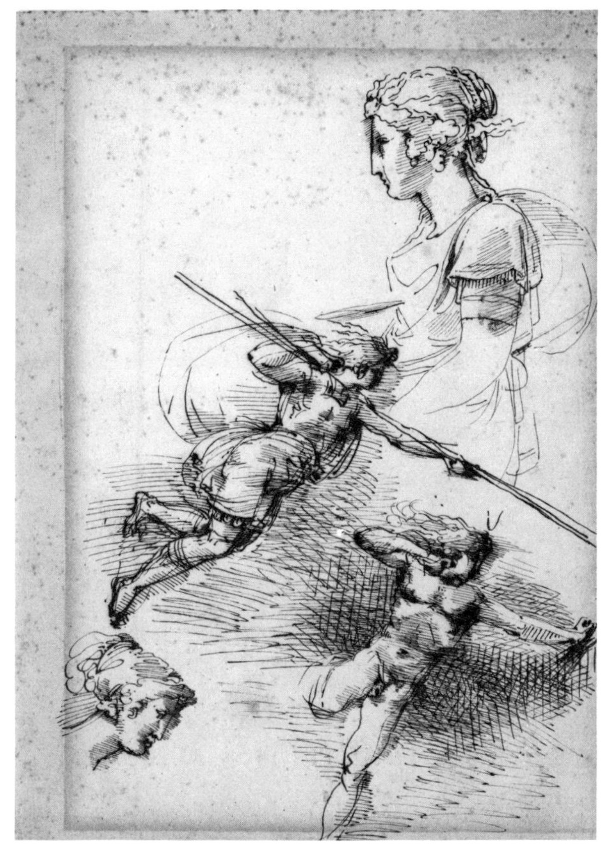

86

1. In conversation.
2. These sheets are an ink study of two ladies' heads accompanied by some calligraphic exercises in the Gabinetto Nazionale delle Stampe, Palazzo della Farnesina, Rome (inv. no. 7553/31357), and an ink and watercolor drawing of a figure with bow and arrows and a trumpet in the Cooper-Hewitt Museum, New York (inv. no. 1938-88-4357). Their attribution to Giani is itself open to question.

ANONYMOUS ITALIAN

87. Jupiter Fleeing the Wrath of Juno

c. 1800
Black ink and gray wash, white gouache heightening, on light brown laid paper
247 x 218 mm (9 3/4 x 8 5/8")
1978-70-240
Provenance: purchased from P. Seligmann, London, 1957
Exhibition: Providence, 1957, no. 146 (as attributed to Felice Giani)

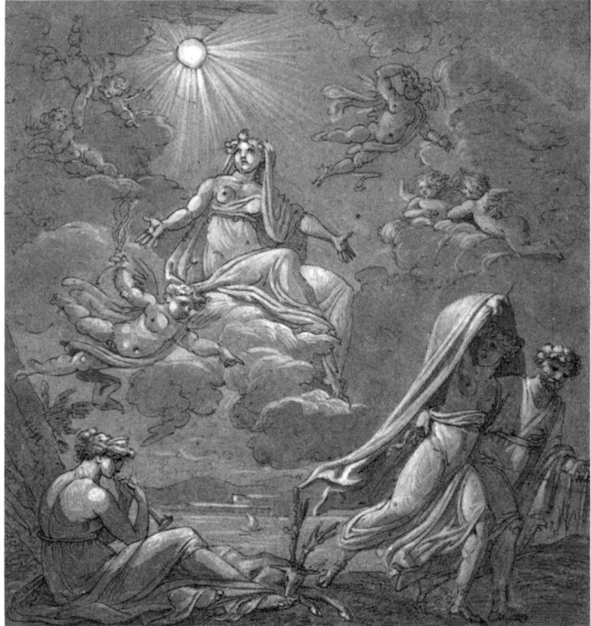

87

The authorship of this mythological scene is difficult to establish precisely. Anthony Clark tentatively attributed it to Giani many years ago, but it is more bland in draughtsmanship and reveals a slight neo-Zuccaresque air that has nothing to do with Giani's style. Clark's suggested attribution to Liborio Coccetti—made with some reserve—is a logical second choice, as Coccetti was also a decorator active in and near Rome at the same time as Giani; the latter, in fact, is supposed to have worked with Coccetti upon first arriving in that city.[1] Little is known about Coccetti's career beyond the existence of the number of painted decorations: for a papal residence at Subiaco (1779); for the Palazzo Baronale at Nerni (1784); for the Palazzo Chigi at Ariccia (1789–90); and, in Rome, for Palazzo Braschi (now the Museo di Roma; 1791–95), Palazzo di Spagna (where Coccetti's work has been confused with Giani's, 1806), Palazzo Taverna (formerly Palazzo Gabrielli, 1809–11), Palazzo Spada, and Palazzo della Consulta.[2] Often executed in a neo-Pompeian mode, most of these decorations remain unpublished or relatively inaccessible, except for those in Palazzo Taverna and Palazzo Braschi.

Virtually no drawings by Coccetti are known at present with which to compare this sheet.[3] Although its figural types are similar to those in some of Coccetti's painted decorations, and although the latter remains the most likely author, the drawing can only be regarded for the present as the work of a still-anonymous late-eighteenth-century artist, probably working in Rome.

The covertly departing couple and the approaching airborne goddess suggest that the subject may be identified with one of Jupiter's amorous escapades.

A.P.

1. Gasparoni, 1863, p. 10.

2. The principal treatment of Coccetti is in Faldi, 1952, pp. 238–40, 244–45, nn. 20–27.

3. Faldi, 1952, p. 245, n. 23, mentions a few pen and watercolor drawings preserved in the Chigi archives in the Vatican, related to Coccetti's decorative projects for a room devoted to subjects from Ariosto in the Palazzo Chigi at Ariccia (repr. di Macco, 1973–74, figs. 9–12).

Attributed to GIOVANNI CECCARINI
active Rome, c. 1816–28

88. Caricature of a Dandy Observed by a Dwarf
1805–15
Signed in gray brown ink at lower right: Ceccarini f; inscribed in gray brown ink on base of column: litto [?]
Gray brown ink and wash on light gray wove paper
152 x 202 mm (6 x 7 15/16")
1978-70-232
Provenance: gift of Fabrizio Apolloni, 1973

The signature on this sheet initially suggested an attribution to Sebastiano Ceccarini (1702–1783), the best-known member of a family of Fanese painters, who was a portraitist as well as a church decorator.[1] Sebastiano worked a number of years in Rome in the 1730s and 1740s before returning to Fano at some unknown date. Anthony Clark, however, believed the modish dress of the dandy to date from a period at least ten years after Sebastiano's death. The costume actually should be dated as late as the decade 1805–15. The above-the-ankle, skintight pantaloons and the disheveled hairdo (*à coup de vent*) were in vogue from the French Revolution to about 1820; the hat, a type designed by the London hatmaker Harrington, was wildly popular in England and Italy between about 1805 and 1818, and the cut of the dress-coat likewise suggests a date within the same period.[2] Therefore, the sheet dates at least twenty years after Sebastiano Ceccarini's death.

The younger of Sebastiano's two artist sons, Giuseppe (1747–1811), could have been the author of the drawing. Probably born in Rome but returning home at an early age with his family, Giuseppe seems to have spent most of his life in Fano, executing portrait and church commissions for various small towns in the Marches.[3] This sheet, to all appearances drawn in Rome, bears something distinctly cosmopolitan in its ironic juxtaposition of a stylish, emaciated, melancholic youth—perhaps a French or English tourist—and the hunchbacked dwarf, a typical and often-caricatured element of contemporary Italian low life. A more likely candi-

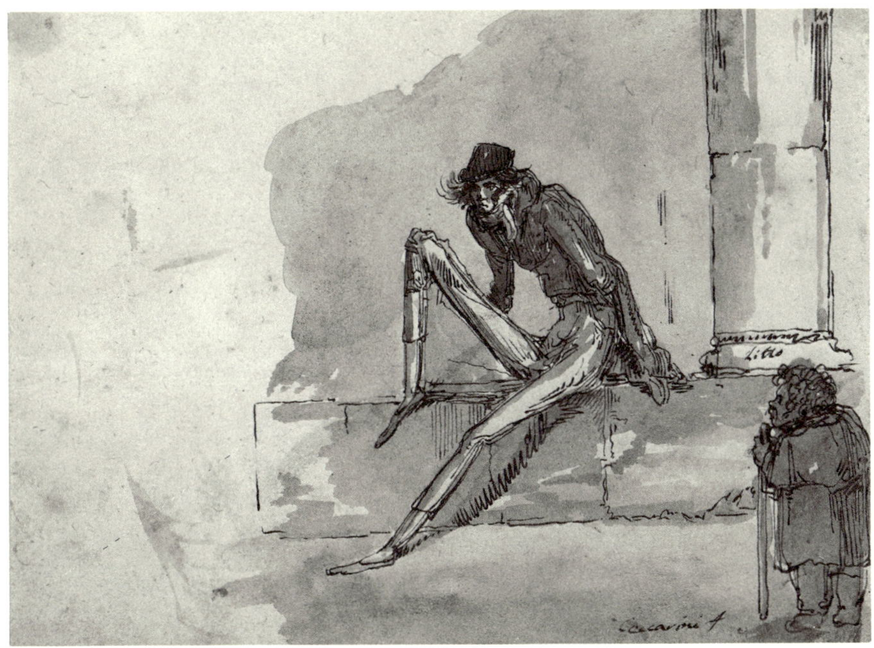

88

date as author than Giuseppe Ceccarini, who was old and living in Fano when the sheet was apparently produced, is a sculptor named Giovanni Ceccarini, about whom little is known except that he seems to have been a pupil of Canova and to have executed several sculptural commissions in and around Rome in the second and third decades of the nineteenth century.[4] Unfortunately not enough is known about the draughtsmanship of either of these artists to make a firm attribution of the Clark sheet.

The drawing—typical of one aspect of Anthony Clark's collecting interests—is not the easily recognizable work of a major figure, but a minor work by a minor figure that heightens our awareness of the style, humor, and daily life of the period.

A.P.

1. *See* especially Busiri Vici, 1968; also, Servolini, 1959.
2. I am most grateful to dott. Andrea Viotti for this information.
3. The births of seven of Giuseppe's children are recorded in Fano between 1780 and 1802, and he died there in 1811 (*see* Paolucci, 1938, especially pp. 26–27, 32–33; Busiri Vici, 1968, pp. 271–73, n. 12).
4. G. Castellani in Thieme-Becker, 1907–50, vol. 6, p. 251; Selvelli, 1931, p. 91; T.C.I. *Roma,* 1977, p. 700.

JOHN FLAXMAN
York 1755—London 1826

89. Study of a Roman Sarcophagus

Verso: *Reprise of Lower Ornamental Frieze* (not illustrated)

c. 1790

Brown ink over black chalk on cream laid paper

93 x 205 mm (3 11/16 x 8 1/8") (the original sheet extended by the artist about 5 mm to the right)

1978-70-275

Provenance: Bishop Percy (?); John Ruskin (?); purchased from Goodspeed's, Boston, 1957

Exhibition: Providence, 1957, no. 58

Bibliography: Friedrich Matz, *Die Dionysischen Sarkophage,* Berlin, 1975, vol. 1, p. 110; vol. 4, p. 548

After training at the Royal Academy, London, Flaxman was employed as a modeler for Josiah Wedgwood before finally undertaking a long-hoped-for trip to Rome in 1787. When the two years scheduled for the trip had expired, Flaxman received the commission from Lord Bristol to execute a colossal statue of *The Fury of Athamus* (Ickworth, Suffolk) and was able to postpone his return to England until 1794.

During his years in Rome Flaxman developed a graphic style noted for its stark, linear simplicity, which was to have an enormous impact on European painting and sculpture of the later-eighteenth and early-nineteenth centuries. His drawings illustrating Homer, Aeschylus, and Dante, executed in the early 1790s and first published in engravings by Tommaso Piroli from 1793, were the first of the sculptor's works to carry his reputation throughout Europe.

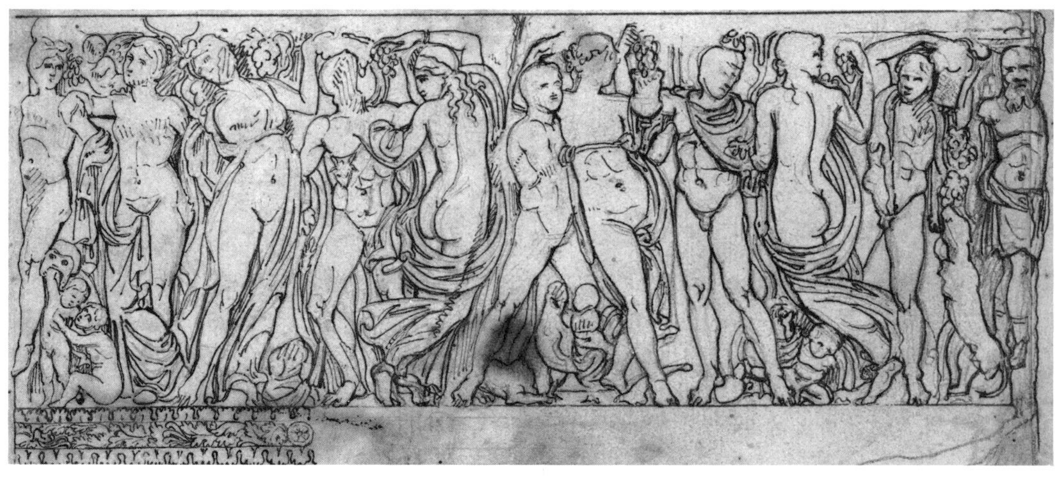

89

Flaxman came to Rome to learn, and soon after his arrival he declared that "my mind has been affected by the fine things I have seen here . . . I find myself more and more immersed every day in such studies as are necessary to make me a good artist."[1] Several of his surviving Italian sketchbooks testify to his diligent pursuits and wide range of interests, containing, as they do, figure studies from life, street scenes, and studies after Renaissance paintings, medieval frescoes and mosaics, and modern sculptures, in addition to the predominantly antique subjects,[2] sarcophagi in particular.

This drawing is a fairly finished study of a Bacchic sarcophagus representing the god with an entourage of maenads, satyrs, and putti engaged in the vintage harvest. Presently located in the atrium of the Capitoline Museum, where it was placed in 1812, the sarcophagus stood in Flaxman's day in the Benedictine cloister of Santa Maria della Concezione in the Campus Martius.[3]

In his drawn study Flaxman omitted the grapes and leaves on the upper border, executed only a partial sample of the lower ornamental frieze, and nearly ignored the large crack that splits the sarcophagus through the middle. In keeping with his predilection for simple figural schemes, and in contrast to the uniformity of treatment of the relief itself, Flaxman greatly emphasized the contours of the figures and set each more clearly against the background.

Probably executed rather early during the artist's stay in Rome, the drawing and its purpose were vividly evoked forty years later when Flaxman in his *Lectures on Sculpture* referred to such sarcophagi as "magnificent . . . compositions from the great poets of antiquity, Homer, Hesiod, Aeschylus, Euripides, and Sophocles—the systems of ancient philosophy, with Greek mysteries, initiations, and mythology. The study of these will give the young artist the true principles of composition, . . . to produce the chief interest of his subject by grand lines of figures without the intrusion of useless, impertinent, or trivial objects. . . ."[4] U.W.H.

1. Constable, 1927, p. 34 (letter of May 25, 1788).
2. *See* Whinney, 1956; Irwin, 1959; for Flaxman, with general literature, Rosenblum, 1967, pp. 158–91; London, 1979.
3. Jones, 1912, vol. 1, p. 29, no. 10A, pl. 7; Matz, op. cit., vol. 1, pp. 110–12, pl. 16; *see also* vol. 4, p. 512, for mention of another drawing by Flaxman of a now-lost sarcophagus with Bacchus and Ariadne in the Metropolitan Museum of Art, New York, inv. no. 61.129.2.
4. John Flaxman, "Ancient Art," in *Lectures on Sculpture,* London, 1829, pp. 287–88.

Attributed to GIUSEPPE VALADIER

Rome 1762—Rome 1839

90. Façade Elevation of a Domed Rotunda

c. 1800

Pen and brown ink, gray and brown washes, over black chalk on cream laid paper

123 x 95 mm (4 7/8 x 3 3/4")

1978-70-424

Provenance: purchased from Eugenio di Castro, Rome, 1968

Giuseppe Valadier was the most distinguished exponent of French Revolutionary neoclassicism practicing in Rome at the end of the eighteenth century. Valadier may have studied in France, and his designs show strong affinities with those of Claude Nicolas Ledoux and Etienne Boullée, particularly in their emphasis on pure geometric forms. There is also a strong element of another international movement in his work: neo-Palladianism. A late work like Valadier's 1833 façade of San Rocco in Rome owes a profound debt to Palladio and is related as well to the Renaissance master's eighteenth-century followers like Tommaso Temanza in Venice, Giacomo Quarenghi in Russia, and Sir William Chambers in England. Valadier's sensitivity to northern European theory and practice, remarkable as it was in Rome during this period, did not isolate him from the historical development of Roman architecture. Indeed, in his works the grand tradition of Baroque classicism that had been initiated by Carlo Fontana and pursued by Luigi Vanvitelli and Giovanni Battista Piranesi was continued well into the nineteenth century.

Valadier is perhaps best known for his part in completing the Piazza del Popolo and the adjacent gardens on the Pincian Hill (1816–24). Situated in these gardens is the handsome Casina Valadier (1809–14), which displays to perfection the architect's imaginative fusion of diverse currents present within the neoclassical style.

While this drawing does not directly relate to any of Valadier's executed buildings, it does bear significant points of similarity with his known designs. The building type—a small, central-plan structure appropriate for a chapel—appears repeatedly in Valadier's work.[1] Moreover, the use of drafted masonry and the frieze that runs beneath the entablature in this drawing recall Valadier's combination of the same elements in the façade of San Pantaleo in Rome (1806).

Before it was acquired by Anthony Clark the drawing was among a group of four studies of domed structures, the verso of one of which was inscribed with Valadier's name.[2] Although the sheet is similar to a number of autograph drawings by Valadier in the collection of the Accademia di San Luca, the analysis of style alone does not permit an unqualified attribution to the architect.[3] However, in its refined application of classical detail to the articulation of basic geometric solids we see an elegant synthesis of Roman tradition and French rationalism—a synthesis that, through the work of Giuseppe Valadier, constituted the dominant architectural force in Rome at the end of the eighteenth century.

J.P.

90

1. The chapel of the Villa Pianciani near Spoleto (1784) and Valadier's design for a "cappella di campagna" based on the Pantheon (1796) are two examples. *See* Marconi, 1964, figs. 1 and 49.
2. The inscribed drawing was subsequently sold to Carlo Sestieri.
3. Marconi, 1974, vol. 2, nos. 2586–2930. It should be noted with reservation, however, that in Valadier's numerous projects for domed structures he shows a marked predilection for profiles with stepped bases like that of the Pantheon and never employs a pure hemisphere as here.

VINCENZO CAMUCCINI
Rome 1771—Rome 1844

91. *Mercury Rewarding Agriculture, Industry, and the Arts*
c. 1806
Acquired in original frame, the back board of which is inscribed in brown ink: fatto da Camuncini [sic] 1806. / dalle [word illegible] Collegi—Santi. mi [?] / al 27 [word illegible] 1816., and: Cav Vincenzo Camuncini [sic]
Black ink and brown wash over traces of black chalk on buff laid paper
188 x 278 mm (7 7/16 x 10 15/16")
1978-70-225
Provenance: gift of Andrew Ciechanowiecki, 1974

Vincenzo Camuccini was the leading Roman painter from the outset of the nineteenth century, and for approximately three and a half decades, second only to Canova during his lifetime, he enjoyed preeminence in the artistic life of the city by virtue both of official appointments and an immense and distinguished international patronage.[1] He served from 1814 until a year before his death as inspector of public paintings for Rome and the Papal States, a post that helped to reinforce his predilection for the work of sixteenth-century masters, and for Raphael and his school in particular.

Camuccini first achieved local celebrity with his cartoon of *The Death of Julius Caesar,* exhibited in 1796. When completed on a monumental scale, this work, to-

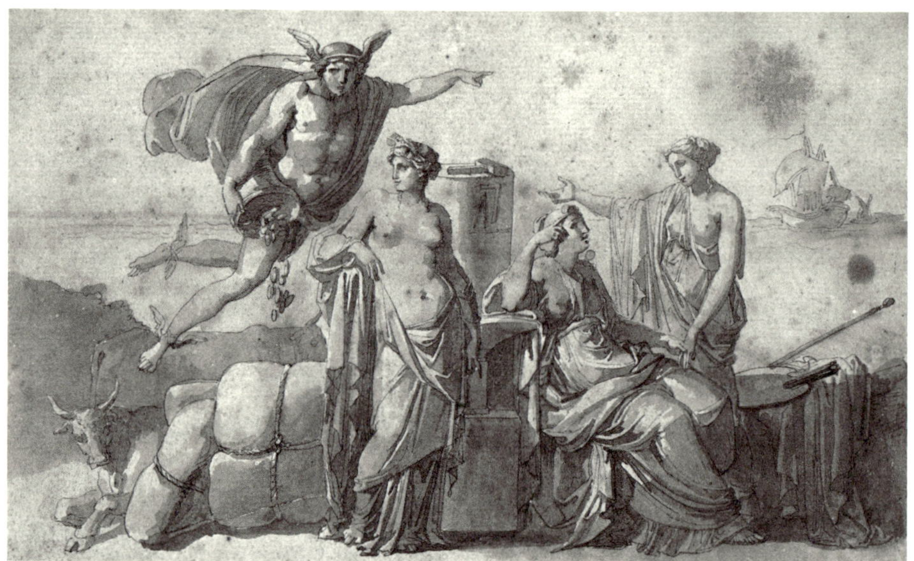

91

gether with its pendant, *The Death of Virginia* of 1804, was considered by many contemporary observers to have placed Italian painting on equal terms with the most advanced standards of neoclassical reform. The austere abstraction and rigorous control of Camuccini's compositions earned him the reputation as one of the ablest draughtsmen of his day. Beginning in the 1790s many artists, Flaxman among them, are recorded among the purchasers of his drawings.

With its clear reflection of antique classical sources, this drawing belongs to Camuccini's most formal and statuesque manner. The date on the back board of the original frame coincides with what we know of Camuccini's style in the middle of the first decade of the nineteenth century, and, even if the inscription is not autograph, it can still be accepted as essentially correct.

The drawing represents Mercury, god of commerce, spilling coins from a cornucopia and gesturing toward a ship in the distance; beside him are posed three female figures representing Agriculture, Industry, and the Arts. Otherwise unrecorded in Camuccini's oeuvre, the nature of the allegory suggests that it was possibly intended for an engraving rather than for a painted composition. The interrelationship of the arts with other branches of industry, as well as the significant commercial advantages derived from the arts by the Papal States, was a theme commonly rehearsed throughout the eighteenth and nineteenth centuries. It was perhaps in the context of Camuccini's official posts, such as those assumed in 1803, when he was made director of the Vatican mosaic studios, and in 1806, when he became *principe* of the Accademia di San Luca, that this allegory may have been created.[2]

U.W.H.

1. For Camuccini, with literature, *see* Hiesinger, 1978; Rome, 1978.

2. Camuccini was *principe* of the academy, 1806–10.

92. *Agrippa and the Pantheon*

c. 1815

Inscribed in pencil or black chalk at bottom center: Agrippa

Black chalk and brown wash on cream wove paper

263 x 442 mm (10 3/8 x 17 3/8")

1978-70-226

Provenance: purchased from Bruscoli, Florence, 1956

Exhibitions: Providence, 1957, no. 43; Minneapolis, 1967, no. 24

Agrippa was the chief general and minister of the Roman emperor Augustus, and according to a dedicatory inscription carried over from an earlier building, he was long believed to have been responsible for the construction of the Pantheon in Rome. In this drawing Agrippa is portrayed as seated on a narrow platform, holding a plan of the Pantheon and gesturing toward the building, which is visible through an opening behind. At the sides are a military trophy and a burning altar marked with a dolphin and trident.

Intended for a lunette decoration, this drawing may have formed part of a series of decorations ordered in 1814 by Joachim Murat, king of Naples, for the royal palace at Caserta. The commission for the Caserta decorations was left unexecuted by Camuccini when Murat was overthrown the following year. Although the exact nature and scope of the project remain to be determined, and although several of Camuccini's lunette designs for it had quite different allegorical subjects, the scarcity of such decorative projects in Camuccini's oeuvre would support the connection to Caserta.

The program implied by the drawing's subject—the patronage of the arts by famous historical figures—has a contemporary, though not directly related parallel in the scheme of decorations ordered by Napoleon for the

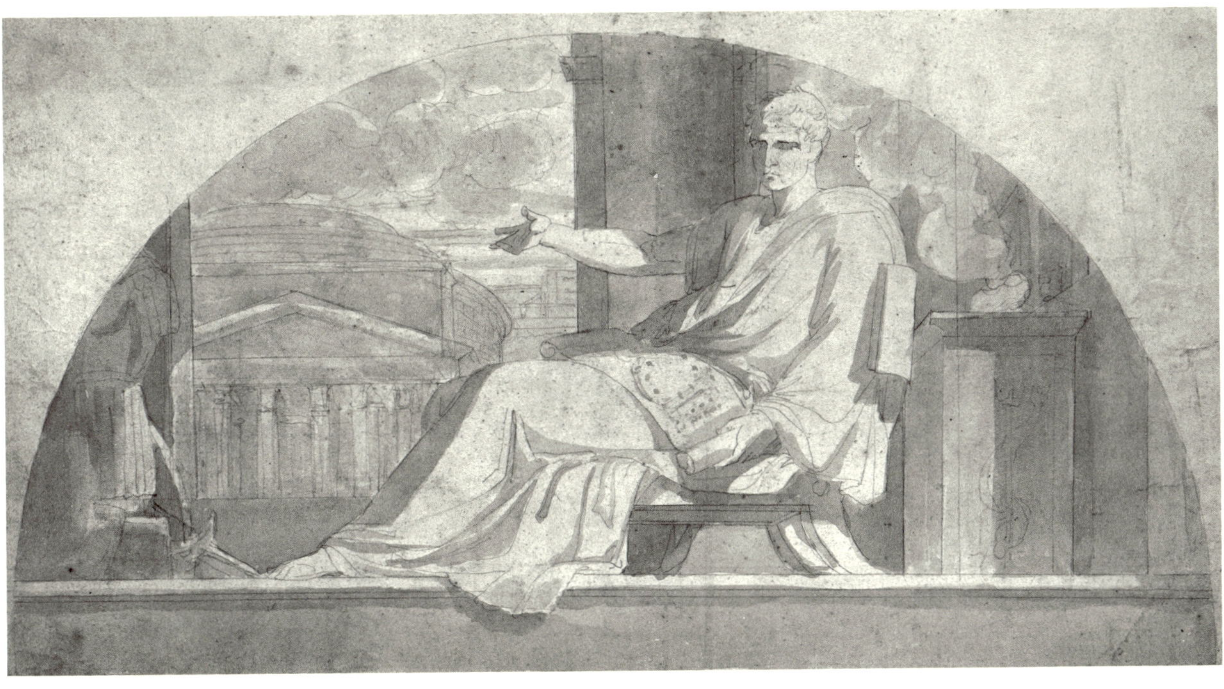

92

Quirinal Palace in Rome, which Camuccini contributed to between the years 1811 and 1813.[1]

U.W.H.

1. *See* Hiesinger, 1978, p. 305. On the Quirinal decorations, *see also* Ternois, 1970.

PIETRO BENVENUTI

Arezzo 1769—Florence 1844

93. Study for "The Triumph of Judith"

1803

Signed on recto in brown ink at lower left: Pietro Benvenuti Fece —; inscribed on verso in pencil at top center: £20 and at bottom center: 56

Black and white chalks on tan prepared paper; verso squared in black chalk

330 x 235 mm (13 x 9 1/4")

1978-70-188

Provenance: Giovanni Piancastelli (?) (1845–1926); Mary and Edward Brandegee (?); Reverend Francis Agius, Inwood, Long Island; purchased from Shepherd Gallery, New York, 1976

Exhibition: New York, 1976, no. 56 (repr.)

Pietro Benvenuti, whose fame and authority in Florence paralleled that of Camuccini in Rome, was the leading neoclassical painter in Tuscany during the first half of the nineteenth century.[1] As students the two artists had, in fact, collaborated during Benvenuti's sojourn in Rome, which he began in 1792 after training in Florence at the Accademia di Belle Arti. In Rome Benvenuti was first recognized as among the three or four best painters in Italy; his success led to his appointment as director of the academy in Florence, where he returned in 1804. Missirini later boasted that this former member of the Accademia di San Luca had "restored the arts in Tuscany" through his own high talents and through his application of "the rigorous principles of the Roman school."[2]

This drawing is a study for the central group of Benvenuti's early and famous composition of *The Triumph of Judith,* which he executed in two monumental canvases. The first of these, signed and dated 1798, is in the Galleria Nazionale, Palazzo di Capodimonte, Naples;[3] the second, completed in 1804, is located in the Cappella della Madonna del Conforto of the cathedral in Arezzo.

The *Judith* was originally commissioned for Arezzo by Bishop Niccolò Marcacci. Benvenuti, at work on this first version by 1797, related in his autobiography that Frederick Hervey, earl of Bristol and bishop of Derry, wished to purchase the painting then in progress and that the artist ceded it to him with a view to making many improvements in a second version.[4] The death of Marcacci in 1799 and the French invasion of Florence evidently delayed work on the second version of the *Judith.* It was eventually begun in Rome in 1803 and at the end of April, 1804, was exhibited in the Pantheon with great success. Afterward shown in Florence, the painting was finally installed in Arezzo at the end of October, 1804.

This drawing, differing in several important respects from either of Benvenuti's finished paintings, appears to

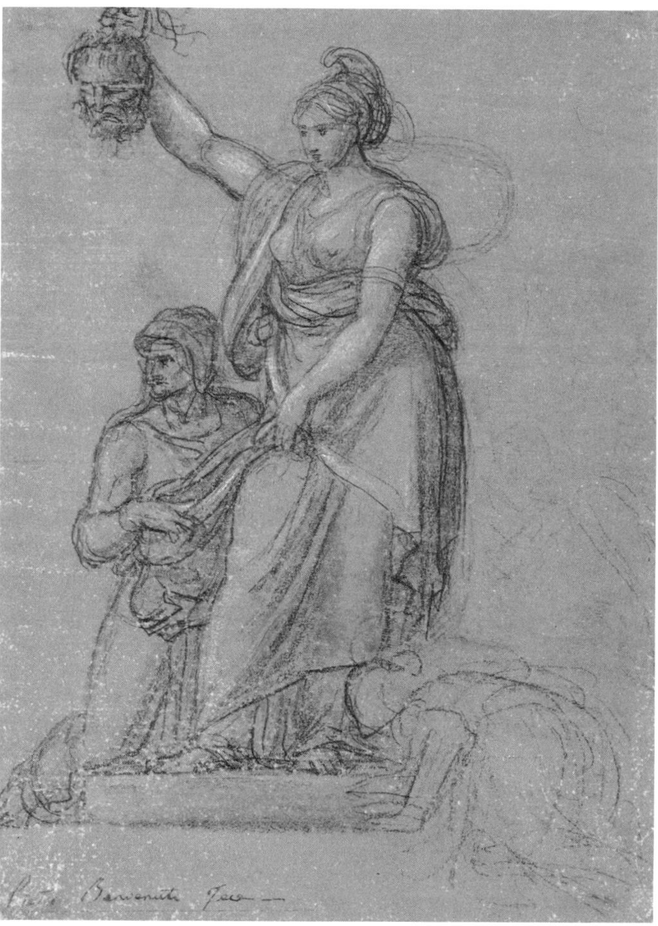

93

represent an interim stage in the development of the second version. In addition to changes made in the positioning of the head and in the headdress and costume, Benvenuti here lowered the left arm of Judith to correspond with the raising of the maid's arm, hoping apparently to promote a greater unity in the group. The final compromise, however, was to return the maid's arm to its original position but to repeat Judith's triumphant gesture with both arms held aloft.

Other preparatory studies for *The Triumph of Judith* are in the Gabinetto dei Disegni e delle Stampe degli Uffizi[5] and in the Casa Sandrelli, Arezzo.[6]

U.W.H.

1. For Benvenuti, with literature, *see* E. Fezzi in *Dizionario biografico,* 1960–, vol. 8, pp. 680–81; Arezzo, 1969; Florence, 1971, nos. 20–24.
2. Missirini, 1823, p. 344.
3. Repr. in Bruno Molajoli, *Notizie su Capodimonte,* Naples, 1958, pl. 106.
4. Salmi, 1913; Viviani, 1922, p. 180.
5. Inv. nos. 12024S, 12022S; Florence, 1971, no. 21.
6. Arezzo, 1969, nos. 1, 2 (repr.).

94. Studies for "The Curse of Cain"

Verso: *Studies for "The Last Judgment"*

c. 1827

Inscribed on verso in pencil at lower left: del Prof. P Benvenuti

Black and white chalks, stumping, on blue green wove paper

440 x 580 mm (17 3/8 x 22 7/8")

1978-70-186

Provenance: purchased from Gonelli, Florence, c. 1957

Exhibition: Providence, 1957, no. 28

On the recto of this sheet are three preliminary studies for the principal foreground figure in *The Death of Abel and the Curse of Cain,* one of the eight large scenes painted by Benvenuti in the cupola of the Cappella dei Principi in the church of San Lorenzo, Florence.[1] This "gigantic undertaking," as Benvenuti described it in his autobiography,[2] consisted of the eight narrative paintings in the sections of the cupola, together with eight hexagons depicting the four Evangelists and Moses, Aaron, David, and Saint John the Baptist.[1] The project, which occupied the artist from 1827 to 1836, was Benvenuti's second major fresco commission, exceeding in scale his better-known cycle for the Sala d'Ercole in the Palazzo Pitti (1817–29) and executed immediately afterward.

Considered suitable for the sepulchral chapel of the Tuscan grand dukes, the program for the cupola centered on the theme of death and redemption, with Old Testament subjects from Genesis each given a counterpart from the New Testament. The scene opposite Cain and Abel represents the Resurrection of Christ.

In the final painted version the figure of Cain is proportioned more compactly and massively, is made to advance forward rather than laterally, and shows the position of the arms reversed, with the right arm drawn across to the opposite side of the head. The natural bluntness and vigor of Benvenuti's style are joined in such later works by a new intensity in treatment of surfaces and greatly increased contrasts of light and shade.

A number of similar, inscribed studies for the project were recorded by Anthony Clark as being on the market at the time this drawing was purchased. A nearly complete set of oil studies for the San Lorenzo cupola frescoes is owned by Benvenuti's descendants in Arezzo.[2]

The verso of this sheet, indicating the oblong frame of the cupola section, contains an early idea for the whole composition of Benvenuti's *Last Judgment.*

U.W.H.

1. Viviani, 1922, p. 185. For the project, *see* Missirini, 1836; for a reproduction of the cupola, Aldo Fortuna, *The Church of San Lorenzo in Florence and the Medicean Chapels,* Florence, 1950, pp. 29–30, 69.
2. Arezzo, 1969, nos. 23 ff.

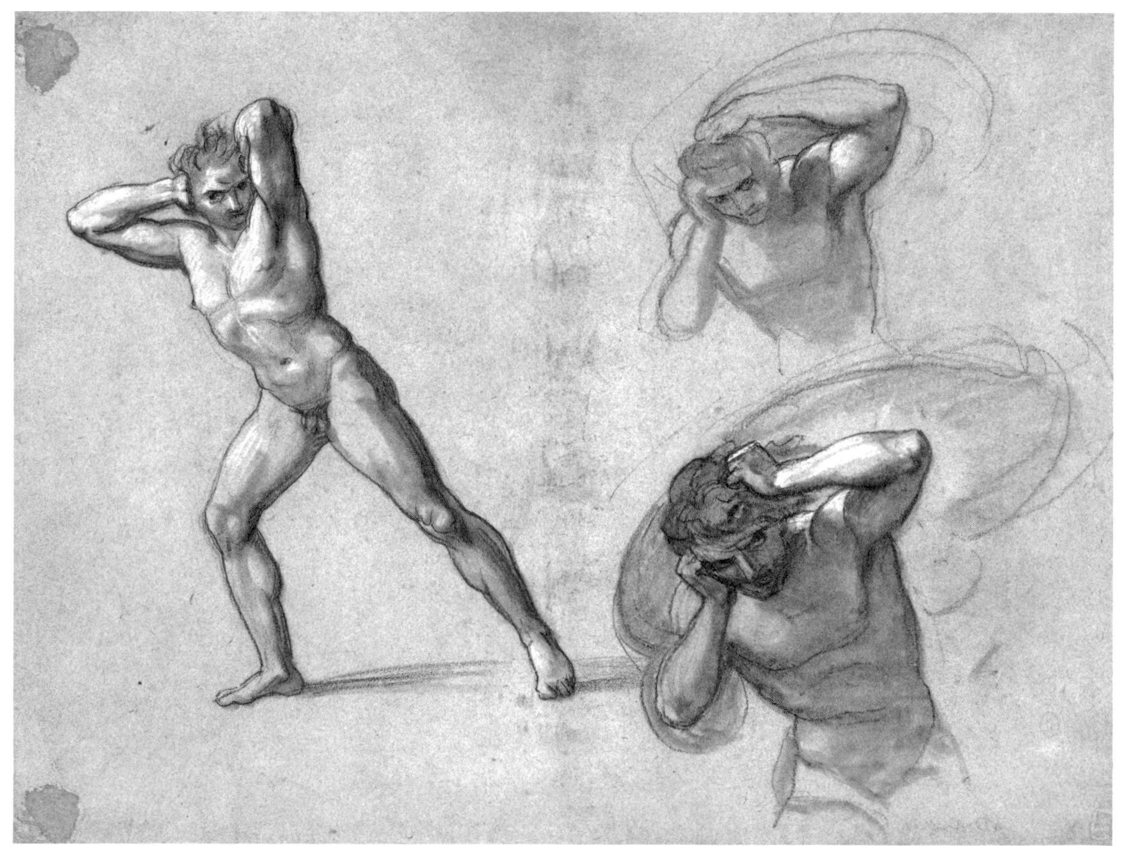
94 Recto

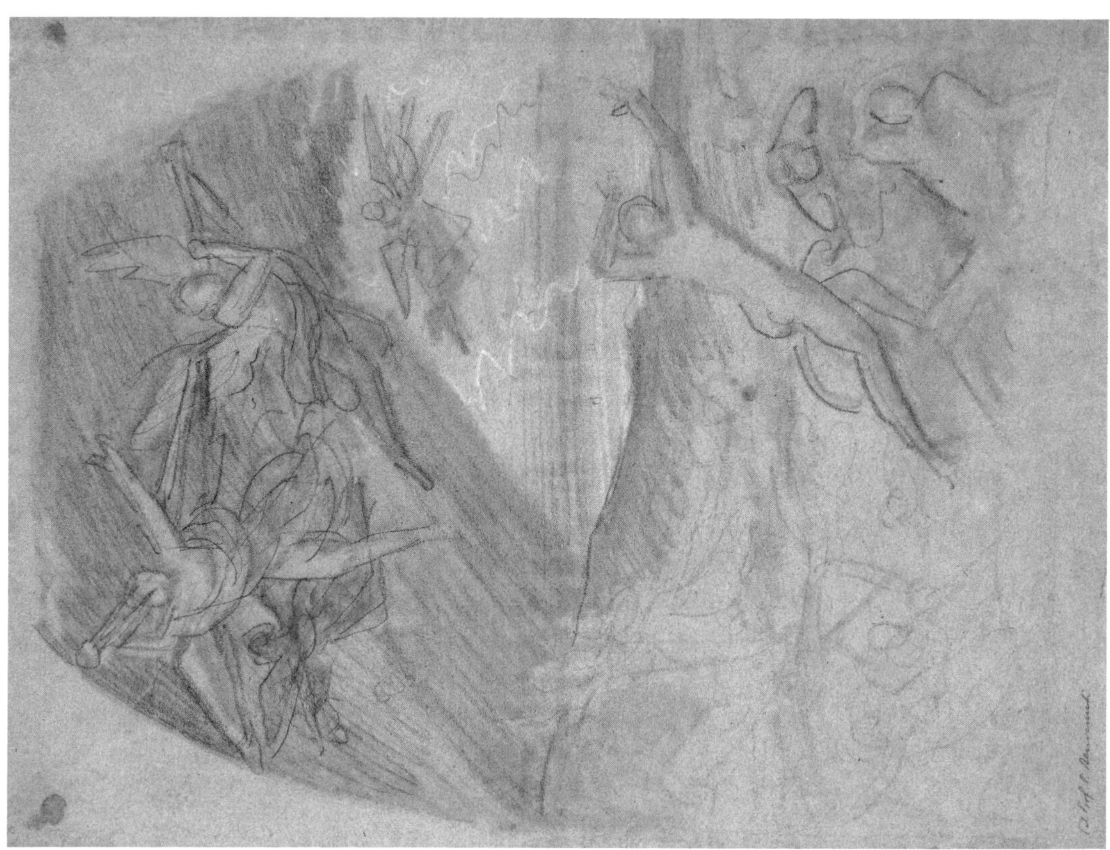
94 Verso

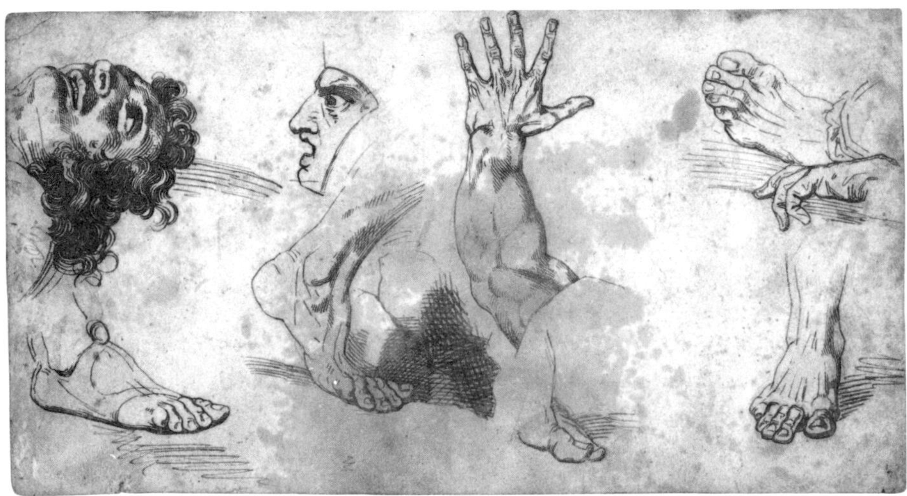
95

LUIGI SABATELLI

Florence 1772—Milan 1850

95. Studies for a Battle Scene

Verso: *Two Black-chalk Sketches of Standing Figures* (not illustrated)

c. 1801

Pen and brown ink on buff wove paper

109 x 203 mm (4 5/16 x 8")

1978-70-402

Provenance: purchased from Gonelli, Florence, 1958

A member of the same generation as Camuccini and Benvenuti, Luigi Sabatelli[1] was regarded with them as one of the principal reformers of Italian painting in the early nineteenth century. His imaginative and emphatic graphic style owed something to Michelangelo and to Fuseli, whose work Sabatelli came to know during a sojourn in Rome between the years 1789 and 1794. A draughtsman of precocious talents, Sabatelli won his own group of admirers in Rome for drawings improvised on themes from Homer, Dante, the Old Testament, and Greek and Roman history. Although this early reputation as *improvisatore pittorico* largely faded from memory, critics who were divided on Sabatelli's merits as a painter continued to view his most significant achievements within his immense output of drawn and engraved compositions.

His designs published in Rome included the series *Pensieri diversi* . . . of 1795, and after he returned to Florence Sabatelli created his most celebrated engraving, *The Plague of Florence* (1801), taken from Bocaccio's *Decameron*. In Florence he also received the commission for a large canvas of *David and Abigail,* the pendant to Benvenuti's *Judith* painted for the cathedral in Arezzo (no. 93). In 1808 Sabatelli was appointed professor of painting at the Accademia di Brera, Milan, where he taught for the remainder of his career. In Milan and throughout Lombardy he executed numerous decorative projects, also returning at intervals to Florence for other commissions, which included the frescoes for the Sala dell'Iliade in the Palazzo Pitti (1820–25) and the Tribuna di Galileo (1841).

These studies apparently relate to a series of engravings representing battles fought between the Greeks and Persians, executed by Sabatelli probably not long after *The Plague of Florence*. The series includes *Arimnestus Slaying Mardonius,* as well as scenes from the battles of Thermopylae, Plataea, Salamis, and Marathon.[2] Within these compositions some seemingly identical parallels to the heads, feet, arms, and hands in the Clark sheet can be found—such as the upraised arm in the *Battle of Thermopylae*—but as all of the studies represent stock elements in Sabatelli's repertory, there is no certainty as to which, if any, of these compositions is directly related to this sheet. The most likely candidate is the scene of the *Battle of Marathon*. Despite its modest scale, the sheet represents a microcosm of Sabatelli's style, remarkable for its dramatic energy and tension, and for its bold, decisive technique.

U.W.H.

1. *See* Sabatelli, 1900; for important recent studies of the artist with earlier literature, *see* Pistoia, 1977, and Florence, 1978.
2. Florence, 1978, nos. 46–49, figs. 48–51.

FORTUNATO DURANTI

Montefortino (Marches) 1787—Montefortino 1863

96. *Kneeling Angel and Putti*

c. 1820–25

Inscribed on verso in pencil: Agrigola [sic]; P369; partially obliterated inscription: 1488 [?]

Pencil with traces of black chalk on buff laid paper

243 x 186 mm (9 5/8 x 7 5/16")

1978-70-271

Provenance: Giovanni Piancastelli (?) (1845–1926); Mary Brandegee (Lugt suppl. 1860c); purchased from Rockman Prints, New York, 1958

An artist of humble origins, Fortunato Duranti showed an intense interest in drawing at an early age. He was sent to Rome at the expense of Cardinal Ercolani, where he studied with a follower of Batoni and became the friend of his exact contemporary Tommaso Minardi. Duranti's acquaintance with Felice Giani (*see* nos. 81–85) is credited with having introduced him to a style of neoclassicism that was evolving into romanticism. Duranti supported himself as a dealer rather than as an artist—no commissions or paintings are known—and as such he set out for the Congress of Vienna in 1815 believing that the large gathering of statesmen and their entourages there would provide a thriving market for art. He was arrested and imprisoned at the Austrian border, however, and his entire stock of paintings and engravings was confiscated, an event which afterward haunted the apparently extremely sensitive Duranti and left him permanently unstable. He lived in Rome, with sojourns in Montefortino, occupied as a dealer of paintings and antiquities until 1840; thereafter he retired permanently to his native town in the Marches, where his last decades were plagued by physical and emotional ill health.

Drawing itself was one of Duranti's many obsessions. He left several thousand sheets that mirror his preoccupations and are often remarkable for the way in which traditional themes, such as the Virgin and Child or the Flight into Egypt, are altered to express the artist's personal fantasies. The influences on Duranti were primarily the works of Raphael, Pontormo, and—especially important for his late drawings, which exhibit a distinctively cursory, "cubist" style—Luca Cambiaso.

It is the style of Pontormo that infuses this particular sheet. Examples of motifs Duranti derived from Pontormo are the angel's profile and the twist of its body (with its extravagantly rendered, full, billowing draperies), as well as the round "pop-eyes" of the putti, the pudgy limbs, and hunched-up shoulder that obscures the chin. Duranti's works in this manner usually have a claustrophobic sense of space, with the figures seen close up and virtually filling the available ground.

The subject of the drawing might be extended from Duranti's fascination with the theme of the Virgin and Child; the two young boys suggest the young Christ and Saint John the Baptist. Black chalk and pencil drawings by Duranti in the same style, representing the Virgin and Child and strongly influenced by Raphael and Pontormo, are in the Cooper-Hewitt Museum in New York and in the Biblioteca Comunale in Fermo. Eitner has dated them early in the artist's career, between about 1820 and 1825.[1]

M.L.M.

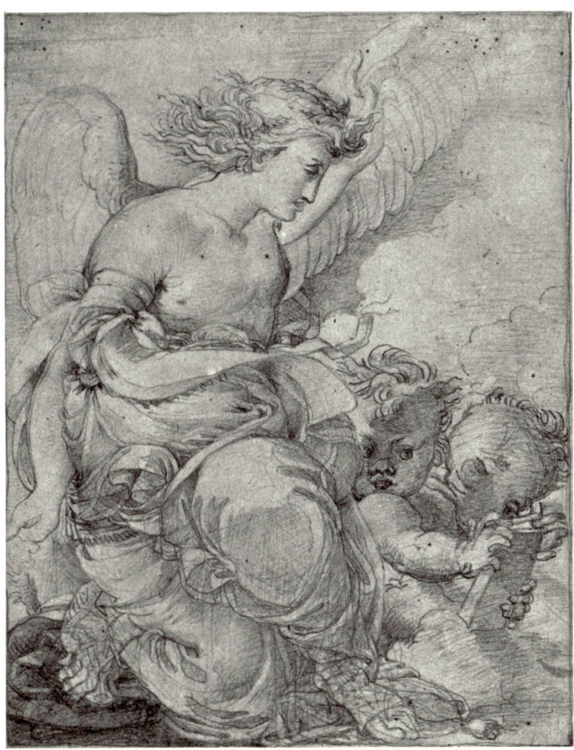

96

1. The best work on Duranti is Palo Alto, 1965, with previous bibliography. *See also* Francini, 1928–29; Pino Adami, 1977. Duranti's drawings have figured in three recent exhibitions: Rome, 1969–70, nos. 17–25; Milan, 1973, nos. 27–35; and Milan, 1977. This drawing is closely related to two drawings at the Cooper-Hewitt Museum, New York: a *Mother and Child* (inv. no. 1938-88-8048; Palo Alto, 1965, no. 8, repr. fig. 4) and a *Virgin Borne Aloft by Putti* (1938-88-8041); both works share the same Piancastelli-Brandegee provenance as the Clark sheet. The pose of the angel is close, though in reverse, to that of an angel on a sheet in a private collection in Fermo (Milan, 1973, no. 28, repr.; Milan, 1977, no. 4, repr.).

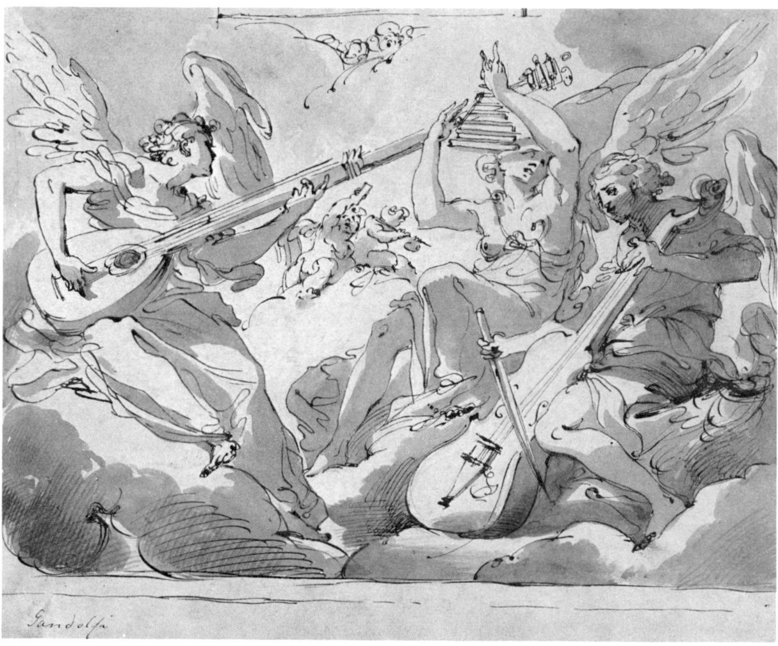

97

Attributed to FILIPPO PEDRINI
Bologna 1763—Bologna 1856
97. A Concert of Angels
after 1830
Inscribed in brown ink at lower left: Gandolfi; inscribed illegibly in pencil on verso
Pen and brown ink with gray wash over traces of pencil on beige wove paper
178 x 210 mm (7 1/16 x 8 1/4")
1978-70-279
Provenance: gift of John Maxon, 1956

Anthony Clark's notes indicate that he considered this drawing near the work of members of the Gandolfi family, Bolognese painters and draughtsmen of the second half of the eighteenth century. He rightly rejected attributions to Ubaldo and Gaetano Gandolfi and was considering a tentative attribution to Gaetano's son Mauro,[1] although none of the characteristic features of Mauro's drawings—an elegant refinement of line, precision of detail, and certain stylistic conceits for the rendering of hands and faces—can be said to appear in the present drawing.

Nevertheless, it is certainly in the immediate circle of the Gandolfi that the author of this drawing must be sought. The late Bolognese artists whose drawings most closely resemble those of the Gandolfi are the two Pedrini: Domenico, the father, a contemporary and follower of Ubaldo, and his son and pupil, Filippo, who carried the Bolognese late Baroque tradition well into the nineteenth century. Domenico's pen and wash drawings, closely resembling those of Ubaldo Gandolfi and frequently confused with them, can be described as lighter, more delicate variations of his master's style. Filippo, while retaining a number of stylistic features clearly derived from Ubaldo, tended, except for a period when he dabbled in neoclassicism, to execute his drawings in a looser, more flowing style.[2]

The *Concert of Angels* appears to be a study for a wall or ceiling decoration (the small square indicated at the top of the drawing may signify the position of a window). Clark noted the similarity between this drawing and one by the same hand in the Albertina, also containing a ceiling study with a concert of angels.[3] The angel on the left appears in the Albertina drawing from a slightly different angle. The two drawings share stylistic idiosyncrasies also reflected in other sheets by Filippo Pedrini, such as the awkward handling of the hands and feet and the very Ubaldesque stylization of the head as seen in the Clark drawing's central angel. Certain parallels can in addition be drawn between the Clark drawing and a fresco of an *Allegory of Victory* in the Palazzo Comunale in Bologna.[4] The fresco likewise represents female figures holding wreaths, seated on clouds and viewed *di sotto in su,* and reveals a similar stylization of facial features together with an almost total inability to cope with the drawing of a hand holding an object.

Roli attributes to Ubaldo Gandolfi another *modello* for a ceiling painting of a *Concert of Angels,* which is surely also by Filippo Pedrini.[5] A convincing comparison can be made between the two angels holding long-necked lutes that appear to the left in almost identical poses in both the *modello* and the present drawing. The central angel in both the drawing and *modello* (holding a lyre in the latter) is in exactly the same relationship to the lute-playing angel.

The artist, who died at the age of ninety-three, had an unusually long working career, and thus it is difficult to date his works; moreover, a complete chronology of Filippo's paintings, on which a chronology of his drawings would depend, has not yet been done. The Clark sheet can tentatively be dated rather late in Filippo's career, after 1830, when he had outgrown both the earlier influence of Ubaldo Gandolfi and the later one of Felice Giani.

M.A.C.

1. Mauro's drawing style, until recently almost invariably confused with that of his father and brother, is only now beginning to be known. *See* Mimi Cazort in Bologna, 1979, nos. 303–9, pls. 302–8.

2. Published material on the two Pedrini is scarce (*see* especially Roli, 1978; Bologna, 1979, nos. 310–19), and the distinction between their respective hands awaits further clarification.

3. Inv. no. 2969; attributed to Gaetano Gandolfi (A. Stix and A. Spitzmüller, *Beschreibender Katalog der Handzeichnungen in der Staatlichen Graphische Sammlung Albertina,* vol. 6, *Die Schulen von Ferrara, Bologna, Parma und Modena, der Lombardei, Genuas, Neapels, und Siziliens,* Vienna, 1941, no. 338, pl. 338). Other drawings forming a stylistically homogeneous group that can now be given to Filippo are: an *Adoration of the Shepherds* in the Albertina (inv. no. 1868; Bologna, 1979, no. 316, repr. pl. 309); a study for a *Ceiling with Bacchus, Ariadne, Diana, and Minerva* in the Art Institute of Chicago (inv. no. 1922.3340; Joachim and McCullagh, 1979, p. 90, no. 148, repr. pl. 153, there tentatively attributed to Ubaldo Gandolfi); a *Justice and Nobility* in the collection of the Pennsylvania Academy of the Fine Arts, Philadelphia (inv. no. 195); a *Study for a Ceiling* in the Staatsgalerie, Stuttgart (collection Koenig-Fachsenfeld, inv. no. 11/1090); and another *Study for a Ceiling* in the Albertina (Stix and Spitzmüller, op. cit., no. 331, pl. 331). It is significant that all the above drawings were previously given to either Ubaldo or Gaetano Gandolfi—and usually to Ubaldo—despite the fact that in some instances the drawings bear old inscriptions to Filippo Pedrini.

4. For a detail reproduced, *see* Roli, 1978, fig. 81a.

5. Roli, 1978, fig. 77a.

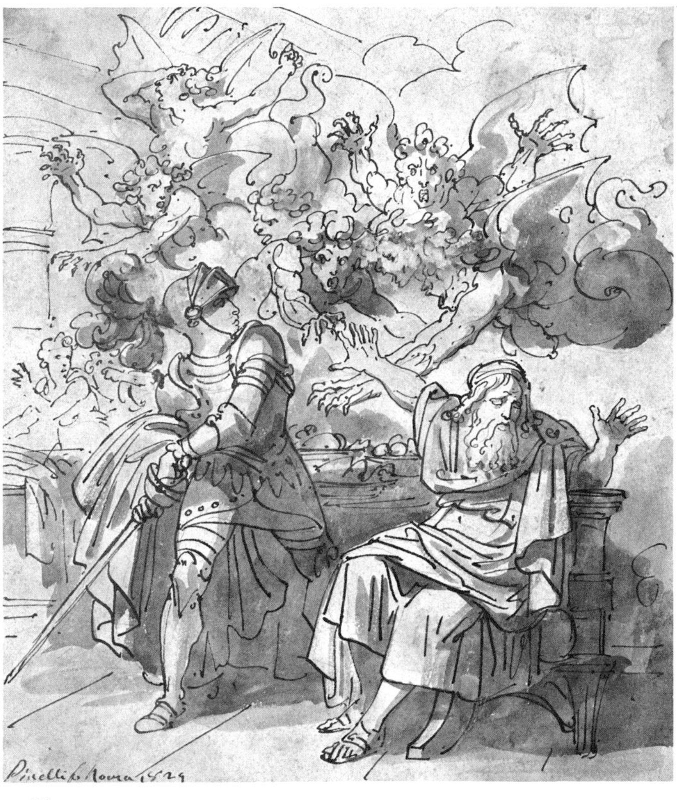

98

BARTOLOMEO PINELLI

Rome 1781—Rome 1835

98. *Illustration to "Orlando Furioso": Astolpho Fights the Harpies at Senapo's Table*

1829

Signed and dated in black ink at lower left: Pinelli f Roma 1829; inscribed on verso in pencil at upper left: 1

Pen and black ink with brown wash, over traces of blue chalk, on cream wove paper

214 x 186 mm (8 7/16 x 7 5/16")

1978-70-389

Provenance: gift of John Maxon, 1958

Exhibition: Minneapolis, Minnesota, The Minneapolis Institute of Arts, "Dreamer of Dreams," September, 1969 (no catalogue)

A versatile artist who practiced as a sculptor, painter, and draughtsman, Bartolomeo Pinelli[1] became most widely known for his drawings and engravings, which ranged from copies after old masters to Roman landscapes and ancient mythologies. Most renowned, however, were his scenes drawn from the local life of Italy portraying colorfully dressed countrypeople, brigands, and the inhabitants of Trastevere; his various *Raccolte di costumi pittoreschi* were issued in many editions and supplements after their first publication in 1809.

Pinelli's watercolors and drawings became great favorites among visitors to Rome after the Restoration, and some measure of the enthusiasm for his work can be gained from Orloff's assessment in 1823 of the young artist, "... endowed with true genius, ... who surpasses all imagination, as much in the composition of his drawings as in the truth of his images and of the regional costumes. Nothing is more exact, nothing is more correct and more bold than his pencil, ... and no foreigner would dare leave Rome without taking away some souvenirs of Pinelli, which are equally as much souvenirs of his native land."[2]

Pinelli created illustrations to a number of literary classics including the *Aeneid*, the *Divine Comedy*, *Gerusalemme liberata*, and *Don Quixote*. This drawing is the study for plate 70 of Ariosto's epic *Orlando furioso* in the edition illustrated by Pinelli in 1828 and 1829;[3] it depicts an episode in which Duke Astolpho comes to the aid of Senapo, the blind king of Nubia, made to suffer perpetual hunger by the Harpies who steal any food set before him:

Behold! the band of Harpies thither flies,
Lured by the scent of victual from the skies...

And seven in number are the horrid band;
Emaciated with hunger, lean, and dry;
Fouler than death; the pinions they expand
Ragged, and huge, and shapeless to the eye...

The fowls are heard in the air; then swoops amain
The covey well nigh in that instant, rends

The food, o'erturns the vessels, and a rain
Of noisome ordure on the board descends.
To stop their nostrils king and duke are fain;
Such an insufferable stench offends.
Against the greedy birds, as wrath excites,
Astolpho with his brandished faulchion smites.[4]

Pinelli's vigorous and fluid style, which owes something to both Fuseli and Giani, transposed a "nobler" neoclassicism into an unstrained and easily digested popular idiom. Even the visionary force of this fantastic scene from Ariosto is muted into a pleasantly theatrical effect.

A rapid worker and a bohemian by nature who reputedly created part of his vast output seated in his favorite *osteria*, Pinelli was able to maintain a strength and a genuine novelty that far outweigh the inevitable repetitions in his oeuvre. Though a prizewinner as a student at the Accademia di San Luca, he was never actually elected an academy member.

Other drawings for the Orlando series are cited as in the Galleria di Palazzo Bianco, Genoa.[5]

U.W.H.

1. For Pinelli, *see* Falconieri, 1835; Raggi, 1835; Rome, 1956.
2. Orloff, 1823, vol. 2, p. 431.
3. *L'Orlando furioso di Messer Lodovico Ariosto / inventato ed inciso all' acquaforte, in cento rami da B. Pinelli Romano* (al costo di paoli tre ogni cinque, ne portiranno dieci stampe il mese), Rome, 1828.
4. *Orlando furioso,* canto 33, ll. 119 ff., from the English translation by William Stewart Rose published in London in 1828.
5. F. Noack and A. Pander, in Thieme-Becker, 1907–50, vol. 27, p. 57.

PRINTS

In the eighteenth century, reproductive prints became an integral part of the vast intellectual and commercial enterprises of Enlightenment Europe.[1] The impact of these prints on previously isolated audiences was immense. Exposing thousands to new schools of art, educating their taste, and sharpening their visual awareness, they were crucial to the formation of the sophisticated public that frequented the salons and academies of the later eighteenth and nineteenth centuries.

This selection of prints, the majority of which are reproductive etchings or engravings, is consistent with what might be sampled in a typical eighteenth-century European collector's cabinet. While only three are by Italians, their subject matter reflects an age preoccupied with Italian art and culture. Prints were the principal means by which transalpine audiences learned about and enjoyed the work of Italian masters from Raphael to Canaletto. The growth throughout eighteenth-century Europe of a large, mainly amateur audience for reproductions of Italian paintings and drawings led to the domination of this sector of the Italian art world by a polyglot collection of dealers, agents, artists, and printsellers.

A glance at the interrelationship of some of the artists and publishers represented in this collection demonstrates the importance of these informal networks in spreading public interest in reproductive prints. In Paris, the comte de Caylus and Nicolas Le Sueur experimented with etching and chiaroscuro woodcuts, which they combined to reproduce drawings in the *Recueil Crozat,* published in 1729 (*see* nos. 102–4). Traveling to Paris in 1720, the Venetian Anton Maria Zanetti learned this technique from Crozat and his collaborator Pierre-Jean Mariette, both of whom he had met previously in Italy; Zanetti then went to England, where he discussed chiaroscuro reproductions of drawings with artists and connoisseurs, and on his return to Venice produced a series of woodcuts after Parmigianino drawings he had purchased in London.[2]

Simultaneously, the English wood engraver John Baptist Jackson, who had worked on the *Recueil Crozat* in Paris, brought to Venice an improved block-printing technique he had developed, which won encouragement from Zanetti, Consul Smith, and a number of distinguished travelers.[3] When another Englishman, Arthur Pond, stopped in Paris in 1727 he met the comte de Caylus and Mariette, studied their prints, and with them started a prosperous trade in prints and old master drawings. In Italy, he had entered the circles of the caricaturist Pier Leone Ghezzi in Rome and probably of Zanetti in Venice. When he returned to London, Pond began to publish prints after drawings in imitation of the *Recueil Crozat* and caricature etchings after Ghezzi (*see* no. 106). He also imported for sale the prints of the Swiss engraver Johann Jakob Frey, then established in Rome (*see* nos. 99–100).[4]

Soon after Pond left Rome, the German engraver Markus Tuscher arrived there and entered the service of the antiquarian Baron Philipp von Stosch (*see* no. 106). Stosch introduced him to Ghezzi, and when in 1741 Tuscher left Italy for the north, he carried with him the caricature drawing that would be published two years later by Ghezzi's London friend Arthur Pond (*see* no. 107).

The wide appeal of contemporary eighteenth-century reproductive prints is exemplified by the many different kinds of people who bought them—artists, tourists, virtuosi, and wealthy consumers filling their leisure hours with art. Professional artists collected reproductions to familiarize themselves with paintings or drawings they could not see or as a permanent record of those they had seen. Art students copied prints to improve their draughtsmanship, while established painters used them as sources for details and poses, especially when an allusion to or "quotation" from a famous work of art was held to enhance the interest of a composition. Tourists—usually English—were mainly interested in the subject matter of the prints and paintings they bought to commemorate their visits and to show to family and acquaintances back home.

For virtuosi—wealthy, leisured people whose main avocation was art—print collections were a principal means of studying the history of art. Among other things, reproductive prints provided a permanent working vocabulary of the distinguishing features of various artists. Partly influenced by limited means of reproduction, experts based their attribution of paintings as much on the elements of composition and design as on coloring or brushwork; engravings could thus supply important information on which to base aesthetic judgments.[5] Drawings were recognized by the inimitable qualities of an artist's "hand," and this, it was believed, could be aided through the study of prints after drawings.

In the early eighteenth century, aristocratic and middle-class patronage for reproductive prints began to develop and as the century progressed swelled to overwhelming proportions. Some of this audience was female, and reproductive prints—published in matched series, elegantly tinted with watercolors, framed in black, and protected by expensive sheets of plate glass—were to become standard features of decoration in hallways, staircases, and dining rooms. Engraved portraits, usually exemplifying their owners' political or religious allegiances, were also collected and displayed. Viewing these collections became a polite eighteenth-century amusement that prefigured the phenomenon of the nineteenth-century photograph album.

L.W.L.

1. The material in this essay is derived from the author's dissertation in progress, "Arthur Pond and the London Art World, 1700–1750" (Princeton University, Department of History).

2. Venice, 1969, p. 15.

3. Jacob Kainen, *John Baptist Jackson, Eighteenth-Century Master of the Color Woodcut,* Washington, 1962.

4. London, British Museum, Add. MS 23,725 ("Papers illustrative of the works of Arthur Pond"), fol. 83.

5. Jonathan Richardson, *The Theory of Painting,* Strawberry Hill, 1792, pp. 10–20.

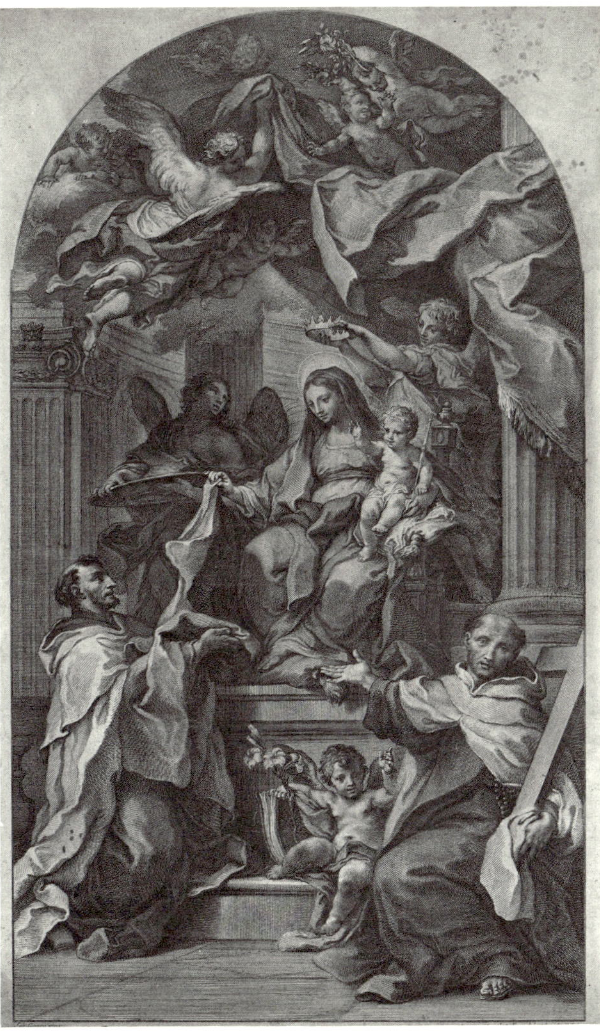

99

JOHANN JAKOB FREY

Hochdorf (Lucerne) 1681—Rome 1752

after Sebastiano Conca

99. *The Madonna and Child Enthroned with Saints Bonaventure and Anthony of Padua*

1719

Inscribed: Seb: Conca pinx. Iac: Frëij del. et Incidit Roae 1719

Engraving with etching

602 x 355 mm (23 11/16 x 13 15/16″) sheet trimmed within plate line

1978-70-571

Johann Jakob Frey[1] arrived in Rome in 1702 and entered the studio of Carlo Maratta around 1709 or 1710. He adapted the loose, painterly technique of Maratta's etchings to his own reproductive printmaking, combining the etching needle and engraver's burin to achieve subtly modeled, accurate renderings of paintings, a style that became highly influential. Frey's oeuvre consisted mainly of engravings after the work of his own contemporaries and of sixteenth- and seventeenth-century masters such as Raphael, Annibale Carracci, Guido Reni, and, especially, Carlo Maratta. Probably around 1723 he purchased from Maratta's heirs their stock of prints and copper plates, which he used as the foundation for his own highly successful firm, becoming one of the oustanding Roman reproductive engravers of his age. Those abroad who wished to follow the state of the arts in Rome, for example, would place standing orders with him, and his price lists are often found among the papers of eighteenth-century artists.[2] His position in Roman art circles was such that in 1723 Clement XII consulted him on the acquisition of the copper plates and engravings for the Calcografia Apostolica that later were to form the nucleus of the Calcografia Nazionale.[3]

Frey reproduced five works after Sebastiano Conca. This engraving is after a painting of 1719 now in the collection of the earl of Leicester at Holkham Hall.[4]

M.L.M./L.W.L.

1. For the most complete listing of Frey's prints, as well as for the details of his life and work, *see* F. Noack in Thieme-Becker, 1907–50, vol. 12, pp. 347–38. *See also* Gori Gandellini, 1808–16, vol. 10, pp. 75–78; Nagler, 1835–52, vol. 4, pp. 485–88.

2. London, British Museum, Add. MS 23,725 ("Papers illustrative of the works of Arthur Pond"), fol. 83, and Add. MS 23,089 ("Notebook of George Vertue"), fols. 46–47.

3. *See* Ozzola, 1910.

4. *See* Sestieri, 1969, p. 328, repr. p. 329, fig. 16; Sestieri, 1970, pp. 132, 135, no. 94.

JOHANN JAKOB FREY

after Carlo Maratta

100. *The Glorification of Clemency*

1719

Inscribed: Carol: Eq: Marat. pinxit. Iac: Freij del: et Incid: Roae 1719 In Aedib. Ill.^{mi} ac Exc.^{mi} Principis D. Gasparis Alterij Em.^{mo} ac Rev.^{mo} Principi Laurentio Alterio S. R. E. Diacono Cardinali

Etching

745 x 355 mm (29 5/16 x 14″) plate line; 759 x 372 mm (29 7/8 x 14 5/8″) sheet

1978-70-574

Under the pontificate of Clement X Altieri (1590–1676; elected pope 1670) the family palace in Rome was rebuilt and redecorated; the ceiling of the enormous reception hall was frescoed by Carlo Maratta between 1674 and 1676.[1] The only known print of the grand ceiling, Frey's etching reproduces an early design for the fresco, the oil sketch now in the Prado. This oil sketch belonged to Maratta's heirs in 1719, the date of the print's publication.[2]

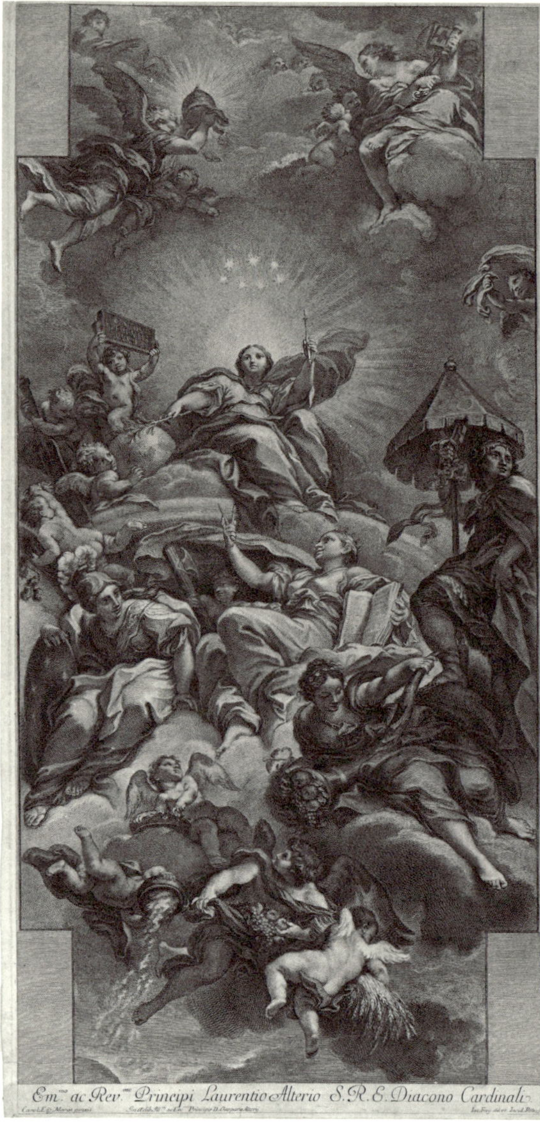

100

The authorship of the ceiling's program is uncertain, but Bellori's lengthy description clarifies some of its complicated imagery.[3] Clemency, seated in the center with a scepter and an olive branch stretched over a globe, indicates Pope Clement's peaceful reign over the Christian world. Beneath her Justice holds a compass and a book of law, and, leftward, Prudence as Minerva rests her hand upon a shield bearing the Altieri stars. The young man at the right with the hexagonal canopy is identified by Bellori as a relative of the pope in the guise of Strength; just below him reclines a woman identified as Public Happiness. The program as a whole is conceived as an illustration of the beneficent rule of Clement X—who is aided by Prudence, Justice, Strength, and Public Happiness—over the earthly and heavenly universe.

Owing perhaps to the exceptionally large size of the copper plate, it was impossible to print this etching upon a single sheet of paper. All known impressions are composed of two sheets, joined horizontally below the bottom-most putto's foot.

A.E.G.

1. *See* Schiavo, 1964, for the history of the family and palace; the ceiling is reproduced on plate 39. For other bibliography on the commission, *see* Storrs, 1973, no. 1 a, b.
2. Inv. no. 1767, Colecciones Reales, published in Alfonso E. Pérez Sánchez, *Museo del Prado, pintura italiana del siglo XVII, conmemorativa del ciento cincuenta aniversario de la fundación de Museo del Prado,* Madrid, 1970, pp. 366–67, no. 119, repr. This oil sketch passed directly from Maratta's heirs to the Spanish royal collections in 1722.
3. Bellori, 1976, p. 596. For the planned but unexecuted frescoes in the spandrels, *see* Montagu, 1978.

NICOLAS DORIGNY

Paris 1657—Paris 1746

after Carlo Maratta

101. Allegories of Art

A. *Academy of Drawing (A giovani studiosi del disegno)*

1728 (second state of two)

Inscribed: Eques Carolus Maratti inven. et delin. Cum priuil Summi Pont. et Regis Christ.mi Rome Apud Iacobum Frey an. 1728 N. Dorigny Sculp.

Etching with some engraving

473 x 325 mm (18 5/8 x 12 3/4") sheet trimmed to plate line

1978-70-552

B. *Ignorance (Agli amatori delle buone arti)*

1728 (second state of two)

Inscribed: Eques Carolus Maratti inu. et delin. Cum priuil Sum. Pont. et Regis Christ.mi et sup. perm. Rome Apud Iacobum Frey an. 1728 N. Dorigny sculp.[1]

Etching, with some engraving

467 x 317 mm (18 3/8 x 12 1/2") sheet trimmed to plate line

1978-70-551

Trained as a lawyer in Paris, Nicolas Dorigny went in 1687 to Rome where, having made the acquaintance of Maratta, he began his career as a printmaker with two prints after that master. In 1711 he left Italy for England and, after returning to Paris, was elected to the French Academy in 1725. His eyesight failing, Dorigny turned to painting and exhibited at the salons between 1739 and 1743.[2]

Maratta's preparatory drawings for these pendant prints survive at Chatsworth and in the Louvre.[3] The early stages of the *Academy* show that the Antinous statue in the background followed the antique model in the Vatican. In the final stage, Maratta transformed the Antinous into a precise copy of the Apollo statue in Raphael's *School of Athens*—a shift in emphasis from the fragmentary antique to the canon of High Renaissance perfection.[4] An early, rare edition of the print's first state, before Frey's address was added, was issued under Maratta's supervision prior to Dorigny's departure from Italy, probably between 1703 and 1705. The 1728 printing by Frey is part of a systematic publication of reproductive images after Maratta and other Roman artists.

As pendants, the prints complement one another in subject, addressing in turn issues of art practice and public appreciation. The *Academy* expresses the need for the aspiring painter not only to master the skills of drawing, perspective, anatomy, and geometry, as well as continually to study antique statuary, but also to possess an intelligence that is divinely granted.[5] Its pendant presents Ignorance as the worst enemy of the arts: Avarice drags Painting before Ignorance, who has snatched away Time's scythe, while Time covers his face in shame; Sculpture and Architecture are cast to earth in the foreground and Poetry and Philosophy flee in the background, while in the heavens Minerva begs Jupiter to aid the sorry state of events.[6] The long inscriptions accompanying each image explain most of the details; probably written by Dorigny, these texts closely reflect Maratta's ideas.

A.E.G.

1. *Ignorance* bears an inscription by the collector Alessandro Maggiori on the verso stating that he bought the print in Rome in 1805. (For other works in the catalogue formerly in Maggiori's collection, *see* nos. 3, 59).

2. The most useful sources for Dorigny's activities are George Vertue, cited in Horace Walpole, *Anecdotes of Painting in England . . . with Additions by the Reverend James Dallaway,* ed. Ralph N. Wornum, London, 1849, vol. 3, pp. 965–67, and Roger-Armand Weigert, *Bibliothèque Nationale, Département des Estampes, Inventaire du Fonds Français: graveurs du XVIIe siècle,* Paris, 1954, vol. 3, pp. 490–507 (with catalogue of 141 prints).

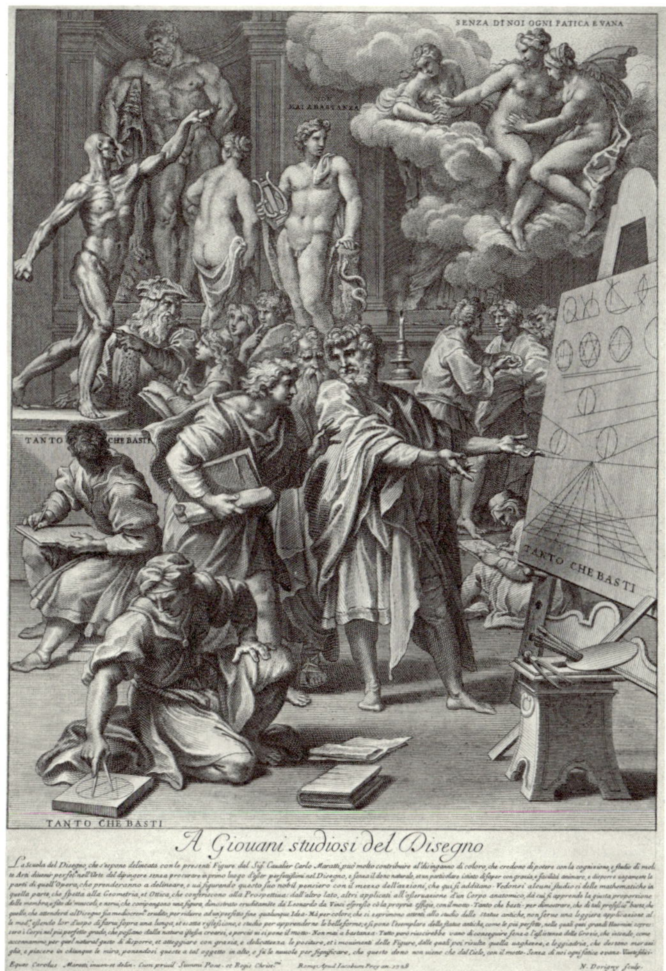

101A

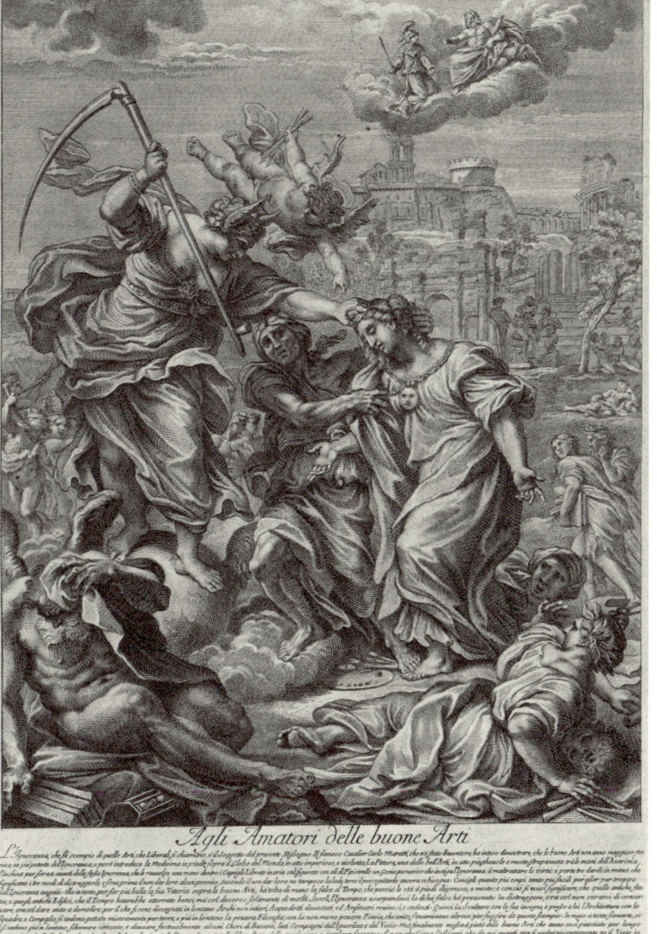

101B

3. The drawing for the *Academy* is at Chatsworth, collection of the duke of Devonshire (inv. no. 646, 402 x 310 mm). The *Ignorance* drawing is in the Louvre, Cabinet des Dessins (inv. no. 17950, 410 x 310 mm). For other aspects of Maratta's involvement with printed images, *see* Pavia, et al., 1977–78; Rudolph, 1978.

4. A preliminary drawing for the *Academy* is at the Wadsworth Atheneum, Hartford, Conn., inv. no. 1967.309a; *see* Amherst, 1974, no. 78, repr. This sheet may be a shop record of a lost finished drawing of an art academy by Maratta, made about 1682 for the marchese del Carpio, don Gaspar Méndez de Haro y Guzman, while he was ambassador to the Papal States (*see* Bellori, 1976, pp. 629–30). Pentimenti in the Chatsworth drawing also show changes in the Antinous figure, as well as elsewhere.

5. For an extended discussion, with reference to this sheet, of the iconographical history of art academies, *see* Oswald Kutschera-Woborsky, "Ein kunsttheoretisches Thesenblatt Carlo Marattas und seine ästhetischen Anschauungen," *Mitteilungen der Gesellschaft für vervielfältigende Kunst. Beilage der "Graphischen Künste,"* nos. 2, 3 (1919), pp. 9–28; *see also* Matthias Winner, "Gemalte Kunsttheorie," *Jahrbuch der* Berliner *Museen,* vol. 4 (1962) pp. 151–85.

6. *See* Andor Pigler, "Neid und Unwissenheit als Widersacher der Kunst," *Acta Historiae Artium,* vol. 1, 1954, pp. 215–35.

NICOLAS LE SUEUR

Paris 1691—Paris 1764
after Sebastiano Conca

102. Diana and Endymion

1729
Inscribed: Diane et Endimion / d'apres le dessein de Sébastien Conca, gravé par Nicolas leSueur. Sous la Conduite de M.[le] Basseporte 134
Chiaroscuro woodcut, with line block printed in black and two tone blocks printed in light and dark greens
450 x 312 mm (17 3/4 x 12 1/4″) image; 522 x 367 mm (20 5/8 x 14 7/16″) sheet
1978-70-600

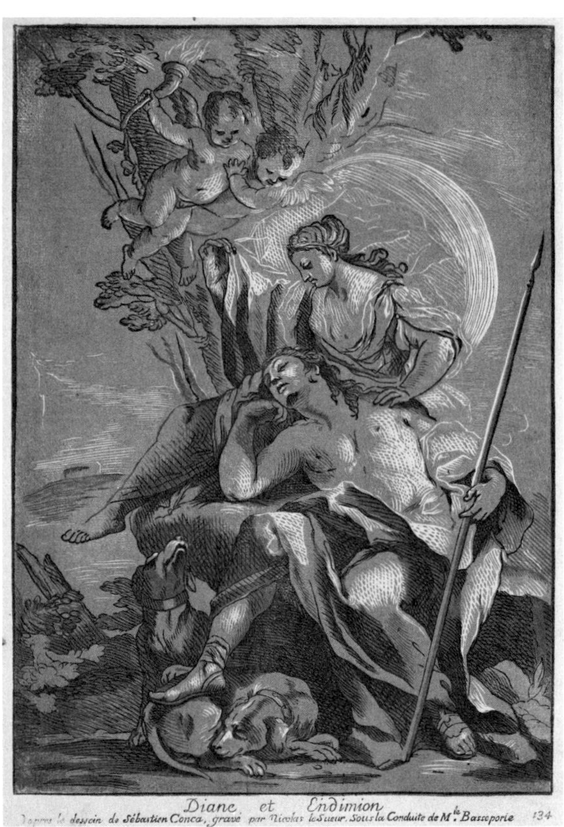

102

This print and numbers 103 and 104 originally were bound into a copy of the lavishly produced folio *Recueil d'estampes d'après les plus beaux tableaux et d'après les plus beaux dessins qui sont en France, dans le Cabinet du Roi, dans celui de Monsigneur le Duc d'Orleans, & dans d'autres Cabinets . . . ,* Paris, 1729, which was commonly called the *Cabinet Crozat,* or *Recueil Crozat,* because many of the works reproduced belonged to Pierre Crozat (1665–1740) and because of his financial support of the project.[1]

The *Recueil Crozat* stands as the first illustrated presentation of the historical and stylistic development of Italian painting and drawing from the Renaissance to contemporary times. The texts on the forty-six Roman and five Venetian artists, ordered chronologically, seem to have been a cooperative endeavor shared by Crozat, Pierre-Jean Mariette (1694–1774), and Anne-Claude-Philippe de Tubières, comte de Caylus, the three keen est connoisseurs in Paris of their time. A collaborative effort among printmakers as well, the *Recueil Crozat* was chiefly illustrated by Caylus as etcher and Nicolas Le Sueur as woodcutter. Most of the prints after drawings combine etched line and relief, with two woodblocks of different colors used to capture accurately effects of pen and ink or chalk and wash on toned paper.

The *Diana and Endymion* is one of three prints made wholly in the medium of woodcut; Conca's original drawing in Dresden is executed in black and white chalks on gray blue paper and corresponds precisely in reverse to the print.[2] No other work by Conca has yet been related to the composition of Diana and Endymion.

A.E.G.

1. The publication was divided into two volumes and comprised 140 oversized plates, after forty-one drawings and ninety-nine paintings by Roman artists. A supplement for Venetian artists of plates after forty paintings and two drawings was prepared during the 1730s and joined with the original Roman plates to form the second edition of 1742.

2. Staatliche Kunstsammlung, Kupferstich Kabinett, Dresden, inv. no. C 562.

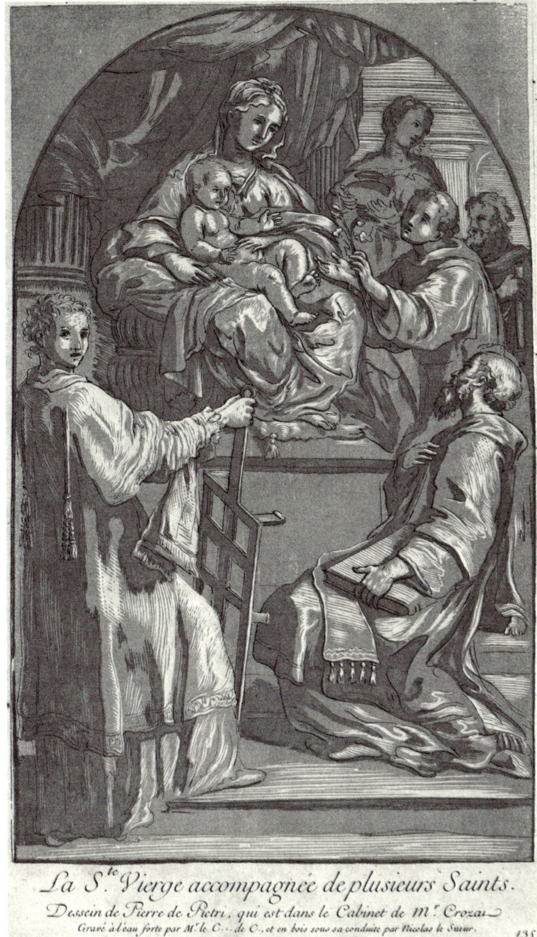

103

ANNE-CLAUDE-PHILIPPE DE TUBIERES, COMTE DE CAYLUS

Paris 1692—Paris 1765

and NICOLAS LE SUEUR

after Pietro de' Pietris

103. The Virgin and Child with Five Saints, including Lawrence, Anthony of Padua, and Praxedes

1729

Inscribed: La S.te Vierge accompagnée de plusieurs Saints. / Dessein de Pierre de Pietri, qui est dans le Cabinet de M.r Crozat / Gravé àl'eau forte par M.r le C. . . de C., et en bois sous sa conduite par Nicolas le Sueur. / 135

Etching, printed in black, with two chiaroscuro woodblocks printed in light and dark greens

420 x 242 mm (16 9/16 x 9 1/2″) plate line; 538 x 388 mm (21 1/4 x 15 1/4″) sheet

1978-70-602

On the *Recueil Crozat*, in which this print was published, *see* number 102. Although its drawn model, once in the Crozat collection, has not been traced, we may assume that it was made in black and white chalks on grayish paper and that the green tones of the print approximate coloristically the drawing's appearance. The design records an early stage in the composition of an altarpiece still *in situ,* painted by Pietro de' Pietris (*see* no. 7) for the first chapel to the left in Santa Maria in via Lata, Rome.[1] The painting contains all the figures present in the drawing reproduced in the *Recueil,* but shows them in rearranged postures and with additional figures in the background. Two other preliminary drawings for the composition exist, in which the poses vary and the figure of Saint Praxedes is omitted.[2]

A.E.G.

1. Gabinetto Fotografico Nazionale, Rome, E 21483. (I am grateful to Stella Rudolph for this reference.)

2. Kunstmuseum Düsseldorf, Kupferstichkabinett (inv. no. FP 3027; *see* Düsseldorf, 1964, no. 130, pl. 38); Windsor Castle, Royal Library (inv. no. 5649; Blunt and Cooke, 1960, p. 86, no. 670, fig. 65).

COMTE DE CAYLUS and NICOLAS LE SUEUR

after Luigi Garzi

Pistoia 1638—Rome 1721

104. Saint Philip Neri's Vision of the Virgin

1729

Inscribed: S. Philippe de Nery. / D'apres le dessein de Louis Garzi, qui est dans le Cabinet de M.r Crozat. / Gravé à l'eau forte par Mr le C . . . de C . . . et en bois sous sa conduite par Nicolas le Sueur. / 133

Etching, printed in black, with two chiaroscuro woodblocks printed in dark and light greens

379 x 250 mm (14 15/16 x 9 7/8″) plate line; 538 x 385 mm (21 1/4 x 15 1/8″) sheet

1978-70-601

Born in Tuscany, the painter Luigi Garzi is recorded in Rome by the age of fifteen as a pupil of Salomon Boccali; he then studied with Andrea Sacchi. A prolific artist who worked primarily in Rome and Naples, he was made a member of the Accademia di San Luca in 1670. While he enjoyed a high reputation during his lifetime, his work has yet to be totally rescued from the obscurity into which it has fallen since his death.[1]

The drawing, belonging to Crozat, that served for this print in the *Recueil Crozat* (*see* no. 102) is now in the Louvre.[2] It records an early stage in the composition for an altarpiece representing the vision of Saint Philip Neri, commissioned from Garzi in 1699 by Padre Domenico Federici (1633–1720), a diplomat who was a prominent citizen of Fano. The altarpiece was executed for the church of San Pietro in Valle, Fano,[3] and is still *in situ.*

A.E.G.

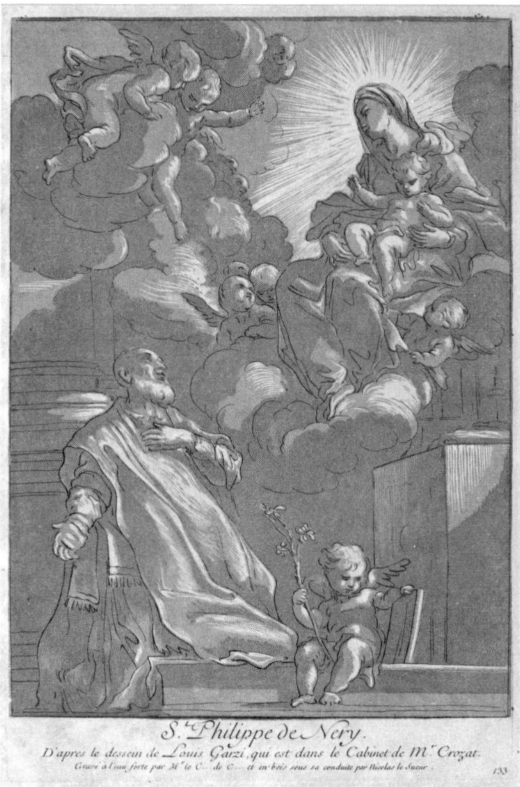

104

1. Basic sources for Garzi are Pascoli, 1730–36, vol. 2, pp. 235–45, and Lanzi, 1968, vol. 1, pp. 397–98. *See also* Sestieri, 1972.

2. Cabinet des Dessins, inv. no. 3110 (pen and brown ink, pale brown wash, touches of white chalk, on blue paper; 358 x 250 mm). The drawing is reversed in the *Recueil* print, which otherwise exaggerates the white heightening, adding whiteness as paper tone to indicate certain highlights.

3. I am grateful to Franco Battistelli, director of the Biblioteca Comunale Federiciana, Fano, for photographing the painting and for making available the information concerning its commission (extracted from the manuscript of c. 1707 by Padre Jacomo Ligi, Biblioteca Comunale Federiciana, MSS Federici, no. 76 ("Congregazione dell'Oratorio de Fano"), fols. 67–68.

PIERRE SUBLEYRAS

Saint-Gilles-du-Gard 1699—Rome 1749

105. The Banquet in the House of Simon the Pharisee

1738

Signed and dated: P. Subleyras inven. Pinxit, et sculp. Romae 1738.

Etching, printed in red brown

249 x 608 mm (9 13/16 x 23 15/16″) plate line; 253 x 614 mm (9 15/16 x 24 1/8″) sheet

1978-70-653

Subleyras's etching, dated 1738 and dedicated to the duc de Saint-Aignan, the French ambassador in Rome, reverses the composition of his painting of *The Banquet in the House of Simon the Pharisee* (on the artist, *see* no. 22). Signed and dated 1737, the painting was commissioned by the canons of the Order of Saint John Lateran for the refectory of their monastery at Asti (Piedmont); it is now in the Louvre, along with one of its *bozzetti.*[1] The influence of Veronese's *Wedding at Cana* has been noted in the graceful disposition of figures in a large architectural setting and especially in the buffet filled with food and vessels. Painted two years after Subleyras's term as a *pensionnaire* had expired and he had decided to stay on in Rome, the painting has been seen as the first witness of his artistic maturity,[2] foreshadowing the renown he was later to earn for his large religious paintings.

Subleyras made nine etchings, most of which are connected with his painted compositions. The use of red brown ink in this impression gives a richer and more painterly effect than is usual in his prints, for the most part printed in black.

M.L.M.

1. *See* Paris, Musée du Louvre, *Catalogue illustré des peintures; école française xviie, et xviiie,* Paris 1974, vol. 2, p. 218, nos. 782–83, p. 107, figs. 782–83. On the painting's preparatory studies and variant versions, including the etching, *see* Odette Arnaud in Dimier, 1928–30, vol. 2, pp. 59–60, 74–75, 86, 90, nos. 21–27, 18, 5, respectively. In 1739 Subleyras married the miniaturist Maria Felice Tibaldi, who often copied his paintings; in 1748 she copied the Louvre *Banquet in the House of Simon* in a miniature now in the Capitoline Museum, Rome (exhibited Rome, 1959, no. 595).

2. Arnaud, in Dimier, 1928–30, vol. 2, p. 60.

ARTHUR POND

London 1701—London 1758

after Pier Leone Ghezzi

106. Two Famous Antiquaries, Stosch and Sabatini

1739

Inscribed: Cav. Ghezzi delin. AP. fecit 1739. Due famosi Antiquari. / Stosch. Sabbatini.

Etching

382 x 262 mm (15 1/16 x 10 5/16″) plate line; 416 x 309 mm (16 3/8 x 12 3/16″) sheet

1978-70-631

Arthur Pond visited Rome in 1726, where he met and drew Pier Leone Ghezzi (*see* nos. 12–14), along with other Italians prominent in the city's social and artistic

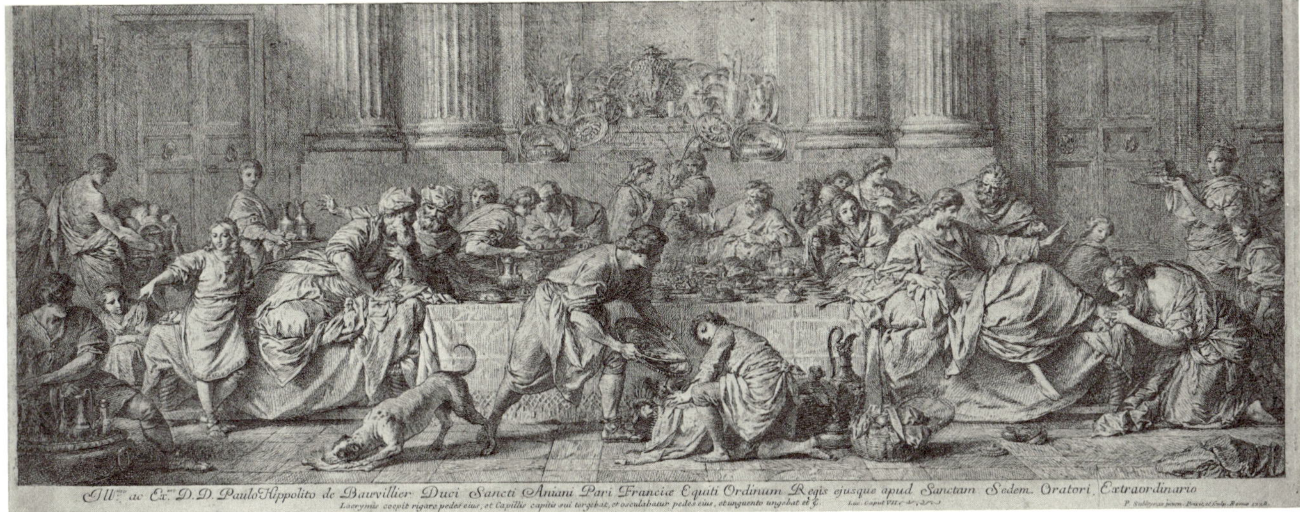

105

life. Between 1736 and 1747 he published a series of twenty-six etched caricatures, of which twelve, including the *Two Famous Antiquaries,* are after drawings by Ghezzi.[1] Born on London Bridge in 1701,[2] Pond dedicated much of his career to the promotion of Italian art in England. He etched a series of prints after sixteenth- and seventeenth-century Italian drawings in imitation of the *Recueil Crozat* (*see* no. 102) and later published several series of engravings after Claude Lorrain, Gaspard Dughet, and Giovanni Paolo Panini. He was also a successful, if rather uninteresting, portrait painter and a famous dealer and collector of drawings and prints. In the 1740s his interest shifted to natural history and he began a comprehensive collection of shells and "fossils," which, in conjunction with his artistic endeavors, led to his election as a fellow of the Royal Society and a member of the Society of Antiquaries in 1752.

Represented avidly examining gems are two of Rome's foremost antiquaries, Baron Philipp von Stosch (1691–1757; *see also* nos. 19, 125) and Marcantonio Sabatini, both of whom appear in one of Ghezzi's best-known caricatures, *A Congress of the Finest Antiquaries of Rome.*[3] Stosch, the better known of the two figures, was a brilliant and outrageous man, a scholar, and a discerning collector of ancient coins and gems. His gem collection, eventually catalogued by Winckelmann,[4] was one of the largest and finest ever assembled, containing over three thousand objects. Born in Prussia, he arrived in Rome in 1715 and soon met everyone of consequence in social, intellectual, and antiquarian circles, becoming good friends with the pope's nephew, Cardinal Alessandro Albani. With the death of Clement XI in 1721 the pension Stosch held from the pope ended, and, to augment his income, he became a secret agent in Rome for the British government. Among the visitors he reported on was Arthur Pond, whom he described as very loyal to the Hanoverians.[5]

It was not by chance that Ghezzi represented Sabatini with Stosch, as they were close friends and often traveled together. A Bolognese aristocrat,[6] Sabatini was granted in 1703 the title of papal antiquary and superintendent of ancient and contemporary buildings. As tutor to Alessandro Albani, he advised the future cardi-

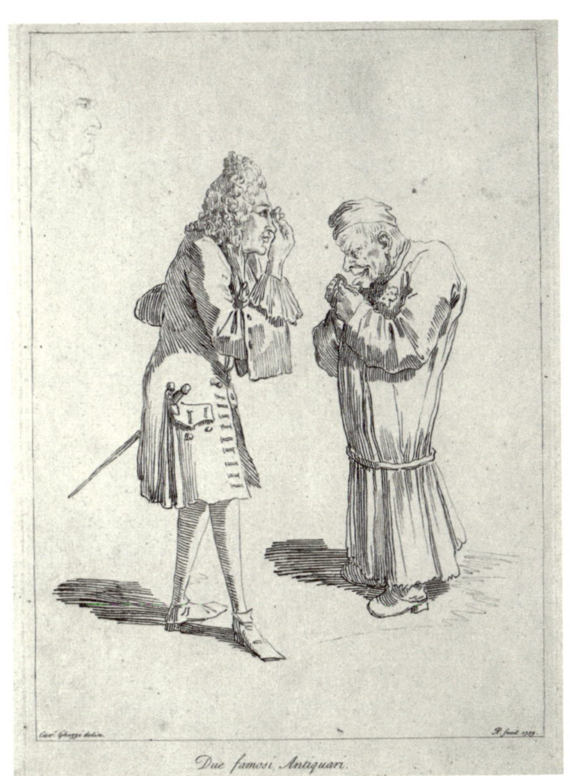

106

nal on matters of collecting and taste. It is not clear whether Sabatini took holy orders, as in *Two Famous Antiquaries* he is shown wearing what may be a cleric's robe, whereas in the *Congress of Antiquaries* he appears in secular dress. Sabatini was himself an avid collector and counted among his possessions the renowned gem called the Strozzi Medusa (*see* no. 11), which Stosch published in his *Pierres antiques gravées*.

L.W.L./M.L.M.

1. On Pond, *see* Hake, 1922 (for the etching, p. 347, no. 74). Ghezzi's drawing for Pond's print is in the collection of the duke of Devonshire at Chatsworth (inv. no. 641; pen and ink, 365 x 255 mm; repr. by Vitzthum, 1971, p. 70, fig. 17).
2. London, Guildhall Library, MS 11361, Parish Register of Saint Magnus the Martyr, 1557–1720 (Baptisms and Burials), fol. 91.
3. Two versions of the caricature exist, one in the Kunsthistorisches Museum, Vienna, dated 1725, and the other in the Vatican Library, dated 1728. For the Vienna version, *see* A. Stix and L. Frölich-Bum, *Beschreibender Katalog der Handzeichnungen, Graphische Sammlung Albertina,* vol. 3, *Die Zeichnungen der toskanischen, umbrischen und römischen Schulen,* Vienna, 1932, p. 85, no. 892, repr. pl. 190; for the Vatican version, *see* Rome, 1959, no. 2449, which gives the inscription identifying the sitters (repr. by Bodart, 1976, p. 26, fig. 20).
4. *See* Winckelmann, 1760.
5. London, Public Record Office, State Papers Foreign, SP 85, vol. 16 (Walton Letters, Rome); this reference communicated by Brinsley Ford. Stosch's career is treated at length in Lewis, 1961; *see also* Lewis, 1967.
6. For information on Sabatini, *see* Justi, 1898, vol. 2, pp. 219, 239, 282, 301. Ghezzi caricatured him alone (*see* Rome, 1959, no. 2440), and an anonymous medal was struck in his honor, dated 1714 (ibid., no. 2441).

MARKUS TUSCHER

Nuremberg 1705—Copenhagen 1751

107. Caricature of Pier Leone Ghezzi

1743

Signed and dated: MT. del. & sculp: Londini 1743; inscribed: Il Famoso Cav[re] delle Caricature

Etching

335 x 203 mm (13 1/4 x 8″) plate line; 379 x 245 mm (14 15/16 x 9 5/8″) sheet

1978-70-656

Pier Leone Ghezzi was a man of many talents, but his fame today is primarily based on his numerous drawn caricatures (*see* nos. 12–14). Tuscher's caricature mimics Ghezzi's own style, showing him in front of the

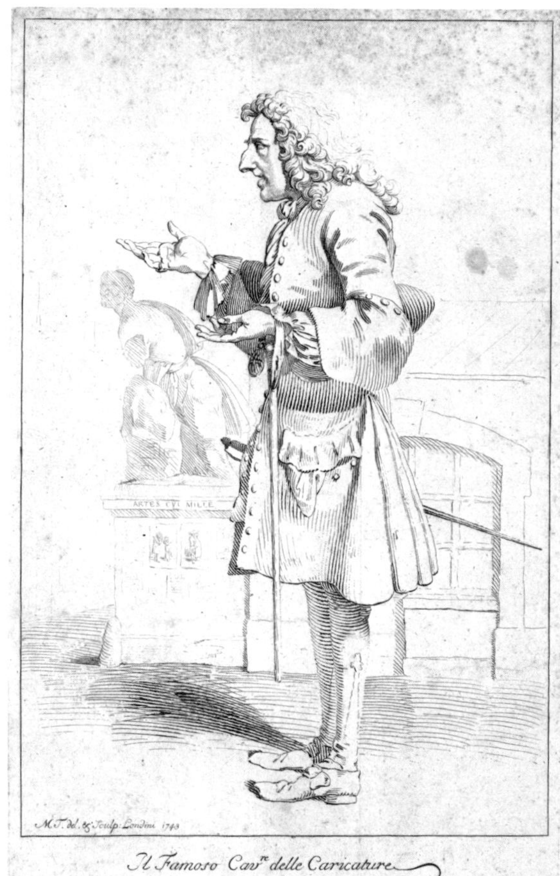

107

statue of Pasquino, to the base of which two of his own caricatures are attached.[1]

Markus Tuscher[2] studied with Nuremberg's leading engraver, Johann Daniel Preissler, before setting off for Rome in 1728 to join his teacher's son, Johann Justin, in the service of Baron Philipp von Stosch. Stosch introduced Tuscher to his wide circle of acquaintances—who commissioned drawings and prints from the young engraver—and to his friend and fellow antiquary Ghezzi. In 1731 Tuscher left Rome for Florence with Stosch to help record the latter's enormous collection of gems and to assist with his "atlas," an antiquarian and topographical history drawn from extant monuments or ruins. By 1732 Tuscher was a member of the Accademia di Belle Arti in Florence, and in 1738 he joined the Accademia di San Luca in Rome. He remained in Florence until 1741, when he left for Paris, Holland, and finally, London, where this caricature was published by Arthur Pond as part of Pond's series of Italian caricatures (*see* no. 106). Invited to the Danish court in 1743, Tuscher prepared the illustrations for Frederik Ludvig Norden's *Voyage d'Egypte et de Nubie.* First published in Copenhagen in 1755, it ranks among the earliest examples of the eighteenth-century taste for Egyptian antiquities and remains the artist's best-known

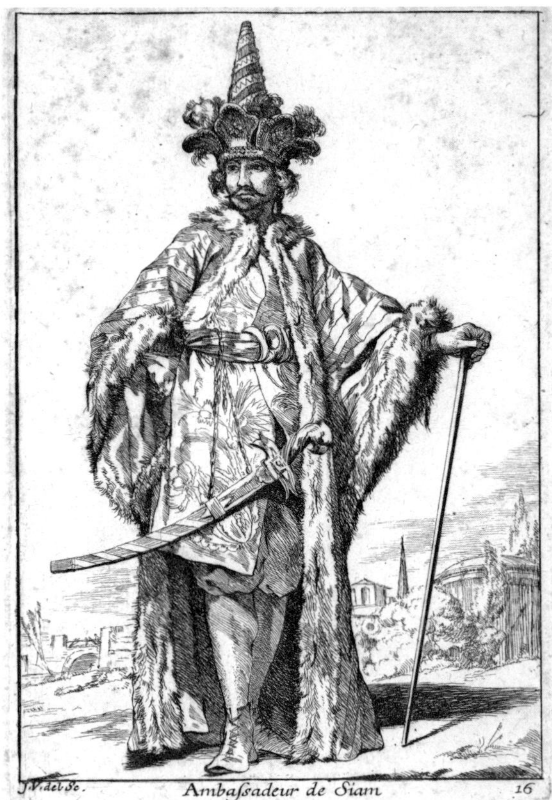

108

work. Tuscher spent the rest of his life in Copenhagen, becoming professor at the Danish academy of painting and drawing in 1748.

M.L.M.

1. The two Ghezzi caricatures, which Tuscher would surely have known, are the ones etched by Pond in London after Ghezzi's drawings, *Two Famous Antiquaries, Stosch and Sabatini* (no. 106) and *Un Pizzicaruolo.* Pasquino is a well-known, weathered fragment of ancient statuary, a male torso, situated along the flank of Palazzo Braschi near Piazza Navona.
2. On Tuscher, *see* Leitschuh, 1886, especially pp. 16–51.

JOSEPH-MARIE VIEN
Montpellier 1716—Paris 1809
108. The Ambassador of Siam
1748
Signed: J. V. del. Sc.; inscribed: Ambassadeur de Siam 16
Etching
203 x 136 mm (8 x 5 3/8″) plate line; 242 x 172 mm (9 1/2 x 6 3/4″) sheet
1978-70-663

Joseph-Marie Vien won the Prix de Rome in 1743 and remained in Rome from 1744 until 1750. Through his association with Mengs and antiquarian circles and his study of the excavations at Herculaneum, the example of ancient paintings—as well as of Italian painters of the sixteenth and seventeenth centuries—figured decisively in a reorientation of his style. Vien was to become of central importance in the development of French neoclassical painting, especially through his teaching; Jacques-Louis David studied under him when Vien was director of the French Academy in Rome from 1775 to 1781.[1]

Each year it was customary for students at the French Academy to participate in Rome's celebration of carnival, and Vien proposed for the carnival of 1748 that the theme adopted should be a Turkish masquerade, with costumes *à la turque* or in some other oriental fashion made out of painted cloth simulating a variety of rich fabrics and luxurious ornaments. The masquerade met with enormous success among the Romans who viewed it, including most of the nobility and the pope. Vien made a series of drawings of the magnificent costumes in his studio afterwards, which he then etched in thirty-one plates with the title *Caravane du Sultan à la Mecque, Masquerade turque donnée à Rome par Messieurs les Pensionnaires de l'Académie de France et leurs amis au Carnaval de l'année 1748.*[2] The ambassador of Siam is plate sixteen in the series; a preparatory drawing is in the Petit Palais, Paris.[3] Several sets of preparatory drawings for the etchings survive, and in one of these the names of the academicians and their friends are inscribed on the sheets; unfortunately, the drawing for *The Ambassador of Siam* has no inscription, and the masquerader's identity is therefore unknown.

The elaborate oriental costumes with their full, sometimes billowing silhouettes have a very rococo quality, as does the etching style. These prints differ greatly from the rigorous neoclassicism of Vien's later paintings, for which he is better known. The artist's interest in classical Rome is expressed, however, by the inclusion of ancient monuments in the backgrounds of this and many other etchings in the set, contrasting with the orientalism of the costumes.

M.L.M.

1. On Vien, *see* Detroit, et al., 1974–75, pp. 659–62.
2. On the *Caravane du Sultan à la Mecque, see* Boucher, 1961, and Boucher, 1962.
3. Regarding the problems of the various sets of drawings and a related series of pictures by the young painter Jean Barbault, one of the participants in the masquerade, *see* Toronto, et al., 1972–73, no. 144, and Beauvais, et al., 1974–75, pp. 25–44, especially nos. 52 and 53.

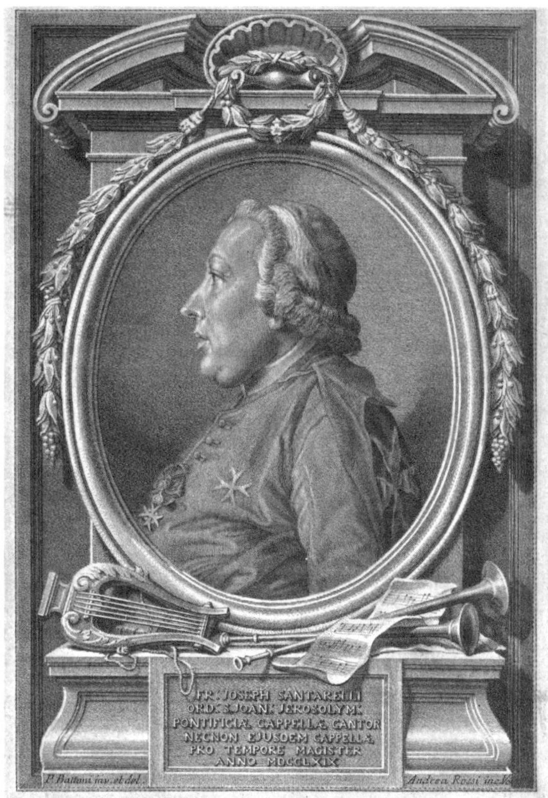

109

ANDREA ROSSI

Venice (?)—active 1770s—Rome (?)

after Pompeo Batoni

Lucca 1708—Rome 1787

109. Portrait of Giuseppe Santarelli

1769

Inscribed: P. Battoni inv. et del. Andrea Rossi inc. Ve; and: FR: JOSEPH SANTARELLI / ORD: S. JOAN: JEROSOLYM: / PONTIFICIAE CAPPELLAE CANTOR / NECNON EJUSDEM CAPPELLAE / PRO TEMPORE MAGISTER / ANNO MDCCLXIX

Engraving

212 x 142 mm (8 5/16 x 5 9/16″) plate line; 319 x 233 mm (12 9/16 x 9 3/16″) sheet

1978-70-643

Giuseppe Santarelli (1710–1790) was a chaplain in the order of the Knights of Malta and was from 1749 onward a soprano in the Sistine Choir.[1] A composer and theoretician, he was in contact with some of the most important writers on music of his time. In 1761 he sought the reform of the Sistine Choir through the offices of Cardinal Albani, an effort that is documented in a printed tract;[2] by 1769, as indicated by the inscription on Rossi's print, he was master of the Sistine Choir. Charles Burney, author of one of the first musical histories in English, met Santarelli in 1770 and described the Italian as "deep in theory, and learned in the history of his profession, . . . having been many years employed in the following curious work, *Della Musica del Santuario e della Disciplina de' suoi Cantori;* or, an Historical Dissertation on Church Music,"[3] a work that was never published.

Andrea Rossi executed prints after the paintings of a number of Venetian artists; Pompeo Batoni is supposed to have noticed these engravings and to have made every effort to secure Rossi's services to engrave his own work.[4] Whether or not Batoni was instrumental in bringing Rossi to Rome,[5] the engraver obviously had a close association with the famous painter; his best-known print is the folio sheet published in 1778 after Batoni's double portrait of Emperor Joseph II with his brother the grand duke Leopold of Tuscany, today in the Kunsthistorisches Museum, Vienna. Rossi's engravings have been praised for their graceful delicacy and for their resemblance to paintings. His print after Batoni's portrait of Santarelli shows his control of nuances of light, which gives such a convincing appearance of three-dimensionality that the image evokes a marble rather than a paper monument to the distinguished musician.

M.L.M.

1. On Santarelli, *see Enciclopedia della musica,* Milan, vol. 4, 1964, p. 111.
2. *See* Rome, 1959, no. 1746.
3. *See* Charles Burney, *The Present State of Music in France and Italy,* London, 1773, 2d ed., pp. 271–73, 279.
4. On Rossi, *see* Giannantonio Moschini, *Dell' incisione in Venezia,* Venice, 1924, pp. 98–99; Le Blanc, 1854–88, vol. 3, p. 365.
5. According to the inscription, Rossi was still in Venice in 1769 when he engraved the portrait of Santarelli. The artist's extensive Roman career included engraving the portraits of four popes and various saints and theologians, as well as making prints after the Roman paintings of artists such as Carlo Maratta, Annibale Carracci, and Pietro da Cortona; he also reproduced catafalques designed by Alessandro Specchi and Filippo Barigioni.

MARCO CARLONI

Rome 1742—Rome 1796

110. Portrait of Pope Pius VI

1778

Signed and dated: Con Priuil. Pontif. Marco Carloni Romano disegnò, e incise A. MDCCLXXVIII; inscribed: PIO · SEXTO · P · M / BONARVM · ARTIVM · PATRONO

Engraving

539 x 366 mm (21 1/4 x 14 3/8″) plate line; 606 x 430 mm (23 7/8 x 16 15/16″) sheet

1978-70-537

Marco Carloni, who practiced both as an engraver and a painter, is remembered today primarily for his engravings of the drawings of Franciszek Smuglewicz and Vincenzo Brenna after the grotesque paintings in the Golden House of Nero; these appeared in 1775 in *Vestigia delle Terme di Tito,* published by Ludovico Mirri. The same publisher issued six of the seven volumes by Giambattista and Ennio Quirino Visconti on the Museo Pio-Clementino; the first volume contains as a frontispiece a portrait by Carloni of Pius VI, seen in three-quarter view instead of in profile but given the same elaborate, ornamented surround.[1]

Giovanni Angelo Braschi (1717–1799), who reigned as Pope Pius VI from 1775, was named treasurer of the Apostolic Chamber (or finance minister of the Papal States) under Clement XIII and was created cardinal in 1771 by his own predecessor, Clement XIV. The Vatican collections of ancient sculpture had become so large by 1770 that Clement XIV had to provide new exhibition space by enclosing the Belvedere courtyard to form the present Cortile Ottagono (*see also* no. 54). Pius VI, whose success as finance minister had furnished the revenues that made Clement's extensive collecting possible, continued both the collections and the building of his predecessor, adding new rooms to create a cohesive complex of small, handsome, connecting galleries at the northern end of the Vatican that together form the Museo Pio-Clementino. Pius was also the founder of the Pinacoteca Vaticana. He died in exile in France, having been taken prisoner by Napoleon's invading armies. Appropriately, the palace he had built for a nephew in 1780, Palazzo Braschi, is today the seat of the Museo di Roma.

M.L.M.

1. *Il Museo Pio-Clementino descritto da Giambattista Visconti prefetto delle antichità di Roma,* Rome, 1782–1807; cited in Borroni, 1954–57, vol. 2, pt. 2, p. 200, no. 2139. This portrait, an impression of which exists in the Clark collection, is reproduced in Borroni, 1954–57, vol. 2, pt. 2, p. 199. In the Visconti volumes at Avery Library the engraving is signed not by Carloni but by Alessandro Mochetti and dated 1790; evidently Carloni's plate was reworked by Mochetti and included in the publication. For a portrait dated 1790 to appear in a volume with an imprint of 1782 may be explained by the fact that such publications were often issued unbound; this copy must have been bound only after 1790. Presumably other copies, bound earlier, exist with Carloni's signature on the plate. That the portrait exhibited here was itself often reworked is shown by another state of the profile, reworked by Carloni, that appears in a folio volume in the Metropolitan Museum of Art with the title page *Nuova raccolta di statue, busti, bassirilievi, e urne esistenti nel nuovo Museo Pio-Clementino nel Vaticano,* Rome, 1784. The volume contains sixty-nine plates, all engraved by Carloni, probably issued separately to be bound at the purchaser's discrimination.

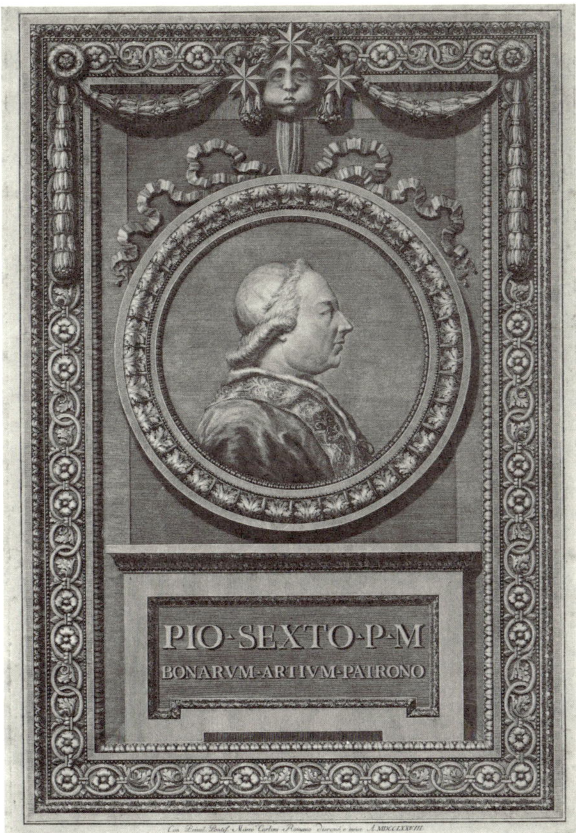

110

GIUSEPPE D'ESTE

Born Modena (?)—active Rome, c. 1808

111. Portrait of Pope Pius VII

1808

Signed: Giuseppe D'Este dis. ed inc.

Engraving

492 x 322 mm (19 7/16 x 12 5/8") plate line; 602 x 424 mm (23 11/16 x 16 11/16") sheet

1978-70-558

Giuseppe d'Este was active in Rome as a draughtsman, engraver, and architect by 1808,[1] the year in which this print appeared as the frontispiece to the catalogue of the Museo Chiaramonti authored by Filippo Aurelio Visconti and Giuseppe Antonio Guattani,[2] a continuation of the magnificent Visconti volumes on the Museo Pio-Clementino (*see* no. 110). The engraving represents a marble bust by Antonio Canova of Pope Pius VII Chiaramonti (1742–1823; elected pope in 1800), placed in the long gallery of the museum he founded in the Vatican Palace to house part of the Vatican's collection of ancient sculpture. The Museo Chiaramonti (*see also* no. 136) is divided into three galleries—the long, thin Galleria Chiaramonti, which conjoins the Galleria Lapidaria, and the Braccio Nuovo, which is set at a right angle to them. The engraver placed the bust at the junc-

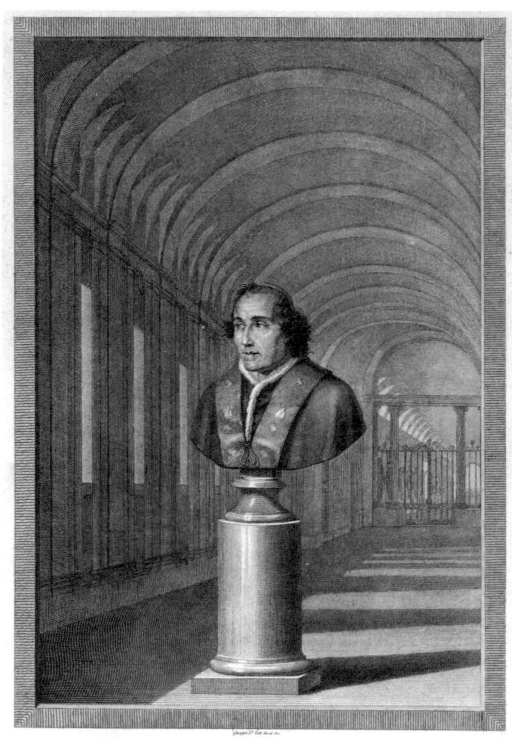

111

ture of the Galleria Chiaramonti and the Galleria Lapidaria, just before the iron grill that separates them. In ignoring or forgetting the question of reversal in engraving, he mistakenly shows the windows on the wrong side of the gallery.

Aristocratic and deeply cultured, Pius VII was elected pope in Venice and returned to a papal city bereft of many of its masterpieces, which had gone to France under the terms of the Treaty of Tolentino in 1797. He began the restoration of a papal collection by ordering statues from Canova in 1801 and in 1805 named the sculptor to the post of inspector general of antiquities and the arts in Rome and the Papal States. After 1816 Canova commissioned young artists to paint episodes of Pius's patronage of the arts in the fifteen lunettes of the Galleria Chiaramonti.[3]

A bust by Canova of Pius VII was made between 1820 and 1822 especially for the opening of the Braccio Nuovo, where it stands today; it is a second version, with much studio intervention, of a marble executed in 1806–7 that was given by Canova to the pope, who in turn donated it in 1820 to the Protomoteca Capitolina on the Campidoglio.[4] Closer in effect to Jacques-Louis David's painted portraits of the pope than to Canova's marble, d'Este's print may represent the engraver's imaginative transposition of the earlier version of Canova's statue to the gallery of the Museo Chiaramonti.

M.L.M.

1. On d'Este, *see* Zani, 1819–22, pt. 1, vol. 8, p. 118.

2. *Il Museo Chiaramonti aggiunto al Pio-Clementino da N.S. Pio VII. P.M. con l'esplicazione de' Sigg. Filippo Aurelio Visconti e Giuseppe Antonio Guattani pubblicata da Antonio d'Este e Gaspare Capparone,* vol. 1, Rome, 1808 (con privilegio Pontificio); cited in Borroni, 1954–57, vol. 2, pt. 2, p. 204, no. 2148. Giuseppe d'Este supplied several of the engraved plates of sculpture for the volume.

3. For this project and the history of the Museo Chiaramonti, *see* Hiesinger, 1978 ("Canova").

4. Pavanello and Praz, 1976, p. 111, no. 158, fig. 158 and color plate 34 for the version in the Protomoteca Capitolina; p. 132, no. 337 for the version in the Braccio Nuovo. Canova first sculpted the pope in 1803–4; this bust was sent as a gift to Napoleon on the occasion of his coronation and is now at Versailles (ibid., p. 111, no. 156, fig. 156).

SCULPTURE

Reproductions of antique and a few chosen "modern" sculptures enjoyed great popularity in Rome in the latter part of the eighteenth century. The manufacture of such small-scale replicas was intended mainly for export and included objects in terracotta and porcelain, as well as the more familiar bronze statuettes. These reproductions, which served either as individual mementos or cabinet pieces, could also be acquired in larger groups to form elaborate ornamental garnitures for the mantelpiece or dining table.

Giacomo and Giovanni Zoffoli, Francesco Righetti, Luigi and Giuseppe Valadier, and Giuseppe Boschi were among the most prominent Roman manufacturers of bronze replicas and ornamental furnishings. Most of these artists had been trained as silversmiths and appear to have contracted for their original models from outside sculptors. The bronzes they created thus depended upon skilled handcraft and free modeling rather than any mechanical processes.

Writing from Rome in 1795, where he had gone to study architecture and acquire works of art, the Englishman Charles Heathcote Tatham appraised the quality and relatively high prices of Roman bronzes in the following manner: "As to the difference between the Prices of the french bronzes and the Roman, no one here is I find at a loss to account for it. . . . The materials used by the french are in the first place very inferior to those used by the Romans, being for the most part of very indifferent metal; their figures in general ill attended as to nature (the ornament only being sometimes good) instead of gilding in solid gold, they are accustomed to use a kind of varnish mixt with gold dust . . . the bronzes themselves were also frequently covered with another mixture of varnish, . . . which is but a faithless representation of a good bronze, added to the rapidity with which they executed them, in consequence of a great demand, enabled them to sell them cheap. The bronze used by the Italians is of the best metal, with what they call a patina, meaning the outward colour, of a good nature, their gilding is always (unless ordered to the contrary) of real sicane gold, the most valuable of the kind for colour weight and substance, and above all their execution is superlatively good, having artists employed who study the antique with Attention and model with great ingenuity and taste. This is the comparison I have been able to make from the best information. The works in question must be left to speak for themselves hereafter, when under the inspection of those of better judgement."[1]

Produced in an era when genuine antiquities were increasingly scarce and expensive, and before industrialization produced a certain casualness about the availability of reproductive works, such bronzes could be, and were, admired for their fine individual craftsmanship. This admiration was enhanced rather than overshadowed by the recollection of the famous sculpted prototypes that they provided for connoisseurs and collectors.

U.W.H.

1. Honour, 1961, p. 201.

FRANCESCO RIGHETTI

Rome 1749—Rome 1819

112. Young Centaur

1787

Signed: F · RIGHETTI · F · ROMAE · 1787. Inscribed on base: ΑΡΙCΤΕΑCRΑΙ ΠΑΠΙΑC ΑΦROAEICCIC [sic]

Bronze

Greatest height 397 mm (15 11/16″); length of base 220 mm (8 11/16″)

1978-70-136

Provenance: purchased from The Drawing Shop, New York, 1969

Francesco Righetti[1] was apprenticed as a youth to the silversmith Luigi Valadier and established his reputation as a producer of bronzes in the 1780s. He became head of the Vatican foundry in 1805 and is known from the latter part of his career for his casting of large-scale bronzes for Antonio Canova, including the Brera *Napoleon* and the equestrian statue of Charles III in Naples.

In addition to producing copies of ancient and modern sculptures, Righetti, in a catalogue issued in 1794, offered his services in the making of bronzes to ornament "des Deserts, des Horologes, des Vases, des Urnes, des Obelisks, & autres objets."[2] Examples of such decorative furnishings by Righetti are recorded as early as 1786, when a marble and bronze *Parnassus* was ordered by the czarina. Some later works include a pair of dated candelabra of 1790 (Rome, Forquet collection), similar perhaps to those ordered by Lord Bristol in 1795; an elaborate altar set in gilt bronze of 1801 commissioned by Pius VII for San Giorgio Maggiore, Venice; and four grand table centerpieces produced for Naples in 1803 in collaboration with the artist's son Luigi.

This bronze, among Righetti's earliest known works, reproduces the younger of a pair of marble centaurs discovered in 1736 during excavations carried by by Monsignor Alessandro Furietti at Hadrian's Villa, Tivoli.[3] Evidently based on a Hellenistic bronze original, the marble centaur bears the signatures—incorrectly reproduced on this small bronze—of Aristeas and Papias, sculptors from Aphrodisias. Famous from the time of their discovery, the Furietti centaurs remained one of the prominent sights for visitors to Roman collections throughout the century. In 1765 they were acquired by Clement XIII and presented to the Capitoline Museum (for the medal commemorating this event, *see* no. 133).

The centaurs were among the reproductions of more than 150 famous sculptures featured in Righetti's catalogue of 1794 and were also represented in the almost contemporary but much smaller catalogue of reproductions offered by the bronzemakers Giacomo and Giovanni Zoffoli (*see* nos. 113, 114). A pair of Furietti centaurs by Righetti is in the Victoria and Albert Museum, London, and a pair by the Zoffoli is in the Nationalmuseum in Stockholm.[4]

U.W.H.

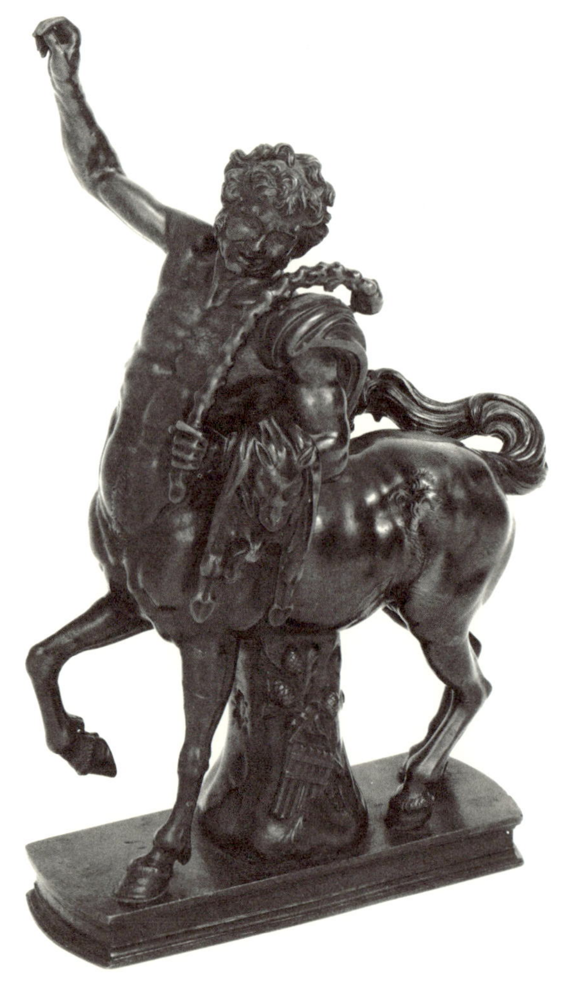

112

1. For Righetti and his works, *see* Righetti, 1940; Righetti, 1941; Honour, 1963; Gonzalez-Palacios, 1976.

2. Honour, 1963, p. 197.

3. This is the centaur drawn by Batoni and published in an engraving by Girolamo Frezza in 1739 (*see* Macandrew, 1978, pp. 137–38, fig. 4). For the marble sculptures, *see* Jones, 1912, pp. 7, 274–75, no. 2, pl. 64.

4. Honour, 1961, p. 202, figs. 5, 6; Honour, 1963, p. 199, figs. 6, 7.

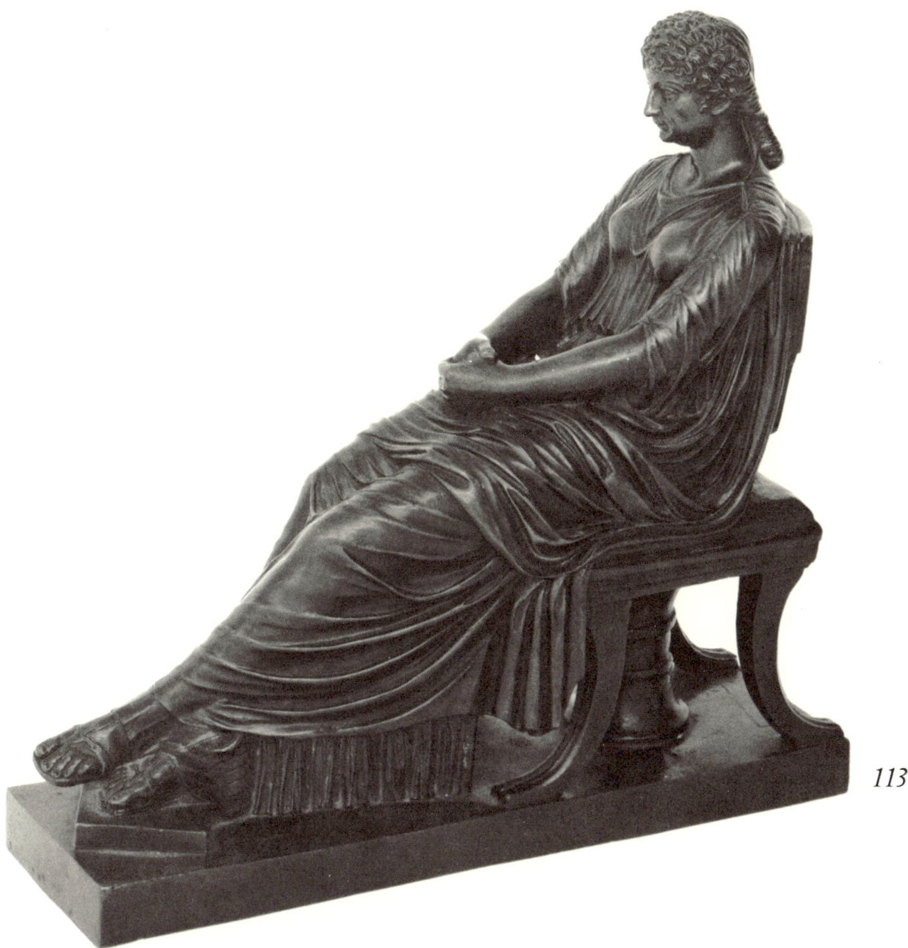

113

GIACOMO or GIOVANNI ZOFFOLI

Giacomo: Rome (?) c. 1731—Rome 1785

Giovanni: Rome (?) c. 1745—Rome 1805

113. Roman Matron (so-called "Agrippina")

c. 1780–90

Signed: G · Zoffoli · F

Bronze

Height 289 mm (11 3/8"); length of base 298 mm (11 11/16")

1978-70-138

Provenance: purchased from The 18th Century Shop, New York, 1956/57

Exhibition: Cleveland, 1964, no. 104, repr.

Bibliography: Honour, 1961, p. 198, fig. 1, p. 205, no. 5

Relatively little is known of the bronzeworkers Giacomo and Giovanni Zoffoli.[1] Giacomo, the more prominent of the two, may have been the elder brother or possibly the uncle of Giovanni. Trained as a worker in precious metals, Giacomo was associated with the goldsmiths' Università dei Lavoranti from 1758 to 1760 and received his license as a master silversmith in 1775. Several silver pieces bearing his mark are still in existence. His earliest known copy after the antique is a replica in Dresden, produced in 1763, of the equestrian statue of Marcus Aurelius. Giacomo is also known to have collaborated in 1783–84 with Tommaso Righi on a large-scale bust of Pius VI for a piazza in Treia (Marches).

Giovanni took over Giacomo's studio in 1785 and carried on the business of making bronze reproductions until his death in 1805. A printed catalogue of works offered for sale by Giovanni existed in 1795, listing fifty-nine items including the *Agrippina, Mother of Nero* here exhibited, which was priced at fifteen zecchins.[2]

Giovanni evidently continued to base his reproductions on models commissioned from outside sculptors—as was the case documented in 1773 and 1774 when Vincenzo Pacetti executed small clay statuettes for Giacomo of the Farnese *Flora* and the Borghese *Hermaphrodite*. Presumably the Zoffoli would execute their own wax models after the ones in terracotta and direct if not execute the castings as well as assume personal charge in the final chasing and finishing of each bronze.

This example reproduces a marble statue of a Roman matron that was part of the Farnese collection in Rome and was later transferred to the royal collection at

Naples (now the Museo Archeologico Nazionale). Although there were always serious doubts about the effort to identify the sitter as Agrippina—an identification disregarded today—the name persisted as a popular designation in the eighteenth century.

In the case of signed bronzes such as this example, which indicates the Christian name of the artist only with the initial G, it is impossible to distinguish authorship beween Giacomo and Giovanni Zoffoli. Another version of the so-called Agrippina, part of a five-piece *garniture de cheminée,* is at Saltram Park, Devon.

U.W.H.

1. *See* Honour, 1961; Honour, 1963; Thieme-Becker, 1907–50, vol. 36, p. 546; Bulgari, 1958–69, vol. 2, pt. 1, p. 558.
2. Honour, 1961, p. 205, no. 5.

114. Flora

c. 1780–90
Bronze
Height 341 mm (13 6/16″)
1978-70-139
Provenance: unknown
Bibliography: Honour, 1961, p. 205, no. 13; Honour, 1963, p. 200, fig. 8

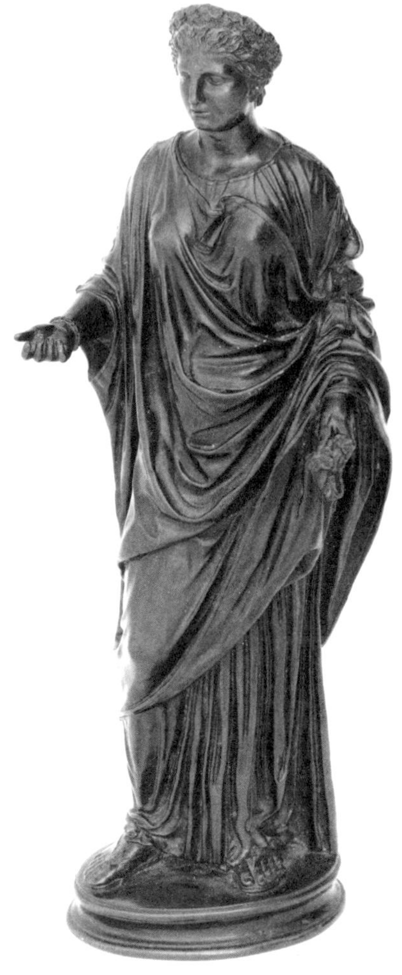

114

This bronze appeared as item thirteen in the Zoffoli catalogue of 1795 as *Flora di Campidoglio, 16* (zecchins). It is based on an antique marble statue found in 1744 at Hadrian's Villa, Tivoli, and presented to the Capitoline Museum by Benedict XIV. Because of her crown of flowers the figure was called Flora in the eighteenth century (the marble's left hand with flowers is a restoration). Also identified as a Muse, or Hora, the statue has more recently been regarded as an idealized portrait of a girl, probably based on a Hellenistic bronze original.

Other versions of the Zoffoli *Flora* are in the Ashmolean Museum, Oxford, and at Saltram Park, Devon.

U.W.H.

MEDALS

Many types of official papal medals were issued to commemorate regular events in the church calendar or, as occurred more exceptionally, in such cases as canonization ceremonies or a papal *possesso*. Medals also marked important secular events including treaties, embassies, and military expeditions, and quite frequently related to public works or artistic projects involving new construction or the restoration and decoration of existing monuments.

Annual medals were created to commemorate a particularly noteworthy event in each pontifical year, being distributed at the Feast of Saints Peter and Paul on June 29. Produced in original editions that included anywhere from 300 to 700 examples in gold and silver as well as bronze, such annual medals served not only as documentary and artistic objects, but as a substantial form of emolument, distributed by careful prearrangement—often in multiple examples—to various dignitaries and church officials.

Medals for exceptional events were likewise distributed to dignitaries participating in the ceremonies. Examples of medals struck to commemorate building projects were usually placed in the foundation stones, and by custom annual medals were also included in papal burials. Pope Clement XI (1700–1721) is thus reported to have been laid to rest with three crimson velvet purses at his feet, each containing versions in gold, silver, and bronze of twenty medals commemorating deeds for each year of his pontificate.

In addition to those medals issued by the Holy See, many others were created for separate ecclesiastical authorities and on private commission. Included in these categories are the medals struck in honor of the Stuart pretenders, and the splendid, framed, gilt-bronze and silver medals awarded as prizes in the student competitions held by the Accademia di San Luca in Rome.

In all fields medal engraving for a long time was virtually monopolized by successive members of the Hamerani family, whose goldsmith's firm operated uninterruptedly in Rome from the mid-seventeenth century until the beginning of the nineteenth century. At the height of wealth and prestige in the first half of the eighteenth century, the Hamerani family enjoyed remarkable prominence as court medalists and mint administrators and as members and officials in the city's various professional guilds and academies. Hamerani medals were considered among the best modern productions, and adding to their reputation was a process invented for patinating bronze medals that was prized by collectors for its brilliant appearance and preservative quality. From the beginning of the eighteenth century the family workshop on the via dei Coronari became a regular stopping place for important foreign visitors who came not only to order medals from the papal series, the dies of which were retained by the family and often used until well worn, but also to admire the Hamerani's collection of coins, medals, prints, casts, and drawings.

In the late eighteenth century the successors of Ottone Hamerani were active though far less dominant in the medalist's profession, evidently preferring "the comfortable life," as one source reported in 1777, of selling restrikes at high prices from the workshop inventory. A number of later Hamerani medals of fine quality were created notwithstanding such accounts. Competition from new generations of engravers must have hastened the waning fortunes of the Hamerani dynasty, nonetheless, and after the turn of the nineteenth century entirely new methods and styles enter the practice of Roman medal engraving.

U.W.H.

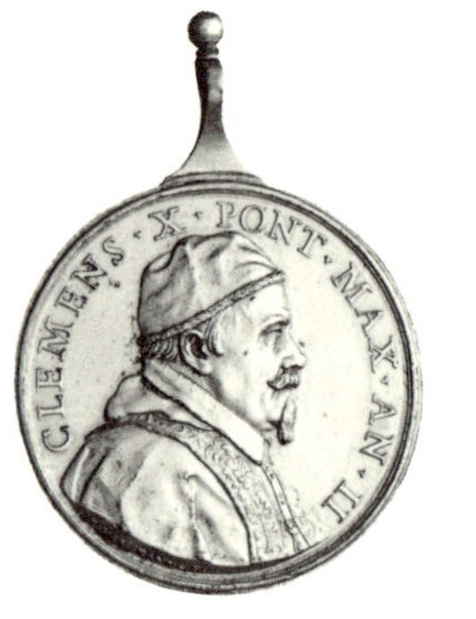

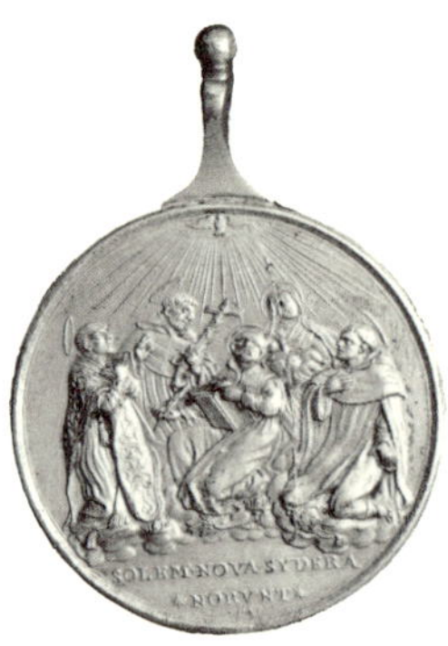

115

ALBERTO HAMERANI

Rome 1620—Rome 1677

115. Clement X / The Canonization of Five Saints

1671

Gilt bronze, ring-mounted for suspension.

Diameter 42 mm

Obverse: Bust of Clement X right, wearing camauro, mozzetta, and stole; inscribed around: CLEMENS · X · PONT · MAX · AN · II ; signed on truncation: ALB · HAMERANVS · F ·

Reverse: A group of five saints beneath the radiance of the Holy Spirit; inscribed in exergue: SOLEM · NOVA · SYDERA / · NORVNT · / III (the last line indistinct)

1978-70-44

Provenance: purchased in New York, 1967

Alberto Hamerani was the first Roman-born son of the German émigré goldsmith Johann Hameran Hermannskircher, scion of the family that was to earn a virtual monopoly over the direction and output of the papal mint from the mid-seventeenth century to the end of the eighteenth century. Alberto, who designed coins at the mints of Rome and Massa Carrara (Tuscany), was established as a goldsmith in the via dei Coronari in 1662. An exceptionally skillful and highly regarded engraver, he was appointed medalist to Clement IX (1667–69) and Clement X (1670–76) and also produced medals for Queen Christina of Sweden (1657; 1659) and other private clients in Rome.

This medal, struck in the second year of Clement X's pontificate, celebrated the canonization in that year of Saint Filippo Benizi, Saint Gaetano Tiene, Saint Francesco Borgia, Saint Lodovico Bertrando, and Saint Rosa di Lima. Three versions of the medal were issued with different legends, created in part with the collaboration of Alberto's son Giovanni.[1]

U.W.H.

1. For Alberto Hamerani, *see* Forrer, 1902–30, vol. 2, pp. 392–94; Noack, 1921–22, pp. 26–27. For the medal, *see* Mazio, 1824, no. 304; Lochner, 1737–44, vol. 5 (Vorrede).

ANONYMOUS ITALIAN

(possibly Hamerani workshop)

116. Pair of Bronze Plaques

c. 1680

A. *Pius V*

Gilt bronze

Diameter 178 mm

Bust of Pius V right, wearing camauro and mozzetta; inscribed around: BEA · PIVS · V · P · O · M · CREATVS DIE 7 IANVAR 1565

1978-70-127

B. *Innocent XI*

Gilt bronze

Diameter 177 mm

Bust of Innocent XI left, wearing camauro, mozzetta, and stole with arabesques; inscribed around: INNOCENTIVS · XI · P · O · M

1978-70-126

Provenance: Sonnenschein collection, Chicago; gift of Alfred R. Bader, 1967

The authorship and precise function of these large bronze decorative plaques remain uncertain. Identical portrait medallions of Pius V and Innocent XI—similarly cast as one-sided reliefs, chased and gilded—are known from the same Roman workshop.[1] The apparent restriction to the same subjects may suggest that these examples were originally designed as pendants. They probably date from the late 1670s; at least a near *terminus post quem* can be established for each by the beatification of Pius V in 1672 and the beginning of the reign of Innocent XI in 1676.

Considerable numbers of other papal medallions were produced in Rome during the same period, both by known and anonymous artists. The most remarkable of these is a large bronze plaque of Clement X in the Museo di Palazzo Venezia, Rome, which was cast—perhaps by Girolamo Lucenti—after a model by Bernini

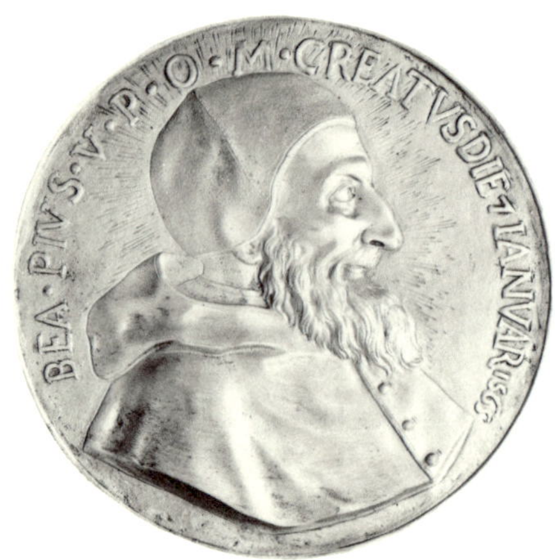

116A

of 1676. To place the present examples within the sphere of influence from Bernini's portraits, as has been done for another replica of the Pius V plaque,[2] seems a sure but overly broad determination. Their style and exceptionally severe workmanship are not unlike the work of Giovanni Martino Hamerani, (*see* nos. 117, 118), and efforts have been made elsewhere to connect them more specifically with the Hamerani workshop[3]—an attribution which at present still awaits a convincing demonstration. While it is known that the Hamerani did trade in articles drawn from their collection of papal medals dating from the fifteenth through eighteenth centuries, it is not known whether they also manufactured such relatively large-scale relief sculptures.

U.W.H.

1. For other examples of the Innocent XI plaque in the Imbert and Ciechanowiecki collections, *see* Imbert, 1941, no. 142; Louisville and Houston, 1969–70, no. 456. For Pius V in the Museo di Palazzo Venezia, Rome, *see* de Caro Balbi, 1974, p. 21, fig. 18.
2. De Caro Balbi, 1974, p. 21; *see* pp. 7 ff. for examples of contemporary portrait bronzes, with literature. For a plaque of Gregory XV, *see* Amherst, 1974, no. 21.
3. Louisville and Houston, 1969–70, no. 456.

GIOVANNI MARTINO HAMERANI

Rome 1646—Rome 1705

117. *Innocent XII / Saint Peter Watching Over the City of Rome*

1694

Gilt bronze, ring-mounted for suspension

Diameter 34 mm

Obverse: Bust of Innocent XII right, wearing camauro, mozzetta, and stole; inscribed around: · INNOCEN · XII · PONT · M · A · III ; signed below bust: HAMERANVS

Reverse: Saint Peter holding Gospels and keys,

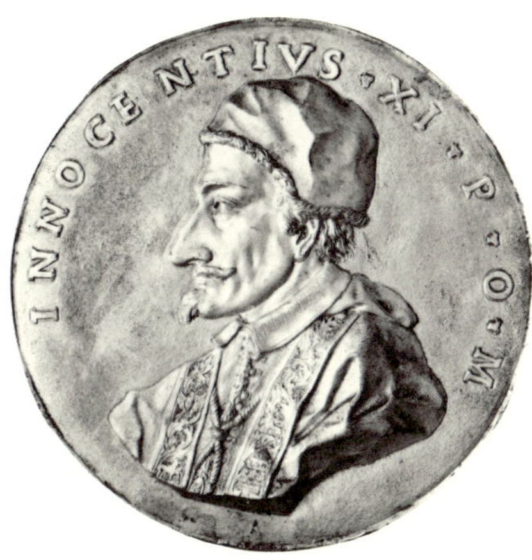

116B

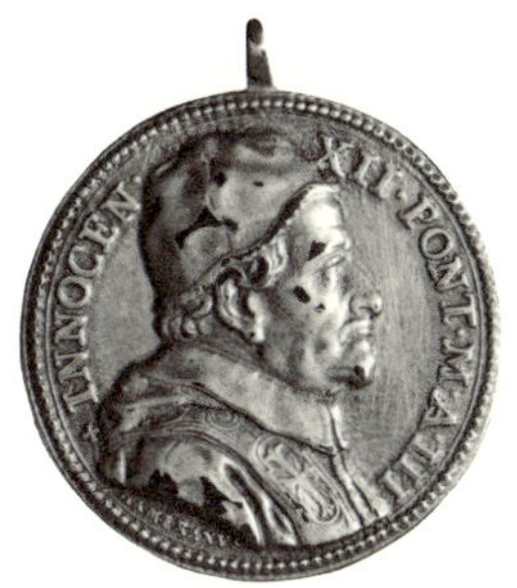

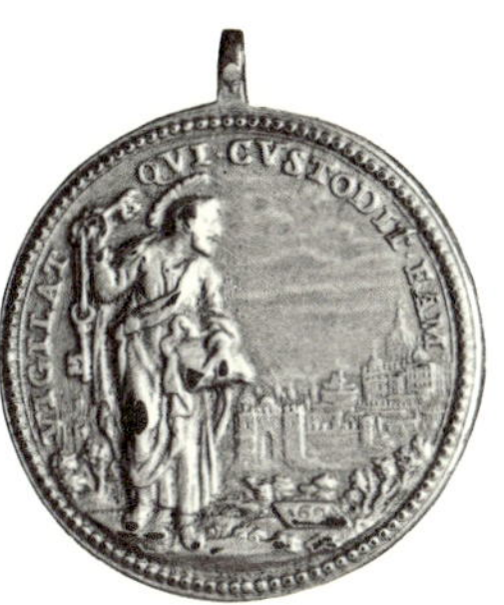

117

overlooking a view of Rome; inscribed around: VIGILAT QVI · CVSTODIT · EAM; on the tablet lower right: 1694

1978-70-59

Provenance: purchased from Blumka Gallery, New York, 1965

Giovanni Martino, the most important artist of the Hamerani family,[1] assisted his father Alberto at the mint of Massa Carrara; after returning to Rome he began to execute independent commissions by at least 1668. He created two medals for Queen Christina of Sweden in 1675 and was first employed by the papal court under Clement X (1670–76). Appointed by Innocent XI (1676–89) as *incisore della zecca,* or mint engraver, in 1679 and confirmed in this position by succeeding popes, he was responsible for an immense output of coins and papal medals that continued through the early years of the pontificate of Clement XI (1700–1721).

Upon Alberto's death, Giovanni was granted renewal of his father's license as a goldsmith and continued to operate the family shop located in the via dei Coronari. He became a member of the Virtuosi del Pantheon in 1676 and served terms as regent between 1685 and 1693. In 1685 Giovanni was made a member of the Accademia di San Luca and nine years later he created the new competition medal for the academy's centenary celebration held in 1695. Among Giovanni's offspring, all distinguished medalists, were Beatrice, who predeceased him, Ermenegildo, and Ottone Hamerani.

This medal, issued in 1694 at the Feast of Saints Peter and Paul, bears on its reverse a portrayal of Saint Peter as the protector of the city of Rome.[2] Its connection to any specific event is uncertain, and it may be that the "vigilance" of the saint was meant as a general allusion to religious reforms effected by the papacy that year.

U.W.H.

1. *See* Noack, 1921–22, pp. 28–30; Noack, in Thieme-Becker, 1907–50, vol. 15, p. 549; Nagler, 1835–52, vol. 5, pp. 532–33; Forrer, 1902–30, vol. 2, pp. 399–403.
2. *See* Mazio, 1824, no. 365; Forrer, 1902–30, vol. 2, p. 402; Bartolotti, 1967, pp. 104, 423.

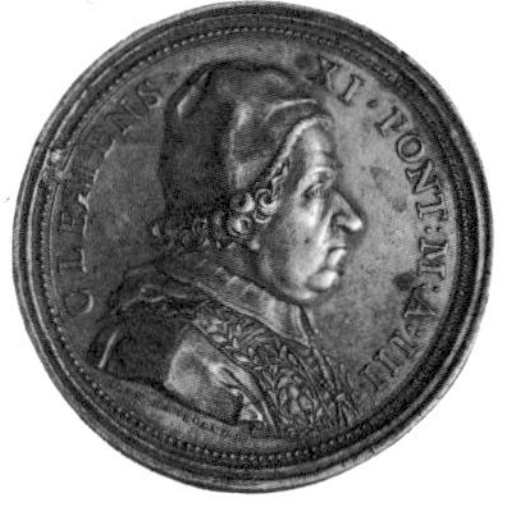
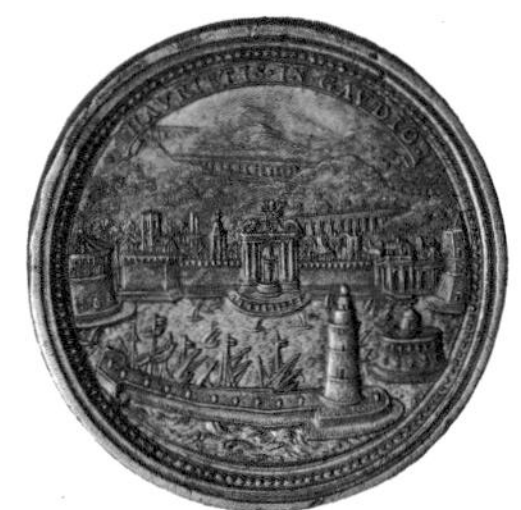

118

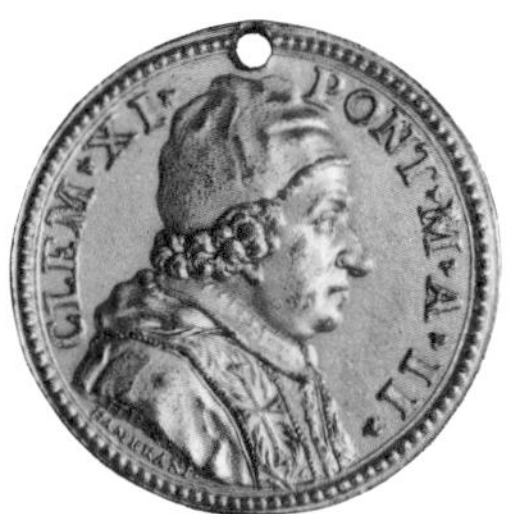
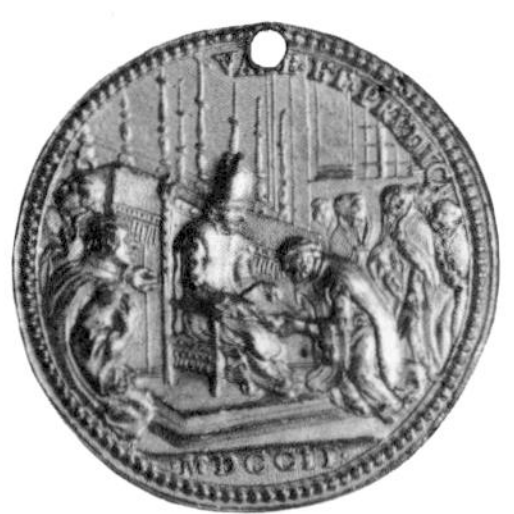

119

118. Clement XI / The Construction of the Aqueduct at Civitavecchia

1703

Bronze

Diameter 55 mm

Obverse: Bust of Clement XI right, wearing camauro, mozzetta, and stole; inscribed around: CLEMENS · XI · PONT: M: A: III; signed below bust: IOAN · HAMERANI · F ·

Reverse: View of the city and harbor of Civitavecchia; inscribed in banderole: HAVRIETIS · IN · GAVDIO

1978-70-69

Provenance: purchased in Rome, 1967

Depicted in a wide panorama on the reverse of this medal[1] is the port city of Civitavecchia, with its breakwater, light tower, fortress, aqueduct, and monumental fountain. Located seventy-two kilometers north of Rome, Civitavecchia was historically the most important military and commercial seaport of the Papal States on the Tyrrhenian Sea. Brought to great prominence during the Renaissance, its role was in decline by the eighteenth century, with the reactivation of the ports at Fiumicino and Anzio. Innocent XII had begun construction of an aqueduct to bring a fresh supply of water to Civitavecchia. Completed under Clement XI—one of many building projects extended to papal territories beyond Rome—the aqueduct was brought to its terminus by a monumental fountain, inaugurated in November, 1702.

U.W.H.

1. *See* Mazio, 1824, no. 384; Forrer, 1902–30, vol. 2, p. 402. For a related medal by Ferdinando de Saint-Urbain, *see* Bartolotti, 1967, p. 114.

ERMENEGILDO HAMERANI

Rome 1683—Rome 1756

119. Clement XI / The Embassy of Monsignor de Tournon to China

1702

Gilt bronze, pierced for suspension

Diameter 33 mm

Obverse: Bust of Clement XI right, wearing camauro, mozzetta, and stole with cross; inscribed around: CLEM · XI · PONT · M · A · II · ; signed on truncation: HER · / HAMERANI ·

Reverse: The pope enthroned before an altar with clerics grouped at either side; kneeling before him, Monsignor de Tournon receives from the pope a copy of the Gospels; inscribed above: VA[D]E · ET · PREDICA; in exergue: MDCCII

1978-70-68

Provenance: purchased from Michael Hall, New York, 1967

The eldest son of Giovanni Martino, Ermenegildo Hamerani was recorded as a master goldsmith as early as 1702 and succeeded his father as *incisore* at the papal mint in 1704. After Giovanni's death Ermenegildo received the license to operate the family business, and with the help of his brother Ottone raised it to its height of power and prestige. At one period or another under Ermenegildo's direction, the Hamerani firm enjoyed monopolies in the assaying of gold and in the recall of old and the minting of new coinage. Named court medalist in 1706, reaffirmed as *incisore della zecca* in 1719 and 1747, Ermenegildo was responsible throughout his career for a prodigious output of papal medals and coinage. He also created medals for the pretender James III, for the courts of Palermo and Sardinia, and for other foreign sovereigns through the sponsorship of his admirer Cardinal Albani. Besides holding official posts in the goldsmith's guild, Ermenegildo was named to the Virtuosi del Pantheon in 1711, later serving as regent of the organization; in 1719 he became a member of the Accademia di San Luca, where for many years he served as secretary.

This small medal,[1] produced while Ermenegildo was

still assistant to his father, commemorated the embassy to China in 1702 of Monsignor Charles Thomas Maillard de Tournon, who was sent as papal legate by Clement XI to resolve a longstanding conflict within the Roman Church over Confucian rites. The Jesuits argued that Confucianism, viewed as a civil and ethical system, could be tolerated among Chinese converts to Christianity. De Tournon was received in cordial ceremony at the court of the emperor K'ang-hsi but, proving himself rigid and tactless in negotiation, was eventually expelled to the Portuguese colony at Macao. He was held there in confinement until his death in 1710, having in the meantime been raised to the cardinalate by Clement XI.

A second version of this medal was engraved by Ermenegildo's sister Beatrice (1677–1704).[2]

U.W.H.

1. *See* Forrer, 1902–30, vol. 2, p. 395; Bartolotti, 1967, p. 113.
2. Rome, 1959, no. 1258.

120. Clement XI / The Reconstruction of the Church of Santi Apostoli

1702

Coppered lead

Diameter 45 mm

Obverse: Bust of Clement XI facing front, wearing camauro, mozzetta and stole; inscribed around: · CLEM · XI · PONT · MAX · ; signed on truncation of bust: HERMENIG: HAMERANVS ·

Reverse: Plan of the church of Santi Apostoli; inscribed around: AVXILIVM · MEVM · A · DOMINO; in exergue: NOVA · BASILICA / SS: XII · APOST / MDCCII

1978-70-70

Provenance: purchased in Rome, 1964

The ancient basilica of Santi Apostoli, found to be in ruinous condition at the beginning of Clement XI's reign, was subsequently scheduled for almost total reconstruction. The program of rebuilding, which preserved only the portico of the old church, was begun in 1701 under the supervision of Francesco Fontana and was continued after the architect's death by his father Carlo. As a former parishioner of the church, Clement XI took a special interest in the project, contributing substantial funds to its beginnings and personally laying the foundation stone early in 1702, when this medal was issued.[1] A second visit was made by the pope in 1708 to inspect the new tribune of the church. Under Clement XI and throughout the century, the church became the focus for many new commissions for paintings and sculptures; it was finally consecrated in 1724, during the reign of Benedict XIII, and in the next century it received a plain façade based on a design by Giuseppe Valadier. (*See* no. 90.)

Ermenegildo's father Giovanni also produced a medal of Santi Apostoli, in the same year and for the same occasion as this one.

U.W.H.

1. Mazio, 1824, no. 383; Forrer, 1902–30, vol. 2, p. 395. For a different version, *see* Rome, 1959, no. 1068.

121. Clement XI / Prize Medal for the Accademia di San Luca

1708

Gilt bronze medal, mounted in gilt bronze frame

Diameter 62 mm

Obverse: Bust of Clement XI left, wearing camauro, mozzetta, and stole; inscribed around: CLEMENS · XI · · PONT · MAX; signed on truncation: HERMEN · HAMERANVS; inscribed around frame: QVIS · VIRTVTEM · AMPLECTITVR · IPSAM · PRAEMIA · SI · TOLLAS · IVVEN. ·

Reverse: Saint Luke at an easel, portraying the Virgin in a cloud of glory above; signed in exergue: · HAMERANO · F · ; inscribed around frame: ACADEMIA · PICTOR · SCVLPTOR · ET · ARCHITECT · VRBIS · · 1708 · (the last numeral separately let in)

1978-70-64

Provenance: purchased in London, c. 1963

This medal, one of three examples of its kind here exhibited (*see* nos. 131 and 132), is from the series of prize medals created by members of the Hamerani family

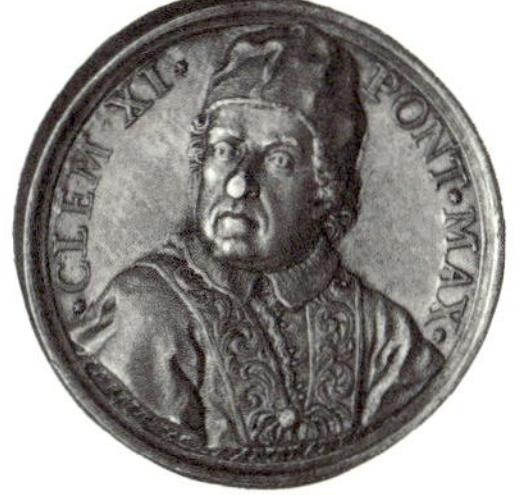

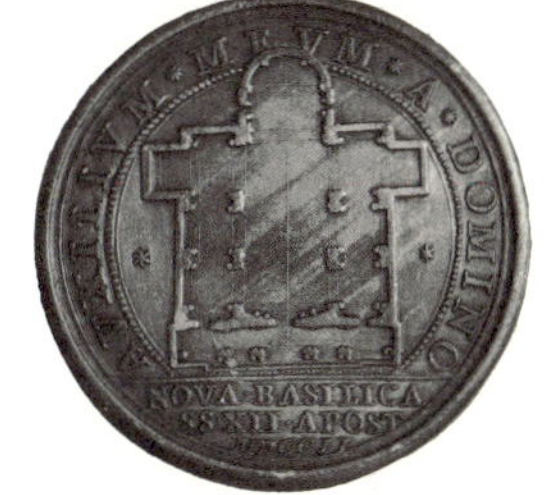

120

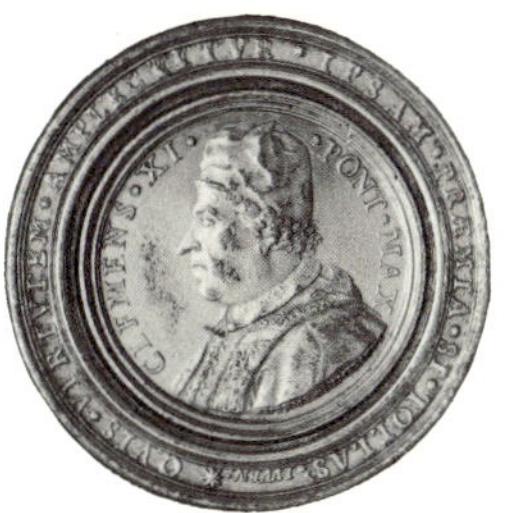

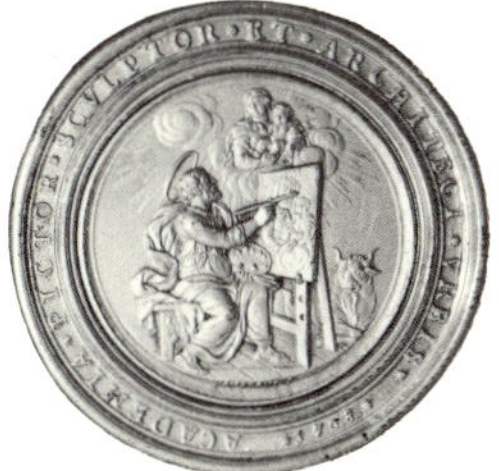

121

over many years and intended for distribution at the award ceremonies climaxing the Accademia di San Luca's student competitions.[1] An annual competition—the Concorso Clementino—was established by Pope Clement XI in 1702. Though later restricted to every two or three years, subject at times to an even more irregular schedule for lack of funds, and eventually alternating in a four-year cycle with the Concorso Balestra founded in 1763, the basic features of the competitions first instituted by Clement XI were to remain in effect throughout the eighteenth and early nineteenth centuries.

The award ceremonies were major festive occasions that took place on the Capitoline Hill, in rooms (the Sale Capitoline) ornamented with tapestries, paintings, and other decorations. The program of events included processions, musical compositions, a period for viewing the winning entries, a lengthy oration on some theoretical or philosophical aspect of the arts, and the recitation of numerous epigrams and sonnets by members of the literary Accademia degli Arcadii, founded in 1690. At an appropriate moment near the close, the academy's master of ceremonies accompanied the winners, one by one, to a designated spot where the cardinal protector of the academy presented each with his prize medals and urged him to even higher achievements.

The distribution of prizes for 1708, the seventh of such celebrations, was held on April 19, with Carlo Maratta serving as *principe* of the academy. As was customary, prizes were given in three progressively advanced classes for each of three separate competitions in painting, sculpture, and architecture. Top prize winners in the most advanced classes received the most costly medals and frames, a hierarchy of value determined by the choice of silver or bronze, the size of the frames, and whether or not the frame and/or medal were gilded.

The usual format of the Hamerani prize medals included an obverse portrait of the reigning pontiff—here by Ermenegildo of Clement XI—and a reverse depicting the academy's patron, Saint Luke, in the act of painting the Virgin. This reverse was designed by Giovanni Martino in 1694 for the academy's centenary competition held in the following year,[2] and it remained standard for as long as the Hamerani produced medals for the academy. Frames for the competition medals were regularly changed in order to introduce new written mottoes, but their reuse is proven in this and other instances (*see* no. 132), where separate metal plugs inserted for the final numerals indicate that an earlier date was altered.

The academy's record of payments to Ermenegildo for the competition of 1708 states that sixty-one medals and frames were made at a cost of 186 scudi. Among the itemized charges were four giulii for each medal and each frame, five scudi for gilding five silver frames, and 7.20 scudi for the gilding of each group of eighteen bronze frames and bronze medals. Of the total, fifty-two medals served as actual student prizes, the large number owing to multiple awards and to the usual practice of giving each winner two medals; of the remaining medals, two went to the pope, two to the orator, and the rest to other officials connected with the ceremony (*see also* no. 132).[3]

U.W.H.

1. For other framed medals, of 1703 and 1705, *see* Louisville and Houston, 1969–70, nos. 267–68; *see also* Hamburg, et al., 1966–, no. 230; *L'Accademia,* 1974, p. 379, no. 19, repr. (dated 1705) and p. 381 (dated 1725).
2. *See L'Accademia,* 1974, p. 377, no. 18 (repr.) and p. 381.
3. From the account presented by Ermenegildo Hamerani, "Nota delle medaglie fatte per L'accademia di S. Luca per il concorso dell'Anno 1708," and other miscellaneous lists in the archives of the Accademia di San Luca. A forthcoming article will deal with these and further documents through the 1760s that describe the various types and distribution schedules of competition medals produced by the Hamerani for the academy.

122. Clement XI / The Restoration of the Church of San Clemente

1715
Bronze
Diameter 38 mm
Obverse: Bust of Clement XI right, wearing camauro, mozzetta, and stole; inscribed around: CLEMENS XI · P · M · A · XV ; signed on truncation: · E · HAMERANVS · S ·
Reverse: View of the quadriportico and façade of the church of San Clemente; inscribed around: TEMPLO · S · CLEMENTIS · INSTAVRATO
1978-70-56
Provenance: purchased in Rome, 1964

San Clemente, one of Rome's most ancient and venerable basilicas and titular church of Clement XI's patron saint, underwent extensive renovation during his reign. The pope visited the church in November, 1701, for the

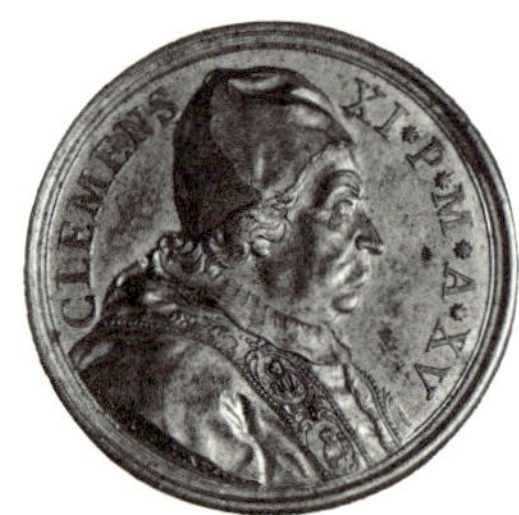

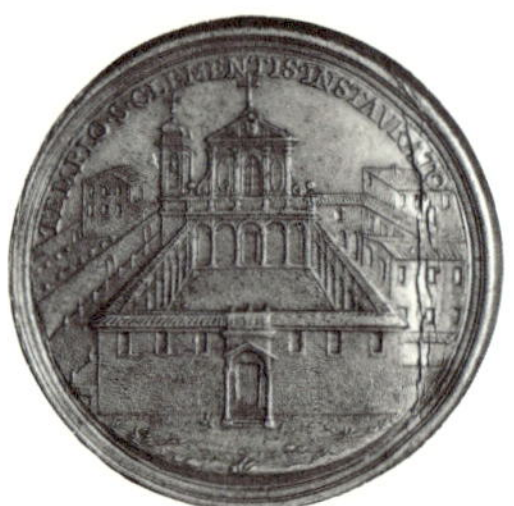

122

purpose of inaugurating the work, and between 1715 and 1719 a new façade and side entrance were built under the direction of the architect Carlo Stefano Fontana.[1] The renovation of the interior included a new nave vault with frescoes by Giuseppe Chiari (*The Glory of Saint Clement*) and other paintings on the life of the saint by Giacomo Triga, Sebastiano Conca, Giovanni Odazzi, and Pier Leone Ghezzi.[2]

U.W.H.

1. For this medal, issued at the commencement of the project, *see* Mazio, 1824, no. 401; Forrer, 1902–30, vol. 2, p. 396; Rome, 1959, no. 1090; Bartolotti, 1967, pp. 126, 426.
2. *See* Gilmartin, 1974.

123. Clement XI / The Decoration of the Church of San Giovanni in Laterano

1718
Silvered bronze
Diameter 40 mm
Obverse: Bust of Clement XI right, wearing tiara and cope embroidered with an image of Saint John the Evangelist; inscribed around: CLEMENS · XI · · PONT · M · A · XVIII; signed on truncation: E · HAMERANI · F ·
Reverse: The personification of the church, radiate and seated, holds the tablet of the Laws in her left arm and points behind with her right to the basilica of San Giovanni in Laterano; two angels at her side bear the cross and the Gospels; inscribed around: SVPER · FVNDAMENTVM · APOSTOLOR · ET · PROPHET ; in exergue: CONSTANTINI · BASILICA / STATVIS · E · PICTVR · / ORNATA
1978-70-63
Provenance: purchased in London, 1964

The decoration of the interior of San Giovanni in Laterano was completed under Clement XI in 1718 by the addition of twelve colossal statues of the apostles, originally projected by Borromini for the niches of the nave, and by a series of painted medallions above depicting the prophets. The cost of each statue—5,000 scudi—was such that the pope personally contributed two of them, while funds for others were solicited from a group of cardinals, the duke of Bavaria, the king of Portugal, and the bishops of Würzburg and Paderborn. Among the eight sculptors employed were Pierre Le Gros and Camillo Rusconi (*see* no. 10), the latter being responsible for the statue of Saint James, which contemporaries considered to be the most successful of the series. The painters chosen for the medallions of prophets were even more numerous and represented virtually all of the best painters in the city. Included were Giuseppe Chiari (*see* no. 6), Sebastiano Conca (*see* nos. 17 and 18), Benedetto Luti (*see* no. 9), Marco Benefial (*see* nos. 26–29), Giovanni Odazzi, Luigi Garzi, Andrea Procaccini, Pier Leone Ghezzi (*see* nos. 12–14), Francesco Trevisani (*see* no. 8), Giovanni Paolo Melchiorri, Giuseppe Nasini, and Domenico Muratori. Ermenegildo's medal[1] celebrated the completion of the decoration.

U.W.H.

1. *See* Mazio, 1824, no. 405; Rome, 1959, no. 1067; Forrer, 1902–30, vol. 2, p. 396; Bartolotti, 1967, pp. 129, 427.

124. Benedict XIII / Equestrian Statue of Charlemagne for Saint Peter's

1725
Gilt bronze
Diameter 49.5 mm
Obverse: Bust of Benedict XIII right, wearing camauro, mozzetta, and stole; inscribed around: BENEDICTVS · XIII · PONT · MAX ; signed on truncation: HAMERANI
Reverse: View of the equestrian statue of Charlemagne by Agostino Cornacchini; inscribed around: · CAROLO · MAGNO · ROMANAE · ECCLESIAE · VINDICI · ; in exergue: ANNO · IVBILEI / MDCCXXV
1978-70-58
Provenance: purchased from Cyril Humphris, London, 1964

This medal commemorates the dedication of Agostino Cornacchini's statue of Charlemagne, which was commissioned by Pope Clement XI and completed under

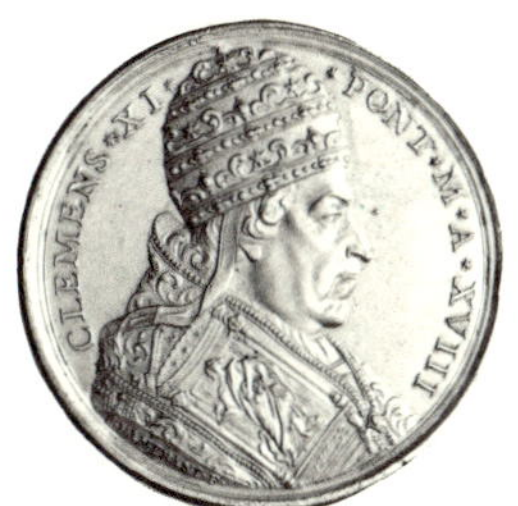
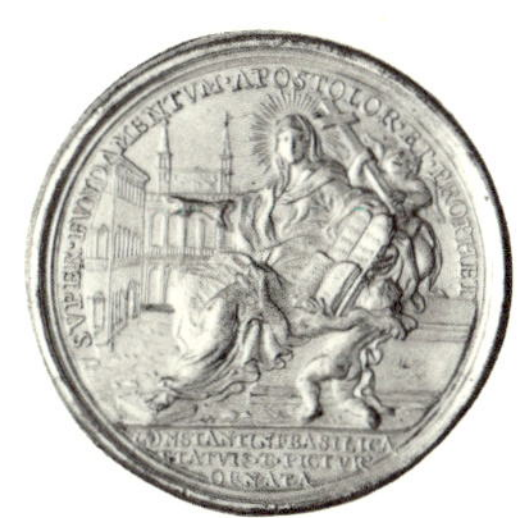

123

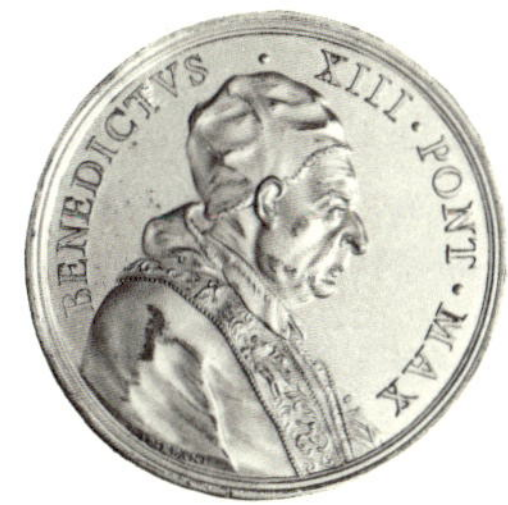
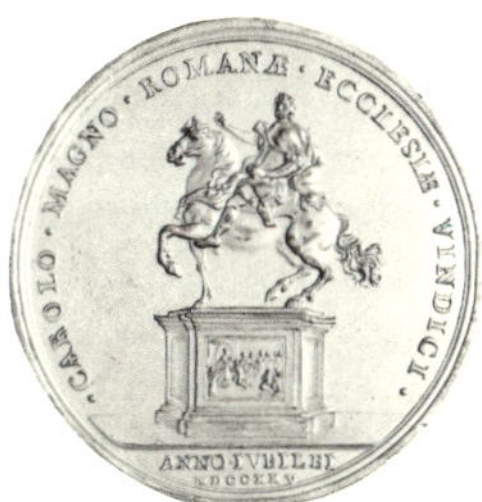

124

Benedict XIII. Placed at the south wall of the portico of Saint Peter's, the statue was intended as the counterpart to Bernini's statue of Constantine of 1670, which stands opposite at the main landing of the Scala Regia.[1]

Cornacchini was a Florentine who came to Rome in 1712, and who, thanks to high patronage and a generous perception of his talents, enjoyed a celebrated career in the capital. A measure of Cornacchini's prestige at the papal court was the privilege granted him after the *Charlemagne* was finished of restoring the Vatican's famous statue of Laocoon. The *Charlemagne* proved Cornacchini's most important commission, and his work on it extended from at least 1720, when the pope inspected a model of the statue, until the ceremonious unveiling of the finished piece in March of the Jubilee Year 1725.

The illustration on the medal[2] rather accurately captures the character of the statue, but it omits the military trophies beneath the horse as well as the elaborate drapery and architectural perspective constructed by Cornacchini on the wall behind. The relief on the statue's base was meant to represent the coronation of Charlemagne, and though recorded elsewhere in an engraving, it was never carried out on the statue itself.

Those outside papal circles found good opportunity to criticize efforts made to compare Cornacchini's *Charlemagne* with Bernini's *Constantine.* At the end of March, 1725, Charles-François Poerson, director of the French Academy in Rome, remarked in a letter that "... this new statue was made by a Florentine, who is said to have had little experience and also not to have had great success. He has had the temerity, supported by a group of rich, ignorant and favored people, to boast of having equalled Bernini; but that [opinion] has been strongly scorned by all who have a little bit of good taste."[3] Pier Leone Ghezzi, in his caricature of Cornacchini, called the statue "pretty bad" ("assai cattivo").

U.W.H.

1. For Cornacchini's *Charlemagne, see* Wittkower, 1961; Enggass, 1976, vol. 1, pp. 200–202.

2. Payments to the medalist Ermenegildo Hamerani from March, June, and December 1725, record the sum of 620.12 scudi paid for "... the medals of Charlemagne ... all the medals of gold, silver, and bronze made on the occasion of the equestrian statue ..." (cited in Wittkower, 1961, p. 473, where these payments are incorrectly related to a series of different oval bronze plaquettes of uncertain authorship; *see* his fig. 333, repr. from Imbert, 1941, no. 139; for another example of this plaquette, *see* Storrs, 1973, no. 43.) For the present medal, *see* Mazio, 1824, no. 423; Louisville and Houston, 1969–70, no. 269.

3. *Correspondance,* 1887–1912, vol. 7, p. 143.

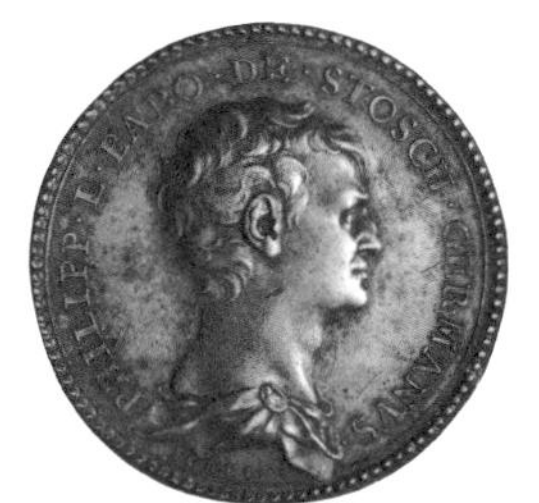

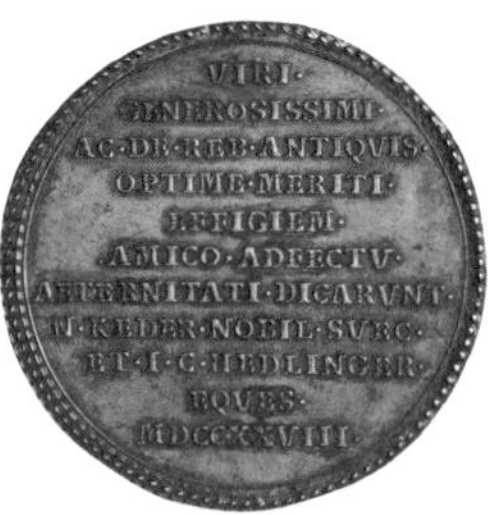

125

JOHANN KARL HEDLINGER

Schwyz (Switzerland) 1691—Schwyz 1771

125. Philipp von Stosch

1728

Bronze

Diameter 42 mm

Obverse: Bust of Philipp von Stosch right; inscribed around: PHILIPP · L · BARO · DE · STOSCH · GERMANVS ; signed below bust: I · C · H · F · 1728

Reverse: Inscribed: VIRI · / GENEROSISSIMI · / AC · DE · REB · ANTIQVIS / OPTIME · MERITI · / EFFIGIEM · / AMICO · ADFECTV · / AETERNITATI · DICARVNT · / N · KEDER · NOBIL · SVEC · / ET · I · C · HEDLINGER · / EQVES · / MDCCXXVIII ·

1978-70-80

Provenance: gift of Andrew Ciechanowiecki, 1968

Johann Karl Hedlinger was one of the most celebrated medalists of the eighteenth century.[1] Active in Switzerland at the beginning of his career, he left in 1716 to work in Nancy and Paris. In 1718 he was invited to Sweden, where Charles XII appointed him chief engraver at the Stockholm mint. He was to remain attached to the Swedish court throughout most of his long career, despite repeated attempts by the sovereigns of Russia, Poland, and Prussia to lure him away. He retired to his native Schwyz for reasons of health in 1745, having been made a court steward and a member of the Stockholm academy. From retirement he continued for many more years to produce medals for various European courts. His collected works were published in engravings in Basel in 1776 and by Johann Kaspar Füssli in Augsburg in 1781.[2] Goethe observed that Hedlinger had not only fulfilled the stylistic promise of Ottone Hamerani but had surpassed the latter's achievements with works of more "agreeable softness and ... painterly effect, ... spirit and liveliness."[3]

Hedlinger visited Rome between November, 1726, and March, 1727, where he is known to have made the acquaintance of many artists and antiquaries including, besides Stosch, Camillo Rusconi, Francesco Trevisani, Pier Leone Ghezzi, Francesco de' Ficoroni, and Cardinal Albani. During his sojourn he executed a portrait medal of Benedict XIII, for which he was decorated with the cross of the Order of Christ.[4] Hedlinger's medal of Baron Stosch—celebrated in 1724 for his publication of the *Pierres antiques gravées* (*see* nos. 19, 106)—was begun in Rome and completed in 1728 after the artist's return to Sweden. A spirit of rivalry as well as admiration for a friend may have prompted its execution, as Hedlinger could already have seen the medal of rather modest quality that Giovanni Pozzo created in honor of Stosch in 1727.[5] Hedlinger's medal is dedicated jointly with the antiquary Nicholas Keder, a Swedish nobleman who was earlier known to have designed medals for the Stockholm mint.

U.W.H.

1. For Hedlinger, *see* Forrer, 1902–30, vol. 2, pp. 455–67, vol. 7, p. 432; Amberg, 1887.
2. de Méchel, 1776; Füssli, 1781.
3. Goethe, 1969, pp. 156–57.
4. For this medal, *see* Noack, 1907, p. 42; Lochner, 1737–44, vol. 2, pp. 113 ff.
5. *See* Forrer, 1902–30, vol. 4, p. 681 (repr.).

OTTONE HAMERANI

Rome 1694—Rome 1761

126. Princess Maria Clementina Sobieski / Clementina's Escape from Innsbruck

1719

Silver

Diameter 49.5 mm

Obverse: Bust of Princess Maria Clementina Sobieski left, wearing diadem; inscribed around: CLEMENTINA · M · BRITAN · FR · ET · HIB · REGINA · ; signed below the bust: OTTO · HAMERANI · F

Reverse: The princess in a chariot drawn by two horses; a landscape with the city of Rome in the distance, and the sun rising from the sea; inscribed around: FORTVNAM · CAVSAMQVE · SEQVOR ; in exergue: DECEPTIS · CVSTODIBVS · / · MDCCXIX ·

1978-70-120

Provenance: purchased from Michael Hall, New York, 1967

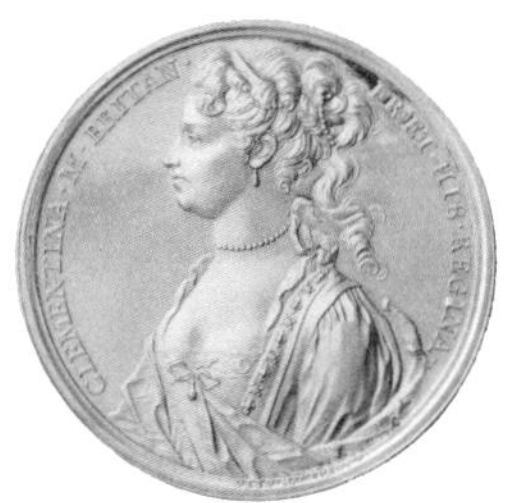

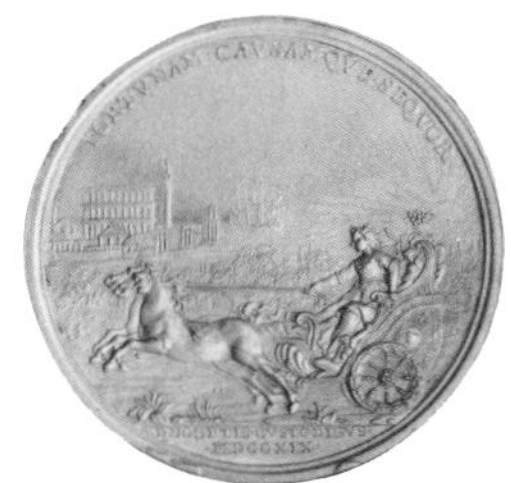

126

Ottone, younger brother of Ermenegildo Hamerani, first studied to be a painter under Benedetto Luti. He had begun making medals by at least 1717 and was eventually to dedicate himself completely to the family profession. Ottone Hamerani was responsible for a long series of medals executed on independent commission as well as in collaboration with his brother Ermenegildo. He occupied the position of papal medalist and die engraver (*incisore della zecca*) and from 1734 was master of the Roman mint. Sharing with Ermenegildo numerous official posts, as well as operations of the family workshop, Ottone is usually mentioned together with his brother in papal records of payments and similar documents.

Popular in upper circles, Ottone became the particular favorite of James III, the Stuart pretender to the English crown, who in 1718 established permanent residence in Rome under the protection of Clement XI. This medal was created to honor Princess Maria Clementina Sobieski, granddaughter of the Polish king John III and the betrothed of James III.[1] The medal reverse commemorated Clementina's escape from Innsbruck, where on her way to Italy she had been imprisoned in a convent by Emperor Charles VI, after George I of England had opposed her marriage to James. The wedding took place at Montefiascone, near Rome, in 1719—an event celebrated in a separate medal by Ottone—and in the following year Maria Clementina gave birth to Prince Charles Edward, heir to James III and elder brother of Prince Henry Benedict, Cardinal York (*see* nos. 127, 135). Clementina died in 1735. Ottone Hamerani also authored a medal portraying her elaborate mausoleum in Saint Peter's, issued under Benedict XIV in 1743.

U.W.H.

1. For the medal, *see* Lochner, 1737–44, vol. 1, pp. 369 ff; Hawkins, 1885, vol. 15, pl. 143, no. 7. Louisville and Houston, 1969–70, no. 96.

127. Prince Charles Edward Stuart / Prince Henry Benedict Stuart

1729

Silver

Diameter 43 mm

Obverse: Bust of Charles Edward Stuart right, wearing cuirass and cloak; a star in the background above the left shoulder; inscribed around: MICAT · INTER · OMNES

Reverse: Bust of Henry Benedict Stuart left, wearing cuirass and sash; inscribed around: ALTER · AB · ILLO ; inscribed around edge: EXTVLIT · OS · SACRVM · COELO · DIE · XXXI · DECEMBR · MDCCXX ·

1978-70-119

Provenance: purchased from Michael Hall, London, 1964

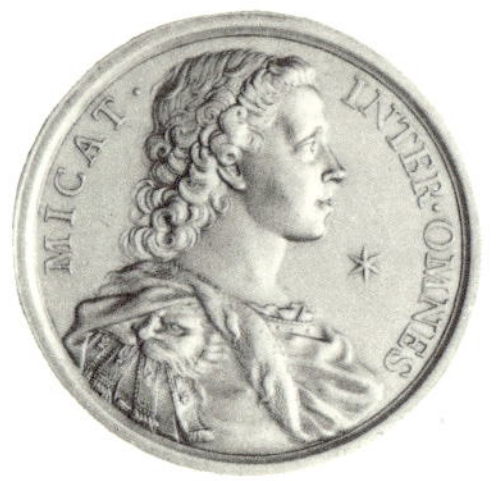
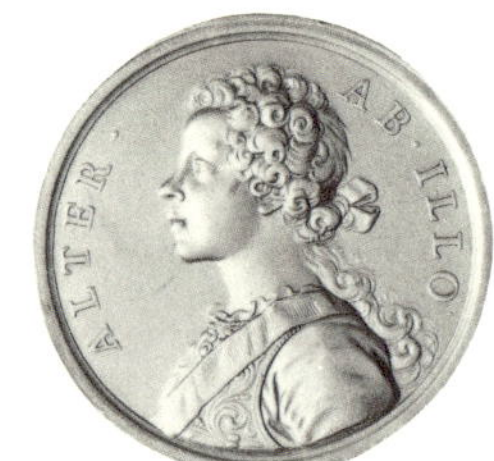

127

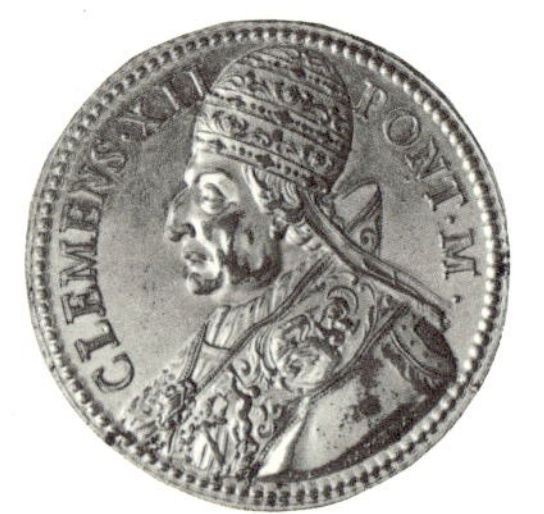
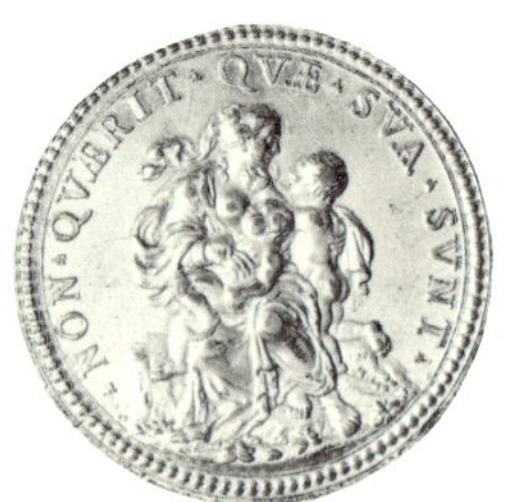

128

This medal,[1] which portrays the heirs of the old pretender, James III, was designed to affirm the continuity of the Stuart line. The inscription on the outer rim refers to the birth of the elder son, Prince Charles Edward, an event that took place in Rome on December 31, 1720, and became the subject of official announcement throughout the courts of Europe. The hopeful inscription accompanying his portrait is adapted from Horace's ode in praise of Augustus and the Julian house ("Micat inter omnes Julium sidus, velut inter ignes luna minores").[2]

Prince Charles Edward, known as the young pretender, carried forward his father's claims to the British throne, landing in Scotland in 1745 to lead an unsuccessful march on London. This adventure, which ended in Charles Edward's flight to France in 1746, was to prove the last serious threat of the Stuart cause in England. Unable to gain royal privileges for himself upon the death in 1766 of James III, Charles Edward accepted exile in Florence, where under the title of count of Albany he lived out his remaining years in physical and moral decline. He had returned to Rome shortly before his death on January 31, 1788. For Prince Henry Benedict, *see* no. 135.

U.W.H.

1. *See* Hawkins, 1885, vol. 15, pl. 150, no. 3.
2. Horace, Odes, I, xii, 46–48.

128. Clement XII / Charity

probably 1730
Gilt bronze
Diameter 38 mm
Obverse: Bust of Clement XII left, wearing tiara and cope embroidered with the Madonna and Child; inscribed around: CLEMENS · XII PONT · M · ; signed on truncation: OT · HAMERANI
Reverse: Figure of Charity seated with two children in her arms; inscribed around: · NON · QVAERIT · QVAE · SVA · SVNT ·
1978-70-77
Provenance: Blumka Gallery, New York; gift of John Maxon, 1971

The personification of Charity is characteristic of those medal reverses designed to celebrate individual attributes or qualities of the various pontiffs. The exceptional liberality of Clement XII, sustained against the staggering economic conditions of his reign, was repeatedly witnessed by the many statues and monuments erected in his honor. This medal, not listed in the series officially issued under Clement XII, reuses a reverse created by Giovanni Hamerani for a medal of Innocent XI of 1686.[1] If not privately created, this problematically mixed issue may have been commissioned from the Hamerani by a city or municipality to commemorate some aid or privilege granted by the pope.

U.W.H.

1. Having noted the reuse of the reverse die by Giovanni, and interpreting the portrait of Clement XII to be copied after one by Peter Paul Werner, Bartolotti considered this issue to be a forgery, albeit a contemporary one, executed at least prior to 1744 (*see* Bartolotti, 1972, pp. 32–34). There seems, however, no good reason for doubting Ottone's authorship of this portrait obverse, which is clearly produced from a die different from Werner's. The "arbitrary joining of dies," cited by Bartolotti, has other parallels and should be unsurprising in light of the Hamerani's practice of making restrikes from their entire stock of earlier medal dies. In the case of prize medals produced for the Accademia di San Luca, a reverse created by Giovanni Hamerani was reused for over a half a century in combination with portrait obverses by Ermenegildo and Ottone. Finding no intrinsic reason to doubt the genuineness of these medals, Bartolotti admits elsewhere (1967, p. 151) that the Hamerani may have joined inconsistent dies for other medals of Clement XII, without, as in this case, using such a circumstance to rule out their authorship. For a similar medal, *see* Hamburg, et al., 1966–, no. 235.

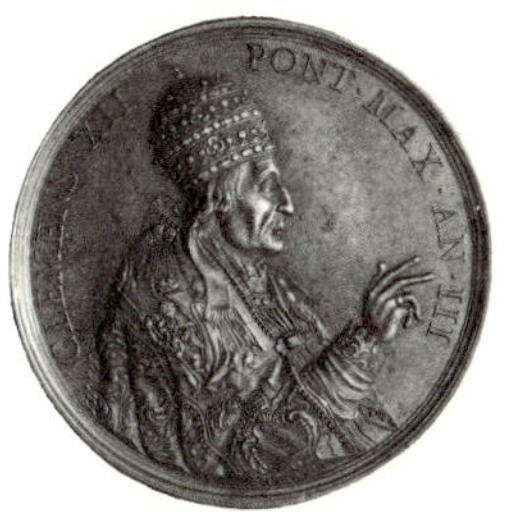
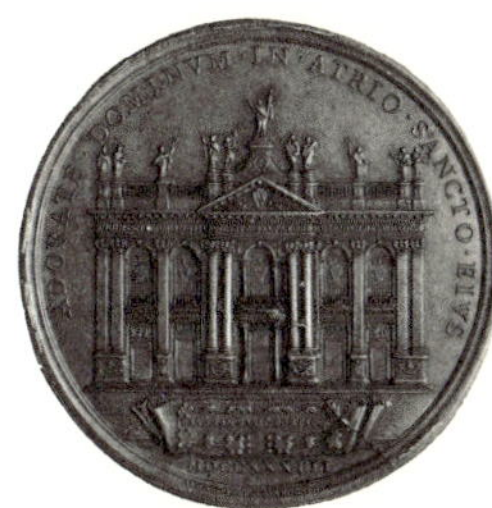

129

129. Clement XII / The Façade of San Giovanni in Laterano

1733
Bronze
Diameter 73.5 mm
Obverse: Bust of Clement XII Corsini right, wearing tiara and cope embroidered with an image of Saint Andrew Corsini and the Corsini arms, his right arm raised in benediction; inscribed around: CLEMENS · XII PONT · MAX · AN · III ; signed on truncation: OTTO HAMERANI · F ·
Reverse: The façade of San Giovanni in Laterano; in a cartouche below, a plan of the church portico; inscribed around: ADORATE · DOMINVM · IN · ATRIO · SANCTO · EIVS ; on the church entablature: CLEM · XII · P · M · AN · IIII CHRISTO · SALVATORI ET · SS · IOAN · BAPT · ET · EV · ; on the portico plan: LATERAN · BASIL · PORTICVS ; signed at the sides of the plan: · O · · H · ; below the plan: MDCCXXXIII ; on the lower edge: ALEX · GALILAEVS · ARCH · INV
1978-70-76
Provenance: purchased from Blumka Gallery, New York, 1971

Through a special committee established in 1731, Clement XII revived the project left unfinished by his predecessors of constructing a main façade for the church of San Giovanni in Laterano. After the rejection of Borromini's earlier plan, a competition for a new design was announced in April 1732, with the resulting twenty-one entries exhibited in the Quirinal Palace in June of that year.[1] Among the artists on the selection committee were many of the most famous names in the city, including Sebastiano Conca, Pier Leone Ghezzi, and Giovanni Paolo Panini. The majority opinion was nearly equally divided between the designs of Luigi Vanvitelli and Alessandro Galilei. The final decision of the pope went to his fellow Florentine Galilei, who was called from Florence to begin work almost immediately.

The complex rendering and exceptional scale of this commemorative medal are a measure of the importance with which the new building project was regarded by the pope, who personally assumed most of its immense costs. The medal's design for the still-unbuilt façade—including the second-story fenestration that was never executed—was based on an engraving by Stefano Pozzo dedicated in October 1733. The ceremonial laying of the foundation stone, scheduled to take place at that time, was finally held on December 8, 1733, having been delayed because the medal was itself not yet completed.[2] As usual for such events, examples of the medal were distributed to a host of dignitaries, in this case on the day preceding the ceremony, while other examples—one each of gold and silver and six of bronze—were placed within the stone itself.

U.W.H.

1. From the diary of Valesio, in Scatassa, 1916.
2. Idem. For a description of the medal and ceremony, *see also* Lochner, 1737–44, vol. 1, pp. 97 ff. For the medal, *see* Mazio, 1824, no. 441; Rome, 1959, no. 1135; Hamburg, et al., 1966–, no. 233; Louisville and Houston, 1969–70, no. 272; Storrs, 1973, no. 54, fig. 15.

130. Clement XII / The Trevi Fountain

1736
Bronze
Diameter 40 mm
Obverse: Bust of Clement XII right, wearing camauro, mozzetta, and stole; inscribed around: CLEMENS XII · P · M · A · V
Reverse: View of the Palazzo dei Duchi di Poli and the Trevi Fountain; inscribed around: FONTE · AQVAE · VIRGINIS · ORNATO · ; signed in exergue: MDCCXXXVI / O H ; an emblem of the she-wolf and twins between the last two letters
1978-70-89
Provenance: purchased from Spink and Son, Ltd., London, 1966

With its spectacular joining of architecture, statuary, and rocky cascades, the Trevi Fountain, created under Clement XII, has remained one of the most conspicuous and famous monuments of eighteenth-century Rome.

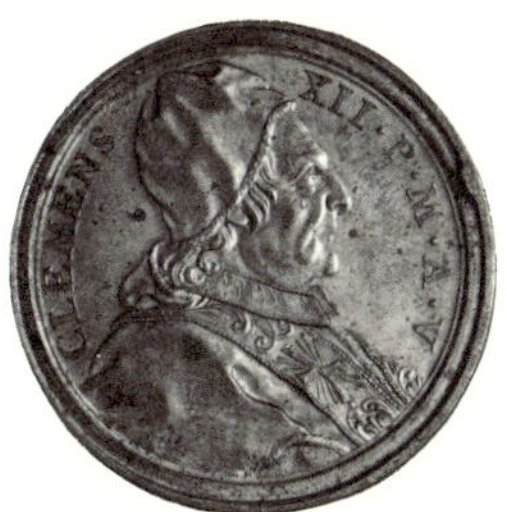
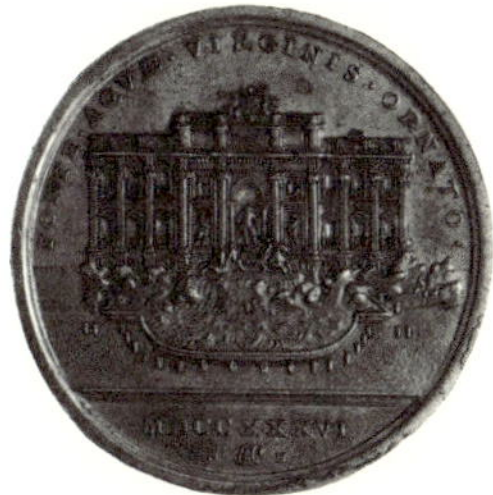

130

Dissatisfied with earlier projects for a fountain to adorn the terminus of the ancient Aqua Virgo, Clement XII established in 1732 a competition for a new design. Sixteen plans were submitted for judgment and were exhibited in the Quirinal Palace. Included among the competition's participants were Luigi Vanvitelli, Edmé Bouchardon, Pietro Bracci, and Giovanni Battista Maini. Although he was said to be at first inclined toward Vanvitelli's plans, the pope ultimately chose that of the Roman Nicolò Salvi, and work on the grandiose project began. In July, 1736, the great inscription was put in place, and in December of that year the arms of the pope were set into the attic. It was upon the latter occasion that this commemorative medal was issued.[1]

The fountain was not completed until 1762, with some alterations being made to the original plan under Salvi's successor, Giuseppe Panini. Pope Clement XII, who had died long before, bequeathed 40,000 scudi for the project's completion.

U.W.H.

1. Mazio, 1824, no. 447; Forrer, 1902–30, vol. 2, p. 405; Rome, 1959, no. 1138; Bartolotti, 1967, pp. 151, 427. Bartolotti cites a number of other medals which, like the Clark example, have the dated reverse coupled with an obverse from the preceding year (Anno V). This may result from a reissue by either the Hamerani or by Mazio in the early nineteenth century.

131. Benedict XIV / Prize Medal for the Accademia di San Luca

1754

Gilt bronze medal, mounted in gilt bronze frame

Diameter 66 mm

Obverse: Bust of Benedict XIV right, wearing camauro, mozzetta, and embroidered stole; inscribed around: BENEDICT · XIV · PONT · MAX · ; signed on truncation: · HAMERANI · ; inscribed around frame: · ACADEMIA · PICTOR · SCVLPTOR · ET · ARCHITECT · VRBIS · ·

Reverse: Saint Luke at an easel portraying the Virgin in a cloud of glory; signed in exergue: · HAMERANO · F · ; inscribed around frame: VIRTVTIS · AMPLISSIMVM · PRAEMIVM · EST GLORIA CIC · PRO · MILO · 1754 (the last two numerals separately let in)

1978-70-65

Provenance: purchased in London or New York, 1963

The distribution of prizes for the competition of 1754 was held on November 24, with Ferdinando Fuga as *principe* of the academy. Among those attending the ceremonies were the old pretender, James III, the ambassadors of France and Venice, and eighteen cardinals. Along with the usual decorations, musical compositions, and oration, the program included the recitation of no less than twenty-seven sonnets and other poetical works by members of the Accademia degli Arcadii.

Prize winners for the combined classes of painting, sculpture, and architecture totaled twenty-seven, with each class of the three faculties being awarded first, second, and third prizes.

The Hamerani produced sixty-five framed prize medals of "diverse quality and size" for 1754 and received for them 298.25 scudi. Forty-one of the medals were of silver, twenty-one of gilt bronze, and three of plain bronze with a patina. The mountings included nine large gilt silver frames, five large plain silver frames, and fifteen plain silver frames in two smaller sizes, as well as thirty-six gilt bronze frames. Although we do not know how and in what numbers these different medals and frames were combined, their distribution was as follows: two medals went to each of the twenty-seven prize winners; two medals each to the pope, the cardinal chamberlain, and the prelate who delivered the oration; and one medal each for the cardinals Albani, the *custode* of the Accademia degli Arcadii and the *principe* and secretary of the Accademia di San Luca[1] (*see also* nos. 121, 132).

U.W.H.

1. Accademia di San Luca archives, medal lists and accounts for 1754.

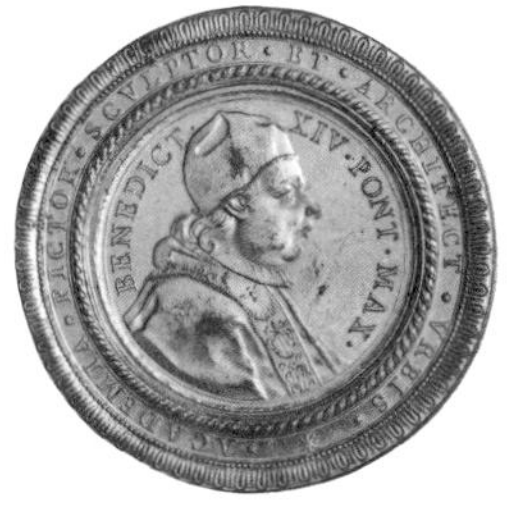

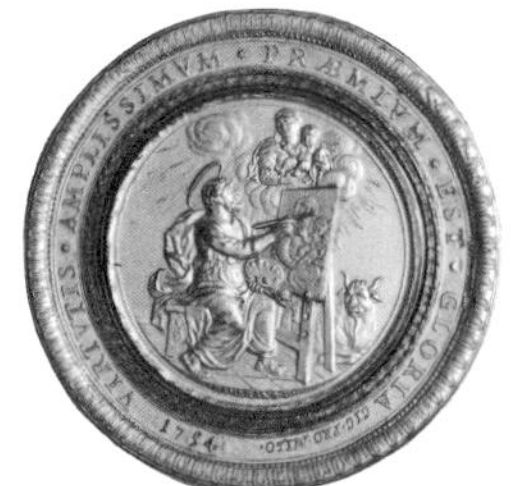

131

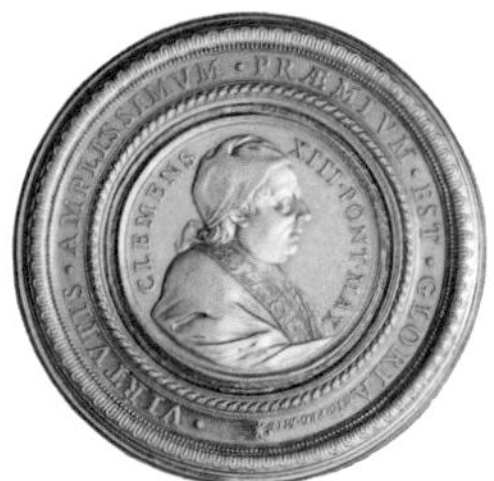

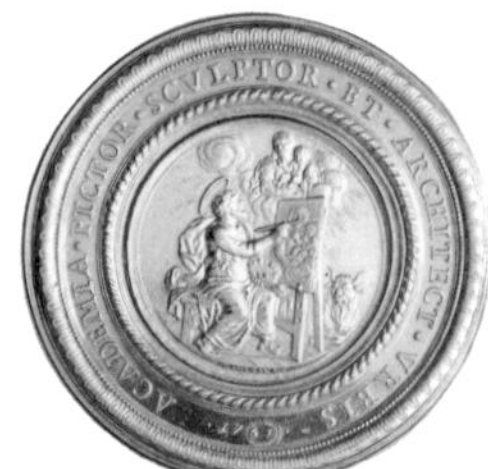

132

132. Clement XIII / Prize Medal for the Accademia di San Luca

1762

Silver medal; mounted in gilt bronze frame

Diameter 76 mm

Obverse: Bust of Clement XIII right, wearing camauro, mozzetta, and stole; inscribed around: CLEMENS XIII · PONT · MAX ; inscribed around frame: · VIRTVTIS · AMPLISSIMVM · PRAEMIVM · EST · GLORIA CIC · PRO · MIL ·

Reverse: Saint Luke at an easel portraying the Virgin in a cloud of glory; signed in exergue: · HAMERANO · F · ; inscribed around frame: ACADEMIA · PICTOR · SCVLPTOR · ET · ARCHITECT · VRBIS · 1762 · (the last two numerals separately let in)

1978-70-66

Provenance: purchased from Cyril Humphris, London, c. 1965

The award ceremony for the Accademia di San Luca's competition of 1762 was held on September 16, under the principate of Mauro Fontana. Because of the death of Ottone Hamerani in the preceding year, the prize medals of 1762 were undoubtedly based on the models created for the academy in 1758, with their actual production supervised by Ferdinando Hamerani, Ottone's son and successor in the family trade.

The academy archives preserve a complete schedule of medals distributed in this year,[1] which permits us for the first time to learn exactly what prizes went to students in every category of the competition. For each of the three classes that comprised the separate faculties of painting, sculpture, and architecture a first, second, and third prize were awarded. Thus the total number of prize winners was twenty-seven, with each winner receiving two medals as follows:

FIRST CLASS—*First Prize:* silver medal / large gilt silver frame and silver medal / large plain silver frame, *Second Prize:* silver medal / medium silver frame and silver medal / gilt bronze frame, *Third Prize:* silver medal / small silver frame and gilt bronze medal / gilt bronze frame; SECOND CLASS—*First Prize:* silver medal / medium silver frame and gilt bronze medal / gilt bronze frame, *Second Prize:* silver medal / small silver frame and gilt bronze medal / gilt bronze frame; *Third Prize:* silver medal / small gilt bronze frame and gilt bronze medal / small gilt bronze frame; THIRD CLASS—*First Prize:* silver medal / medium gilt bronze frame and gilt bronze medal / medium gilt bronze frame, *Second Prize:* silver medal / small gilt bronze frame and gilt bronze medal / small gilt bronze frame, *Third Prize:* silver medal / small gilt bronze frame and bronze medal with patina / small gilt bronze frame.

It is worth noting that all prize winners received at least one silver medal, although the size and/or material of the frame varied greatly. The second, or duplicate medal, tended to be a less valuable example, and except for top prizes in the first class, was either of gilt bronze or, as in the last category, of plain, patinated bronze.

In addition to the award of fifty-four student prize medals, twelve silver medals were distributed to officials and participants in the ceremony. These were all framed in silver, distinguished as before by the size and treatment of their mounts and by the numbers given. Medals in large gilt silver frames were received by the pope (two), Cardinal Chamberlain Colonna (two), Cardinal Rezzonico (one), Cardinal Alessandro Albani (one), and Cardinal Giovanni Francesco Albani (one). The prelate who delivered the oration (Monsignor Onofrio Alfani) also received one of the same, plus another silver medal in a large, plain silver frame. The *principe* of the academy and the *custode* of the Arcadii each received one silver medal in a medium-sized, plain silver frame, and the secretary of the academy received a medal in a small, plain silver frame (*see also* nos. 121, 131).

U.W.H.

1. Accademia di San Luca archives, "Nota distinta de Premj da dispensarsi dall'Insigne Accademia di S. Luca nel Concorso dei 16. Sett. 1762."

FERDINANDO HAMERANI

Rome 1730—Rome 1789

133. Clement XIII / The Gift of the Furietti Centaurs to the Capitoline Museum

1765

Bronze

Diameter 40 mm

Obverse: Bust of Clement XIII right, wearing tiara and embroidered cope with arabesques; inscribed around: CLEMENS XIII · PONT · M · A · VII ; signed on truncation: HAMERANI

Reverse: View of the façade of the Capitoline Museum; in the foreground the two Furietti centaurs;

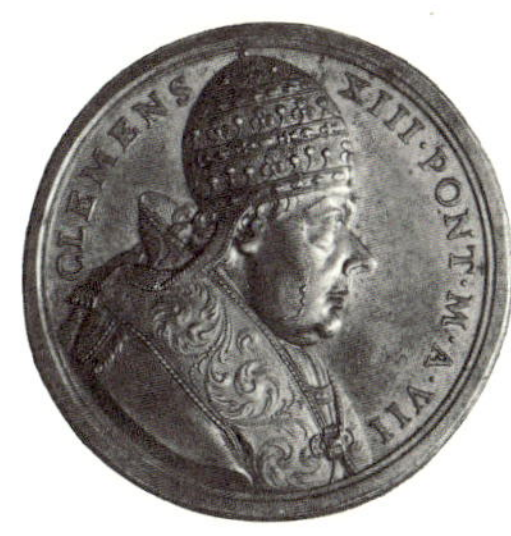

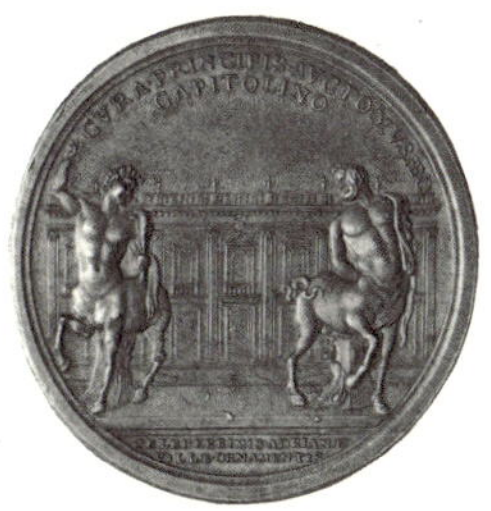

133

inscribed around: CVRA · PRINCIPIS · AVCTO · MVSAEO CAPITOLINO ; in exergue: CELEBERRIMIS · ADRIANAE / VILLAE · ORNAMENTIS

1978-70-85

Provenance: purchased in Rome, 1966

Pope Benedict XIV had sought for years to acquire for the Capitoline collection the two famous marble centaurs discovered at Hadrian's Villa by Monsignor Giuseppe Alessandro Furietti in 1736 (*see* no. 112). Furietti was a devoted antiquary and author of a widely admired history of ancient mosaics. His decision to keep the sculptures is said to have cost him a cardinalate under Benedict XIV, and during the period when pressure was greatest, Furietti reportedly feared becoming known as "Cardinal Centaur" if he agreed to give up the statues. He was raised to the purple within a year of the accession of Clement XIII who, incidentally, had little of his predecessor's extreme devotion to antiquity. After Furietti's death in 1764, Clement XIII purchased the two centaurs from his estate for 14,000 scudi, together with the celebrated "dove mosaic" by Sosus of Pergamum. This medal by Ferdinando Hamerani[1] was issued to commemorate the gift of these objects to the Capitoline Museum.

U.W.H.

1. On Ferdinando and the question of whether he was an engraver or only supervised the production of medals, *see* Noack, 1921–22, pp. 36–37; for the medal, *see* Mazio, 1824, no. 493; Forrer, 1902–30, vol. 2, p. 407; Hamburg, et al., 1966–, no. 237; Bartolotti, 1967, p. 184.

GIOACCHINO HAMERANI

Rome 1761—Rome 1797

134. Pius VI / The Restoration of the Via Appia

1788

Silver

Diameter 40 mm

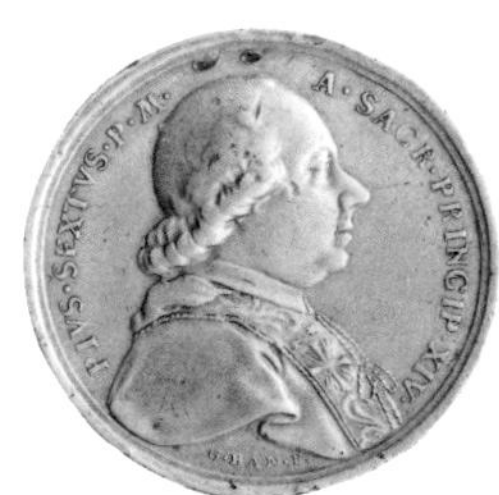

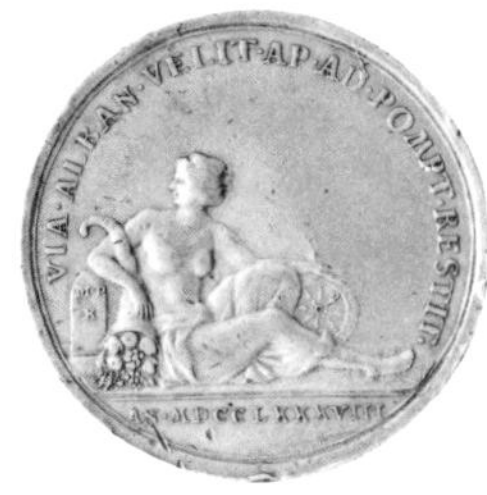

134

Obverse: Bust of Pius VI right, wearing birettino, mozzetta, and stole; inscribed around: PIVS · SEXTVS · P · M · A · SACR · PRINCIP · XIV · ; signed below bust: G. HAM · F ·

Reverse: Female personification of the via Appia, holding a cornucopia and wheel, and reclining against a milestone inscribed: M · P / X ; inscribed around: VIA · ALBAN · VELIT · AN · AD · POMPT · RESTIT · ; in exergue: AN · MDCCLXXXVIII

1978-70-78

Provenance: gift of Cyril Humphris, London, 1970

This medal commemorates the completion of work ordered by Pius VI to restore the ancient via Appia, a major thoroughfare that ran south from Rome through the Pontine Marshes. Seeking to improve travel and to control the chronic flooding in the area, Pius VI ordered the removal of the successive layers of paving that had raised the level of the ancient road and thereby blocked the water draining from the marshes to the sea. Work was completed in 1787, with a new roadway built to extend the route to Terracina, the southernmost city in the Papal States.

Since Giovanni Hamerani (1763–1846), younger brother of Gioacchino, was unknown to both Nagler and Forrer,[1] some confusion has resulted in the attribution of medals produced in the late eighteenth and early nineteenth centuries that bear variations of the signatures G. HAM. or J. HAM.

Friedrich Noack was of the opinion that Gioacchino, although an official of the mint from at least 1789, was not active artistically.[2] He also affirmed that Giovanni, having early practiced architecture, did not work as a medalist until after the death of Gioacchino in 1797. In any case, it is certain that the medals signed J. HAM. that appeared between 1797 and at least 1807 belong to Giovanni (J. was also the initial adopted by Giovanni's great-grandfather Giovanni Martino), whereas we must conclude that Gioacchino authored the numerous examples, like this one,[3] produced under Pius VI (1775–99) and bearing the signature G. HAM.

U.W.H.

1. Nagler, 1835–52, vol. 5, pp. 537–38; Forrer, 1902–30, vol. 2, pp. 398–99.
2. Noack, 1921–22, pp. 37–38 (". . . was however not personally active").
3. *See,* in addition to the works cited in note 1, Mazio, 1824, no. 529; Bartolotti, 1967, p. 211.

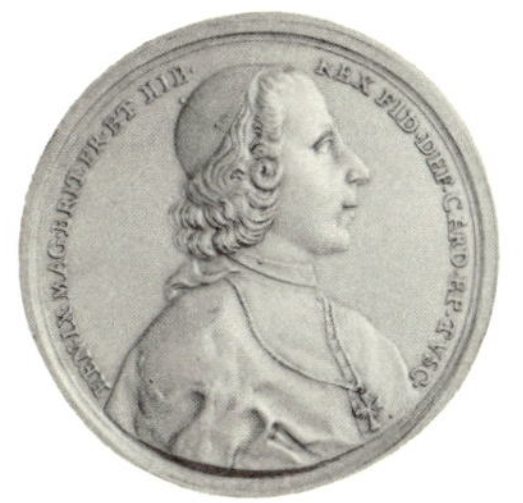
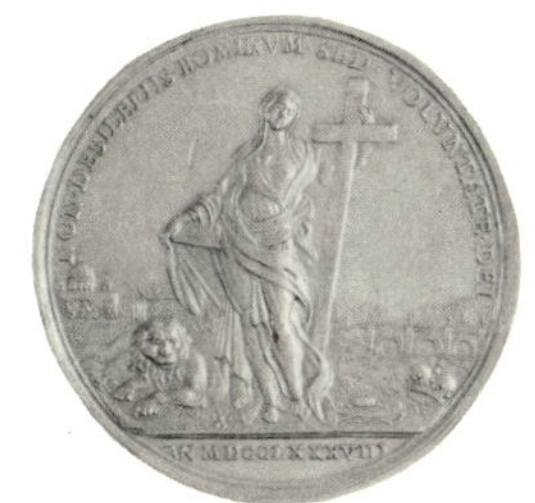

135

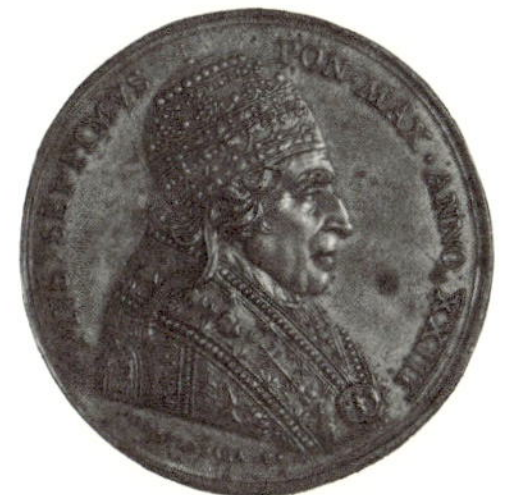
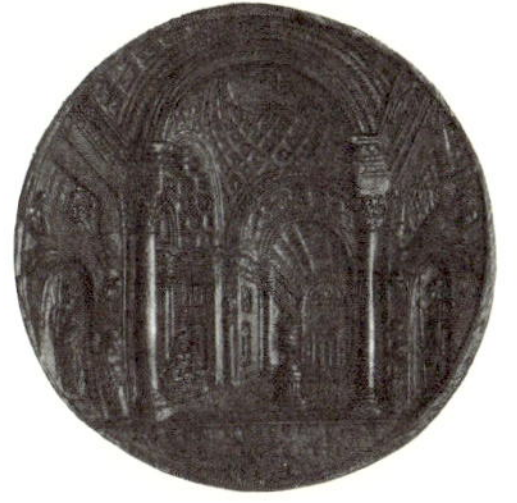

136

135. Henry Stuart, Cardinal Duke of York / Religion
1788
Silver
Diameter 54 mm
Obverse: Bust of Henry Stuart, cardinal duke of York right, wearing birettino and mozzetta; inscribed around: HEN · IX · MAG · BRIT · FR · ET · HIB · REX · FID · DEF · CARD · EP · TVSC ·
Reverse: Religion holding the Gospels and a cross, a lion at her feet; a cardinal's hat and a royal crown set on the ground, and in the background a view of Rome; inscribed around: NON · DESIDERIIS · SED · VOLUNTATE · DEI ; in exergue: AN MDCCLXXXVIII
1978-70-55
Provenance: gift of Michael Hall, 1965

Henry Benedict Stuart (1725–1807), the second son of James III and Maria Clementina Sobieski, received the title of duke of York shortly after his birth. After assisting his brother from France during the unsuccessful Jacobite rebellion of 1745–46, he was created cardinal by Benedict XIV in 1747. In 1759 he became titular archbishop of Corinth and in 1761 cardinal-bishop of Frascati where for many years he showed himself a sincere and pious administrator. With the death of the young pretender, Charles Edward, in 1788, Cardinal York assumed the title of King Henry IX of Great Britain. Issued in honor of the occasion, this medal incorporates the new royal title but as usual portrays the cardinal in ecclesiastical costume. The wistful attitude of Religion on the reverse seems to echo something of the reluctance and pious dutifulness with which, as the legend proclaims, Cardinal York assumed his—by then purely fictional—sovereign role. He was buried in the Vatican Grottoes alongside James III and Charles Edward.

Although this medal is unsigned, identical ones bearing the signature G. HAM. F.[1] make its attribution to Gioacchino Hamerani reasonably certain. Together with the medal of Pius VI here catalogued (no. 134), it is among the earliest known medals by Gioacchino.

U.W.H.

1. *See* Forrer, 1902–30, vol. 2, p. 399.

GIUSEPPE CERBARA
Rome 1770—Rome 1856

136. Pius VII / The Braccio Nuovo of the Museo Chiaramonti
1822
Bronze
Diameter 43.5 mm
Obverse: Bust of Pius VII right, wearing tiara and cope embroidered with the Chiaramonti arms; inscribed around: PIVS SEPTIMVS PON · MAX · ANNO XXIII; signed below the bust: GIU · CERBARA F ·
Reverse: Interior view of the Braccio Nuovo; inscribed in exergue: NOVUM MUSEUM PIUM / A · D · MDCCCXXII / CERBARA · F
1978-70-107
Provenance: purchased in Rome, 1966

Giuseppe Cerbara began his career as assistant to his father Giovanni Battista Cerbara (d. 1811), a Roman gem cutter celebrated for his classical subjects and portraits of famous contemporaries. Until his appointment as engraver at the papal mint in 1821 Giuseppe was also known principally for his engraved gems—the basis of his election to the Accademia di San Luca in 1812—and produced works for patrons such as the duc de Blacas, Count Sommariva, and Czar Alexander. Renewed in his appointment as mint engraver, Giuseppe was eventually responsible for a long series of medals commemorating events in papal history through the reigns of Popes Leo XII, Pius VIII, Gregory XVI, and Pius IX.[1] This medal, the first in his official career, was issued on the completion of the Braccio Nuovo, a major new sculpture gallery that formed part of the recently established Museo Chiaramonti (*see* no. 111). The latter collection was organized by Pius VII (1800–1823) after the example of the Museo Pio-Clementino and was initially intended to offset the loss of Vatican antiquities taken to France in 1797.[2] Antonio Canova was given responsibility for the selection and installation of the new collections, part of which, in the eastern wing of Bramante's corridors, was opened to the public in 1810. The Braccio Nuovo, one of the great neoclassical interiors in Rome, was built across the Cortile del Belvedere on the design of Raphael Stern between 1817 and 1822. The steep perspective view of the medal shows the domed central crossing that joins the two long wings of the gallery.

U.W.H.

1. For Cerbara, *see* Nagler, 1835–52, vol. 2, p. 472; Bolzenthal, 1840, p. 306; Thieme-Becker, 1907–50, vol. 6, p. 291; Forrer, 1902–30, vol. 7, p. 172; Patrignani, 1933, pp. 29 ff; de Caro Balbi ("Accademico").

2. For the Museo Chiaramonti, its history and pertinent literature, *see* Hiesinger, 1978 ("Canova"). For the medal, *see* Mazio, 1824, no. 568; Patrignani, 1930, no. 108, pl. 6; Bartolotti, 1967, p. 240; de Caro Balbi, 1974 ("Accademico"), p. 24, fig. 25, and p. 27.

GIUSEPPE CAPUTI

active Rome, c. 1810–40

137. Cardinal Pacca

1830

Bronze

Diameter 35 mm

Obverse: Bust of Cardinal Pacca right, wearing birettino and mozzetta; inscribed around: B: C · PACCA S · C · DECANVS ; signed below bust: CAPVTI

Reverse: Inscribed: ADSERTORI / FELICITATIS / PVBLICAE / S · P · Q · V / MDCCCXXX

1978-70-108

Provenance: purchased Rome, 1966/67

Giuseppe Caputi (also known as "Capucci") was a rather obscure gem engraver and medalist who practiced in Rome in the first half of the nineteenth century, evidently after some earlier activity in Paris and London. He produced medals for Popes Leo XII (1823–29) and Pius VIII (1829–30), as well as numerous gems with portraits and classical subjects.[1]

Bartolomeo Cardinal Pacca (1756–1844) reached the height of his long and influential career as a church statesman during the reign of Pius VII (1800–1823). Created cardinal by that pope in 1801, Pacca was named pro-secretary of state upon the French occupation of Rome in 1808 and presided over promulgation of the bull that excommunicated Napoleon after he annexed Rome in the next year. Pacca was arrested and taken from the city together with Pius VII and was afterward imprisoned at Fenestrelle for three years. He later joined the pope at Fontainebleau and, having been named cardinal chamberlain, accompanied him to Rome in triumph in 1814. After the Restoration he was instrumental in reestablishing the Jesuit order, which had been suppressed in 1773. Named pro-secretary of state for a second time during Cardinal Consalvi's absence at the Congress of Vienna, Pacca earned the latter's reproach for his harsh reprisals against former supporters of the French.

Cardinal Pacca authored several memoirs and histories; though his role as a patron is yet to be explored, he was reputed to be a generous supporter and friend to artists and literary figures. His casino outside the gates of Rome was kept as a small museum for the display of a collection that included antiquities excavated by him at Porto and Ostia. It was for his official role as protector of the Accademia di San Luca that Melchior Missirini dedicated to Pacca his well-known history of the academy published in 1823.

In 1829 Cardinal Pacca was named cardinal-deacon and bishop of Ostia and Velletri. As Velletri was raised to the status of apostolic legation, Pacca, its first legate, was honored in his new position by this medal, sponsored by the senate and people of Velletri.

U.W.H.

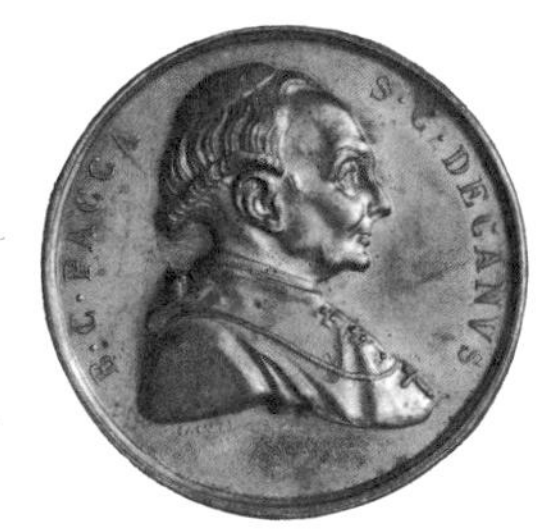

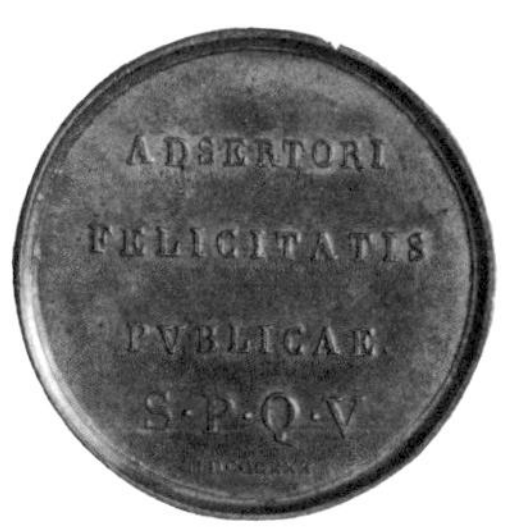

137

1. For Caputi, *see* Forrer, 1902–30, vol. 1, p. 341, and vol. 7, p. 151; Thieme-Becker, 1907–50, vol. 5, p. 559; Nagler, 1835–52, vol. 2, p. 352. For this medal, cf. Patrignani, 1929, p. 159, no. 19; Moroni, 1840–61, vol. 50, pp. 86–87.

NICOLA CERBARA

Rome 1796—Montepulciano 1869

138. Cardinal Alessandro Albani / The Villa Albani

1830

Bronze

Diameter 70 mm

Obverse: Bust of Cardinal Albani left, wearing birettino and mozzetta; inscribed around: MAGNO PATRVO ALEXANDRO CARD · ALBANO ; signed on truncation: NIC. CERBARA F.

Reverse: View of the façade of the Villa Albani; inscribed around: BONARVM ARTIVM CVLTORI PERITISSIMO ; in exergue: IOSEPHVS CARD · ALBANVS /[1] MDCCCXXX ; signed at lower rim: NICOLAVS CERBARA FECIT ROMAE

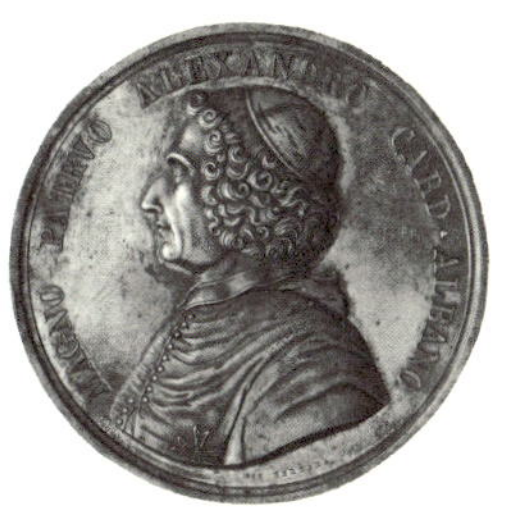
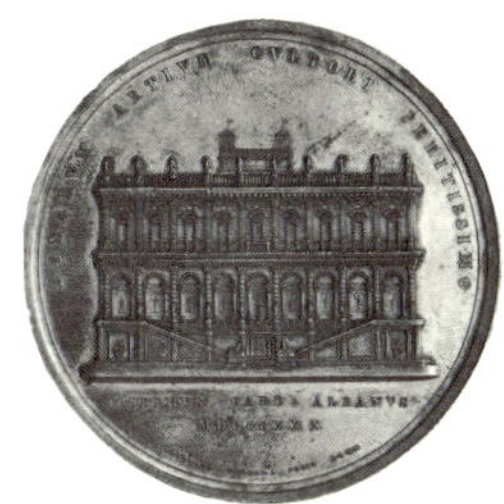

138

1978-70-101
Provenance: London, Spink and Son, Ltd.; purchased from John Harris, London, 1967

Nicola Cerbara, brother of Giuseppe (*see* no. 136), was a prolific medalist, coin, and gem engraver active in Rome during the reigns of Pius VIII (1829–30), Gregory XVI (1831–46), and Pius IX (1846–78). As engraver—and later director—at the mint in Rome his medalic production centered on depictions of great figures from Italian history. His best-known effort was the medalic series produced in collaboration with Pietro Girometti (*see* no. 140), *Serie iconografica numismatica dei più famosi italiani*.[2]

Alessandro Cardinal Albani (1692–1779) was a figure of unrivaled prominence in the artistic and political life of Rome in the eighteenth century. A nephew of Pope Clement XI, Alessandro was created cardinal in 1712 and gained a central role in state affairs by functioning simultaneously as the cardinal protector of Sardinia and Austria and serving through many decades as ally and unofficial sponsor of the English government in policies directed against the Jacobites based in Rome.

Best known perhaps for his patronage of the archaeologist Johann Joachim Winckelmann in the late 1750s and 1760s, Albani throughout his life was a generous supporter of scholars and artists, among them many of the Englishmen who visited and worked in Rome. A prodigious collector of antiquities, medals, gems, and drawings, Albani had already assembled—and then sold in time of need—two collections of ancient sculpture before forming the last and most important collection housed in his famous villa outside the Porta Salaria. The Villa Albani, built between 1743 and 1763 by the architect Carlo Marchionni (*see* no. 44), was the cardinal's grandest undertaking. Largely despoiled of its contents by Napoleon, the villa served in the eighteenth century as a virtual museum, celebrated as no other of its time for the splendor of its gardens and collections and for interior decorations that, in the gallery of the casino, included Raphael Mengs's famed *Parnassus* of 1761.

U.W.H.

1. Giuseppe Cardinal Albani (1750–1834).
2. For the birth date of Nicola and the most recent literature, *see* de Caro Balbi, 1974, ("Accademico"), p. 32, n. 20; also the standard references—Forrer, 1902–30, vol. 1, pp. 386–88, and vol. 7, p. 172; Thieme-Becker, 1907–50, vol. 6, p. 291; Nagler, 1835–52, vol. 2, p. 472. For this medal, *see* Louisville and Houston, 1969–70, no. 279.

ANTONIO FABRIS

Udine 1792—Udine 1865

139. Antonio Canova / The Tempio Canova at Possagno

1831
Silver
Diameter 53 mm
Obverse: Bust of Antonio Canova right; inscribed around: ANTONIVS CANOVA ; signed below the bust: A · FABRIS VTINENSIS SCVLP ·
Reverse: View of the Tempio Canova at Possagno; inscribed around: CHARITAS IN PATRIAM ; in exergue: DEDIC · AN · M · DCCC · XXXI ·
1978-70-115
Provenance: purchased from David Peel, London, 1965

Antonio Fabris was a goldsmith prior to becoming a medalist. Following his first studies in Rome he worked in Florence at some point after 1829 and was eventually employed as chief engraver at the Venice mint in the latter part of his career. Fabris's first medal, produced in 1823, was a small edition of two hundred examples issued to commemorate the death of Antonio Canova (1757–1822). A second medal representing Canova's funeral monument in Venice was executed in 1828. The present medal, created to mark the dedication of the Tempio Canova at Possagno, was viewed by some as Fabris's masterpiece, regarded for its "pains and delicacy of the execution [as] almost unbelievable."[1]

The Tempio at Possagno was constructed under the personal sponsorship of Canova and was intended to re-

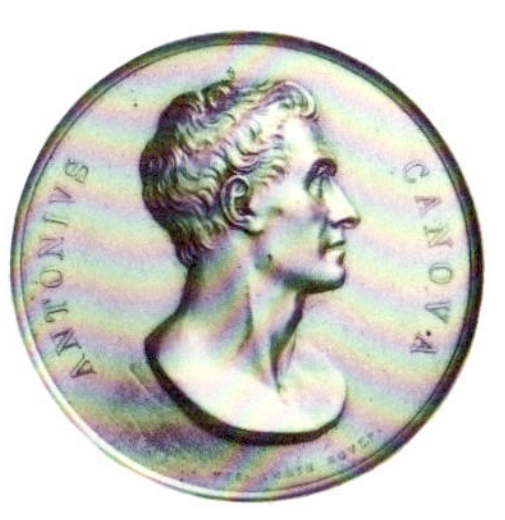

139

place the small parochial church of his native village.[2] Built with the aid of the architect Giovanni Antonio Selva (1753–1819), it is one of several edifices of the period aimed at synthesizing the Parthenon's portico with the rotunda of the Pantheon. The cornerstone was laid in 1819, and after the sculptor's death, work on the building continued until 1830. The Tempio houses the tomb of Canova, marked by his *Pietà,* which was cast in bronze in 1830. Among other works preserved there is Canova's self-portrait in marble (1812), which served as the model for Fabris's medal.

U.W.H.

1. Nagler, 1835–52, vol. 4, p. 211. For Fabris, *see also* Forrer, 1902–30, vol. 2, pp. 64–65, and vol. 7, p. 286; Thieme-Becker, 1907–50, vol. 11, p. 168; Bolzenthal, 1840, p. 306. For other Canova medals by Girometti and Putinati, *see* Louisville and Houston, 1969–70, nos. 319, 321; Eidlitz, 1927, no. 217; *L'Accademia,* 1974, p. 385, no. 31.
2. Missirini, 1833. For the Tempio Canova, *see* Meeks, 1966, pp. 155, 171, 186, 188, 190.

PIETRO GIROMETTI

Rome 1812—Rome 1859

140. Ennio Quirino Visconti / Allegory of Antiquity

1832

Silvered bronze

Diameter 52 mm

Obverse: Bust of Ennio Quirino Visconti right; inscribed around: ENNIVS QVIRINVS VISCONTI ROMANVS ; signed below bust: PETRVS · GIROMETTI · F ·

Reverse: A female seated beneath a radiant star holds a scroll in her left hand, and points to a round temple inscribed: ICONOGI ; at her feet the Torso Belvedere; at right a winged putto kneeling on a plinth inscribed: ☧· VAL · SA , holds a tablet inscribed: DM ; behind, the columns of a temple; inscribed around: LVX · TEMPORVM · VITA · MEMORIAE · NVNCIA · VETVSTATIS · ; in exergue: MDCCCXXXII / ROMAE

1978-70-102

Provenance: purchased from Luigi de Nicola, Rome, 1967

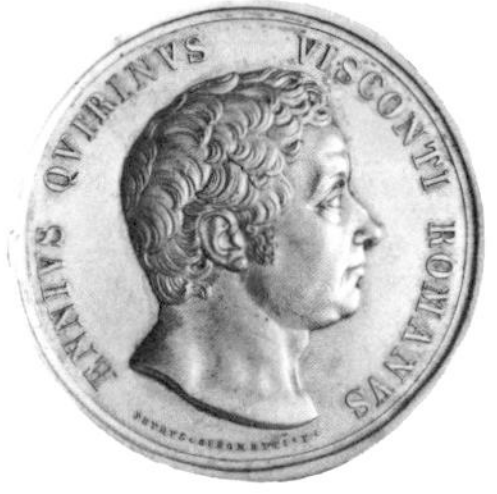
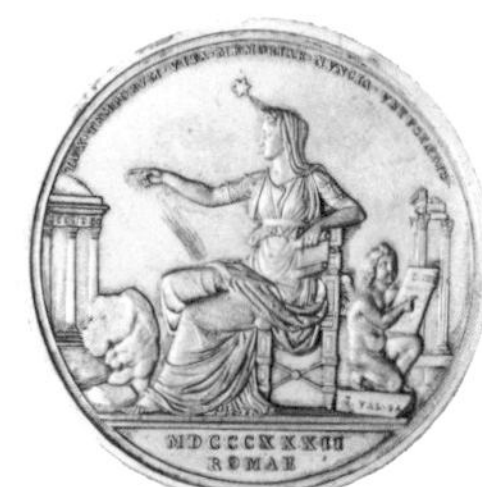

140

Son of the more famous medalist and gem engraver Giuseppe Girometti, Pietro worked in Rome during the pontificates of Gregory XVI (1831–46) and Pius IX (1846-78) and is best known for his contributions to the medallic series of famous Italians undertaken jointly by his father Giuseppe and Nicola Cerbara, *Serie iconografica numismatica dei più famosi italiani* (*see* no. 138).[1]

Ennio Quirino Visconti (1751–1818), the most celebrated archaeologist of the late eighteenth and early nineteenth centuries, was the son of Giovanni Battista Visconti, superintendent of antiquities in Rome under Popes Clement XIII, Clement XIV, and Pius VI. A genuine prodigy, the young Visconti was reputedly able to identify the series of Roman emperors at age two and could read Greek and Latin at age three. His first publication, at age fourteen, was a translation of Euripides' *Hecuba,* printed in Rome in 1765.

After serving as librarian to Prince Sigismondo Chigi, with Carlo Fea as underlibrarian, Visconti was named conservator of the Capitoline Museum, having lost to his brother during a period of parental disfavor the nomination to the superintendency of antiquities. With publication in 1782 of the first volume of the *Museo Pio-Clementino,* which ranks among his most important publications, Visconti's celebrity was permanently established. Six ensuing volumes were published throughout the 1780s and 1790s, with a final volume appearing in 1807. Among other catalogues written by Visconti were those for the collections of Thomas Jenkins and Marcantonio Borghese. As the author of innumerable books and essays on the mythology and monuments of classical antiquity, Visconti's work was consistently distinguished by an astonishing erudition and by the brief, precise logic of his arguments. On frequent occasions he is also mentioned as one to whom young artists turned for advice on classical subjects and opinions concerning the style of the ancients.

Visconti's participation in the occupation government of General Berthier, and his service as one of the five consuls of the Roman Republic of 1798, obliged him to flee the city when Neapolitan troops captured Rome in the following year. His flight to Paris coincided with the arrival there of the antiquities surrendered from Italy, and Visconti was appointed to a series of positions at the museum then being formed at the Louvre. In Paris he continued to publish unceasingly and produced under the sponsorship of Napoleon the first three Greek volumes of his famous *Iconographie grecque et romaine* (1808). Near the end of his career Visconti was called by parliament to London to give his appraisal and set a price for the purchase of Lord Elgin's marbles. His observations on the Parthenon sculptures, published on his return to Paris, were the first to identify the Panathenaic procession.

Representatives of nearly all the European countries attended his funeral in Paris, and memorial ceremonies were subsequently held at the academy of archaeology and the Accademia di San Luca in Rome. In summing up Visconti's career one biographer wrote: "Winckelmann has brought us to love the science of antiquity, Visconti has illuminated for us its entire domain."

U.W.H.

1. For Girometti, *see* Forrer, 1902–30, vol. 2, p. 274, and vol. 7, p. 368; Thieme-Becker, 1907–50, vol. 14, p. 190; Bolzenthal, 1840, p. 305.

141. Cardinal Zurla / Religion Protecting the Arts and Sciences
1833
Bronze
Diameter 55 mm
Obverse: Bust of Cardinal Zurla right, wearing birettino and mozzetta; inscribed around: PLACIDVS · TIT · SESSOR · S · R · E · CARD · ZVRLA · VICE · SACRA · VRB · ANTIST · S · CONGR · STVD · REG · PRAEF ·
Reverse: At center the enthroned figure of Religion holding a cross; at left Geography is seated with a globe inscribed: ASIA , and bears a scroll inscribed: M / POLO ; to the right with hammer and chisel the personification of the Arts; beside her a palette, architect's square, and a bust of Athena, the plinth nearby inscribed: RAPHAEL / CANOVA ; inscribed around: HOC SIDERE ; signed in exergue: IN OBSEQVIVM TANTI VIRI SCVLPS · / PETRVS GIROMETTI / ROMAE / MDCCCXXXIII
1978-70-100
Provenance: gift of Andrew Ciechanowiecki, 1968

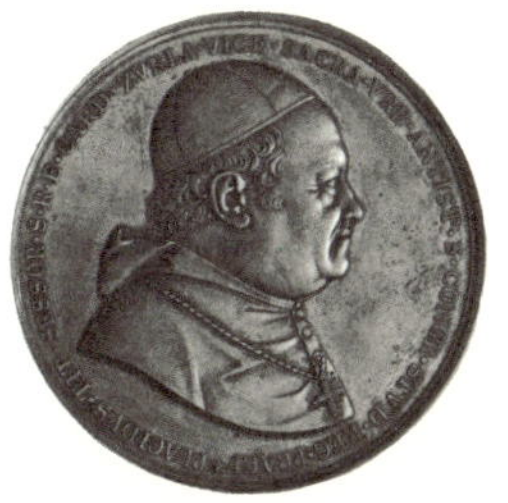

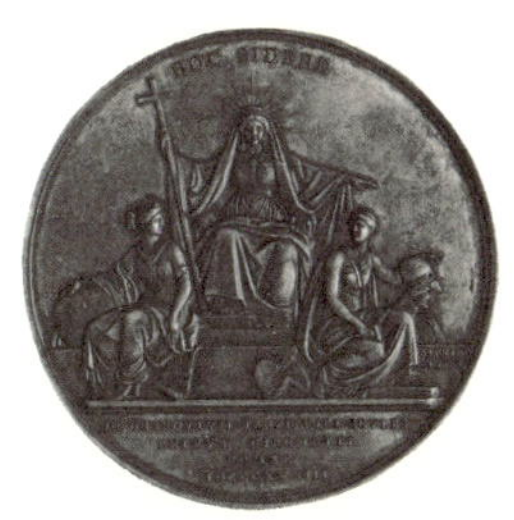

141

This medal was produced in 1833 to honor Placido Cardinal Zurla (1769–1834), a genial, scholarly figure who played a prominent role in the literary, scientific, and artistic life of Rome after the Restoration.[1] Zurla spent the greater part of his career in monastic centers in his native Veneto, where he taught and published works on theology and the natural sciences. His particular devotion to geography and to the study of early travelers resulted in his most famous work, *Di Marco Polo e degli altri viaggiatori veneziani* (Venice, 1818–19).

During a visit to Rome in 1821 Zurla was instantly celebrated for a dissertation delivered on the subject of the benefits conferred by the Catholic religion on geography and other sciences ("De'vantaggi derivati dalla Religione Cattolica alla geografia e all'altre scienze"). Official appointments made first by Pius VII kept him permanently in Rome, where he became active in cultural circles and in the reform of various ecclesiastical and learned institutions. Created cardinal in 1823, Zurla was named vicar general of Rome under Leo XII (1823–29) and was a special friend of Gregory XVI, for whom he served as confessor and to whom he left his estate. As a noted *amateur* and friend of Antonio Canova and Vincenzo Camuccini, the cardinal owned a number of drawings, oil sketches, and paintings by these artists, as well as a wide-ranging collection of engraved gems, sculptures, inscriptions, books, prints, bronze objects, and minerals.

After Zurla's death, which occurred in Palermo while he was touring the monuments of Sicily, copies of Girometti's medal were placed in his tomb in the church of San Gregorio de'Camaldolesi in Rome. The allegory on the medal's reverse was designed to symbolize the specific pursuits and patronage of the cardinal, which were regarded as especially praiseworthy for their combination of religious, scientific, and artistic disciplines. A similar tribute occurred with the posthumous publication of Zurla's writings, which included his treatises on Raphael's *Transfiguration,* the religious works of Canova, and the relation of religion to geography and science.[2]

U.W.H.

1. The medal is described by Gaspare Servi, *Il Tiberino,* July 5, 1834; *see also* Patrignani, 1929, no. 25. For Cardinal Zurla, *see* Moroni, 1840–61, vol. 103, pp. 493–514.

2. *Dissertazioni del cardinal d. Placido Zurla: De'vantaggi recati dalla religione cattolica alla geografia e scienze annesse: Sull'unità del soggetto nel quadro della Trasfigurazione di Raffaele: Sul gruppo della Pietà, e le altre opere di religioso argomento di Antonio Canova: ora per la prima volta insieme riunite.* Rome, 1835 (published by P. A. Visconti).

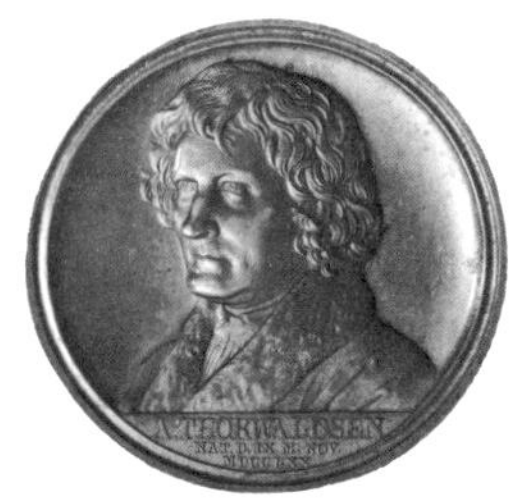

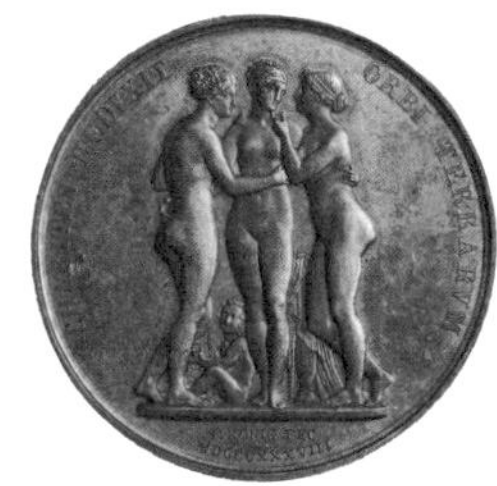

142

FRIEDRICH KÖNIG

Breslau 1794—Dresden 1844

142. Bertel Thorvaldsen / The Three Graces

1838

Bronze

Diameter 40 mm

Obverse: Bust of Bertel Thorvaldsen three-quarter view left; inscribed in exergue: A· THORWALDSEN / NAT. D. IX M. NOV. / MDCCLXX

Reverse: The Three Graces; inscribed around: CHARITES REDVXIT ORBI TERRARVM ; signed in exergue: F. KÖNIG FEC. / MDCCCXXXVIII

1978-70-103

Provenance: purchased in Copenhagen, 1966

Friedrich König's early career followed the movements of his father Anton, a celebrated medalist active in Breslau and Berlin. Assistant to his father at the Berlin mint from 1811, Friedrich was called to Dresden in 1824 and there spent the remainder of his career. A long series of medals commemorating celebrated personalities and many members of the German royal houses was produced throughout the 1820s and 30s. His most famous work, a medal created after Friedrich Schinkel's designs in honor of Prince Blücher, was issued in 1817.[1]

This medal, of 1838, coincided with the return of the sculptor Bertel Thorvaldsen to his native Copenhagen. Thorvaldsen had practiced in Rome since 1797, first as the rival of Canova and later as a celebrity of comparable international fame. He made the journey home in the company of all of his sculptures, traveling on a Danish frigate supplied by the government. Regarded as a national hero, he was given a triumphal reception in Copenhagen, which at one point he compared to the treatment accorded the pope at Rome. This is one of a number of medals created in Thorvaldsen's honor. Others were issued by the Copenhagen academy to serve as prizes for students in sculpture and by the Accademia di San Luca in Rome (1836).

Thorvaldsen's *Three Graces,*[2] which is pictured on the reverse of this medal, was one of the sculptor's most widely known works, produced in Rome between 1817 and 1819 and intended as a reply to Canova's own celebrated group of the same subject. U.W.H.

1. For König, *see* Forrer, 1902–30, vol. 3, pp. 195–96, and vol. 7, p. 511. Thieme-Becker, 1907–50, vol. 21, pp. 148–49.
2. *See* Cologne, 1977, nos. 53 and 59.

HENRY WEIGALL

born c. 1800—London (?) 1883

143. John Flaxman / Mercury and Pandora

1854

Bronze

Diameter 57 mm

Obverse: Bust of John Flaxman left; inscribed: FLAXMAN ; signed below bust: HENRY WEIGALL SC :

Reverse: Mercury in flight bearing Pandora; signed lower left and right: H. WEIGALL.· FECIT.; impressed around edge: ART-UNION OF LONDON 1854.

1978-70-73

Provenance: gift of Michael Hall, 1966

The commission for a medal to honor John Flaxman was first initiated by the Art Union of London in 1846, at the twentieth anniversary of the sculptor's death. After earlier attempts by W. Wilson and W. Wyon, the medal was finally produced in 1854 by Henry Weigall[1] and used as a prize by the Art Union in that year. The portrait is after a bust by the former pupil of Flaxman, Edward Hodges Baily. The reverse depicts Flaxman's relief of *Mercury Descending to Earth with Pandora,*[2] designed originally for a silver vase commemorating the battle of Trafalgar and exhibited by Flaxman in 1805.

U.W.H.

1. For Weigall, a sculptor, gem engraver, and modeler, *see* Forrer, 1902–30, vol. 6, pp. 422–23; Thieme-Becker, 1907–50, vol. 35, p. 276; for the medal, Beaulah, 1967, p. 132, no. 6; London, 1979, no. 181.
2. For versions at University College, London, *see* Whinney and Gunnis, 1967, p. 25, no. 32, pl. 5a; and in Copenhagen, *see* London, 1979, no. 122.

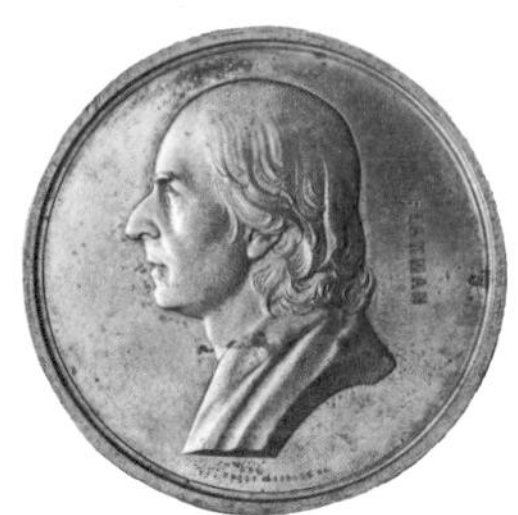

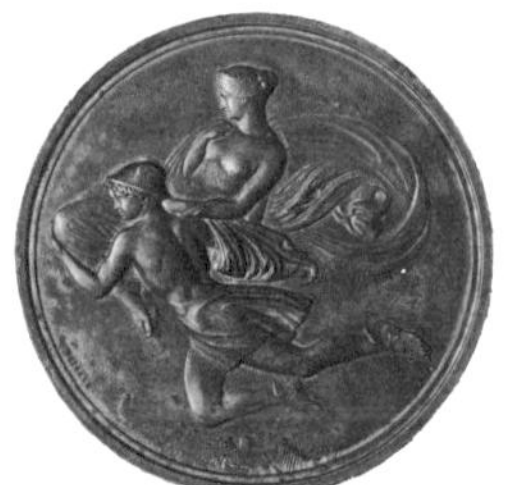

143

CHECKLIST OF DRAWINGS

Luigi Agricola (Italian, 1750/59–1821)
1. *An Angel Appearing to a Warrior (Study for an Engraving)*
Black chalk on cream wove paper
209 x 155 mm (8 1/4 x 6 1/8")
1978-70-152

Domenico Amici (Italian, c. 1808–after 1874)
2. *View of the Alban Hills,* 1874
Watercolor on cream wove paper
267 x 374 mm (10 9/16 x 14 11/16")
1978-70-153

Napoleone Angiolini (Italian, 1797–1864)
3. *Hercules Wrestling the Nemean Lion*
Black chalk on cream laid paper
197 x 310 mm (7 3/4 x 12 3/16")
1978-70-155

Attributed to Andrea Appiani (Italian, 1754–1817)
4. *Study for a Cupola Section, Assumption of the Virgin*
Brown ink on cream laid paper
Verso: *Studies of a Putto*
Brown ink and black chalk
259 x 255 mm (10 3/16 x 10 1/16")
1978-70-156

Attributed to Francesco Appiani (Italian, 1704–1792)
5. *A Group of Goddesses and River Gods*
Verso: *Head of a God*
Black chalk on cream laid paper
120 x 237 mm (4 3/4 x 9 5/16")
1978-70-157

Attributed to Robert van Audenaerd (Flemish, 1663–1743)
After Carlo Maratta (Italian, 1625–1713)
6. *Madonna del Rosario*
Red chalk, some black chalk or pencil, on cream laid paper
649 x 429 mm (26 1/8 x 16 7/8")
1978-70-158

Pompeo Batoni (Italian, 1708–1787)
7. *Old Pilgrim Walking with a Staff*
Red chalk on buff laid paper
130 x 95 mm (5 1/8 x 3·3/4")
1978-70-162

8. *Study for the Merenda "Ecce Homo"*
Black and white chalks on blue prepared paper
170 x 120 mm (6 11/16 x 4 3/4")
1978-70-166

9. *Twenty-one Sheets from a Sketchbook*
Black and red chalks on cream laid paper
Each sheet approximately 130 x 100 mm (5 1/8 x 3 7/8")
1978-70-175[a-n, p-r, u-x]

Attributed to Pompeo Batoni
10. *Studies of a Small Girl with a Lamb and a Baby*
Black and white chalks on tan prepared paper
281 x 431 mm (11 1/8 x 17")
1978-70-176

11. *Portrait of a Cleric (Study for an Engraving)*
Red chalk on buff laid paper
207 x 155 mm (8 3/16 x 6 1/8")
1978-70-177

Anonymous, after Pompeo Batoni
12. *Portrait of the Emperor Joseph II*
Black chalk and watercolor on cream laid paper
172 x 138 mm (6 3/4 x 5 7/16")
1978-70-178

Circle of Pompeo Batoni
13. *Two Putti*
Black and white chalks on tan prepared paper
210 x 223 mm (8 1/4 x 8 3/4")
1978-70-179

Attributed to Claudio Francesco Beaumont (Italian, 1694–1766)
14. *Study for a Wall Decoration with Allegorical Figures*
Brown ink, brown and gray washes, on beige laid paper
200 x 144 mm (7 7/8 x 5 5/8")
1978-70-180

Stefano della Bella (Italian, 1610–1664)
15. *View of the Villa Medici Gardens*
Brown ink over traces of black chalk on cream laid paper
231 x 366 mm (9 1/8 x 14 3/8")
1978-70-181

Pietro Benvenuti (Italian, 1769–1844)
16. *The Courage of Portia*
Black and white chalks on blue paper, mounted down
181 x 244 mm (7 1/8 x 9 5/8")
1978-70-187

Niccolò Berrettoni (Italian, 1637–1682)
17. *Study of an Angel Appearing to Saint Anthony Abbot*
Brown ink and wash over red chalk on cream laid paper
182 x 146 mm (7 3/16 x 5 3/4")
1978-70-189

Antonio Bianchini (Italian, active c. 1800–1850)
18. *Saints Gregory (?) and Lawrence in Glory*
Brown washes over pencil on cream wove paper, squared
265 x 245 mm (10 7/16 x 9 5/8")
1978-70-190

Giuseppe Bernardino Bison (Italian, 1762–1844)
19. *The Resurrection of Christ*
Brown ink over black chalk on beige wove paper
289 x 215 mm (11 3/8 x 8 3/8")
1978-70-191

Attributed to Jan Frans van Bloemen, called Orizzonte (Dutch, 1662–1749)

20. *Landscape with Trees and a Bridge*
Black and white chalks on beige laid paper
189 x 259 mm (7 7/16 x 10 3/16″)
1978-70-193

21. *Study of a Landscape with a Tree and Gate*
Black and white chalks on beige laid paper
201 x 267 mm (7 7/8 x 10 1/2″)
1978-70-194

22. *Sketches of Trees*
Black chalk on buff laid paper
Verso: red chalk
214 x 157 mm (8 7/16 x 6 3/16″)
1978-70-195

Giuseppe Bottani (Italian, 1717–1784)
23. *Study for the Portrait of a Gentleman*
Red and white chalks on orange prepared paper
231 x 175 mm (9 1/8 x 7 11/16″)
1978-70-198

24. *Studies of a Standing Apostle and an Arm*
Black and red chalks on cream laid paper
Verso: *Study of a Hand*
Red chalk
307 x 190 mm (12 1/8 x 7 1/2″)
1978-70-199

Attributed to Karl Pavlovitsch Briullov (Russian, 1799–1852)
25. *The Vestal Virgins Leaving Rome before the Gauls*
Brown ink and wash over black chalk on cream laid paper
138 x 233 mm (5 7/8 x 9 3/16″)
1978-70-202

Sir Edward Burne-Jones (English, 1838–1898)
26. *Studies of a Male Nude*
Black chalk or pencil on buff laid paper
293 x 220 mm (11 1/2 x 8 3/4″)
1978-70-203

Giuseppe Cades (Italian, 1750(?)–1799)
27. *Caricature of a Man with a Cane*
Brown ink over black chalk on cream wove paper
230 x 168 mm (9 1/16 x 6 5/8″)
1978-70-205

28. *Caricature of the Artist with the Engraver Tommaso Piroli*
Brown ink over black chalk on cream laid paper
156 x 168 mm (6 1/8 x 6 5/8″)
1978-70-206

29. *Orpheus Charming the Animals (The Invention of Music?)*
Gray brown ink and brown washes over black chalk on buff laid paper
210 x 335 mm (8 1/4 x 13 3/16″)
1978-70-214

30. *Two Reclining Allegorical Figures Flanking a Vase*
Gray ink and brown wash over black chalk on blue laid paper, mounted down
158 x 232 mm (6 1/4 x 9 3/16″)
1978-70-217

31. *Studies of Two Gentlemen and a Man's Head*
Black chalk, watercolor, and brown ink on cream laid paper
Verso: *Studies of the Head of a Man in a Tricorn Hat and a Piece of Drapery*
Black and red chalks and brown ink
246 x 216 mm (9 11/16 x 8 1/2″)
1978-70-219[a-b]

Attributed to Giuseppe Cades
32. *The Flagellation of Christ*
Verso: *Studies of the Flagellation*
Black chalk on beige laid paper
183 x 146 mm (7 1/4 x 5 3/4″)
1978-70-220

33. *Saint Lawrence Crowned by an Angel*
Brown ink over black chalk on buff laid paper, mounted down
209 x 151 mm (8 1/4 x 6″)
1978-70-221

Attributed to Giacinto Calandrucci (Italian, 1646–1707)
34. *Putti under a Tree*
Brown ink over red chalk on cream laid paper
Verso: *Sketches of Putti*
Red chalk
110 x 106 mm (4 5/16 x 4 1/8″)
1978-70-222

Vincenzo Camuccini (Italian, 1771–1844)
35. *Saint Paul,* after 1801
Black chalk on buff wove paper
230 x 183 mm (9 1/16 x 7 3/16″)
1978-70-224

Attributed to Vincenzo Camuccini
36. *Classical Scene*
Brown ink and washes on buff wove paper
192 x 234 mm (7 9/16 x 9 1/4″)
1978-70-227

Attributed to Agostino Carracci (Italian, 1557–1602)
37. *The Triumph of Venus*
Brown ink and wash on cream laid paper, mounted down
152 x 242 mm (6 x 9 9/16″)
1978-70-228

Attributed to Antonio Cavallucci (Italian, 1752–1795)
38. *The Virgin and Christ Enthroned with Saints*
Pencil on cream laid paper, squared
344 x 272 mm (13 9/16 x 10 11/16″)
1978-70-230

Attributed to Giacomo Cavedone (Italian, 1577–1660)
39. *Head of a Woman*
Verso: *Studies of Arms*
Black chalk on blue laid paper
247 x 182 mm (9 3/4 x 7 1/8″)
1978-70-231

Louis Cheron (French, 1660–1723)
40. *Liriope and Narcissus (after a bas-relief)*
Brown ink on buff laid paper
185 x 166 mm (7 5/16 x 6 9/16″)
1978-70-233

Carlo Cignani (Italian, 1628–1719)
41. *Saint Anthony of Padua and the Christ Child*
Red chalk on cream paper, mounted down
130 x 101 mm (5 1/8 x 4″)
1978-70-236

Giovanni Battista Cipriani (Italian, 1727–1785)
42. *Studies of a Man and Two Women*
Verso: *Studies of a Man with a Sack*
Gray ink and brown washes on cream laid paper
190 x 160 mm (7 1/2 x 6 1/4″)
1978-70-237

Attributed to Liborio Coccetti (Italian, late-18th century–early-19th century)
43. *Design for a Wall Decoration*
Gray ink over black chalk on cream laid paper
170 x 210 mm (6 3/4 x 8 1/4″)
1978-70-238

44. *The Arms of Pius VII (Design for a Lunette)*
Brown ink and washes on cream paper, mounted down
96 x 196 mm (3 3/4 x 7 3/4″)
1978-70-239

Charles Nicolas Cochin (French, 1715–1790)
45. *Victorious Love*
Black chalk on cream laid paper, squared
128 x 96 mm (5 1/8 x 3 3/4″)
1978-70-241

Sebastiano Conca (Italian, c. 1680–1764)
46. *Saint Mary Magdalen*
Brown ink and wash with white gouache over black chalk on brown paper, mounted down
162 x 120 mm (6 3/8 x 4 3/4″)
1978-70-244

47. *Innocence or Flora*
Black chalk and purple washes, contours reinforced in pencil, on gray paper, mounted down
130 x 101 mm (5 1/8 x 4″) (oval)
1978-70-246

Attributed to Sebastiano Conca
48. *Immacolata*
Brown ink and blue and gray washes over red and black chalks on cream laid paper, squared
258 x 198 mm (10 3/16 x 7 3/4″)
1978-70-247

49. *Saint Michael Conquering Satan*
Black chalk and gray wash on cream laid paper, mounted down
259 x 167 mm (10 3/16 x 6 5/8″)
1978-70-248

Tommaso Maria Conca (Italian, 1735–1822)
50. *Head of a Boy*
Black chalk on cream laid paper, mounted down
222 x 177 mm (8 3/4 x 7″)
1978-70-249

51. *The Rest on the Flight into Egypt*
Verso: *Fragment of a draft or letter dated 1798*
Brown ink on cream laid paper
123 x 134 mm (4 7/8 x 5 1/4″)
1978-70-253

52. *A Flying Angel*
Black chalk on buff laid paper
273 x 193 mm (10 3/4 x 7 5/8″)
1978-70-254

53. *Parnassus*
Brown ink over black chalk on cream laid paper, squared
152 x 235 mm (6 x 9 1/4″)
1978-70-255

54. *Seated Minerva*
Black and white chalks on gray prepared paper
291 x 220 mm (11 1/2 x 8 5/8″)
1978-70-257

Attributed to Pietro da Cortona (Italian, 1596–1669)
55. *Sketch of the Rape of Europa*
Brown ink on beige paper, mounted down
35 x 60 mm (1 3/8 x 2 3/8″)
1978-70-258

56. *Sketch after a Painting (?) of Two Female Figures*
Brown ink on buff paper, mounted down
58 x 75 mm (2 5/16 x 3″)
1978-70-259

57. *Male Academy, Seated, and a Caricature of a Man's Head*
Red chalk on buff laid paper, mounted down
417 x 265 mm (16 5/16 x 10 7/16″)
1978-70-260

School of Pietro da Cortona
58. *The Virgin and Child Seated in a Landscape, with the Infant John the Baptist*
Black chalk, gray and brown washes, and white gouache on brown laid paper
265 x 310 mm (10 1/2 x 12 3/8″)
1978-70-261

Maria Cosway (Italian, 1759–1838)
59. *Design for a Fan*
Black chalk, brown ink and washes, on cream laid paper
Verso: *Sketches of Figures*
Black chalk
138 x 184 mm (5 1/2 x 7 1/4″)
1978-70-264

60. *Sketches of Jupiter with Outstretched Arms and Other Figures*
Brown ink over black chalk on cream wove paper
Verso: *Sketch of a Seated Girl*
Black and red chalks
182 x 222 mm (7 3/16 x 8 3/4″)
1978-70-265

Donato Creti (Italian, 1671–1749)
61. *Sketch of Saint Jerome*
Purplish brown ink on cream laid paper
98 x 89 mm (4 x 3 5/8″)
1978-70-266

Nathaniel Dance (English, 1735–1811)
62. *Portrait of Man in a Hat with a Rose (Study for an Engraving?)*
Black chalk on cream laid paper
216 x 163 mm (8 1/2 x 6 7/16″)
1978-70-267

John Deare (English, 1759–1798)
63. *Nude Man on a Rearing Horse*
Brown ink on cream laid paper
181 x 124 mm (7 1/8 x 4 15/16″)
1978-70-268

Gaspare Diziani (Italian, 1689–1767)
64. *Sketch of an Embattled King (?) in a Chariot*
Brown ink and washes over red chalk on cream laid paper
204 x 143 mm (8 1/16 x 5 9/16″)
1978-70-269

Giovanni Dupré (Italian, 1817–1882)
65. *Sketch of a Seated Man in a Cloak*
Black chalk on cream wove paper
140 x 127 mm (5 1/2 x 5 1/16″)
1978-70-270

Attributed to Richard Earlom (English, 1742–1822)
66. *Piping Pan with a Muse*
Oil over black chalk on grayish pink prepared paper
Verso: *Head of a Man*
Black chalk
184 x 187 mm (7 1/4 x 7 3/8″)
1978-70-272

Attributed to Giovanni Andrea de' Ferrari (Italian, 1598–1669)
67. *Standing, Draped Female Figure*
Red chalk, touches of brown ink, on cream paper, mounted down
271 x 192 mm (10 9/16 x 7 9/16″)
1978-70-273

Domenico Ferri (Italian, 1797–1869)
68. *Stage Design*
Gray and pink washes with white gouache over pencil on cream wove paper
201 x 221 mm (7 15/16 x 10 11/16″)
1978-70-274

John Flaxman (English, 1755–1826)
69. *Homer Inspired by his Muse*
Brown ink and washes over black chalk on cream laid paper
153 x 124 mm (6 1/8 x 5")
1978-70-276

Bénigne Gagnereaux (French, 1756–1795)
70. *Study of Dawn Dispelling Demons from an Awakening Man*
Verso: *Studies of Figures and Heads*
Brown ink over black chalk on cream laid paper
188 x 256 mm (7 7/16 x 10 1/8")
1978-70-278

Mauro Gandolfi (Italian, 1764–1834)
71. *Putto in a Hat and Cloak*
Brown ink, green and brown washes, over traces of black chalk on cream laid paper
154 x 205 mm (6 1/8 x 8 1/16")
1978-70-280

Attributed to Luigi Garzi (Italian, 1638–1721)
72. *Study of a Soldier Killing a King*
Brown ink and wash over black chalk on beige laid paper
Verso: *Christ(?) Standing*
Black chalk
222 x 168 mm (8 3/4 x 6 5/8")
1978-70-281

Giovanni Battista Gaulli (Italian, 1639–1709)
73. *Study of an Angel Crowning a Kneeling Bishop with a Wreath*
Brown ink and gray wash on buff laid paper, mounted down and squared in red chalk
205 x 151 mm (8 1/16 x 6")
1978-70-282

Attributed to Giovanni Battista Gaulli
74. *The Rest on the Flight into Egypt*
Brown ink and gray washes over black chalk on beige laid paper
192 x 156 mm (7 9/16 x 6 1/8")
1978-70-283

After Giovanni Battista Gaulli
75. *Copy of Two Pendentives in the Church of the Gesù, Rome*
Black and white chalks on blue laid paper, mounted down
131 x 183 mm (5 1/8 x 7 3/8")
1978-70-284

Attributed to J. M. Gault (English [?], 1765–1818)
76. *Eight Small Decorative Studies*
Black and gray washes and white gouache on cream paper, each cut out and mounted down
Each approximately 30/40 x 25 mm (1 3/8 / 1 5/8 x 1") (ovals and lozenges)
1978-70-285

Pier Leone Ghezzi (Italian, 1674–1755)
77. *Caricature Head of a Cleric in Traveling Costume (Cardinal Marconi?)*
Brown ink on brown laid paper, mounted down
396 x 329 mm (15 5/8 x 13")
1978-70-288

78. *Caricature of a Female Nude ("La ninfa Egeria")*
Brown ink and wash on cream laid paper
267 x 178 mm (10 1/2 x 7 1/16")
1978-70-291

79. *Study of a Hilly Landscape*
Brown ink over black chalk on white laid paper
203 x 321 mm (8 x 12 5/8")
1978-70-292

Attributed to Pier Leone Ghezzi
80. *Perseus Turning Polydectes and His Followers to Stone*
Brown ink and wash on buff laid paper
240 x 366 mm (9 7/16 x 14 3/8")
1978-70-293

Felice Giani (Italian, 1758–1823)
81. *Sketch of a Youth's Head*
Red chalk on cream wove paper
91 x 96 mm (3 5/8 x 3 3/4")
1978-70-297

Corrado Giaquinto (Italian, c. 1699–1765)
82. *Christ Appearing to Saint Theresa and Other Carmelite Saints*
Red chalk on beige paper, mounted down
461 x 252 mm (18 1/8 x 9 15/16")
1978-70-300

John Gibson (English, 1790–1866)
83. *Cupid Carrying Psyche (?)*
Pencil on beige wove paper
211 x 159 mm (8 5/16 x 6 1/4")
1978-70-301

Anne-Louis Girodet Trioson (French, 1767–1824)
84. *The Blind Belisarius,* 1806
Brown ink and washes on buff paper, mounted down
194 x 84 mm (7 11/16 x 3 5/16")
1978-70-302

Attributed to Hugh Douglas Hamilton (Irish, 1739–1808)
85. *Two Heads in Profile (Study for an Engraving?)*
Black chalk on cream laid paper
103 x 85 mm (4 1/16 x 3 5/16")
1978-70-303

Constantin Hansen (Danish, 1804–1880)
86. *Studies of a Kneeling Man for the "Argonaut" Frescoes in the Vestibule of the University of Copenhagen*
Pencil on buff wove paper
258 x 337 mm (10 3/16 x 13 1/8")
1978-70-304

Benjamin Robert Haydon (English, 1786–1846)
87. *Studies of Two Classical Heads*
Pencil and white chalk on brown wove paper
Verso: *Mouth and Ears of a Horse*
Black chalk
502 x 330 mm (19 3/4 x 13")
1978-70-305

James Holland (English, 1800–1870)
88. *View of the Villa Albani and its Environs*
Watercolor over pencil on cream wove paper
206 x 321 mm (8 1/8 x 12 5/8")
1978-70-306

Francesco Fernandi, called Imperiali (Italian, 1679–1741)
89. *Study of a Saint Performing a Miracle*
Red chalk, some stumping, on cream laid paper, mounted down
198 x 211 mm (7 13/16 x 8 5/16")
1978-70-308

90. *Study of the Head of the Priest in "The Martyrdom of Saint Eustace," Church of Sant' Eustachio, Rome*
c. 1726
Red and white chalks on buff paper, mounted down
202 x 153 mm (8 x 6 1/16")
1978-70-309

Feodor Ivanovitsch (Russian, 1765–1832)

91. *Study of Helen and the Elders of Ilium*
Brown ink over pencil on cream laid paper
289 x 427 mm (11 3/8 x 16 13/16")
1978-70-310

Attributed to Martin Knoller (Austrian, 1725–1804)

92. *Aurora Waking Puck (?)*
Black and white chalks on tan prepared paper
384 x 248 mm (15 1/8 x 9 3/4")
1978-70-312

Michel Koch (German, 1853–after 1900)

93. *Study of an Eagle Bearing an Urn to a Woman*
Brown ink and washes over pencil on cream wove (?) paper
Verso: *Study of the Virgin and Child*
Black chalk on paper prepared gray green
346 x 291 mm (13 5/8 x 11 1/2")
1978-70-313

Friedrich Anton Joseph Kühne (German, c. 1782–after 1840)

94. *Portrait of a Man*
Pencil on gray wove paper
149 x 101 mm (6 x 4") (oval)
1978-70-314

Attributed to Thaddäus Kuntz (Polish, c. 1731–1793)

95. *Study for an Allegory of Religion, Agriculture, and the Arts*
Black chalk on cream laid paper
212 x 149 mm (8 3/8 x 6")
1978-70-315

Carlo Labruzzi (Italian, 1748–1817)

96. *Caricature of an Elegant Hunchback (Gianni Soetta)*
Pencil on buff paper, mounted down
149 x 152 mm (6 x 6 1/16")
1978-70-316

97. *The Roman Baths at Albano*
Watercolor over black chalk on cream laid paper
Verso: *Study of a Field*
Brown ink over black chalk
234 x 556 mm (9 3/16 x 22 5/16")
1978-70-317

Etienne de Lavallée-Poussin (French, c. 1733–1793)

98. *Sketches of Female Peasant Costumes*
Black chalk on cream laid paper
156 x 198 mm (6 1/8 x 7 15/16")
1978-70-318

Sir Thomas Lawrence (English, 1769–1830)

99. *Sketch for a Portrait of Mrs. Wolff*
Oil over brown ink on buff laid paper
97 x 84 mm (3 13/16 x 3 3/16")
1978-70-319

Pietro Locatelli (Italian, active c. 1744–62)

100. *Study of the Head of a Male Saint*
Black and white chalks on blue laid paper, mounted down
172 x 167 mm (6 3/4 x 6 5/8")
1978-70-321

Benedetto Luti (Italian, 1666–1724)

101. *Study for "The Last Communion of the Magdalen," Church of Santa Caterina da Siena, Rome*
Brown ink and wash over black chalk on cream laid paper
144 x 173 mm (5 11/16 x 6 13/16")
1978-70-322

Daniel Maclise (English, 1806–1870)

102. *Sketch of a Seated Woman, Bust Length*
Brown ink on cream laid paper, mounted down
146 x 108 mm (5 3/4 x 4 1/4") (oval)
1978-70-324

103. *Sketch of the Bust of a Woman*
Brown ink on cream laid paper, mounted down
145 x 108 mm (5 3/4 x 4 1/4") (oval)
1978-70-325

Antonio Manno (Italian, 1739–1831)

104. *Immacolata (Design for a Ceiling)*
Brown ink and wash over black chalk on cream laid paper
311 x 219 mm (12 1/4 x 8 5/8")
1978-70-326

Carlo Maratta (Italian, 1625–1713)

105. *Studies of Putti*
Red chalk on blue paper, mounted down
264 x 411 mm (10 3/8 x 16 3/16")
1978-70-327

106. *Study of a Boy's Head*
Red and white chalks on blue paper, mounted down
327 x 231 mm (12 5/16 x 9 1/8")
1978-70-328

Circle of Carlo Maratta

107. *Study for a Rest on the Flight into Egypt*
Brown ink and wash on cream laid paper
144 x 133 mm (5 5/8 x 5 1/4")
1978-70-330

Carlo Marchionni (Italian, 1702–86)

108. *Caricature Sketches of Heads and Architectural Sketches*
Black chalk and brown ink on cream laid paper
Verso: *Caricature Sketches of Heads*
Brown ink
236 x 206 mm (9 5/16 x 8 1/16")
1978-70-331

Cesare Mariani (Italian, 1826–1901)

109. *Woman Holding a Mirror (Design for a Half-lunette)*
Black and white chalks on blue wove paper
424 x 261 mm (16 11/16 x 10 5/16")
1978-70-334

Agostino Masucci (Italian, 1691–1758)

110. *Allegory with Four Continents (Study for an Architectural Decoration)*
Brown ink over black chalk on cream laid paper
149 x 337 mm (6 x 13 1/2")
1978-70-335

111. *Saint Vincent Ferrer*
Black chalk on cream laid paper
147 x 98 mm (5 3/4 x 3 7/8")
1978-70-337

Jean-Louis-Ernest Meissonier (French, 1815–1891)

112. *Farmyard Scene (Page from a Sketchbook)*
Pencil on cream wove paper
111 x 171 mm (4 3/8 x 6 3/4")
1978-70-338

Anton Raphael Mengs (German, 1728–1779)

113. *Sketch of Saint John the Baptist, Seated*
Black chalk on cream paper, mounted down
90 x 6 mm (3 1/2 x 2 3/4")
1978-70-346

Attributed to Anton Raphael Mengs

114. *Copy after Correggio, Lunette Fresco of Saint John the Evangelist, San Giovanni Evangelista, Parma*
Red chalk on buff laid paper
161 x 253 mm (6 3/8 x 10")
1978-70-343

Attributed to Anton Raphael Mengs or his studio
Sixteen sheets of red-chalk counterproofs, all on Galippe mounts:

115. *Cain Killing Abel*
220 x 164 mm (8 5/8 x 6 1/2")
1978-70-348

116. *Jacob Blessing Essau*
223 x 169 mm (8 13/16 x 6 11/16")
1978-70-349

117. *God Appearing to a Patriarch*
231 x 159 mm (9 1/16 x 6 1/4")
1978-70-350

118. *The Expulsion of Hagar*
229 x 162 mm (9 x 6 3/8")
1978-70-351

119. *The Ascension of Christ*
222 x 166 mm (8 3/4 x 6 1/2")
1978-70-352

120. *Copy after a Madonna and Child with Saints, School of Correggio*
479 x 352 mm (18 7/8 x 13 7/8")
1978-70-353

121. *God the Father*
233 x 240 mm (9 3/16 x 9 7/16")
1978-70-354

122. *Studies of Saint Anne for the Caserta "Presentation of the Virgin"*
328 x 257 mm (12 15/16 x 10 3/16")
1978-70-355

123. *A Woman Holding Drapery*
247 x 311 mm (9 3/4 x 12 1/4")
1978-70-356

124. *Pentecost*
516 x 231 mm (20 5/16 x 9 1/16")
1978-70-357

125. *A Saint Healing a Blind Man before an Altar*
371 x 312 mm (14 5/8 x 12 1/4")
1978-70-358

126. *The Clemency of Scipio*
320 x 461 mm (12 9/16 x 18 3/16")
1978-70-359

127. *Sketches of the Holy Family and the Virgin and Child*
274 x 187 mm (10 3/4 x 7 3/8")
1978-70-360

128. *Seated Man in Heavy Drapery*
224 x 183 mm (9 x 7 1/4")
1978-70-361

129. *The Adoration of the Shepherds*
297 x 184 mm (11 3/4 x 7 1/4")
1978-70-362

130. *Sketches of the Holy Family and the Virgin and Child*
269 x 228 mm (10 9/16 x 9")
1978-70-363

Studio of Anton Raphael Mengs

131. *Adoration of the Shepherds with God the Father*
Red chalk over black chalk on cream laid paper
456 x 205 mm (17 15/16 x 8 1/16")
1978-70-344

132. *Study of a Youth's Head*
Black chalk, some stumping, touches of white chalk, on gray prepared paper
125 x 113 mm (5 x 4 1/2")
1978-70-345

Studio of Anton Raphael Mengs or Anton von Maron (Austrian, 1733–1808)

133. *Copy of the Ceiling of the Church of Sant' Eusebio, Rome*
Brown washes and white gouache over black chalk on beige laid paper
511 x 241 mm (20 1/8 x 9 1/2")
1978-70-347

Friedrich Edouard Meyerheim (German, 1808–1879)

134. *Copy after a Statue of a Dying Warrior Supported by a Genius,* 1834
Pencil on cream paper, mounted down
263 x 311 mm (11 1/4 x 12 1/4")
1978-70-364

Tommaso Minardi (Italian, 1787–1871)

135. *Copy after "Charity," by Andrea del Sarto*
Brown ink and washes, white gouache, on buff paper, mounted down
1978-70-365

136. *Comic Muse (Study for an Engraving?)*
Pencil on cream wove paper
202 x 198 mm (7 15/16 x 7 13/16")
1978-70-366

Giovanni Maria Morandi (Italian, 1622–1717)

137. *The Holy Family*
Red chalk on buff laid paper
309 x 242 mm (12 3/16 x 9 1/2")
1978-70-367

Attributed to Domenico Morelli (Italian, 1826–1901)

138. *Study of a Man's Left Arm*
Black chalk and stump, white gouache, on brown wove paper
164 x 86 mm (6 7/16 x 3 3/8")
1978-70-368

Gustav Heinrich Naeke (German, 1786–1835)

139. *Studies of a Kneeling Woman and Hands*
Pencil on cream wove paper
116 x 232 mm (4 3/16 x 9 1/8")
1978-70-369

Charles Joseph Natoire (French, 1700–1777)
140. *Portrait of an Artist*
Black and white chalks on blue laid paper
Verso: *Study of a Man's Leg*
Black chalk
193 x 157 mm (7 9/16 x 6 3/16″)
1978-70-370

Jonas Ninbach (German, 1624–1693)
141. *Study of the Virgin and Child*
Black ink and gray wash over black chalk on cream laid paper, mounted down
81 x 52 mm (3 3/16 x 2 1/16″)
1978-70-372

Attributed to Giovanni Odazzi (Italian, 1663–1731)
142. *Study for "The Conversion of Saint Paul"*
Black chalk, brown washes, and white gouache on buff laid paper
Verso: *Sketch of a Man Supporting a Fallen Figure*
Brown ink and red chalk
476 x 321 mm (18 3/4 x 12 5/8″)
1978-70-374

Giovanni Battista Paggi (Italian, 1554–1627)
143. *Study for "Cephalus and Procris"*
Brown ink and wash on buff paper, mounted down and squared in black chalk
207 x 211 mm (8 1/8 x 8 5/16″) (octagonal)
1978-70-375

Attributed to Giovanni Paolo Panini (Italian, c. 1691–1765)
144. *Sketches of Two Workmen*
Black chalk on cream laid paper, mounted down
120 x 176 mm (4 3/4 x 6 15/16″)
1978-70-377

Charles Percier (French, 1764–1838)
145. *Copy of an Antique Frescoed Wall*
Pencil, watercolor, and gouache on cream paper, mounted down
204 x 169 mm (8 1/16 x 6 11/16″)
1978-70-380

Ernst Christian Frederick Petzholdt (Danish, 1805–1838)
146. *Male Academy, Standing*
Pencil on cream laid paper
239 x 169 mm (9 7/16 x 6 11/16″)
1978-70-381

Giovanni Antonio Pichler (Italian, 1734–1791)
147. *Hercules Wrestling the Cretan Bull*
Pencil and brown wash on beige wove paper, squared
110 x 87 mm (4 5/16 x 3 7/16″)
1978-70-384

Pietro de' Pietris (Italian, 1663–1716)
148. *Study for "The Presentation of Christ in the Temple," Church of Santa Maria in Via Lata, Rome*
Red chalk over black chalk on buff laid paper
Verso: *Studies of Kneeling Figures, an Angel, and the Presentation of Christ*
Red chalk
248 x 184 mm (9 3/4 x 7 1/4″)
1978-70-386

149. *Study for "The Assumption of the Virgin," Church of Santa Maria alle Fornaci, Rome*
Brown ink and washes on gray laid paper
Verso: *Studies of Heads and Arms*
Red chalk
270 x 338 mm (10 5/8 x 13 5/16″)
1978-70-387

Bartolomeo Pinelli (Italian, 1781–1835)
150. *Study for "Nero with His Lyre at the Burning of Rome"*
Pencil on cream laid paper
295 x 394 mm (11 5/8 x 15 7/16″)
1978-70-388

151. *Study of an Amazon Spearing a Fallen Rider*
Pencil on cream wove paper
218 x 292 mm (8 5/8 x 11 1/2″)
1978-70-390

Tommaso Redi (Italian, 1665–1726)
152. *Portrait of Senator Buonarrotti (Study for an Engraving)*
Black and white chalks, black ink, on blue paper, mounted down
342 x 212 mm (13 1/2 x 8 5/16″)
1978-70-394

Angelo Ricci (Italian, 1749–1827)
153. *Copy (?) after a Print of an Allegorical Figure*
Dark brown ink on cream laid paper
249 x 176 mm (9 13/16 x 6 15/16″)
1978-70-395

Attributed to Marco Ricci (Italian, 1676–1729)
154. *Studies of Two Farm Huts*
Brown washes over black chalk on cream laid paper, mounted down
204 x 130 mm (8 1/16 x 5 1/8″)
1978-70-396

Michelangelo Ricciolini (Italian, 1654–1715)
155. *Study of Saint Jerome*
Brown ink and wash over black chalk on cream laid paper, mounted down
138 x 134 mm (5 7/16 x 5 1/4″)
1978-70-397

C. (?) Rinchlacke (German, 19th century)
156. *Male Academy*
Black and white chalks on blue paper
612 x 407 mm (24 1/8 x 16 1/16″)
1978-70-398

W. Spence Robinson (English [?], active 1839)
157. *Portrait of Samuel Prout*
1839
Pencil and watercolor on cream paper, mounted down
199 x 162 mm (7 15/16 x 6 3/8″)
1978-70-399

Giuseppe Sabatelli (Italian, 1813–1843)
158. *Farinata degli Uberti Attempting to Save Ceci Buondelmonti at the Battle of Serchio*
Brown ink over pencil on cream paper, mounted down
251 x 187 mm (9 7/8 x 7 3/8″)
1978-70-401

Jean-Pierre Saint-Ours (French, 1752–1809)
159. *Study for "The Examination of the Infants of Sparta"*
Black chalk on gray laid paper
Verso: *Back of a Female Nude*
Black chalk
123 x 186 mm (4 3/4 x 7 5/16″)
1978-70-403

Attributed to G. B. Schorr (Austrian, 17th century)
160. *Designs for Two Pedestals*
Black chalk and brown wash on buff laid paper
163 x 138 mm (6 9/16 x 5 7/16″)
1978-70-404

Attributed to Daniel Seiter
(Austrian, 1649–1705)
161. *Diana and Endymion*
Brown ink on beige laid paper, mounted down
122 x 133 mm (4 13/16 x 5 1/4")
1978-70-405

Johan Tobias Sergel (Swedish, 1740–1814)
162. *Sketches of Antique Statues*
Red chalk on cream laid paper
262 x 334 mm (10 5/16 x 13 3/16")
1978-70-406

Francesco Solimena (Italian, 1657–1747)
163. *Study of a Warrior Presenting a Vase to a Seated Woman*
Black chalk on cream laid paper, mounted down
136 x 195 mm (5 3/8 x 7 11/16")
1978-70-407

Thomas Stothard (English, 1755–1834)
164. *Sketch of a Religious Procession*
Brown ink and gray wash over black chalk on gray laid paper
71 x 120 mm (2 3/4 x 4 3/4")
1978-70-409

Claude Thiénon (French, 1772–1846)
165. *Sketch of Buildings at Tivoli*
Pencil on cream laid paper
159 x 92 mm (6 1/4 x 3 5/8")
1978-70-410

166. *Sketch of the Capuchin Convent at Tivoli*
Pencil on white wove paper
105 x 181 mm (4 1/8 x 7 1/8")
1978-70-411

167. *Sketch of Towers at Tivoli*
Pencil on white wove paper
181 x 108 mm (7 1/8 x 4 1/4")
1978-70-412

Bertel Thorvaldsen (Danish, (1768–1844)
168. *A Winged Youth Riding an Elephant*
Pencil and brown washes on gray laid paper
Verso: *Study of Two Classically Dressed Female Figures*
Pencil
122 x 154 mm (4 3/4 x 6 1/16")
1978-70-415

Attribued to Bertel Thorvaldsen
169. *Study of Faith*
Brown ink and wash on cream wove paper
261 x 164 mm (10 1/4 x 6 7/16")
1978-70-413

Circle of Bertel Thorvaldsen
170. *Hercules Between Virtue and Vice*
Brown ink over black chalk on buff laid paper, squared
167 x 228 mm (6 9/16 x 9")
1978-70-414

Attributed to Stefano Tofanelli
(Italian, 1752–1812)
171. *Clio and Thalia*
Brown wash, white and gray gouache, over black chalk on cream laid paper
173 x 193 mm (6 13/16 x 7 5/8")
1978-70-416

Francesco Trevisani (Italian, 1656–1746)
172. *Study of an Ointment Jar and a Scourge*
Black and white chalks on brown laid paper
172 x 149 mm (6 3/4 x 5 7/8")
1978-70-418

Attributed to Francesco Trevisani
173. *Studies of Saint Mark (for a Pendentive)*
Verso: *Study of a Saint (?)*
Brown ink and blue washes over black chalk on cream laid paper
233 x 351 mm (9 3/16 x 13 13/16")
1978-70-419

174. *Study of Legs (Fragment)*
Red chalk on cream laid paper, mounted down
111 x 204 mm (4 3/8 x 8 1/16")
1978-70-420

Studio of Francesco Trevisani
175. *King David at His Harp*
Black and white chalks on blue green prepared paper, mounted down
328 x 214 mm (12 15/16 x 8 5/8")
1978-70-421

176. *Portrait of Cardinal Annibale Albani*
Pastel and brown wash on buff paper, mounted down
229 x 161 mm (9 1/16 x 6 5/16")
1978-70-422

Attributed to Luigi Vanvitelli
(Italian, 1700–1773)
177. *Landscape with an Italian Hill Town*
Brown ink and washes over red chalk on buff laid paper
206 x 300 mm (8 1/8 x 11 13/16")
1978-70-425

François Verdier (French, 1651–1730)
178. *Study for "Diana Preventing Aesculapius from Reviving Hippolytus"*
Black chalk on brown laid paper
124 x 167 mm (4 7/8 x 6 9/16")
1978-70-426

179. *A Saint Led to Martyrdom*
Black and white chalks, gray wash, on blue paper, mounted down
139 x 243 mm (5 1/2 x 9 9/16")
1978-70-427

Carle Vernet (French, 1758–1836)
180. *Peasant on a Horse*
Oil on paper, mounted down
48 x 80 mm (1 15/16 x 3 1/8")
1978-70-428

Joseph Vernet (French, 1714–1789)
181. *Study of a Seated Peasant*
Black chalk on cream laid paper
153 x 95 mm (6 1/16 x 3 3/4")
1978-70-429

Giovanni Maria Viani (Italian, 1636–1700)
182. *Christ Appearing to Saint Margaret of Hungary*
Brown ink and wash, white gouache, over black chalk on cream paper, squared and mounted down
230 x 177 mm (9 1/16 x 7")
1978-70-430

Francisco Vieira de Mattos, called "il Lusitano" (Portuguese, 1699–1783)
183. *Christ and the Lamb Appearing to Saint Leocadia (Study for an Engraving)*
Red chalk on buff laid paper
222 x 298 mm (8 3/4 x 11 3/4")
1978-70-431

Attributed to Jacques Antoine ("Chevalier") Volaire (French, 1729–1802)
184. *Study of a Standing Gentleman*
Brown ink and white gouache over black chalk on cream paper, mounted down
247 x 167 mm (9 3/4 x 6 5/8")
1978-70-432

Benjamin West (American, 1738–1820)
185. *Sketch of Jael and Sisera (?)*
Brown ink over black chalk on cream laid paper
87 x 90 mm (3 3/8 x 3 9/16")
1978-70-434

Attributed to Joseph Wilton (English, 1722–1803)
186. *Studies for Decorations for a Nave Arch in Saint Peter's*
Brown ink and wash over black chalk on cream laid paper
123 x 216 mm (5 1/4 x 8 1/2")
1978-70-435

Jacob de Wit (Dutch, 1695–1754)
187. *Study of Saint Paul*
Black and white chalks on blue laid paper
404 x 218 mm (15 7/8 x 8 5/8")
1978-70-436

Antonio Zucchi (Italian, 1726–1795)
188. *The Capture of Cupid*
Black ink and gray washes on buff laid paper
188 x 190 mm (7 7/16 x 7 1/2")
1978-70-437

Anonymous Sienese, 16th century
189. *Saint James Healing a Man*
Brown ink and wash, white gouache, over black chalk on blue paper mounted down
299 x 364 mm (11 3/4 x 14 5/16")
1978-70-441

Anonymous Italian, 16th century
190. *Joseph in Egypt*
Brown ink and wash, black and white chalks, on cream laid paper
368 x 276 mm (11 1/2 x 10 7/8")
1978-70-442

Anonymous Italian, c. 1600
191. *Sketches of a Papal Procession*
Black chalk on cream laid paper
199 x 243 mm (7 5/8 x 9 9/16")
1978-70-443

Anonymous Bolognese, early 17th century
192. *Studies of a Statue of a Woman and a Man's Head*
Brown ink and wash on cream paper, mounted down
242 x 175 mm (9 1/2 x 6 7/8")
1978-70-444

Anonymous Venetian, c. 1650
193. *The Holy Family*
Watercolor over black chalk on buff laid paper
132 x 109 mm (5 1/4 x 4 1/4")
1978-70-445

Anonymous Italian, c. 1650
194. *Ceremony with a Statue of Neptune*
Red chalk on cream laid paper, mounted down
121 x 161 mm (4 3/4 x 6 5/16")
1978-70-446

Anonymous Florentine, c. 1650–1700
195. *Studies of a Stretching Figure and Hands*
Red chalk on blue laid paper
Verso: *Studies of Legs and Drapery*
Black and red chalks
244 x 388 mm (9 5/8 x 15 1/4")
1978-70-447

Anonymous French, c. 1650–1700
196. *Sketch of an Angel Holding a Mirror*
Red chalk on cream laid paper
146 x 154 mm (5 3/4 x 6 1/16")
1978-70-448

Anonymous Roman, c. 1650–1700
197. *Diana and Endymion*
Brown ink and wash over red chalk on cream paper, mounted down
156 x 213 mm (6 1/8 x 8 3/8")
1978-70-449

Anonymous Roman, 17th or 18th century
198. *Head of a Woman (Daphne?)*
Red chalk on buff laid paper
198 x 155 mm (7 13/16 x 6 1/8")
1978-70-450

Anonymous Roman, c. 1700
199. *Study of Saint Michael Conquering Satan*
Brown ink and wash on cream laid paper, mounted down
133 x 96 mm (5 1/4 x 3 3/4")
1978-70-451

Anonymous Italian, c. 1700
200. *Design for a Decorated Ceiling*
Brown ink and wash on cream laid paper
Verso: *Sketch of Architectural Elements and a Statue*
Brown ink
281 x 203 mm (11 1/16 x 8")
1978-70-452

Anonymous Italian, c. 1700
201. *Caricature of an Artist*
Brown ink on cream laid paper, mounted down
119 x 110 mm (4 11/16 x 4 5/16")
1978-70-453

Anonymous French or Italian, 18th century
202. *The Resurrection of Christ*
Black and gray washes, white gouache, on buff laid paper
193 x 118 mm (7 5/8 x 4 5/8")
1978-70-454

Anonymous Roman, 18th century
203. *View of Civitavecchia*
Brown ink, brown and gray washes, on buff wove paper
Verso: *Architectural Sketches*
Pencil
187 x 240 (7 3/8 x 9 1/2")
1978-70-455

Anonymous German or Italian, c. 1700–1750
204. *Saint Peter Blessing a Kneeling Bishop*
Brown ink and gray washes on cream laid paper
73 x 169 mm (2 7/8 x 6 5/8")
1978-70-456

Anonymous Italian, c. 1700–1750
205. *Study of a Reclining Female Figure in Drapery*
Black and white chalks, some stumping, on brown prepared paper, mounted down
193 x 238 mm (7 5/8 x 9 3/8")
1978-70-457

Anonymous Bolognese, c. 1700–1750
206. *Studies of Hands*
White and black chalks on gray laid paper
135 x 218 mm (5 5/8 x 8 9/16")
1978-70-458

Anonymous Italian or French, c. 1700–1750
207. *Study for a Statue of Justice*
Red chalk on cream laid paper, mounted down
372 x 155 mm (14 5/8 x 6 1/8″)
1978-70-459

Anonymous Venetian, c. 1700–1750
208. *The Resurrection of Lazarus*
Brown ink over black chalk on cream laid paper
258 x 188 mm (10 3/16 x 7 7/16″)
1978-70-460

Anonymous Italian, c. 1700–1750
209. Recto and Verso: *Portrait of a Hunter with Rifle and Dog*
Black chalk and brown wash on cream laid paper
136 x 98 mm (5 3/8 x 4 7/8″)
1978-70-461

Anonymous Roman, c. 1700–1750
210. *Immacolata*
Verso: *Sketch of an Artist at an Easel*
Black and white chalks on brown laid paper
240 x 163 mm (9 1/2 x 6 7/16″)
1978-70-462

Anonymous Italian, early 18th century
211. *Unidentified Scene with a Heroine before a Monarch (?)*
Brown ink on buff laid paper
165 x 215 mm (6 1/2 x 8 1/2″)
1978-70-464

Anonymous Roman, c. 1720
212. *Design for a Monument to a Bishop*
Brown ink and gray wash over black chalk on cream laid paper
282 x 216 mm (11 1/8 x 8 1/2″)
1978-70-463

Anonymous Italian, c. 1725
213. *Design for the Tomb of a Cleric*
Black ink and gray wash on cream laid paper
388 x 242 mm (11 5/16 x 9 1/2″)
1978-70-508

Anonymous Italian, c. 1730
214. *Elevation of an Apse*
Black ink and gray wash on cream laid paper
152 x 131 mm (6 x 5 1/8″)
1978-70-465

Anonymous Italian, c. 1740
215. *Study for a Flight into Egypt*
Verso: *Study of the Madonna and Child*
Black chalk on cream laid paper
229 x 180 mm (9 x 7 1/16″)
1978-70-466

Anonymous Italian, c. 1740
216. *Portrait of Father Gerolamo di Ligi*
Black chalk on cream paper, mounted down
91 x 79 mm (3 9/16 x 3 1/8″)
1978-70-467

Anonymous Italian, c. 1740
217. *Portrait of the Blessed Nicholas Albergati*
Black chalk on cream paper, mounted down
124 x 91 mm (4 7/8 x 3 9/16″)
1978-70-468

Anonymous Italian, c. 1750
218. *Elevation of an Arch*
Brown ink and gray wash on cream laid paper
479 x 320 mm (18 7/8 x 12 5/8″)
1978-70-469

Anonymous Italian, c. 1750
219. *Sketch of Argus (?)*
Black chalk on cream laid paper
119 x 82 mm (4 3/4 x 3 5/8″)
1978-70-470

Anonymous French, German, or Venetian, c. 1750–1800
220. *Portrait of a Lady and her Daughter*
Black and red chalks on cream laid paper, mounted down
134 x 113 mm (5 1/4 x 4 1/2″)
1978-70-471

Anonymous Roman, c. 1750–1800
221. *Studies of a Male Nude*
Black chalk on cream paper, mounted down
248 x 370 mm (9 5/8 x 14 1/2″)
1978-70-472

Anonymous Italian, c. 1750–1800
222. *Two Studies of the Head of a Bearded Man*
Black chalk on blue laid paper
166 x 217 mm (6 9/16 x 8 9/16″)
1978-70-473

Anonymous Roman, c. 1750–1800
223. *Study of a Bishop Holding a Book*
Black and white chalks on gray laid paper
258 x 201 mm (10 3/16 x 8 1/16″)
1978-70-474

Anonymous Italian or German, late 18th century
224. *Lot and his Daughters*
Brown ink on cream paper, mounted down
165 x 108 mm (6 1/2 x 4 1/4″)
1978-70-476

Anonymous Italian, late 18th century
225. *Saint Theresa and a Crippled Boy*
Brown ink, brown and gray washes, on cream laid paper
358 x 470 mm (14 1/8 x 18 1/2″)
1978-70-477

Anonymous Roman, late 18th century
226. *Euripides*
Brown washes, gray and white gouache, on chicken skin (?), mounted down
179 x 147 mm (7 x 5 3/4″)
1978-70-479

Anonymous Roman, late 18th century
227. *Cicero*
Brown washes on chicken skin (?), mounted down
136 x 114 mm (5 3/8 x 4 1/2″)
1978-70-480

Anonymous Italian, late 18th century
228. *Sketch of Marcus Curtius Leaping into the Gulf*
Brown ink on cream laid paper
64 x 108 mm (2 5/8 x 4 1/4″)
1978-70-481

Anonymous Roman, c. 1775
229. *Studies of the Head of Minerva and a Male Figure*
Black and white chalks on gray prepared paper
267 x 386 mm (10 1/2 x 15 1/4″)
1978-70-475

Anonymous Italian, c. 1785
230. *A Countryman and Countrywoman*
Gouache over chalk or pencil on gray laid paper
246 x 183 mm (9 11/16 x 7 1/4″)
1978-70-482

Anonymous Italian, c. 1790–1800
231. *Sketches of Hercules and Antaeus and Other Figures*
Black chalk on white laid paper, squared
259 x 393 mm (10 1/4 x 15 1/2″)
1978-70-483

Anonymous Roman, c. 1790
232. *Study of the Muse of Comedy*
Black and white chalks on buff laid paper
291 x 259 mm (11 1/2 x 10 1/4")
1978-70-484

Anonymous Italian, c. 1790
233. *The Fantastic Dream of a Heroine*
Black chalk and white gouache on cream laid paper
277 x 338 mm (10 15/16 x 13 5/8")
1978-70-485

Anonymous German, c. 1800
234. *Raphael Drawing Angels near the Farnesina*
Brown ink, brown and gray washes, and white gouache on buff paper, mounted down
287 x 518 mm (11 1/4 x 20 3/8")
1978-70-486

Anonymous Italian, c. 1800
235. *Study of a Beggar*
Brown ink and washes on cream laid paper
Verso: *Sketches of a Male Nude*
Brown ink
133 x 137 mm (5 1/4 x 5 1/2")
1978-70-487

Anonymous Italian, c. 1800
236. *Design for an Architectural Relief*
Brown and gray washes over pencil on cream laid paper, mounted down
125 x 182 mm (4 7/8 x 7 3/16")
1978-70-488

Anonymous Roman, c. 1800
237. *The Toilet of Venus*
Black chalk on cream wove paper
201 x 271 mm (7 15/16 x 10 11/16")
1978-70-489

Anonymous Italian, c. 1800
238. *Portrait of Cardinal Gazzoli (Study for an Engraving)*
Black chalk on buff wove paper
227 x 181 mm (8 15/16 x 7 1/8")
1978-70-490

Anonymous Italian, c. 1800
239. *Study of the Return of the Prodigal Son*
Brown ink, brown and black washes, over black chalk on cream laid paper
238 x 306 mm (9 3/8 x 12 1/16")
1978-70-491

Anonymous English, c. 1800–1850
240. *Study of a Seated Female Figure*
Black and white chalks and stump on cream wove paper
327 x 234 mm (12 7/8 x 9 1/4")
1978-70-493

Anonymous North Italian, early 19th century
241. *The Virgin Mary in Glory, Crowned by a Putto*
Brown ink and gray wash on cream paper, mounted down
202 x 149 mm (8 x 5 7/8")
1978-70-492

Anonymous Italian, early 19th century
242. *Papas with a Fan before a Chapel*
Watercolor on cream wove paper
209 x 163 mm (8 1/4 x 6 7/8")
1978-70-494

Anonymous Italian, early 19th century
243. *Peasant Carrying a Jug and Spade*
Watercolor on white wove paper
229 x 174 mm (9 x 6 7/8")
1978-70-495

Anonymous Italian, early 19th century
244. *Studies of a Foot and Christ at the Column*
Verso: *Head of a Bearded Man*
Red chalk on white laid paper
198 x 181 mm (7 13/16 x 7 1/8")
1978-70-496

Anonymous Italian, c. 1810
245. *Sketch of a Boy Carrying a Basket or Sack*
Brown ink on cream laid paper, mounted down
61 x 54 mm (2 3/8 x 2 1/8")
1978-70-497

Anonymous Italian, c. 1810
246. *Hector Inciting Paris to Virile Pursuits*
Brown ink on cream laid paper
234 x 345 mm (9 1/4 x 13 5/8")
1978-70-498

Anonymous Italian, c. 1820
247. *Study of an Angel with a Sword and Two Figures*
Verso: *Study of an Angel with a Sword and Keys and Three Men*
Black chalk on cream laid paper
246 x 181 mm (9 3/4 x 7 1/8")
1978-70-499

Anonymous Italian, active 1821
248. *View of Bagnaia with an Artist Sketching,* 1821
Pencil on cream wove paper
414 x 269 mm (16 1/4 x 10 5/8")
1978-70-500

Anonymous Venetian, c. 1825
249. *Upper Half of a Male Academy*
Black chalk on beige wove paper
223 x 241 mm (8 5/8 x 9 1/2")
1978-70-501

Anonymous German, c. 1830
250. *Sketch of a Trattoria*
Pencil on cream wove paper
123 x 183 mm (4 7/8 x 7 1/4")
1978-70-502

Anonymous Roman, c. 1830–40
251. *Sketch of the Flight into Egypt*
Pencil on cream wove paper
194 x 271 mm (7 5/8 x 10 5/8")
1978-70-503

Anonymous German, c. 1830–40
252. *Sketch of the Ponte Quattro Capi, Rome*
Verso: *Sketches of Houses and Men*
Pencil on cream laid paper
189 x 274 mm (11 3/8 x 10 11/16")
1978-70-504

Anonymous Italian, c. 1840
253. *Study of an Allegorical Female Figure Writing on a Tablet*
Black ink and gray wash on brown wove paper
108 x 81 mm (4 1/4 x 3 1/8")
1978-70-505

Anonymous Italian, c. 1850
254. *Study of Saint Peter Gonzales in a Quatrefoil*
Black chalk on brown wove paper, squared
321 x 397 mm (12 5/8 x 15 5/8")
1978-70-506

Anonymous English, 19th century
255. *View of the Temple at Agrigento*
Pencil on cream wove paper
209 x 336 mm (8 1/4 x 13 1/4")
1978-70-507

LIST OF ABBREVIATIONS FOR WORKS CITED

Abecedario, 1851/53–1859/60
Abecedario de P. J. Mariette et autre notes inédites de cet amateur sur les arts et les artistes. Edited by Philippe de Chennevières and Anatole de Montaiglon. 6 vols. Paris, 1851/53–1859/60.

L'Accademia, 1974
L'Accademia Nazionale di San Luca. Rome, 1974. Contributions by Carlo Pietrangeli, Stefano Susinno, Luigi Salerno, et al.

Acquaviva and Vitali, 1979
Stefano Acquaviva and Marcella Vitali. *Felice Giani, un maestro nella civiltà figurativa faentina.* Faenza, 1979.

Amberg, 1887
Johannes Amberg. *Der Medailleur Johann Karl Hedlinger.* Einsiedeln, 1887.

Amherst, 1974
Amherst, Massachusetts, Amherst College, Mead Art Building. *Major Themes in Roman Baroque Art from Regional Collections.* April 7–30, 1974. Catalogue published in conjunction with Five College Roman Baroque Festival. Introduction by W. Chandler Kirwin.

Arezzo, 1969
Arezzo, Galleria Comunale d'Arte Contemporanea. *Pietro Benvenuti, 1769–1844: Mostra di opere inedite nel secondo centenario della nascita.* September, 1969. Catalogue edited by Carlo Del Bravo.

Arisi, 1961
Ferdinando Arisi. *Gian Paolo Panini.* Piacenza, 1961.

Averini, 1973
Riccardo Averini. "I dipinti di Pompeo Batoni nella Basilica del Sacro Cuore all'Estrela." *Estudos Italianos em Portugal,* vol. 36 (1973), pp. 75–102. [Also published as "As pinturas de Pompeo Batoni na Basílica dō Sagrado Coração de Jesus da Estrela." *Bracara augusta, actas do congresso a arte em Portugal, no. séc. XVIII,* vol. 27, no. 64 (1973), pp. 465–94.]

Baldinucci, 1950
Francesco Saverio Baldinucci. "Cammillo Rusconi, scultor, Milanese." In Vite di pittori, edited by S. S. Ludovici. Florence. MS, Biblioteca Nazionale Centrale. Published in *Archivi d'Italia,* vol. 2, no. 17 (1950), pp. 216–17.

Bartolotti, 1967
Franco Bartolotti. *La medaglia annuale dei romani pontefici da Paolo V a Paolo VI, 1605–1967.* Rimini, 1967.

Bartolotti, 1972
Franco Bartolotti. "Appunti di medaglistica papale." *Medaglia,* vol. 2, no. 4 (December, 1972), pp. 29–34.

Baudi di Vesme, 1963–68
Alessandro Baudi di Vesme. *Schede Vesme. L'Arte in Piemonte dal XVI al XVIII secolo.* 3 vols. Turin, 1963–68.

Bean, 1979
Jacob Bean. *17th Century Italian Drawings in the Metropolitan Museum of Art.* New York, 1979.

Beaulah, 1967
G. K. Beaulah. "The Medals of the Art Union of London." *British Numismatic Journal,* vol. 36 (1967), pp. 179–85.

Beauvais, et al., 1974–75
Beauvais, Musée Départemental de l'Oise. *Jean Barbault (1718–1762).* October 3–November 15, 1974. Also shown at Angers, Musée des Beaux-Arts, December 1, 1974–January 15, 1975, and Valence, Musée des Beaux-Arts, February 1–March 15, 1975. Catalogue by Nathalie Volle and Pierre Rosenberg.

Belli Barsali, 1973
Isa Belli Barsali. "Documenti vaticani per il Batoni." *Studi Romani,* vol. 21, no. 3 (July–September, 1973), pp. 366–72.

Bellori, 1976
Giovanni Pietro Bellori. *Le vite de'pittori, scultori e architetti moderni.* Edited by Evelina Borea and Giovanni Previtali. Turin, 1976. [Originally published Rome, 1672.]

Berlin, 1969
Berlin, Staatliche Museen Preussischer Kulturbesitz, Kupferstichkabinett. *Römische Barockzeichnungen aus dem Berliner Kupferstichkabinett.* January–June, 1969. Catalogue by Peter Dreyer.

Berliner, 1958–59
Rudolf Berliner. "Zeichnungen von Carlo und Filippo Marchionni." *Münchner Jahrbuch der bildenden Kunst,* s. 3, vols. 9–10 (1958–59), pp. 267–396.

Biavati, 1977
Eros Biavati. "Giovanni Volpato di Bassano (1732–1803) incisore, produttore di porcellane, terraglie uso Inghilterra e maioliche a Roma." *Faenza,* vol. 63, no. 6 (1977), pp. 132–40.

Blunt and Cooke, 1960
Anthony Blunt and Hereward Lester Cooke. *The Roman Drawings of the XVII and XVIII Centuries in the Collection of Her Majesty the Queen at Windsor Castle.* London, 1960.

Blunt, 1969
Anthony Blunt. [Review of Gaus, 1967.] *The Burlington Magazine,* vol. 111, no. 792 (March, 1969), pp. 162–65.

Bodart, 1967
Didier Bodart. "Disegni giovanili inediti di P. L. Ghezzi nella Biblioteca Vaticana." *Palatino,* s. 4, vol. 11, no. 2 (April–June, 1967), pp. 141–54.

Bodart, 1976
Didier Bodart. "Pier Leone Ghezzi disegnatore." *Print Collector,* vol. 7, no. 31 (March–April, 1976), pp. 12–31.

Bollea, 1942
Luigi Cesare Bollea. *Lorenzo Pecheux.* Turin, 1942.

Bologna, 1979
Bologna, Palazzi del Podestà e di Re Enzo *L'Arte del Settecento Emiliano: La pittura; l'Accademia Clementina.* September 8–November 25, 1979. (X Biennale d'Arte Antica: l'Arte del Settecento in Emilia e in Romagna.) Catalogue by Andrea Emiliani, Eugenio Riccòmini, Renato Roli, et al.

Bolzenthal, 1840
Heinrich Bolzenthal. *Skizzen zur Kunstgeschichte der modernen Medaillen-Arbeit (1492–1840).* Berlin, 1840.

Boni, 1787
Onofrio Boni. *Elogio di Pompeo Girolamo Batoni.* Rome, 1787.

Borea, 1977
Evelina Borea. "L'*Armida che tenta di uccidersi* di Giuseppe Bottani e una biografia aggiornata al 1769." In *Per Maria Cionini Visani, scritti di amici,* pp. 133–35. Turin, 1977. Edited by Elia Bordignon Favero, Tamara and Nino Maccotta, et al.

Borroni, 1954–57
Fabia Borroni. *"Il Cicognara," bibliografia dell'archeologia classica e dell'arte italiana.* 12 vols. Florence, 1954–57.

Borroni, 1974
Fabia Borroni. "Francesco Maria Niccolò Gabburri e gli artisti contemporanei." *Annali della Scuola Normale Superiore di Pisa,* s. 3, vol. 4, pt. 4 (1974), pp. 1503–64.

Bottari and Ticozzi, 1822–25
Giovanni Bottari and Stefano Ticozzi. *Raccolta di lettere sulla pittura, scultura ed architettura scritte da'piu celebri personaggi....* 8 vols. Milan, 1822–25.

Boucher, 1961
François Boucher. "An Episode in the Life of the Académie de France à Rome, an Eighteenth-Century Mascarade *'à l'Orientale'.*" *The Connoisseur,* vol. 148, no. 596 (October, 1961), pp. 88–91.

Boucher, 1962
François Boucher. "Les dessins de Vien pour la Mascarade de 1748, à Rome." *Bulletin de la Société de l'Histoire de l'Art Français,* 1962 (published 1963), pp. 69–76.

Bowron, 1979
Edgar Peters Bowron. "The Paintings of Benedetto Luti (1666–1724)." Ph.D. Dissertation, New York University, 1979.

Bregenz and Vienna, 1968–69
Bregenz, Vorarlberger Landesmuseum. *Angelika Kauffmann und ihre Zeitgenossen.* July 23–October 13, 1968. Also shown at Vienna, Österreichisches Museum für Angewandte Kunst, November 8, 1968–February 1, 1969. Catalogue by Martin Butlin, Anthony M. Clark, et al.

Brigante Colonna, 1932
Gustavo Brigante Colonna. *Porporati e artisti nella Roma del Settecento (Albani–Winckelmann–Kaufmann–Goethe).* Rome, 1932.

Bulgari, 1958–69
Costantino Bulgari. *Argentieri gemmari e orafi d'Italia.* 3 vols. Rome, 1958(?)–69.

Busiri Vici, 1967
Andrea Busiri Vici. "La 'prima maniera' di Andrea Locatelli." *Palatino,* s. 4, vol. 11, no. 4 (October–December, 1967), pp. 366–74.

Busiri Vici, 1968
Andrea Busiri Vici. "Ritratti di Sebastiano Ceccarini, pittore fanese a Roma." *Palatino,* s. 4, vil. 12, no. 3 (July–September, 1968), pp. 263–73.

Busiri Vici, 1974
Andrea Busiri Vici. *Andrea Locatelli.* Rome, 1974.

Busiri Vici, 1977
Andrea Busiri Vici. "Ritratti a Roma di Domenico Duprà." *L'Urbe,* n.s., vol. 40, no. 2 (March–April, 1977), pp. 1–16.

Butlin, 1970
Martin Butlin. "An eighteenth-century art scandal: Nathaniel Hone's 'The Conjuror'." *The Connoisseur,* vol. 174, no. 699 (May, 1970), pp. 1–9.

Canova, 1959
Antonio Canova. *I quaderni di viaggio (1779–1780).* Venice, 1959. Edited by Elena Bassi.

Caracciolo, 1973
Maria Teresa Caracciolo. "Per Giuseppe Cades." *Arte Illustrata,* vol. 6, no. 52 (1973), pp. 2–14.

Caracciolo, 1977
Maria Teresa Caracciolo. "L'ispirazione letteraria di Giuseppe Cades." *Antologia di Belle Arti,* vol. 1, no. 3 (September, 1977), pp. 246–65.

Caracciolo, 1978
Maria Teresa Carraciolo. "Un album di Giuseppe Cades. Appunti di viaggio e disegni." *Meddelelser fra Thorvaldsens Museum,* 1978, pp. 6–47.

Caracciolo, 1978 ("Storia")
Maria Teresa Carraciolo. "Storia antica e mitologia nell'arte di Giuseppe Cades." *Quaderni sul Neoclassico,* no. 4 (1978), pp. 73–95.

Casale, et al., 1976
Vittorio Casale, Giorgio Falcidia, Fiorella Pansecchi, et al. *Ricerche in Umbria,* vol. 1. Rome, 1976.

Cassirer, 1922
Kurt Cassirer. "Die Handzeichnungssammlung Pacetti." *Jahrbuch der Preuszischen Kunstsammlungen,* vol. 43 (1922), pp. 63–96.

Chiarini, 1970
Marco Chiarini. " 'Monsù Alto', le maître de Locatelli." *Revue de l'Art,* no. 7 (1970), p. 18.

Chiarini, 1972
Marco Chiarini. *I disegni italiani di paesaggio, 1600–1750.* Treviso, 1972.

Chicago, et al., 1970–71
Chicago, The Art Institute of Chicago. *Painting in Italy in the Eighteenth Century: Rococo to Romanticism.* September 19–November 1, 1970. Also shown at Minneapolis, Minnesota, The Minneapolis Institute of Arts, November 24, 1970–January 10, 1971, and Toledo, Ohio, The Toledo Museum of Art, February 7–March 21, 1917. Catalogue edited by John Maxon and Joseph J. Rishel, with an introduction by Ellis K. Waterhouse.

Cholet, 1973
Cholet, Musée de Cholet. *Pierre-Charles Trémolières (Cholet, 1703–Paris, 1739).* June 29–September 30, 1973. Catalogue by Jean-François Méjanès, with an introduction by Pierre Rosenberg.

Clark, 1959
Anthony M. Clark. "Some Early Subject Pictures by Pompeo Batoni." *The Burlington Magazine,* vol. 101, no. 675 (June, 1959), pp. 232–38.

Clark, 1961
Anthony M. Clark. "Roman Eighteenth-Century Drawings in the Gilmor Collection." *The Baltimore Museum of Art News,* vol. 24, no. 3 (Spring, 1961), pp. 5–12.

Clark, 1962
Anthony M. Clark. [Review of Lewis, 1961.] *The Art Bulletin,* vol. 44, no. 2 (June, 1962), pp. 150–51.

Clark, 1963
Anthony M. Clark. "Pier Leone Ghezzi's Portraits." *Paragone,* vol. 14, no. 165 (September, 1963), pp. 11–21.

Clark, 1963 ("Neo-classicism")
Anthony M. Clark. "Neo-classicism and the Roman Eighteenth-Century Portrait." *Apollo,* n.s., vol. 78, no. 21 (November, 1963), pp. 352–59.

Clark, 1964
Anthony M. Clark. "An Introduction to the Drawings of Giuseppe Cades." *Master Drawings,* vol. 2, no. 1 (1964), pp. 18–26.

Clark, 1964 ("Imperiali")
Anthony M. Clark. "Imperiali." *The Burlington Magazine,* vol. 106, no. 734 (May, 1964), pp. 226–33.

Clark, 1964 ("Introduction")
Anthony M. Clark. "Introduction to Pietro Bianchi." *Paragone,* vol. 15, no. 169 (January, 1964), pp. 42–47.

Clark, 1964–65
Anthony M. Clark. "Three Roman Eighteenth-Century Portraits." *The Journal of The Walters Art Gallery,* vols. 27–28 (1964–65), pp. 48–56.

Clark, 1966
Anthony M. Clark. "Manners and Methods of Benefial." *Paragone,* vol. 17, no. 199 (September, 1966), pp. 21–33.

Clark, 1967
Anthony M. Clark. "Batoni's Three Marys at the Tomb." *Jahrbuch der Staatlichen Kunstsammlungen in Baden-Württemberg,* vol. 4 (1967), pp. 109–14.

Clark, 1967 ("Conca")
Anthony M. Clark. "Sebastiano Conca and the Roman Rococo." *Apollo,* n.s., vol. 85, no. 63 (May, 1967), pp. 328–35.

Clark, 1967 ("Masucci")
Anthony M. Clark. "Agostino Masucci: A Conclusion and a Reformation of the Roman Baroque." In *Essays in the History of Art Presented to Rudolf Wittkower.* London, 1967, pp. 259–64.

Clark, 1967 ("Portraits")
Anthony M. Clark. "The Portraits of Artists Drawn for Nicola Pio." *Master Drawings,* vol. 5, no. 1 (1967), pp. 3–23.

Clark, 1968
Anthony M. Clark. "An Introduction to Placido Costanzi." *Paragone,* vol. 19, no. 219 (May, 1968), pp. 39–54.

Cleveland, 1964
Cleveland, Ohio, Cleveland Museum of Art. *Neo-Classicism: Style and Motif.* September 23–November 1, 1964. Catalogue by Henry Hawley.

Cologne, 1977
Cologne, Kunsthalle. *Bertel Thorvaldsen.* February 5–April 3, 1977. Catalogue by Gerhard Bott, Siegfried Gohr, Frank Otten, et al.

Constable, 1927
William George Constable. *John Flaxman, 1755–1826.* London, 1927.

Corbara, 1950
Antonio Corbara. "Ancora sul Giani preromantico." *Paragone,* vol. 1, no. 9 (September, 1950), pp. 45–50.

Correspondance, 1887–1912
Correspondance des directeurs de l'Académie de France a Rome avec les Surintendants des Bâtiments, publiée d'après les manuscrits des Archives Nationales. Edited by Anatole de Montaiglon and Jules Guiffrey. 17 vols. Paris, 1887–1912.

de Caro Balbi, 1974
Silvana de Caro Balbi. "Gian Lorenzo Bernini e la medaglia barocca romana." *Medaglia,* vol. 4, no. 7 (June, 1974), pp. 7–26.

de Caro Balbi, 1974 ("Accademico")
Silvana de Caro Balbi. "Un Accademico di Merito di San Luca: Giuseppe Cerbara." *Medaglia,* vol. 4, no. 8 (December, 1974), pp. 23–32.

de Keller, 1830
Enrico de Keller. *Elenco di tutti i pittori scultori architetti miniatori incisori in gemme e in rame scultori in metallo e mosaicisti.* 2d edition. Rome, 1830.

della Pergola, 1962
Paola della Pergola. *Villa Borghese.* Rome, 1962.

Delogu, 1930
Giuseppe Delogu. *Pittori veneti minori del Settecento.* Venice, 1930.

de Méchel, 1776
Chrétien de Méchel. *Oeuvre du Chevalier Hedlinger ou recueil des médailles . . . précédées de la vie de l'auteur.* Basel, 1776.

de Rinaldis, 1948
Aldo de Rinaldis. *L'arte in Roma dal Seicento al Novecento.* Istituto di Studi Romani, Storia di Roma, vol. 30. Bologna, 1948.

de Rossi, 1796
Giovanni Gherardo de Rossi. *Vita di Antonio Cavallucci da Sermoneta.* Venice, 1796.

de Rossi, 1811
Giovanni Gherardo de Rossi. *Vita di Angelica Kauffman pittrice.* Pisa, 1811. [Facsimile edition, London, 1970.]

Detroit and Florence, 1974
Detroit, Michigan, The Detroit Institute of Arts. *The Twilight of the Medici: Late Baroque Art in Florence, 1670–1743.* March 27–June 2, 1974. Also shown at Florence, Palazzo Pitti, June 28–September 30, 1974. Catalogue by Harold Acton, Klaus Lankheit, Jennifer Montagu, et al.

Detroit, et al., 1974–75
Detroit, Michigan, The Detroit Institute of Arts. *French Painting, 1774–1830: The Age of Revolution.* March 5–May 4, 1975. Also shown at New York, The Metropolitan Museum of Art, June 12–September 7, 1975, and Paris, Grand Palais, November 16, 1974–February 3, 1975. Organized by Frederick J. Cummings, Pierre Rosenberg, and Robert Rosenblum.

DiFederico, 1972
Frank R. DiFederico. "A Group of Trevisani Drawings in the Uffizi." *Master Drawings,* vol. 10, no. 1 (1972), pp. 3–14.

DiFederico, 1977
Frank R. DiFederico. *Francesco Trevisani.* Washington, D.C., 1977.

di Macco, 1973–74
Michela di Macco. "Graecia vetus, Italia nova." *Annuario dell'Istituto di Storia dell'Arte,* Università degli Studi di Roma, Facoltà di lettere e filosofia, 1973–74, pp. 345–65.

Dimier, 1928–30
Louis Dimier. *Les peintres français du XVIIIe siècle.* 2 vols. Paris and Brussels, 1928–30.

Dizionario biografico, 1960–
Dizionario biografico degli Italiani. 21 volumes to date. Rome, 1960–.

Dowley, 1962
Francis H. Dowley. "Some Drawings by Benedetto Luti." *The Art Bulletin,* vol. 44, no. 3 (September, 1962), pp. 219–36.

Dowley, 1970
Francis H. Dowley. [Review of Nieto Alcaide, 1965]. *The Art Bulletin,* vol. 52, no. 4 (December, 1970), pp. 456–60.

Dreyer, 1971
Peter Dreyer. "Notizen zum malerischen und zeichnerischen Oeuvre der Maratta-Schule: Giuseppe Chiari—Pietro de'Pietri—Agostino Masucci." *Zeitschrift für Kunstgeschichte,* vol. 34, no. 3 (1971), pp. 184–207.

Düsseldorf, 1964
Düsseldorf, Kunstmuseum Düsseldorf. *Italienische Handzeichnungen des Barock aus den Beständen des Kupferstichkabinetts im Kunstmuseum Düsseldorf.* March–May, 1964. Catalogue by Eckhard Schaar.

Düsseldorf, 1969–70
Düsseldorf, Kuntsmuseum Düsseldorf. *Meisterzeichnungen der Sammlung Lambert Krahe.* November 14, 1969–January 11, 1970. Catalogue by Eckhard Schaar and Dieter Graf.

Eidlitz, 1927
Robert James Eidlitz. *Medals and Medallions Relating to Architects, Compiled and Edited and Reproduced in Great Part from the Collection of Robert James Eidlitz.* New York, 1927.

Emmerling, 1931
Ernst Emmerling. "Pompeo Batoni, Handzeichnung-Klebeband der Sammlung Haussmann Berlin, Katalog und Pausen/1931, von Ernst Emmerling." Ingelheim, Germany, MS, collection Ernst Emmerling.

Emmerling, 1932
Ernst Emmerling. *Pompeo Batoni, sein Leben und Werk.* Darmstadt, 1932.

Enggass, 1976
Robert Enggass. *Early Eighteenth-Century Sculpture in Rome.* 2 vols. University Park, Pennsylvania, and London, 1976.

Eriksen, 1974
Svend Eriksen. *Early Neo-Classicism in France: The Creation of the Louis Seize Style in Architectural Decoration.* Translated and edited by Peter Thornton, London, 1974.

Faenza, 1979
Faenza, Palazzo Milzetti. *L'età neoclassica a Faenza, 1780–1820.* September 9–November 26, 1979. (X Biennale d'Arte Antica: l'Arte del Settecento in Emilia e in Romagna). Catalogue by Anna Ottani Cavina, Phyllis Dearborn Massar, Laura Capon Piperno, et al.

Falcidia, 1964
Giorgio Falcidia. "Per un ritratto di Marco Benefial." *Bollettino dei Musei Comunali di Roma,* vol. 11, nos. 1–4 (1964), pp. 19–33.

Falcidia, 1966
Giorgio Falcidia. "Nuove proposte per Marco Benefial ritrattista." *Paragone,* vol. 17, no. 195 (May, 1966), pp. 60–68.

Falcidia, 1978
Giorgio Falcidia. "Per una definizione del 'caso' Benefial." *Paragone,* vol. 29, no. 343, (September, 1978), pp. 24–51.

Falconieri, 1835
Carlo Falconieri. *Memorie intorno alla vita e alle opere di Bartolomeo Pinelli.* Rome, 1835.

Faldi, 1952
Italo Faldi. "Opere romane di Felice Giani." *Bollettino d'Arte,* vol. 37, no. 3 (1952), pp. 234–46.

Faldi, 1955
Italo Faldi. "La festa patriottica della federazione in due dipinti di Felice Giani." *Bollettino dei Musei Comunali di Roma,* vol. 2, nos. 1–2 (1955), pp. 14–18.

Faldi, 1970
Italo Faldi. *Pittori viterbesi di cinque secoli.* Rome, 1970.

Faldi, 1971
Italo Faldi. [Review of Chicago, et al., 1970–71]. *The Burlington Magazine,* vol. 113, no. 882 (September, 1971), pp. 563–71.

Faldi, 1977
Italo Faldi. "Gli inizi del neoclassicismo in pittura nella prima metà del Settecento." In *Nuove idee e nuova arte nel '700 italiano, Atti dei Convegni Lincei,* no. 26, Rome, Accademia Nazionale dei Lincei, May 19–23, 1975. Rome, 1977, pp. 495–523.

Ferrara, 1974–75
Luciana Ferrara. "Domenico Corvi nella Galleria Borghese." *Rivista dell'Istituto Nazionale di Archeologia e Storia dell'Arte,* vols. 21–22 (1974–75), pp. 169–217.

Fleming, 1958
John Fleming, "Cardinal Albani's Drawings at Windsor: Their Purchase by James Adam for George III." *The Connoisseur,* vol. 142 (November, 1958), pp. 164–69.

Fleming, 1962
John Fleming. *Robert Adam and his Circle in Edinburgh and Rome.* Cambridge, Massachusetts, 1962.

Fleming, 1963
John Fleming. "Piedmontese Sculpture in the Eighteenth Century." *Apollo,* n.s., vol. 77, no. 13 (March, 1963), pp. 188–93.

Florence, 1971
Florence, Gabinetto dei Disegni e delle Stampe degli Uffizi. *Disegni italiani del XIX secolo.* 1971. Catalogue by Carlo Del Bravo.

Florence, 1972
Florence, Palazzo Pitti. *Cultura neoclassica e romantica nella Toscana Granducale.* July 8–September 25, 1972. Catalogue edited by Sandra Pinto. Con-

tributions by Anna Rita Caputo Calloud, Paolo Dal Poggetto, Alvar Gonzalez-Palacios, et al.

Florence, 1977
Florence, Gabinetto dei Disegni e delle Stampe degli Uffizi. *Disegni di Giovan Battista Foggini.* 1977. Catalogue by Lucia Monaci.

Florence, 1978
Florence, Gabinetto dei Disegni e delle Stampe degli Uffizi. *Luigi Sabatelli, disegni e incisioni.* 1978. Catalogue by Beatrice Paolozzi Strozzi.

Forrer, 1902–30
Leonard Forrer. *Biographical Dictionary of Medallists; Coin, Gem, and Seal-engravers, Mint Masters, &c., Ancient and Modern, with Reference to their Works,* B.C. *500*–A.D. *1900.* 8 vols. London, 1902–30.

Forster-Hahn, 1975
Françoise Forster-Hahn. "After Guercino or After the Greeks? Gavin Hamilton's 'Hebe': Tradition and Change in the 1760s." *The Burlington Magazine,* vol. 117, no. 867 (June, 1975), pp. 365–71.

Francini, 1928–29
Alberto Francini. "Un singolare ottocentista: Fortunato Duranti (1787–1863)." *Pinacoteca,* vol. 1 (1928–29), pp. 335–48.

Füssli, 1781
Johann Kaspar Füssli. *Des Ritters Johann Karl Hedlingers Medaillen-Werke gezeichnet von J. C. Füssli und in schwarzer Kunst bearbeitet von J. E. Haid.* Augsburg, 1781.

Gabrielli, 1934
R. Gabrielli. "Artisti piceni, cav. Giuseppi Ghezzi." In *Comunanza del Littorio e i suoi artisti.* Ascoli, 1934, pp. 11–17. [Originally published in *Vita Picena,* July 29, 1933.]

Gasparoni, 1863
Francesco Gasparoni. "Cenni biografici del pittore da decorazione Felice Gianni." *Arti e lettere,* vol. 1, no. 1 (1863), pp. 10–12.

Gaus, 1967
Joachim Gaus. *Carlo Marchionni: Ein Beitrag zur römischen Architektur des Settecento.* Cologne, 1967.

Gilmartin, 1974
John Gilmartin. "The Paintings Commissioned by Pope Clement XI for the Basilica of San Clemente in Rome." *The Burlington Magazine,* vol. 116, no. 855 (June, 1974), pp. 305–10.

Giornale, 1784–87
Giornale delle belle arti e della incisione antiquaria, musica, e poesia. 4 vols. Rome, 1784–87.

Goethe, 1969
Johann Wolfgang von Goethe. *Winckelmann und sein Jahrhundert* Leipzig, 1969. [Originally published Tübingen, 1805.]

Goldstein, 1978
Carl Goldstein. "Art History without Names: A Case Study of the Roman Academy." *The Art Quarterly,* n.s., vol. 1, no. 2 (1978), pp. 1–16.

Golfieri, 1950
Enno Golfieri. "Felice Giani." *Paragone,* vol. 1, no. 7 (July, 1950), pp. 23–29.

Golzio, 1945
Vincenzo Golzio. "Il pittore Antonio Cavallucci da Sermoneta." *Capitolium,* vol. 20, nos. 4–6 (April–June, 1945), pp. 17–21.

González-Palacios, 1976
Alvar Gonzalez-Palacios. "I mani del Piranesi." *Paragone,* vol. 27, no. 315 (May, 1976), pp. 33–48.

Gori Gandellini, 1808–16
Giovanni Gori Gandellini. *Notizie istoriche degli intagliatori.* 2d edition with additions by Luigi de Angelis. 15 vols. Siena, 1808–16.

Grassi, 1979
Luigi Grassi. *Teorici e storia della critica d'arte,* vol. 2. *Il Settecento in Italia.* Rome, 1979.

Guerrini, 1971
Lucia Guerrini. *Marmi antichi nei disegni di Pier Leone Ghezzi.* Vatican City, 1971.

Hake, 1922
Henry M. Hake. "Pond's and Knapton's Imitations of Drawings." *The Print Collector's Quarterly,* vol. 9 (1922), pp. 324–49.

Hamburg, et al., 1966–
Hamburg, Hamburger Kunsthalle. *Italienische Medaillen und Plaketten von der Frührenaissance bis zum Ende des Barock.* May 28–July 3, 1966. Also shown at eleven other German cities, Utrecht, and Brussels. Catalogue by Franco Panvini Rosati.

Harris and Schaar, 1967
Ann Sutherland Harris and Eckhard Schaar. *Die Handzeichnungen von Andrea Sacchi und Carlo Maratta.* Kataloge des Kunstmuseums Düsseldorf, Handzeichnungen, vol. 1. Düsseldorf, 1967.

Hartmann, 1957
J. B. Hartmann. "Appunti su alcune opere minori di Canova e Thorvaldsen." In *Arte Neoclassica, Atti del Convegno,* Venice, Fondazione Giorgio Cini, October 12–14, 1957. Venice and Rome, 1964 [?], pp. 145–170.

Hautecoeur, 1910
Louis Hautecoeur. "I musaicisti sanpietrini del Settecento." *L'Arte,* vol. 13 (1910), pp. 450–60.

Hawkins, 1885
Edward Hawkins. *Medallic Illustrations of the History of Great Britain and Ireland to the Death of George II.* Edited by A. W. Franks and H. A. Grueber. 2 vols. London, 1885. [Plates published separately, London, 1904–11.]

Hiesinger, 1978
Ulrich Hiesinger. "The Paintings of Vincenzo Camuccini, 1771–1844." *The Art Bulletin,* vol. 60, no. 2 (June, 1978), pp. 297–320.

Hiesinger, 1978 ("Canova")
Ulrich Hiesinger. "Canova and the Frescoes of the Galleria Chiaramonti." *The Burlington Magazine,* vol. 120, no. 907 (October, 1978), pp. 655–65.

Honisch, 1965
Dieter Honisch. *Anton Raphael Mengs und die Bildform des Frühklassizismus.* Recklinghausen, 1965.

Honour, 1959
Hugh Honour. "Filippo della Valle." *The Connoisseur,* vol. 144, no. 581 (November, 1959), pp. 172–79.

Honour, 1961
Hugh Honour. "Bronze Statuettes by Giacomo and Giovanni Zoffoli." *The Connoisseur,* vol. 148, no. 597 (November, 1961), pp. 198–205.

Honour, 1961 *(Chinoiserie)*
Hugh Honour. *Chinoiserie: The Vision of Cathay.* London, 1961.

Honour, 1963
Hugh Honour. "After the Antique: Some Italian Bronzes of the Eighteenth Century." *Apollo,* n.s., vol. 77, no. 13 (March, 1963), pp. 194–200.

Honour, 1967
Hugh Honour. [Review of Lucca, 1967.] *The Burlington Magazine,* vol. 109, no. 774 (September, 1967), pp. 549–50.

Honour, 1967 ("Statuettes")
Hugh Honour. "Statuettes after the Antique: Volpato's Roman Porcelain Factory." *Apollo,* n.s., vol. 85, no. 63 (May, 1967), pp. 371–73.

Howard, 1973
Seymour Howard. "An Antiquarian Handlist and Beginnings of the Pio-Clementino." *Eighteenth Century Studies,* vol. 7 (1973), pp. 40–61.

Imbert, 1941
Eugenio Imbert. *Le placchette italiane secolo XV–XIX, contributo alla conoscenza della placchetta italiana.* Milan, 1941.

Incisa della Rocchetta, 1932
Giovanni Incisa della Rocchetta. "Le vicende di tre quadri d'altare." *Roma,* vol. 10 (1932), pp. 255–70.

Irwin, 1959
David Irwin. "Flaxman: Italian Journals and Correspondence." *The Burlington Magazine,* vol. 101, no. 675 (June, 1959), pp. 212–17.

Irwin, 1962
David Irwin. "Gavin Hamilton: Archaeologist, Painter, and Dealer." *The Art Bulletin,* vol. 44, no. 2 (June, 1962), pp. 87–102.

Joachim and McCullagh, 1979
Harold Joachim and Suzanne Folds McCullagh. *Italian Drawings in The Art Institute of Chicago.* Chicago and London, 1979.

Jones, 1912
Henry Stuart Jones. *The Sculptures of the Museo Capitolino.* A Catalogue of the Ancient Sculptures Preserved in the Municipal Collections of Rome, vol. 1. Oxford, 1912.

Justi, 1898
Carl Justi. *Winckelmann und seine Zeitgenossen.* 3 vols. 2d edition. Leipzig, 1898.

Kerber, 1968
Bernhard Kerber. "Giuseppe Bartolomeo Chiari." *The Art Bulletin,* vol. 50, no. 1 (March, 1968), pp. 75–86.

Kerber, 1971
Bernhard Kerber. *Andrea Pozzo.* Berlin and New York, 1971.

Kurz, 1955
Otto Kurz. *Bolognese Drawings of the XVII and XVIII Centuries in the Collection of Her Majesty the Queen at Windsor Castle.* London, 1955.

Lalande, 1769
Joseph Jérôme Lalande. *Voyage d'un françois en Italie, fait dans les années 1765 & 1766.* 8 vols. Paris, 1769.

Lankheit, 1962
Klaus Lankheit. *Florentinische Barockplastik.* Munich, 1962.

Lanzi, 1968
Luigi Lanzi. *Storia pittorica della Italia dal risorgimento delle belle arti fin presso al fine del XVIII secolo.* Edited by Martino Capucci. 3 vols. Florence, 1968. [Originally published Bassano, 1795–96.]

Lazareff, 1925
Victor Lazareff. "Ein Bild des Francesco Solimena." *Belvedere,* vol. 7 (January–July, 1925), pp. 120–26.

Le Blanc, 1854–88
Charles Le Blanc. *Manuel de l'amateur d'estampes.* 4 vols. Paris, 1854–88.

Le Moël and Rosenberg, 1969
Michel Le Moël and Pierre Rosenberg. "La collection de tableaux du duc de Saint-Aignan et le catalogue de sa vente illustré par Gabriel de Saint-Aubin." *Revue de l'Art,* no. 6 (1969), pp. 51–67.

Leitschuh, 1886
Franz Friedrich Leitschuh. *Die Familie Preisler und Markus Tuscher.* Leipzig, 1886.

Lewis, 1961
Lesley Lewis. *Connoisseurs and Secret Agents in Eighteenth Century Rome.* London, 1961.

Lewis, 1967
Lesley Lewis. "Philipp von Stosch." *Apollo,* n.s., vol. 85, no. 63 (May, 1967), pp. 320–27.

Ljubljana, 1978
Ljubljana, Narodna Galerija. *Franc Kavčič / Caucig, 1755–1828.* Ljubljana, 1978. Catalogue by Ksenija Rozman.

Lo Bianco, 1977
Anna Lo Bianco. "Pier Leone Ghezzi a Torre in Pietra." *Storia dell'Arte,* vol. 29 (January–April, 1977), pp. 61–66.

Lochner, 1737–44
Johann Hieronymous Lochner. *Sammlung Merkwürdiger Medaillen.* 8 vols. Nuremberg, 1737–44.

London, 1972
London, The Royal Academy and The Victoria and Albert Museum. *The Age of Neo-Classicism.* September 9–November 19, 1972. (The Fourteenth Exhibition of the Council of Europe.) Catalogue by Hugh Honour, L. D. Ettlinger, Herbert von Einem, et al.

London, 1972 *(Lady Hamilton)*
London, The Arts Council of Great Britain. The Iveagh Bequest, Kenwood. *Lady Hamilton in Relation to the Art of her Time.* July–October, 1972. Catalogue by Patricia Jaffé.

London, 1979
London, The Royal Academy of Arts. *John Flaxman, R.A.* October 26–December 9, 1979. Also shown at Hamburg, Hamburger Kunsthalle, April 20–June 3, 1979. Catalogue edited by David Bindman.

Longhi, 1952
Roberto Longhi. "Due disegni del Giani." *Paragone,* vol. 3, no. 27 (March, 1952), p. 62.

Longhi, 1966
Roberto Longhi. "Un appunto su due opere del Benefial." *Paragone,* vol. 17, no. 195 (May, 1966), pp. 68–70.

Louisville and Houston, 1969–70
Louisville, Kentucky, The J. B. Speed Art Museum. *Sculpture in Miniature:*

The Andrew S. Ciechanowiecki Collection of Gilt & Gold Medals and Plaquettes. October 20–November 23, 1969. Also shown at Houston, Texas, The Museum of Fine Arts, December 10, 1969–February 1, 1970. Catalogue by Jacques Fisher, in collaboration with Gay Seagrim.

Lucca, 1967
Lucca, Palazzo Ducale. *Mostra di Pompeo Batoni.* July–September, 1967. Catalogue edited by Isa Belli Barsali with an introduction by Anthony M. Clark.

Lugt
Frits Lugt. *Les Marques de collections de dessins & d'estampes.* Amsterdam, 1921.

Lugt suppl.
Frits Lugt. *Les Marques de collections de dessins & d'estampes: Supplément.* The Hague, 1956.

Macandrew, 1978
Hugh Macandrew. "A Group of Batoni Drawings at Eton College, and Some Eighteenth-Century Italian Copyists of Classical Sculpture." *Master Drawings,* vol. 16, no. 2 (1978), pp. 131–50.

Marconi, 1964
Paolo Marconi. *Giuseppe Valadier.* Rome, 1964.

Marconi, et al., 1974
Paolo Marconi, et al. *I disegni di architettura dell'archivio storico dell'Accademia di San Luca.* 2 vols. Rome, 1974.

Marcucci, 1944
Luisa Marcucci. "Pompeo Batoni a Forlì." *Emporium,* vol. 99, nos. 592–94 (April–June, 1944), pp. 95–105.

Marrini, 1766
Orazio Marrini. *Serie di ritratti di celebri pittori dipinti di propria mano . . . esistente appresso l'abate Pazzi . . . con notizie compilate da Orazio Marrini.* 2 vols. Florence, 1766.

Massar, 1976
Phyllis Dearborn Massar. "Felice Giani Drawings at the Cooper-Hewitt Museum." *Master Drawings,* vol. 14, no. 4 (1976), pp. 396–420.

Matteucci, 1974
Anna Maria Matteucci. "L'attività giovanile di Pelagio Pelagi nei disegni dell'Archiginnasio di Bologna." *Annali della Scuola Normale Superiore di Pisa,* s. 3, vol. 4, pt. 2 (1974), pp. 461–78.

Mayer, 1972
Dorothy Moulton Mayer. *Angelica Kauffmann, R. A., 1741–1807.* Gerrards Cross, 1972.

Mazio, 1824
F. Mazio. *Serie dei conj di medaglie pontificie da Martino V fino a tutto il pontificato di Pio VII esistenti nella pontificia zecca di Roma.* Rome, 1824.

Meeks, 1966
Carroll L. V. Meeks. *Italian Architecture, 1750–1914.* New Haven and London, 1966.

Memorie, 1785–88
Memorie per le belle arti. 4 vols. Rome, 1785–88.

Meyer, 1870–85
Julius Meyer. *Allgemeines Künstler-Lexikon.* 3 vols. Leipzig, 1870–85.

Milan, 1973
Milan, Stanza del Borgo. *Eco neoclassica.* 1973.

Milan, 1977
Milan, Stanza del Borgo. *Tenebre e luci —l'arte del Duranti, disegni di Fortunato Duranti.* 1977.

Miller, 1971
Dwight Miller. "Some Unpublished Drawings by Marcantonio Franceschini and a Proposed Chronology." *Master Drawings,* vol. 9, no. 2 (1971), pp. 119–38.

Minneapolis, 1967
Minneapolis, Minnesota, The Minneapolis Institute of Arts. "Roman Eighteenth-Century Drawings from a Private Collection." February 11–March 19, 1967. Checklist by Anthony M. Clark.

Minneapolis, 1970–71
Minneapolis, Minnesota, The Minneapolis Institute of Arts. "Eighteenth-Century Italian Paintings, Drawings, Sculpture, and Decorative Arts." November 24, 1970–January 10, 1971 (no catalogue). Organized by Edgar Peters Bowron, Anthony M. Clark, and Ann Rogers.

Minor, 1980
Vernon Hyde Minor. "Della Valle's Last Commission." *The Burlington Magazine,* vol. 122, no. 922 (January, 1980), pp. 60–61.

Missirini, 1823
Melchior Missirini. *Memorie per servire alla storia della Romana Accademia di S. Luca fino alla morte di Antonio Canova.* Rome, 1823.

Missirini, 1833
Melchior Missirini. *Del tempio eretto in Possagno da Antonio Canova.* Venice, 1833.

Missirini, 1836
Melchior Missirini. *Della Cappella de'Sepolcri Medicei in S. Lorenzo di Firenze e della grande cupola ivi dipinta dal commendatore Pietro Benvenuti.* Florence, 1836.

Montagu, 1978
Jennifer Montagu. "Bellori, Maratti and the Palazzo Altieri." *Journal of the Warburg and Courtauld Institutes,* vol. 41 (1978), pp. 334–40.

Morazzone, 1935
G. Morazzone. *Le porcellane italiane.* Milan, 1935.

Moroni, 1840–61
Gaetano Moroni. *Dizionario di erudizione storico-ecclesiastica da S. Pietro sino ai nostri giorni.* 103 vols. Venice, 1840–61.

Moschini, 1957
Vittorio Moschini. "Antonio Zucchi veneziano." *Arte Veneta,* vol. 11 (1957), pp. 168–72.

Nagler, 1835–52
G. K. Nagler. *Neues allgemeines Künstler-Lexicon.* 22 vols. Munich, 1835–52.

New Haven, 1979
New Haven, Connecticut, Yale Center for British Art. *The Fuseli Circle in Rome: Early Romantic Art of the 1770s.* September 12–November 11, 1979. Catalogue by Nancy L. Pressly.

New York, 1971
New York, The Metropolitan Museum of Art and The Pierpont Morgan Library. *Drawings from New York Collections III: The Eighteenth Century*

in Italy. Exhibition held at the Metropolitan Museum of Art, January 30–March 21, 1971. Catalogue by Jacob Bean and Felice Stampfle.

New York, 1975
New York, The Metropolitan Museum of Art. *Architectural and Ornament Drawings: Juvarra, Vanvitelli, the Bibiena Family, and Other Italian Draughtsmen.* New York, 1975. Catalogue by Mary L. Myers.

New York, 1976
New York, Shepherd Gallery. *Italian 19th Century Drawings and Watercolors, an Album.* April, 1976. Catalogue by Roberta J. M. Olson, et al.

New York, 1976–77
New York, The Metropolitan Museum of Art. *Roman Artists of the 17th Century: Drawings and Prints.* November 2, 1976–January 16, 1977.

New York, 1978
New York, The Metropolitan Museum of Art. *Artists in Rome in the 18th Century: Drawings and Prints.* February 28–May 7, 1978.

New York, et al., 1978–80
New York, et al., Cooper-Hewitt Museum. *Crosscurrents: French and Italian Neoclassical Drawings and Prints from the Cooper-Hewitt Museum.* September 19–November 5, 1978. Also shown at five other American and two Canadian cities. Catalogue by Catherine Bernard.

Nieto Alcaide, 1965
Victor Manuel Nieto Alcaide. *Carlo Maratti: Cuarenta y tres dibujos de tema religioso.* Dibujos de la Real Academia de San Fernando. Madrid, 1965.

Noack, 1907
Friedrich Noack. *Deutsches Leben in Rom 1700 bis 1900.* Stuttgart and Berlin, 1907. [Reprint. Bern, 1971.]

Noack, 1919
Friedrich Noack. "Marco Benefial, ein Bahnbrecher des Klassizismus." *Monatshefte für Kunstwissenschaft,* vol. 12 (1919), pp. 125–29.

Noack, 1921–22
Friedrich Noack. "Die Hamerans in Rom." *Archiv für Medaillen- und Plaketten-kunde,* vol. 3, pt. 1 (1921–22), pp. 23–40.

Noack, 1927
Friedrich Noack. *Das Deutschtum in Rom.* 2 vols. Stuttgart, 1927. [Reprint. Darmstadt, 1974.]

Orlandi, 1733
Pellegrino Antonio Orlandi. *L'Abecedario pittorico.* Naples, 1733.

Orloff, 1823
Count Gregoire Orloff. *Essai su l'histoire de la peinture en Italie, depuis les temps les plus anciens jusqu'à nos jours.* 2 vols. Paris, 1823.

Ottani Cavina, 1979
Anna Ottani Cavina. "Felice Giani e la Francia: la decorazione di palazzo Baciocchi." In *Florence et la France: Rapports sous la Révolution et l'Empire,* Publications de l'Institut Français de Florence, s. 4, Histoire de l'Art, no. 1. Florence and Paris, 1979, pp. 273–88.

Ovidi, 1902
Ernesto Ovidi. *Tommaso Minardi e la sua scuola.* Rome, 1902.

Ozzola, 1910
Leandro Ozzola. "Gli editori di stampe a Roma nei sec. XVI e XVII." *Repertorium für Kunstwissenschaft,* vol. 33 (1910), pp. 400–411.

Palo Alto, 1965
Palo Alto, California, Stanford University, Department of Art and Architecture. *Fortunato Duranti, 1787–1863.* 1965. Catalogue by Lorenz Eitner.

Paolucci, 1938
Riccardo Paolucci. "Il pittore Sebastiano Ceccarini e la sua famiglia." *Studia Picena,* vol. 13 (1938), pp. 23–41.

Paponi, 1958
Maria Enrica Paponi. "Appunti su Marco Benefial a Città di Castello." *Paragone,* vol. 9, no. 97 (January, 1958), pp. 59–63.

Pascoli, 1730–36
Lione Pascoli. *Vite de' pittori, scultori, ed architetti moderni.* 2 vols. Rome, 1730–36. [Reprint. Rome, 1965.]

Patrignani, 1929
Antonio Patrignani. *Le medaglie di Gregorio XVI (1831–1846).* Rome, Pescara, and Livorno, 1929. [Reprint. Bologna, 1967.]

Patrignani, 1930
Antonio Patrignani. *Le medaglie di Pio VII (1800–1823).* Pescara and Chieti, 1930. [Reprint. Bologna, 1967.]

Patrignani, 1933
Antonio Patrignani. *Le medaglie di Leone XII (1823–1829).* Catania, 1933.

Pavanello and Praz, 1976
Giuseppe Pavanello and Mario Praz. *L'opera completa del Canova.* Milan, 1976.

Pavia, et al., 1977–78
Pavia, Musei Civici del Castello Visconteo. *L'opera incisa di Carlo Maratti.* Also shown at Milan, Castello Sforzesco, and Rome, Gabinetto Nazionale delle Stampe. 1977–78. Catalogue by Paolo Bellini.

Pericoli Ridolfini, 1964
Cecilia Pericoli Ridolfini. "La villa Aldini a Montmorency in un gruppo di disegni di Felice Giani." *Bollettino dei Musei Comunali di Roma,* vol. 11, nos. 1–4 (1964), pp. 34–45.

Perina [Tellini], 1961
Chiara Perina [Tellini]. "Considerazioni su Giuseppe Bottani." *Arte Lombarda,* vol. 6, no. 1 (1961), pp. 51–59.

Perina Tellini, 1973
Chiara Perina Tellini. "Per il Bottani." *Antichità Viva,* vol. 12, no. 5 (1973), pp. 12–21.

Piccolini, 1942–43
Celestino Piccolini. "La famiglia di Carlo Marchionni architetto di S. Pietro in Vaticano." *Atti e Memorie della Società Tiburtina di Storia e d'Arte,* vols. 22–23 (1942–43), pp. 233–56.

Pietrangeli, 1959
Carlo Pietrangeli. "L'Accademia del Nudo in Campidoglio." *Strenna dei Romanisti,* vol. 20 (1959), pp. 123–28.

Pietrangeli, 1962
Carlo Pietrangeli. "L'Accademia Capitolina del Nudo." *Capitolium,* vol. 37, no. 3 (March, 1962), pp. 132–34.

Pietrangeli, 1963
Carlo Pietrangeli. "La 'Sala Nuova' di Don Abbondio Rezzonico." *Capitolium,* vol. 38, no. 5 (May, 1963), pp. 244–47.

Pino Adami, 1977
Alessandra Pino Adami. "La singolare opera grafica di Fortunato Duranti (1787–1863)." *Antichità Viva,* vol. 16, no. 6 (1977), pp. 58–63.

Pio, 1977
Nicola Pio. *Le vite di pittori, scultori et architetti.* Transcribed and edited by Catherine and Robert Enggass. MS, Vatican Library, cod. Capponiana 257. Vatican City, 1977.

Pirotta, 1969
Luigi Pirotta. "I *direttori* dell'Accademia del Nudo in Campidoglio." *Strenna dei Romanisti,* vol. 30 (1969), pp. 326–34.

Pistoia, 1977
Pistoia. *Disegni di Luigi Sabatelli della collezione di Tommaso Puccini.* 1977. Catalogue by C. Mazzi and C. Sisi.

Popham, 1936–37
A. E. Popham. "Sebastiano Resta and His Collections." *Old Master Drawings,* vol. 11 (June 1936–March 1937), pp. 1–19.

Praz, 1971
Mario Praz. *Conversation Pieces: A Survey of the Informal Group Portrait in Europe and America.* University Park, Pennsylvania, 1971.

Princeton, 1977
Princeton, New Jersey, The Art Museum, Princeton University. *Eighteenth-Century French Life-Drawing: Selections from the Collection of Mathias Polakovits.* April 2–May 8, 1977. Foreword by Pierre Rosenberg. Catalogue by James Henry Rubin and David Levine.

Providence, 1957
Providence, Rhode Island, Museum of Art, Rhode Island School of Design. *The Age of Canova: An Exhibition of the Neo-Classic.* November 6–December 15, 1957. Catalogue by Anthony M. Clark.

Raggi, 1835
Oreste Raggi. *Cenni intorno alla vita ed alle opere principali di Bartolomeo Pinelli.* Rome, 1835.

Richardson, 1719
Jonathan Richardson. *Two Discourses.* London, 1719.

Richardson, 1722
Jonathan Richardson. *An Account of the statues, bas-reliefs, drawings and pictures in Italy, France, etc.* London, 1722.

Righetti, 1940
Romolo Righetti. "Fonditori in bronzo romani del Settecento e dell'Ottocento, i Valadier e i Righetti." *L'Urbe,* vol. 5 (November, 1940), pp. 2–16.

Righetti, 1941
Romolo Righetti. "Fonditori in bronzo romani del Settecento e dell'Ottocento, i Valadier e i Righetti." *L'Urbe,* vol. 6 (January, 1941), pp. 2–8.

Röttgen, 1976
Steffi Röttgen. "Antonio Cavallucci: un pittore romano fra tradizione e innovazione." *Bollettino d'Arte,* s. 5, vol. 61, nos. 3–4 (1976), pp. 193–212.

Röttgen, 1977
Steffi Röttgen. "Mengs, Alessandro Albani und Winckelmann, Idee und Gestalt des Parnass in der Villa Albani." *Storia dell'Arte,* vols. 30–31 (May–December, 1977), pp. 87–151.

Röttgen, 1980
Steffi Röttgen. "Das Papyruskabinett von Mengs in der Biblioteca Vaticana: ein Beitrag zur Geschichte und Idee des Museo Pio-Clementino." *Münchner Jahrbuch der bildenden Kunst,* s. 3, vol. 31 (1980) [in press].

Roli, 1978
Renato Roli. *Pittura bolognese, 1650–1880: dal Cignani ai Gandolfi.* Bologna, 1978.

Rome, 1956
Rome, Palazzo Braschi. *Bartolomeo Pinelli.* May–July, 1956. Catalogue by Giovanni Incisa della Rocchetta.

Rome, 1959
Rome, Palazzo delle Esposizioni. *Il Settecento a Roma.* March 19–May 31, 1959. Catalogue by Emilio Lavagnino, Antonino Santangelo, et al.

Rome, 1969–70
Rome, Gabinetto Nazionale delle Stampe. *Disegni dell'Ottocento.* November 21, 1969–March 8, 1970. Catalogue by E. Beltrame-Quattrocchi and S. Lazzaro Morrica.

Rome, 1973–74
Rome, Palazzo Braschi. *Roma giacobina.* December 18, 1973–January 31, 1974. Catalogue by Maria Elisa Monti Tittoni and Lucia Palladini Cavazzi.

Rome, 1976
Rome, Académie de France à Rome, Villa Medici. *Piranèse et les Français, 1740–1790.* Also shown at Dijon, Palais des Etats de Bourgogne, and Paris, Hôtel de Sully. May–November, 1976. Catalogue by Georges Brunel, Marianne Roland-Michel, Jean-François Méjanès, et al.

Rome, 1978
Rome, Galleria Nazionale d'Arte Moderna. *Vincenzo Camuccini (1771–1844), bozzetti e disegni dallo studio dell'artista.* October 17–December 31, 1978. Catalogue by Gianna Piantoni de Angelis.

Rosenblum, 1967
Robert Rosenblum. *Transformations in Late Eighteenth Century Art.* Princeton, 1967.

Rudolph, 1977
Stella Rudolph. "Felice Giani: da Accademico 'de'Pensieri' a Madonnero." *Storia dell'Arte,* vols. 30–31 (May–December, 1977), pp. 175–86.

Rudolph, 1978
Stella Rudolph. "The Toribio Illustrations and Some Considerations on Engravings after Carlo Maratti." *Antologia di Belle Arti,* vol. 2, nos. 7–8 (December, 1978), pp. 191–203.

Sabatelli, 1900
Cenni biografici sul Cav. Prof. Luigi Sabatelli, scritti da lui medesimo e raccolti dal figlio Gaetano. Milan, 1900.

St. Louis, 1972
St. Louis, Missouri, The St. Louis Art Museum. *Italian Drawings Selected from Mid-Western Collections.* February 25–April 16, 1972. Catalogue by Nancy Ward Neilson.

Salerno, 1965
Luigi Salerno. "Inediti di Luigi Vanvitelli e del Pannini. L'appartamento settecentesco di Palazzo Sciarra." *Palatino,* s. 4, vol. 9, nos. 1–3 (January–March, 1965), pp. 4–8.

Salmi, 1913
Mario Salmi. "Pietro Benvenuti e la decorazione della Cappella della Madonna del Conforto ad Arezzo." *Arte e Storia*, vol. 32 (1913), p. 178–80.

Scatassa, 1916
Ercole Scatassa. "I papi e l'arte in un diario romano." *Arte e Storia*, vol. 35 (1916), pp. 334–40.

Schiavo, 1964
Armando Schiavo. *Palazzo Altieri*. Rome, 1964.

Schlegel, 1969
Ursula Schlegel. "Alcuni disegni di Camillo Rusconi, Carlo Maratta e Angelo de' Rossi." *Antichità Viva*, vol. 8, no. 4 (1969), pp. 28–41.

Selvelli, 1931
Cesare Selvelli. *Fano e Senigallia*. Bergamo, 1931.

Servolini, 1952–53
Luigi Servolini. "Un romantico in anticipo: il 'focoso pittore' Felice Giani (1758–1823)." *L'Arte*, n.s., vol. 18 (1952–53), pp. 31–62.

Servolini, 1959
Luigi Servolini. *Sebastiano Ceccarini*. Milan, 1959.

Sestieri, 1969
Giancarlo Sestieri. "Contributi a Sebastiano Conca—I." *Commentari*, n.s., vol. 20 (October–December, 1969), pp. 317–41.

Sestieri, 1970
Giancarlo Sestieri. "Contributi a Sebastiano Conca—II." *Commentari*, n.s., vol. 21 (January–June, 1970), pp. 122–38.

Sestieri, 1972
Giancarlo Sestieri. "Per la conoscenza di Luigi Garzi." *Commentari*, n.s., vol. 23 (January–June, 1972), pp. 89–111.

Sestieri, 1976
Giancarlo Sestieri. "Sebastiano Conca." *Print Collector*, vol. 7, nos. 33–34 (September–December, 1976), pp. 80–102.

Spinosa, 1978
Nicola Spinosa. "Gli arazzi del Belvedere a Palazzo Reale." *Antologia di Belle Arti*, vol. 2, no. 5 (March, 1978), pp. 12–23.

Storrs, 1973
Storrs, Connecticut, The University of Connecticut, William Benton Museum of Art. *The Academy of Europe: Rome in the 18th Century*. October 13–November 21, 1973. Catalogue by Frederick den Broeder, et al.

Strambi, 1964
Michela Strambi. "La cultura dei Collino, scultori del ultimo '700 in Piemonte." *Bollettino della Società Piemontese di Archeologia e di Belle Arti*, n.s., vol. 18 (1964), pp. 120–34.

Susinno, 1970
Stefano Susinno. "Giuseppe Bottani, dipinti e disegni." M.A. Thesis, Istituto di Storia dell'Arte Medioevale e Moderna, Università degli Studi, Rome, 1970.

Susinno, 1971
Stefano Susinno. "Aureliano Milani e Sebastiano Conca per la SS. Trinità dei Missionari a Roma." *Bollettino della Unione Storia ed Arte*, n.s., vols. 1–2 (1971), pp. 1–16.

Susinno, 1976
Stefano Susinno. "Per Giuseppe Bottani al Museo di Roma: i disegni per la *Merca* ed un gruppo di famiglia." *Bollettino dei Musei Comunali di Roma*, vol. 23, nos. 1–4 (1976), pp. 32–44.

Susinno, 1978
Stefano Susinno. "Gli scritti in memoria di Maria Cionini Visani ed un contributo a Giuseppe Bottani, pittore di storia." *Antologia di Belle Arti*, vol. 2, nos. 7–8 (December, 1978), pp. 308–12.

Sutton, 1956
Denis Sutton. "The Roman Caricatures of Reynolds." *Country Life Annual* (1956), pp. 113–16.

T.C.I., *Roma*, 1977
Guida d'Italia del Touring Club Italiano. *Roma e dintorni*. 7th ed. Milan, 1977.

Ternois, 1970
Daniel Ternois. "Napoléon et la décoration du palais impérial de Monte Cavallo en 1811–13." *Revue de l'Art*, no. 7 (1970), pp. 68–89.

Thieme-Becker, 1907–50
U. Thieme and F. Becker. *Allgemeines Lexikon der Bildenden Künstler*. 37 vols. Leipzig, 1907–50.

Toronto, et al., 1972–73
Toronto, Art Gallery of Ontario. *French Master Drawings of the 17th and 18th Centuries in North American Collections*. September 2–October 15, 1972. Also shown at Ottawa, The National Gallery of Canada, November 3–December 17, 1972, San Francisco, California Palace of the Legion of Honor, January 12–March 11, 1973, and New York, The New York Cultural Center, April 4–May 6, 1973. Catalogue by Pierre Rosenberg.

University Park, 1975
University Park, Pennsylvania, The Pennsylvania State University Museum of Art. *Carlo Maratti and his Contemporaries: Figurative Drawings from the Roman Baroque*. January 19–March 16, 1975. Catalogue by Jean K. Westin and Robert H. Westin.

Vasco, 1973
Sandra Vasco. "Due pale d'altare inedite di Sebastiano Conca e Stefano Pozzi a Roccantica." *Commentari*, n.s., vol. 24 (January–June, 1973), pp. 114–19.

Venice, 1978
Venice, Museo Correr. *Venezia nell'età di Canova, 1780–1830*. October–December, 1978. Catalogue by E. Bassi, A. Dorigato, et al.

Vinci, 1795
Giambattista Vinci. *Elogio storico del celebre pittore Antonio Cavallucci da Sermoneta*. Rome, 1795.

Vitzthum, 1970
Walter Vitzthum. [Review of Düsseldorf, 1969–70.] *The Burlington Magazine*, vol. 112, no. 804 (March, 1970), p. 188.

Vitzthum, 1971
Walter Vitzthum. *Il barocco a Roma*. Milan, 1971.

Viviani, 1922
U. Viviani. "Le opere di Pietro Benvenuti." In *Arezzo e gli Aretini*. Arezzo, 1922, pp. 178–85.

Volkmann, 1777
Johann Jacob Volkmann. *Historisch-kritische Nachrichten von Italien*. 2 vols. Leipzig, 1777.

von Einem, 1973
Herbert von Einem. "Anton Raphael Mengs. Briefe an Raimondo Ghelli und Anton Maron." *Abhandlungen der Akademie der Wissenschaften in Göttingen.* Philologisch-historische klasse, vol. 3, no. 82. Göttingen, 1973.

von Heinecken, 1771
Karl Heinrich von Heinecken. *Idée générale d'une collection complète d'éstampes.* Leipzig and Vienna, 1771.

von Huyssen, 1701
Heinrich von Huyssen. *Curieuse und vollstandige Reiss-Beschreibung von ganz Italien.* Freiburg, 1701.

von Kutschera-Woborsky, 1917
Oswald von Kutschera-Woborsky. "Die Geschichte einer Solimena-Komposition." *Repertorium für Kunstwissenschaft,* vol. 40 (1917), pp. 38–58.

Voss, 1924
Hermann Voss. *Die Malerei des Barock in Rom.* Berlin, 1924.

Walch, 1977
Peter Walch. "An Early Neoclassical Sketchbook by Angelica Kauffman." *The Burlington Magazine,* vol. 119, no. 887 (February, 1977), pp. 98–111.

Washington, 1978–79
Washington, D.C., National Gallery of Art. *Hubert Robert, Drawings and Watercolors.* November 19, 1978–January 21, 1979. Catalogue by Victor Carlson.

Waterhouse, 1954
Ellis Waterhouse. "The British Contribution to the Neo-Classical Style in Painting." Lecture on Aspects of Art, Henriette Hertz Trust, British Academy. *Proceedings of the British Academy,* vol. 40 (1954), pp. 57–79.

Waterhouse, 1958
Ellis Waterhouse. "Francesco Fernandi detto d'Imperiali." *Arte Lombarda,* vol. 3, no. 1 (1958), pp. 101–6.

Waterhouse, 1962
Ellis Waterhouse. *Painting in Britain, 1530 to 1790.* 2d ed. Harmondsworth, Baltimore, and Melbourne, 1962.

Waterhouse, 1971
Ellis Waterhouse. "Painting in Rome in the Eighteenth Century." *Museum Studies (The Art Institute of Chicago),* vol. 6 (1971), pp. 7–21.

Waterhouse, 1976
Ellis Waterhouse. *Roman Baroque Painting: A List of the Principal Painters and their Works in and around Rome.* London, 1976.

Westfall, 1969
Carroll William Westfall. "Antolini's Foro Bonaparte in Milan." *Journal of the Warburg and Courtauld Institutes,* vol. 32 (1969), pp. 366–85.

Whinney, 1956
Margaret Whinney. "Flaxman and the Eighteenth Century." *Journal of the Warburg and Courtauld Institutes,* vol. 19 (1956), pp. 269–82.

Whinney and Gunnis, 1967
Margaret Whinney and Rupert Gunnis. *The Collection of Models by John Flaxman, R.A., at University College, London.* London, 1967.

Winckelmann, 1760
Johann Joachim Winckelmann. *Description des pierres gravées du feu baron de Stosch dediée à son eminence monseigneur le cardinal Aléxandre Albani.* Florence, 1760. [Facsimile edition in *Kunsttheoretische Schriften,* vol. 9. Baden-Baden and Strasbourg, 1970.]

Wittkower, 1961
Rudolf Wittkower. "Cornacchini's Reiter-statue Karls der Grossen in St. Peter." In *Miscellaniae Bibliothecae Hertzianae.* Munich, 1961, pp. 464–73.

Wittkower, 1973
Rudolf Wittkower. *Art and Architecture in Italy, 1600–1750.* 3rd rev. ed. Harmondsworth, Baltimore, and Victoria, 1973.

Wynne, 1974
Michael Wynne. "The Milltowns as Patrons: Particularly concerning the picture-collecting of the first two Earls." *Apollo,* n.s., vol. 99, no. 144 (February, 1974), pp. 104–11.

Zamboni, 1961
Silla Zamboni. "Per gli inizi di Felice Giani." *Arte Antica e Moderna,* vols. 13–16, pt. 1 (1961), pp. 459–61.

Zani, 1819–22
Pietro Zani. *Enciclopedia metodica critica-ragionata delle belle arti.* 28 vols. Parma, 1819–22.

Zeri, 1976
Federico Zeri. *Italian Paintings in the Walters Art Gallery.* 2 vols. Baltimore, 1976.

INDEX OF ARTISTS

*The numbers below refer to catalogue entry numbers. An asterisk indicates that the artist is included in the Checklist of Drawings (*see *page 149).*

This book has been set in Granjon types
by Deputy Crown, Incorporated
with display in Elizabeth by Pickering Press
Printed by the Meriden Gravure Company

Designed by John Anderson